The Troubadour Guitar Chord Book

I0170730

A Complete Library of Chords in Standard Tuning

HARVEY REID

WOODPECKER
MULTIMEDIA

York, Maine USA

© 2013-2015 by Harvey Reid
ALL RIGHTS RESERVED

ISBN: 978-1-63029-011-5

Library of Congress Control# 2013951626

WOODPECKER
MULTIMEDIA

PO Box 815 York Maine 03909 USA

www.woodpecker.com

CONTENTS

About This and Other Guitar Chord Books	i
What's In This Book	iii
What's Not In This Book	v
About the Diagrams in This Book	ix
A	1
A#/Bb	26
B	31
C	40
C#/Db	50
D	55
D#/Eb	71
E	75
F	93
F#/Gb	101
G	108
Ab /G#	123
APPENDIX: About Chord Structure	127
Other Guitar Resources by Harvey Reid	137

About This and Other Guitar Chord Books

As you would suspect, there are a number of other encyclopedic guitar chord books already on the market, though I find all of them to be both missing a lot of what I personally look for in a chord book, and full of things I don't really want. I can only imagine the frustration other troubadours must also feel who are trying to learn to play the guitar better, and who have to work with instructional materials that are made for a different type of player. I am hoping that this chord compendium will be readable, user-friendly and accessible, as well as detailed and complete.

This chord book has grown out of my lifelong fascination with the complexity and diversity of guitar chords. I have been a professional acoustic guitar player my entire adult life, and now after 45 years playing guitar, I find myself probing deeper than ever into the mysteries of what make different chords and chord voicings behave the way they do.

I built this library of chords amid a several-year project to explore more carefully the new opportunities offered by partial capos. While studying several hundred ways to use partial capos in dozens of tunings, my ears began to prick up when I would find a combination of notes or a new chord voicing that sounded fresh or unusual to me. I began to wonder whether these chords I was finding really were new to my ears.

I realized that I wanted to know if each new and interesting chord I found could be played in standard tuning. I thus began building this collection of thousands of chords, so that when I found a sequence of notes in a chord voicing in an unusual tuning, I could quickly search my standard tuning list and find out if that chord had ever been available to guitarists before, or if it was some kind of fresh, virgin musical territory.

In my chord research I have built a database that now contains nearly 20,000 guitar chords in dozens of different tunings. I am sure that I am by no means exhausting all the possibilities offered by 6 strings and 4 fingers. It will be interesting to see as I continue to map the guitar fingerboard landscape, whether I will ever feel like I have a sense of the vastness of its entirety, with all the tunings and capo-ings considered. By sifting through my database, I have been able to determine just how many times a given chord voicing is repeated in the list, and which ones are rare or unique. The results have been surprising. More than half of all those thousands of chords are voicings that only show up once, so instead of finding the same chords over and over again, I have been finding a wide variety of variations, each with a unique sound.

All the chords in this book are playable, and they have all been "hand-tested" and are not generated with software merely cranking out permutations of notes.

The chords and voicings were optimized for solo and acoustic guitarists, and most have 5 or 6 strings sounding. Both open-string and barre chord forms are included.

The list of A major chords at the beginning of this book, for example, shows 24 ways to make sure that all the strings ringing are sounding an A, C# or E note. That seems like a lot, since some "chord bible" publications show only two or three A major chords. My chord database now numbers over 125 distinct ways to voice an A chord, without including the really useless ones that have multiple C#'s on the bottom, for example. I have become increasingly fascinated with how many total possibilities there are, and how much diversity and complexity can come from even something like a simple major or minor chord, with just 3 notes occupying the guitar landscape.

Jazz players are apparently bored with major or minor chords and barely discuss them in their zeal to explore more extended chords. Books made for folk, country and other "non-jazz" players trivialize the whole guitar fingerboard and show only a handful of the possible chord voicings.

I have become increasingly intrigued with all the decisions and possibilities that come from trying all the ways to play a certain group of notes on a 6-string fingerboard. Finding as many fingerings as possible, and trying to determine which ones were both playable and musical became a pastime. After countless hours of studying chords and logging the results, my conclusions surprised me.

There are far more ways to play and voice many chords than I ever imagined. The A7, A9 and A6/9 chords are near the top of the list, with many dozens of choices for each of them. I think A9 is the current winner, with 74 different voicings in the book. There is sometimes just no way at all to play a chord, such as a Bbm11 chord, and other chords may only offer 2 or 3 options. You can quickly see which ones are rare or common from the way this book is laid out. Certain keys favor a certain type of chord, and you'll notice that there are lots of Dm13 chords, but no Bm13. There is only one Fmadd9 chord, but more than a dozen ways to play an Emadd9.

The other crucial thing I learned is that there is a very big, shadowy library of chords and voicings that have musical value, but that simply cannot be played in standard tuning. This is not evident from this book, but some of my other guitar chord books unveil thousands of them. This should be very exciting to composers, songwriters and arrangers who are looking for fresh sounds. This is the reason that so many prominent players are exploring alternate tunings, but because the guitar education world is inextricably tied to standard tuning, I have never seen a scholarly discussion of the musical possibilities that altered tunings or partial capos present. Self-taught, non-sight-reading, "un-schooled" guitarists all over the world are pumping out huge amounts of interesting and fresh guitar music in hundreds of tunings, yet the guitar education books and classes often go on as if this other body of guitar music did not exist. Paging through the chords in this book you get the feeling that the guitar fingerboard is vast and nearly infinite at times, but in truth, the chords here are only a fraction of what the guitar can do if you push its boundaries. There are also a mind-boggling number of other chords and voicings that can be accessed only from altered tunings and by using partial capos on guitar, or using both ideas together.

It would seem that these nearly 3000 chords would be enough for anyone, and like the chess board, few of us would dare claim that we have exhausted all the possibilities and thus we want more options. There is a common mind-set that says "I'll learn standard tuning first, and then maybe I'll explore some alternate tunings after I feel like I really understand the guitar." It's really a matter of memory more than anything, and there are limits to how much of the fingerboard geometry our brains can retain. It makes sense to compile books of chords in various tunings rather than trying to memorize them all.

There are literally hundreds of non-standard tunings that have been used throughout history, and each of them offers a unique set of possibilities, and a new set of chord and scale fingerings. Each tuning presents a new group of trade-offs, where you lose access to some things and you gain others. Some players choose to spend their entire careers playing in one non-standard tuning, and it would certainly be possible to compile exhaustive chord books like this for each of them. (As part of this series of chord books, I may publish a few of them.)

Likewise, each way to put a partial capo on a guitar opens some doors and closes others, and it is a delicate and difficult task to try them all and find the ones that offer the most new music. (This is the goal of my extensive series of *Capo Voodoo* books.) Some of the most fruitful fingerboard environments I have found involve combining different tunings with partial capos, and in some of them, over 90% of the chords I have logged are not found in this book. I am in the midst of building a number of other chord books to chart the terrain in many of these new partial capo configurations, to show where to put the capos and where to put your fingers.

I have been preaching the idea of partial capos since the 1970's, and most of that time I have explained them as a way to imitate the drone-string resonances and rich sound of open tunings, without the difficulties of retuning the strings and thus changing the geometry of chord and scale fingerings. Now as a result of this chord research, I have more "scientific" evidence that there are indeed significant numbers of fascinating new combinations of notes available that not even the best players on earth have ever been able to play before.

Recently I have also found a way to "map" guitar chords onto the piano keyboard to see visually where the notes lie, and have been quite surprised by the results of that also. Since I don't play the piano, I always assumed that with 10 fingers and two hands there can't be much on a guitar fingerboard that can't be duplicated on a keyboard. With notes in 4 octaves on the guitar, I have indeed found a significant number of guitar chord voicings that are not "reachable" on the piano.

The chords in this book represent the "possible," and show the benchmark of what players have had to work with in the more than 400 years that standard tuning has been widespread in the guitar world.

What's In This Book

This chord book is tailored to the needs of the "troubadour guitarist." I use this word because it implies that there is a person generating music on the guitar, and not just someone playing in a band or ensemble. A troubadour most often plays an acoustic instrument, where open-string chords are very common. The majority of guitar chord books date back to the "big band" era and are focused almost entirely on movable, closed (barre) chords. They tend to feature 4-string chords, often with muted inner strings.

It's one thing to play a chord that "fits" in a band arrangement, but solo guitarists need the best possible chord with the fullest sound, because there is no band or bass player.

All the chords in this book are playable, and they have all been "hand-tested" and are not generated with software merely cranking out permutations of notes. There is no substitute for taking time to carefully try each chord fingering, and I have done that for you in this book.

Chord books for "folk guitar" tend to be incomplete and simplistic, and don't even hint at the depth and complexity of the guitar fingerboard or all the musical options. There is a surprising amount of complexity and diversity in the voicings and fingerings of any kind of chord, including the simplest ones, and jazz guitarists are not the only ones interested in chord theory.

Modal Chords

A good example of what makes this chord book different is that it includes modal or "power" chords. Nearly all skilled troubadours make some use of this simple chord (that is technically not even a chord, since it has only 2 notes in it) that is just a root and a fifth with no third, commonly written with a numeral 5 as the suffix.

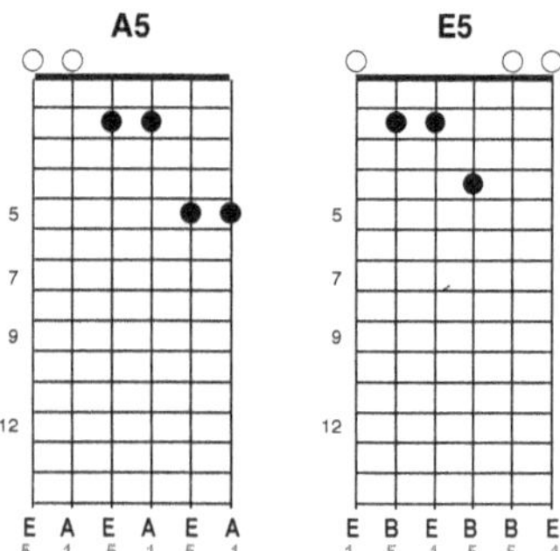
A5
E5
5
7
9
12
E A E A E A
5 1 5 1 5 1
E B E B B E
1 5 1 5 5 1

Jazz-oriented chord books generally omit this chord entirely as if it did not exist. (If triads like major and minor chords are boring, this one is super-boring!) There are no movable barre versions of this chord, and you can only play a few A5, C5, D5 G5, or E5 chords on guitar in standard tuning. (There are about 25 in this book.) Modal chords are musically powerful and widely used, and deserve a place in a chord book. Similarly, other chord books even sometimes ignore the suspended 4th chord, where the musical 3rd is replaced by a 4th. Troubadours use this chord constantly, regardless of whether music professors consider it a legitimate "triad."

Guitar chords are deceptively complicated, and there are often a startling number of ways to play almost any set of notes on a guitar fingerboard. The notes that make up any chord can be in different orders, and some notes may be repeated (doubled) or missing. The ways the notes combine and react with each other musically, due to their positions in the chord, are endlessly interesting and subtle.

The whole fingerboard is shown for each chord, making it much easier to identify and use chords.

You can visually see the "logic" of a chord as you scan all the ways to play it. You can't see this at all on 4-fret diagrams the way other chord books show them.

Possibly the most important feature in this book is that the letter names and musical function of every note in every chord are shown. This is a wonderful theory lesson, and allows you to see the voicing and structure of every chord.

All the chords in this book are playable, and they have all been "hand-tested" and are not generated with software merely cranking out permutations of notes. Some of them are very difficult. Like dictionaries of words, choices had to be made about what to include and leave out.

Why do you even need different ways to play chords? Probably the most important reason is when you are playing a solo guitar arrangement of a song or instrumental piece. Most solo troubadours like to keep as many strings ringing as possible to keep a full sound, and most of us will work very hard to have a bass string sounding underneath and supporting whatever else we are doing. When we don't have a bass player or a band, we generally need to keep as much rhythm, harmony, melody and bass going all at once as we can. As the melody of a song moves around or changes octaves, it often requires us to switch voicings of the chord to keep the song flowing.

We also need both open and closed-position voicings of chords so we can either let open strings ring and resonate, or if we want to play more staccato, bouncier rhythm changes, which require barre chords.

Another vital reason to know multiple voicings of a chord is that often a particular chord voicing has a sound that the others don't. So many classic songs have been built around the sound of a specific guitar chord, and there are still chords out there that no one has made into a memorable guitar part. Maybe you will find one, though the reachable chords in standard tuning have been picked over for 400 years by millions of players.

A final reason to know many ways to play a chord is that if you are playing with another guitarist, it usually sounds better if you play different versions of the chord, often on different parts of the fingerboard where the tone is also different. A lot of famous artists (*The Rolling Stones* and *The Allman Brothers* are good examples) have built a distinctive sound around the way two guitars play together.

Please relax about names of chords. There are no "official names" for chords, and people use different symbols and abbreviations, like dialects of language. You will often see a capital M7 for major 7th, an add2 or sus2 for an add9, sus for sus4, add4 for add11, etc. A minus sign is often used for minor. I used *Adim* in this book for diminished because there is no typographic symbol in my computer book software for A0, with the superscript zero, a common symbol used.

Some chords have special names and other types don't. It's not uncommon for the same group of notes to have more than one name. The most common example of this is that a minor 7th chord has the same notes as a 6th chord. (Am7= A C E G and C6 = C E G A, for example.) Minor 9th chords are often the same notes as major 7th chord, and I have frequently included both.

Many chords in chord books are difficult or nearly impossible to finger. My rule was that I did not include a chord that I would not personally use in a song or instrumental piece. I have a good left hand, and if I can't play it, I left it out of this book. We can't just use computers to choose chords: humans have to make decisions, and I rejected a lot of chords that I thought were unreasonably hard to play. I sometimes wish I could have put some kind of a difficulty index into this book, since some chords are vastly harder than others. (This is of course subjective, and different players favor different kinds of shapes.) It would be fun to make a guitar chord book for professional basketball players, since their hands are so much larger than most of ours.

I thought long and hard about barre chord symbols. All players don't make the same decisions about whether to use a barre or partial barre, and it is not that hard to find the fingering that is best for you. If there are more than 4 dots on the fingerboard, it's a sign that there are some barred notes.

There are a lot of "gray areas" in naming and discussing chords. A group of notes can function as more than one chord, depending on which note is the root, and how it is used in the context of a song. You may not agree with my choices, and you may find the same chord shape with more than one name in this book. This is a big part of the reason I did the work to include the note names of every chord.

Augmented & diminished chords take up a lot of space. There are many ways to play these chords, though there are few good barre chords and a lot of muted (x) strings. Each has multiple names and they have a lot of useful and nearly equivalent inversions, so they take up a lot of room in a book like this, though troubadours don't use them often. They are important, so they were included, though they tend to be awkward to finger, and neither of them fit well on an instrument tuned in 4ths. They are usually used as "passing" or "transitional" chords, and you don't usually strum them.

It's unclear what to do about "slash" chords. These are often notated as a slash followed by a letter, such as C/A. This means play a C chord, but with an A bass note. It is a rather common thing that guitarists do: a lot of well-known songs such as "*Mr. Bojangles*" or "*Friend of the Devil*" feature a moving bass, usually starting on the 1 bass note. The bass notes start with C on the A string and descend down. You are not really strumming a chord with a B and then an A root– as a player you are thinking that you are holding a C chord and just doing a walk-down on the lower strings. The effect is really not as if you are strumming discrete chords. The slash notation allows us to describe what is going on without trying to invent names for a C chord with a B bass, followed by a C chord with an A bass, and so on. A number of these kinds of passing chords are useful and beautiful, but they don't work well in a "snapshot gallery" of chords like this book.

The slash followed by a number, such as 6/9 or 9/11, means that the chord has more than one "added tone." A Cadd9 chord has C-E-G-D and a Cadd11 has C-E-G-F. The C 9/11 chord is C-E-G-D-F, which you could call add9/add11 or add9/11.

Have fun exploring...

What's Not In This Book

Obviously, this kind of book is bound to have some errors and omissions, so the chords that I neglected to put in are not here. Hopefully they are few and not really important ones...

Left-hand finger numbers are not shown here because not everyone plays any chord the same way. The truth is, if you play guitar, you will constantly be learning new fingerings, so get used to always changing. You'll be a better player if you can learn to use alternate fingerings whenever it makes sense. The very first chord in this book (A major) can be fingered at least 6 ways, and none of them is more right or wrong than any other.

There are no double sharps or double flats. There are valid musical reasons for using double accidentals, but there is physically no room for them in my chord diagrams, and they are confusing, so I vetoed them. This book is designed for people who don't have degrees in music theory. It's hard enough to tell people that the 2nd fret of the high E string is sometimes called F# and sometimes a Gb. To insist that an A note is sometimes a G## and sometimes a Bbb is being a little too rigorous. If you know enough music theory to be bothered by the lack of double accidentals then you should understand what is going on and not be bothered. The purpose of the book is to show you a lot of chords and choices for chords, and what notes are in them.

Here is how double flats can occur: diminished chords are technically triads, with just 3 notes in them, but they are almost always played on guitar as four-note diminished 7th chords, with three minor 3rds stacked up instead of 2. (You can't play a chord with only C-Eb-Gb notes on a guitar without skipping inner strings.) The Cdim chords in every guitar book in the world have an A note along with the C-Eb-Gb diminished triad. I have "illegally"called it an A, since "technically" it should be called a Bbb. Diminished chords are unusual, and each one has 4 names, and the notes in them get renamed if you give the chord a different name. The key is A, which has the 6th note of F#, but the "rules" say the note in the chord has to be called a Gb.

This kind of situation is an example of where the terminology and explanations become more obscure as they try to be more clear. It happens in pronunciation and grammar also. We follow rules to avoid doing things like ending sentences with prepositions, and we end up saying things like "*That is something up with which I shall not put.*"

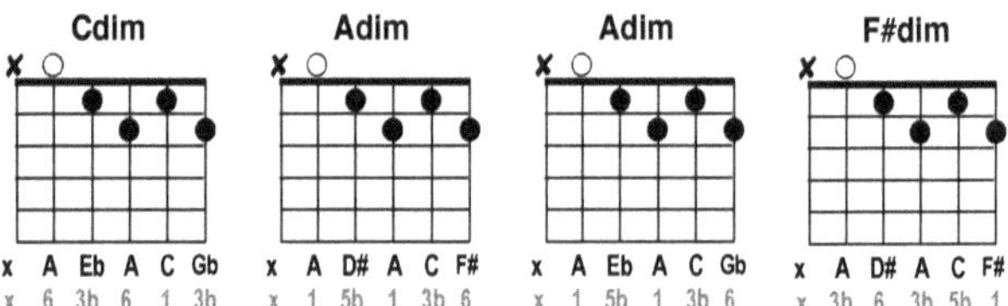

Cdim
x A Eb A C Gb
x 6 3b 6 1 3b
Adim
x A D# A C F#
x 1 5b 1 3b 6
Adim
x A Eb A C Gb
x 1 5b 1 3b 6
F#dim
x A D# A C F#
x 3b 6 3b 5b 1

A prominent web discussion on *Yahoo.com* said this to "explain" the apparent A note when someone asked why there is an A in a Cdim chord: "*The distance from C to B is a Major 7th. The distance from C to Bb is a minor 7th. The distance from C to Bbb is a diminished 7th. In no way is it a 6th. That would be from a C of some sort up to an A of some sort. There is a logic to our theoretical terminology. There are many things implied in the spelling of a chord, not the least of which is actual intonation. A and Bbb are NOT the same pitch. Another implication is one of voice leading. And there is the question as to what the root of the chord is. Spelled the proper way, the root is C. Spelled your way the root becomes A. Then it would be an A diminished 7th. (A C Eb Gb) Are you then going to insist that the Gb be respelled as an F#?? Oops -- then we have an F# diminished 7th -- F# A C Eb -*"

I am not sure this is clearer. Likewise a C# augmented (+) chord would have the notes C# E# G##, which if rigorously enforced, would indeed mean that we would have to tell troubadours to be ready to call an F# a Gb, but that they should be ready to call a G an Abb or an F##. To us guitar players, the G string is the G string, it's not the F## string sometimes. In this book, you'll see the C#+ chords incorrectly show an F and not an E#, and an A instead of the G##. My apologies.

Speaking of rules, the system of rules that says that we must accept double flats and sharps also says that you are not supposed to use parallel 5ths, 4ths or octaves in harmony. Every guitar player on Earth who can play barre chords has played this chord progression:

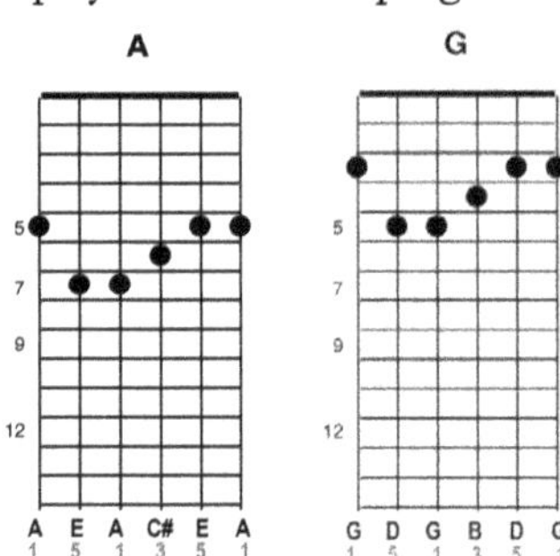

A
G
5
7
9
12
A E A C# E A
1 5 1 3 5 1
G D G B D G
1 5 1 3 5 1

It's rife with parallel 5ths, 4ths and octaves. So what? It's something guitarists do. Just because pianists don't do that (and probably can't even play these chords) doesn't mean we can't. Who says it's breaking rules? Just because pianists developed this language and notation doesn't really give them permanent license to make and enforce rules that really don't make sense to guitarists.

There are no warnings here telling you not to use your thumb to fret notes on the guitar. I'd like to go on record as saying in print that it is fine to use your thumb. It's almost some kind of inside joke or conspiracy among guitar teachers, like the police who won't tell you it's OK to go over the speed limit, though we know they will let us to some extent. Virtually all guitarists use their thumbs, and good players go back and forth as often as they need to. Some chords are hard to play unless your thumb can hang over the bass end. Almost all players use their thumb to mute the bass E string on a D major chord, and most of them actually fret the 2nd fret F# also. This A major chord is one that you can only play if your hand and guitar neck allow you to hang the thumb over on the bass string:

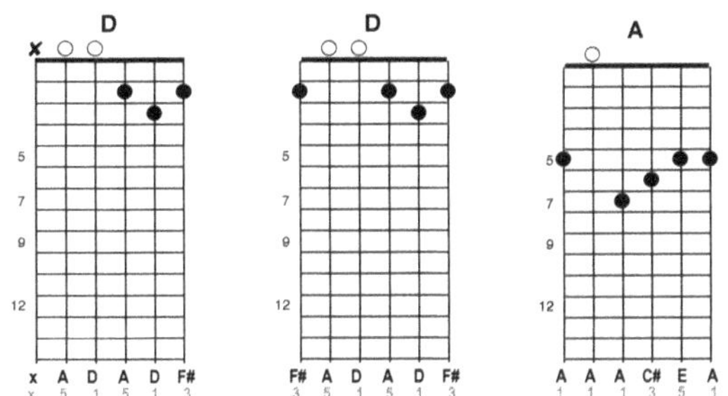
D
D
A
5
7
9
12
x A D A D F#
x 5 1 5 1 3
F# A D A D F#
3 5 1 5 1 3
A A A C# E A
1 1 1 3 5 1

I have a collection of guitar instruction books, and only one of them, an old jazz guitar book by Gene Leis, contains a photograph of someone with their thumb prominently hanging over the fingerboard. Many guitar instruction books have strongly worded warnings against using the thumb. The truth is that when your thumb is over the edge of the fingerboard, it greatly limits the reach you have with your 4th finger. If you need to stretch a long way across the fingerboard, put your thumb in back. If you need to use your thumb, use it and quit worrying.

I left out a lot of chord types that are associated only with jazz. For example, the book would have been nearly twice as long if I had included these: *b5, augmented 9th, 7 flat5, 9 flat5, 9#11, 7#9, 7 b9, 13b9, 13b5, minor 7 flat5, b7b9, minor 9 flat5, minor-major 7th, minor major 9th, b13b9, 13b5b9, 13b5b9, 11b9.* I included some A+7 chords to illustrate the point, but did not show any other augmented 7ths because there are a lot of them and they are marginally useful to troubadours. I doubt many people will miss them.

I even left out the *minor-major 7th*: 1-3b-5-7 that you learn about in any music theory curriculum. Structurally this chord is pretty simple, since it has the flat 3rd and the unflatted 7th notes, but it is pretty dissonant and hard to use in campfire-style guitar. Here is an "A minor major 7th" chord, also written as mM7, mΔ7, -Δ7, mM7, m/M7, m(M7), minmaj7, m⑦

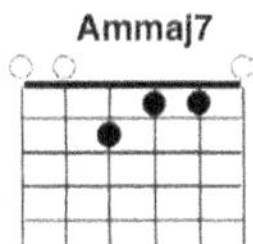
Ammaj7

The Beatles used this chord in *Magical Mystery Tour,* and *Pink Floyd* used it in *Us and Them.* (It is sometimes called the "Hitchcock chord" because it was used effectively by composer Bernard Herrmann in the horror movie *Psycho.*) A handful of songs use them, but hundreds of millions of songs use major, minor and 7th chords, so I made the executive decision to leave them out of this book of so-called "troubadour chords." This was done by conscious choice and not ignorance of their existence.

Things Like the "Tristan Chord" Music theorists have written long treatises on the dissonant "Tristan" chord that Wagner began his opera *Tristan & Isolde* with in 1865. It has a spelling of 1-3b-5b-7b, which isn't that different from a standard minor 7th chord, but seems to defy normal music theory explanations. It is credited with things like triggering the onset of the 20th century atonality movement. It is not a "troubadour chord" so I have left them out, like quite a number of other kinds of odd or unusual chords that we really don't use.

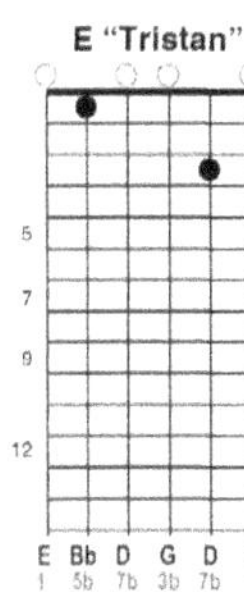
E "Tristan"
5
7
9
12
E Bb D G D E
1 5b 7b 3b 7b 1

It's not hard to play this example, but it's not something you'll use in a song. Technically, Wagner's Tristan chord is just the bottom 4 notes of this chord: E-Bb-D-G, and the D and E repeating on top in this example aren't notes he used. You could add a 3rd fret G on the high string also. Wagner's were actually a half-step higher: F-B-D#-G#.) This example is a "strummer's Tristan chord," which highlights one of the problems of making a guitar chord book. The famous *Neapolitan* chord that Beethoven and other composers have used is also not a troubadour chord, and is not in this book, though you can read extensively about it on the internet if you like.

There is nothing in the chord-naming systems to indicate if notes are doubled (repeated) or omitted. An 11th chord may or may not have a 7th or 9th in it, for example, and though technically something like a 6th chord is an "extension" of a major chord, and should have 1-3-5-6 scale notes, you will find voicings that are missing the 3rd or 5th. This is part of what gives each voicing its own sound, and the only way to know what is going on inside each chord is to study the letters and numbers for every chord.

A modal 7th chord, which is important in blues guitar, has no name, and is generally just put in the pile with the other 7th chords, even though it has no 3rd, and has just the 1-5-7b notes. You'll have to study the small scale degree numbers under the chords to find these. To my ears, Big Joe Williams' classic song "*Baby Please Don't Go*" doesn't sound right to me unless you use one. Similarly, an augmented chord with no 3rd is just 1 and 5# notes. If you don't call it an augmented chord, then it really has no name. It's not really just an interval when there are 4 or 5 notes in it.

This book doesn't use the open circle symbol to show an optional fingering. It's a common and useful thing to do, but it interferes with the way the letter names and the scale degrees of every note are shown under each chord in this book. (You can't really show the note names and scale degrees for the optional fingerings.) A chord diagram with several open circles is more of a puzzle than a chord, and it is not simple to extract the usable fingerings.

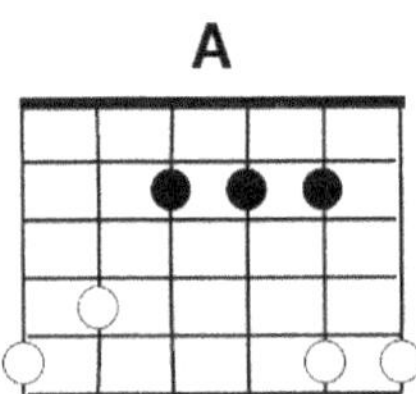
A

This chord diagram appears in the well-known Ted Green "*Chord Chemistry*" book, and seems to say a lot about the different ways to play an A major chord at fret 2. It might be very informative and helpful, but it might also be as confusing as it is helpful. It actually parses down to 12 different fingerings that take some effort to extract from the diagram. 8 of them are in this book. Since you can only play one of them at a time, I chose to show you the 8 choices one at a time. They are at the beginning of this book with the other A major chords.

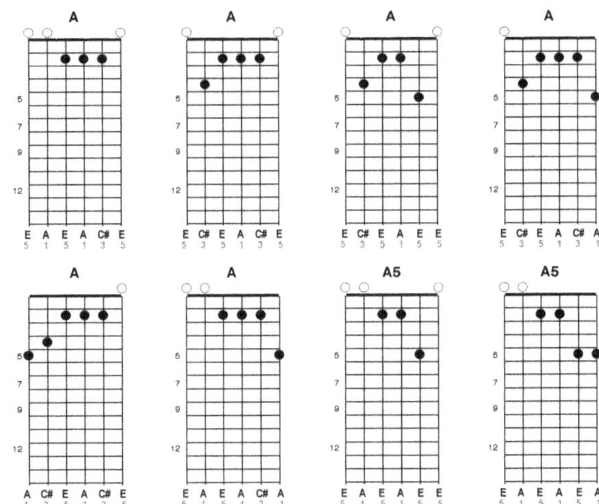
A
A
A
A
E A E A C# E
5 1 5 1 3 5
E C# E A C# E
5 3 5 1 3 5
E C# E A E E
5 3 5 1 5 5
E C# E A C# A
5 3 5 1 3 1
A
A
A5
A5
A C# E A C# E
1 3 5 1 3 5
E A E A C# A
5 1 5 1 3 1
E A E A E E
5 1 5 1 5 5
E A E A E A
5 1 5 1 5 1

Since we are being precise, here are the four I left out. They are playable by some of us, but impractical:

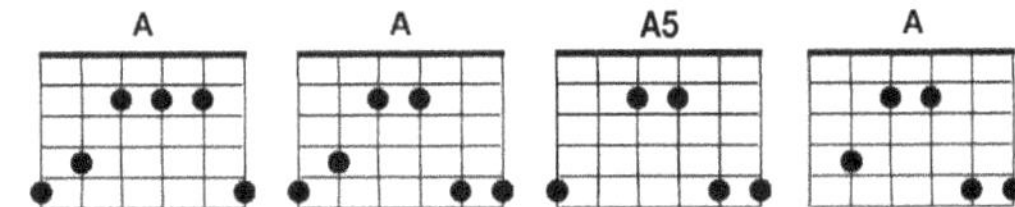
A
A
A5
A

Ted Green's diagram might better represent how a skilled guitarist conceptualizes a nut position A chord, and it might not. You could also just show the whole fingerboard of A-C#-E notes, which is also what a skilled guitarist "sees" on the fingerboard to represent an A chord:

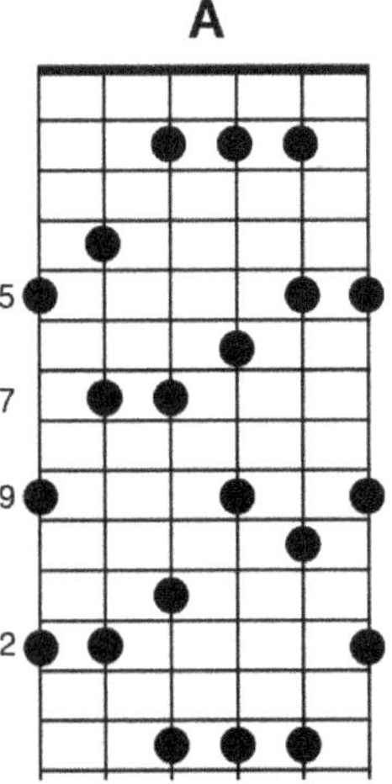
A
5
7
9
12

Again, this is more of a puzzle than a chord chart, and though all possible A chords are encoded here, the diagram is of questionable value to someone who wants to learn the different ways to play an A chord. This the kind of information that computer-generated chord charts and apps give you, but I don't think there is any substitute for a human editor who makes decisions about what chords don't sound good or are too hard to finger. I chose to show you the 24 A chords in the chart instead of just this diagram.

Arpeggiated Chords

The Italian word *arpeggio* literally means "broken chord" and the choice of whether the notes in a chord are played all at once or in staggered time can make a world of difference in the sound of the chord.

For example, we fingerpickers love chords like those that I call 9/11 chords, which have the added 11th (which is the same as the 4th) and the 9th, which is shown as a 2. An A9/11 would have the A-C#-E triad with D and B added to it. This really means that you now have 1-2-3-4-5 scale notes all in the same chord, which can sound quite dissonant when strummed, yet haunting and harp-like when arpeggiated.

Before you decide that a chord in this book is "no good," make sure you play it forward and backwards in arpeggio, and also in a strummed form. Many of them really come to life when they are arpeggiated.

How Many Chords is Best?

Many readers who are opening this book are beginners and intermediate players, and the question arises as to whether it is better to include more or fewer chords, or perhaps to draw some lines in terms of difficulty or complexity.

If you have a lot of chords, you inevitably include "not-so-great" voicings and very difficult fingerings along with the easier and good-sounding chords. Is it perhaps better to just have the most vital and most common chords? In the spirit of do-it-yourself, I decided to include a lot of choices of ways to play more common chords, and to not include more "obscure" types of chords. I don't think it hurts anyone to have a chord book with a lot of choices, any more than it hurts to have a dictionary with words in it than most of us will never really use.

Guitar chord books and even songbooks of popular songs often show chords with just 4 strings sounding, when no troubadour anywhere would play them that way. I own a Bob Dylan songbook that shows "*Blowin' In the Wind*" in Eb, with the bottom 2 strings muted on all the chords. Bob didn't play it that way and neither would anybody else. It was probably put in this key to make pianists happy, and the 4-note chords probably harken back to the early days of music publishing, when tenor guitar (4 strings) and ukulele chords were put in the sheet music along with the piano arrangements. It also satisfies something in people who have studied music theory, where so much of harmony and chord theory is built around 4-part voicings and 4-note "*tetrachords*" as the building blocks of harmony. It has remained common in guitar chord books dating back 100 years to show mostly 4-string chords. You'll notice that I have included only a few really common ones, and there are a vast majority of 5 and 6-string chords here, with very few chords with inner strings muted. (Only 50 of these chords other than augmented and diminished chords have 2 muted strings.) There are lot of other chord encyclopedias that show thousands of movable 4-string chords.

This kind of thinking also brings up the issues of what is hard or easy, and what is common or useful. If you like dissonant music, then what is a useful chord to you is not the same as it would be for someone who had more mainstream tastes and who liked consonance. Our tastes change as we get older also, and as we have life experiences. I had to make a lot of tough decisions about what chords to include, and I might have put in a chord on a day when I was feeling generous, and I may have tossed some out on other days when I was feeling differently.

A guitar chord book is somewhat of an artistic statement, and reflects the personality as well as the musical tastes and skills of the author. I hope you like this one. I really had a lot of fun making it, and it really stirred up in me a constant and ever-deepening sense of awe at all the things a troubadour can do with 6 strings tuned to E-A-D-G-B-E, 4 fingers and a thumb.

In this digital world, where there is an endless torrent of new gadgets, software, and new interfaces, there is something profoundly satisfying about focusing entirely on a centuries-old thing like a guitar fingerboard.

About the Diagrams in This Book

Some guitars have a lot more frets than others, and it's unclear how high to go up the fingerboard when you make a chord book. The note at the 12th fret is the same letter name as the open string and the fingerboard starts repeating at that point. Modern acoustic guitars generally have 14 frets to the body, so the chord diagrams in this book go up to fret 14. If you have an electric guitar or a double cutaway you will have access to some other chord fingerings in the higher frets that are not in this book.

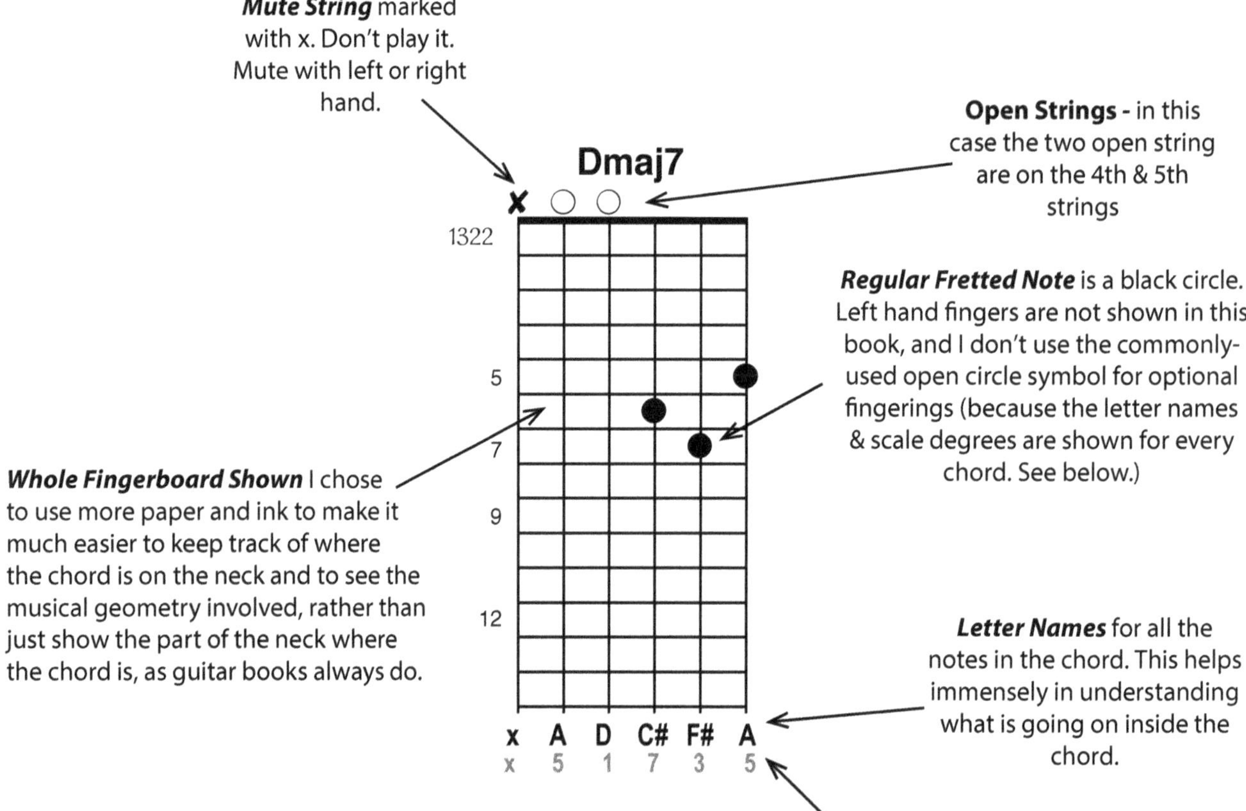

Mute String marked with x. Don't play it. Mute with left or right hand.
Open Strings - in this case the two open string are on the 4th & 5th strings
Dmaj7
1322
5
7
9
12
Regular Fretted Note is a black circle. Left hand fingers are not shown in this book, and I don't use the commonly-used open circle symbol for optional fingerings (because the letter names & scale degrees are shown for every chord. See below.)
Whole Fingerboard Shown I chose to use more paper and ink to make it much easier to keep track of where the chord is on the neck and to see the musical geometry involved, rather than just show the part of the neck where the chord is, as guitar books always do.
Letter Names for all the notes in the chord. This helps immensely in understanding what is going on inside the chord.
x A D C# F# A
x 5 1 7 3 5

Scale Degrees of each note-- showing you the inversions, *"spelling"* and *voicing* of each chord. A big part of what gives each chord its musical identity is determined by which numbers are present. The order in which they appear, and which of them are absent or *doubled* (repeated) is also a vital factor. There are many voicings of any chord, and only a limited number of them are available on a guitar.

In this example, D is the root or 1, so the 3rd of that scale is the F#, the 5th of a D scale is A and the (major) 7th is a C#. These numbers show you the structure and help you analyze and understand the sound of each chord.

Sorting The chords in this book are sorted by root note first. and then by chord type, fret position and number of fingers in the chord. A 3-finger chord that starts at fret 4 will appear before a 3 finger barre chord at that same fret position. In a few instances I have moved a very common voicing to the front. Instead of trying to sort chord types by complexity, I put them in order of how often we use them. This is both helpful and frustrating, since it's hard to know if a minor 6th is more useful than a major 9th.

Troubadour Guitar Chords

TUNING: E A D G B E (Standard)

A

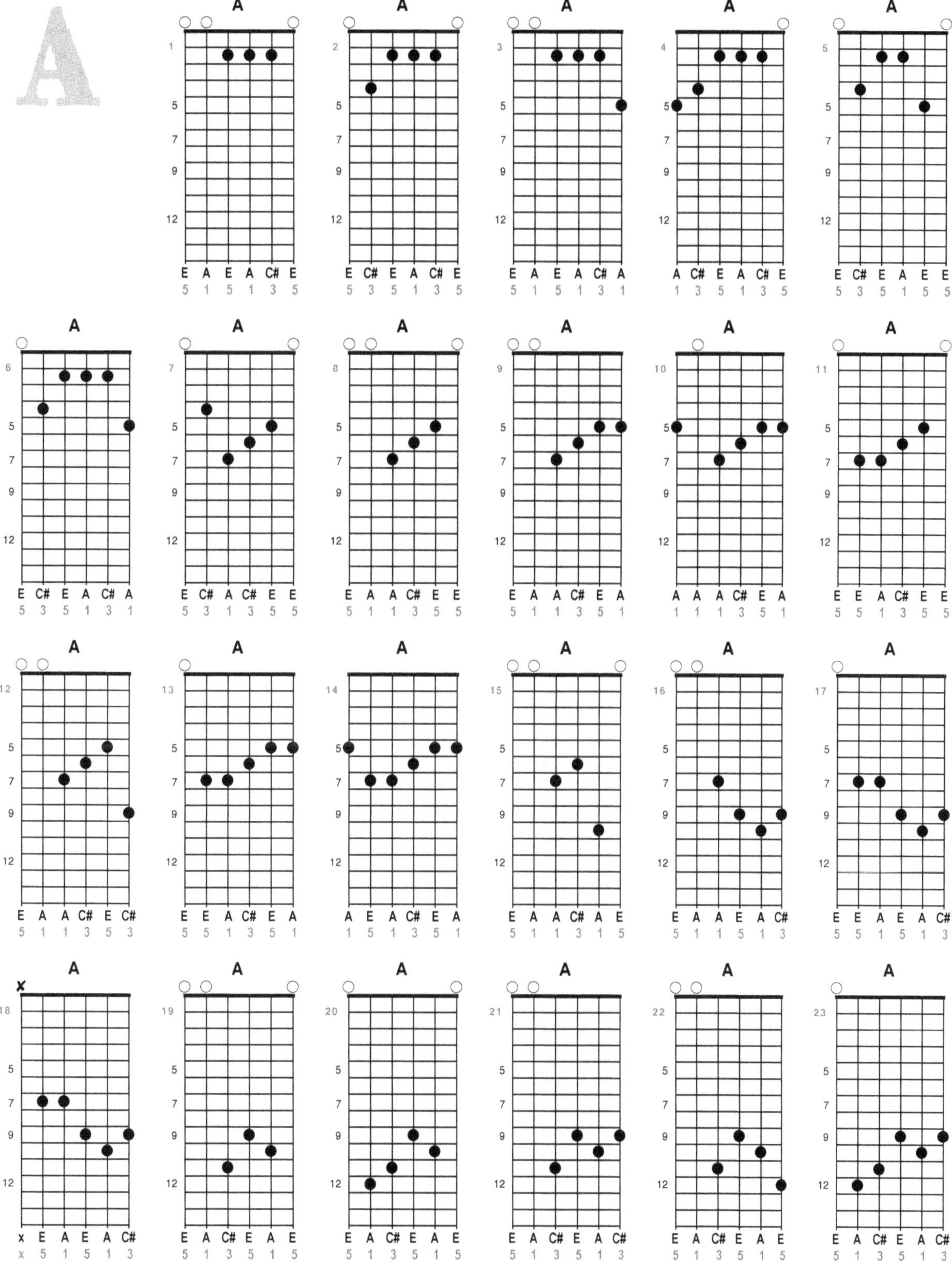

Troubadour Guitar Chords

TUNING: E A D G B E (Standard)

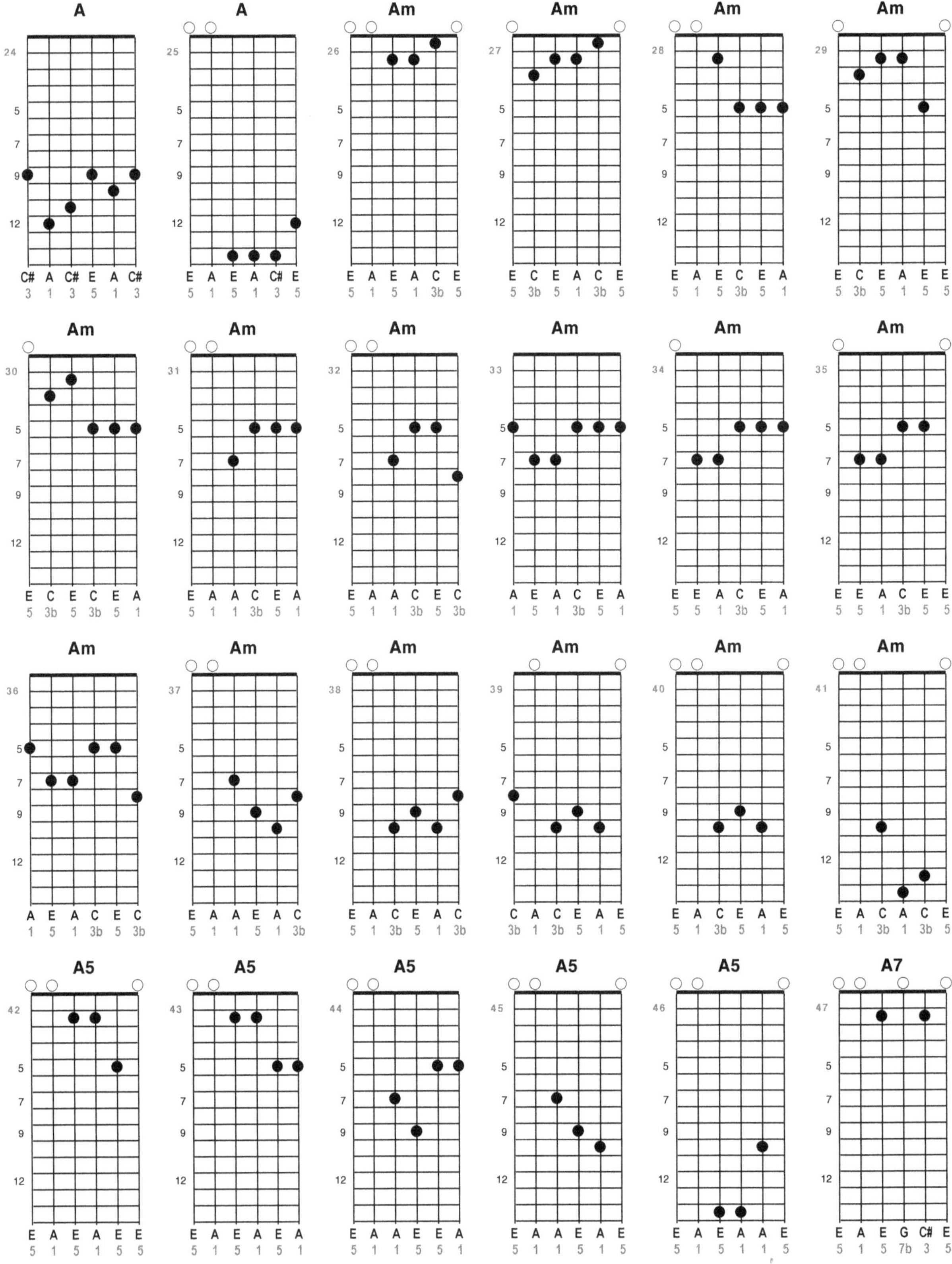

A
24
C# A C# E A C#
3 1 3 5 1 3
A
25
E A E A C# E
5 1 5 1 3 5
Am
26
E A E A C E
5 1 5 1 3b 5
Am
27
E C E A C E
5 3b 5 1 3b 5
Am
28
E A E C E A
5 1 5 3b 5 1
Am
29
E C E A E E
5 3b 5 1 5 5
Am
30
E C E C E A
5 3b 5 3b 5 1
Am
31
E A A C E A
5 1 1 3b 5 1
Am
32
E A A C E C
5 1 1 3b 5 3b
Am
33
A E A C E A
1 5 1 3b 5 1
Am
34
E E A C E A
5 5 1 3b 5 1
Am
35
E E A C E E
5 5 1 3b 5 5
Am
36
A E A C E C
1 5 1 3b 5 3b
Am
37
E A A E A C
5 1 1 5 1 3b
Am
38
E A C E A C
5 1 3b 5 1 3b
Am
39
C A C E A E
3b 1 3b 5 1 5
Am
40
E A C E A E
5 1 3b 5 1 5
Am
41
E A C A C E
5 1 3b 1 3b 5
A5
42
E A E A E E
5 1 5 1 5 5
A5
43
E A E A E A
5 1 5 1 5 1
A5
44
E A A E E A
5 1 1 5 5 1
A5
45
E A A E A E
5 1 1 5 1 5
A5
46
E A E A A E
5 1 5 1 1 5
A7
47
E A E G C# E
5 1 5 7b 3 5

Troubadour Guitar Chords

TUNING: E A D G B E (Standard)

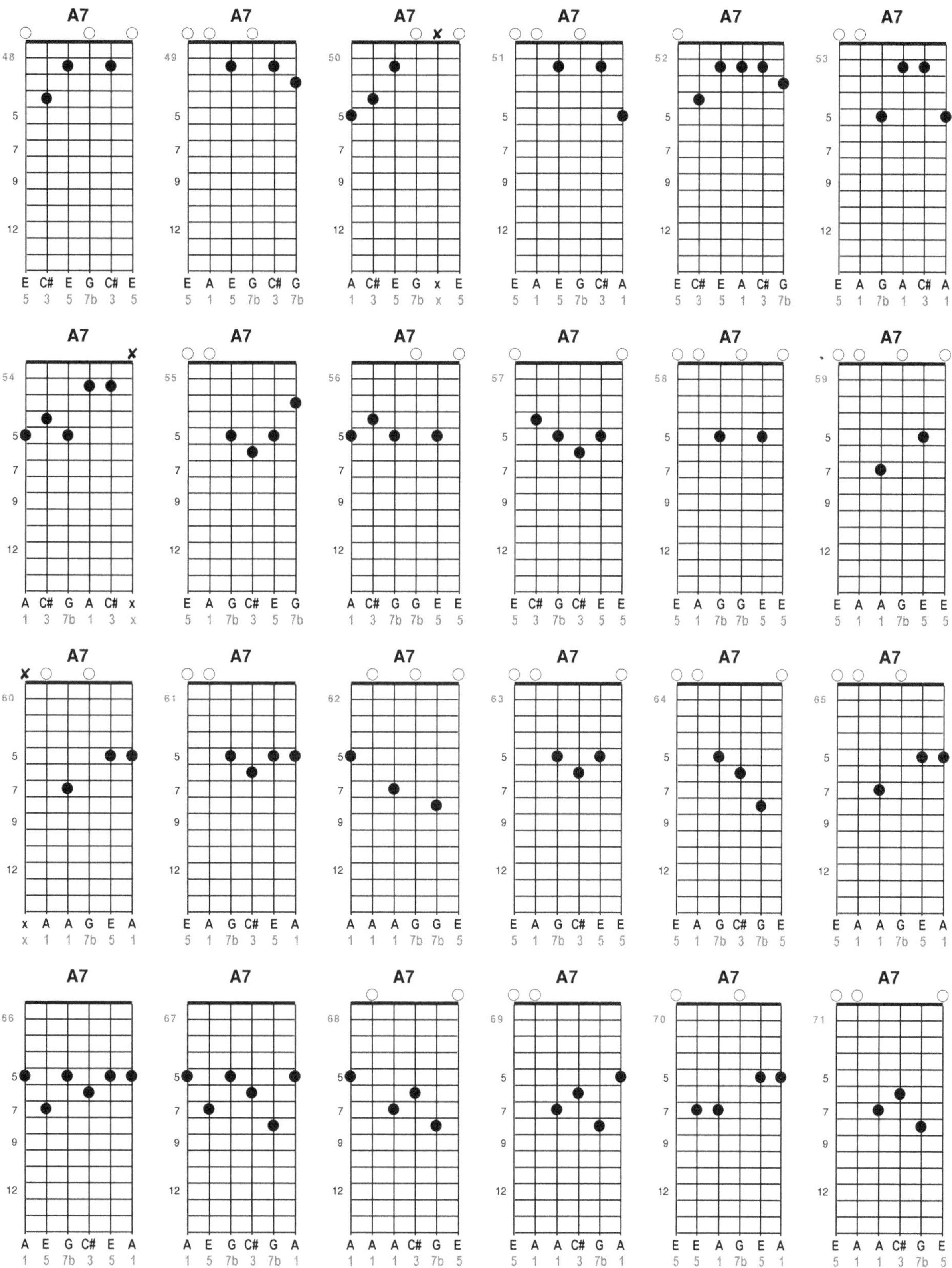

Troubadour Guitar Chords

TUNING: E A D G B E (Standard)

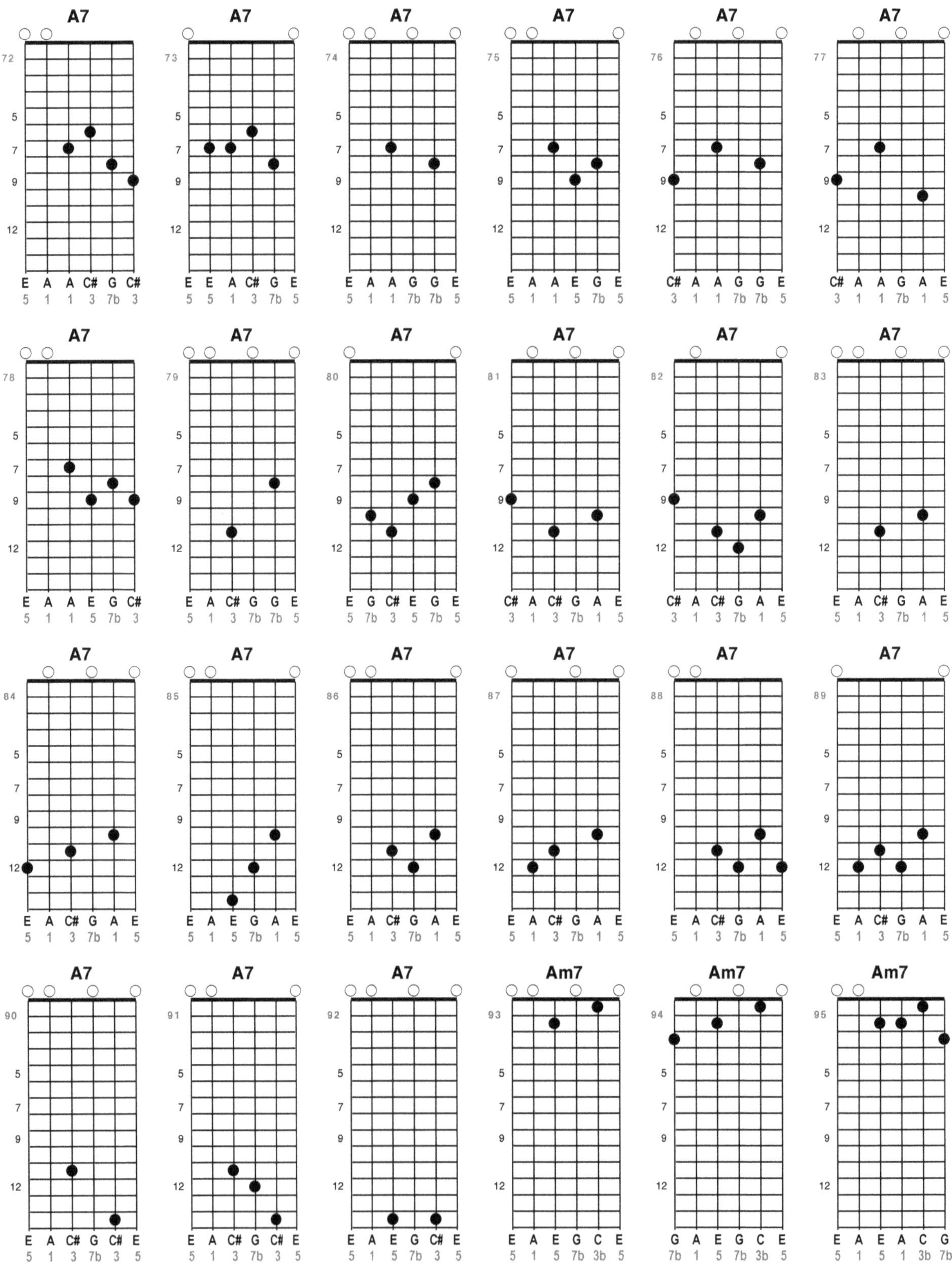

A7
72
E A A C# G C#
5 1 1 3 7b 3
A7
73
E E A C# G E
5 5 1 3 7b 5
A7
74
E A A G G E
5 1 1 7b 7b 5
A7
75
E A A E G E
5 1 1 5 7b 5
A7
76
C# A A G G E
3 1 1 7b 7b 5
A7
77
C# A A G A E
3 1 1 7b 1 5
A7
78
E A A E G C#
5 1 1 5 7b 3
A7
79
E A C# G G E
5 1 3 7b 7b 5
A7
80
E G C# E G E
5 7b 3 5 7b 5
A7
81
C# A C# G A E
3 1 3 7b 1 5
A7
82
C# A C# G A E
3 1 3 7b 1 5
A7
83
E A C# G A E
5 1 3 7b 1 5
A7
84
E A C# G A E
5 1 3 7b 1 5
A7
85
E A E G A E
5 1 5 7b 1 5
A7
86
E A C# G A E
5 1 3 7b 1 5
A7
87
E A C# G A E
5 1 3 7b 1 5
A7
88
E A C# G A E
5 1 3 7b 1 5
A7
89
E A C# G A E
5 1 3 7b 1 5
A7
90
E A C# G C# E
5 1 3 7b 3 5
A7
91
E A C# G C# E
5 1 3 7b 3 5
A7
92
E A E G C# E
5 1 5 7b 3 5
Am7
93
E A E G C E
5 1 5 7b 3b 5
Am7
94
G A E G C E
7b 1 5 7b 3b 5
Am7
95
E A E A C G
5 1 5 1 3b 7b

Troubadour Guitar Chords

TUNING: E A D G B E (Standard)

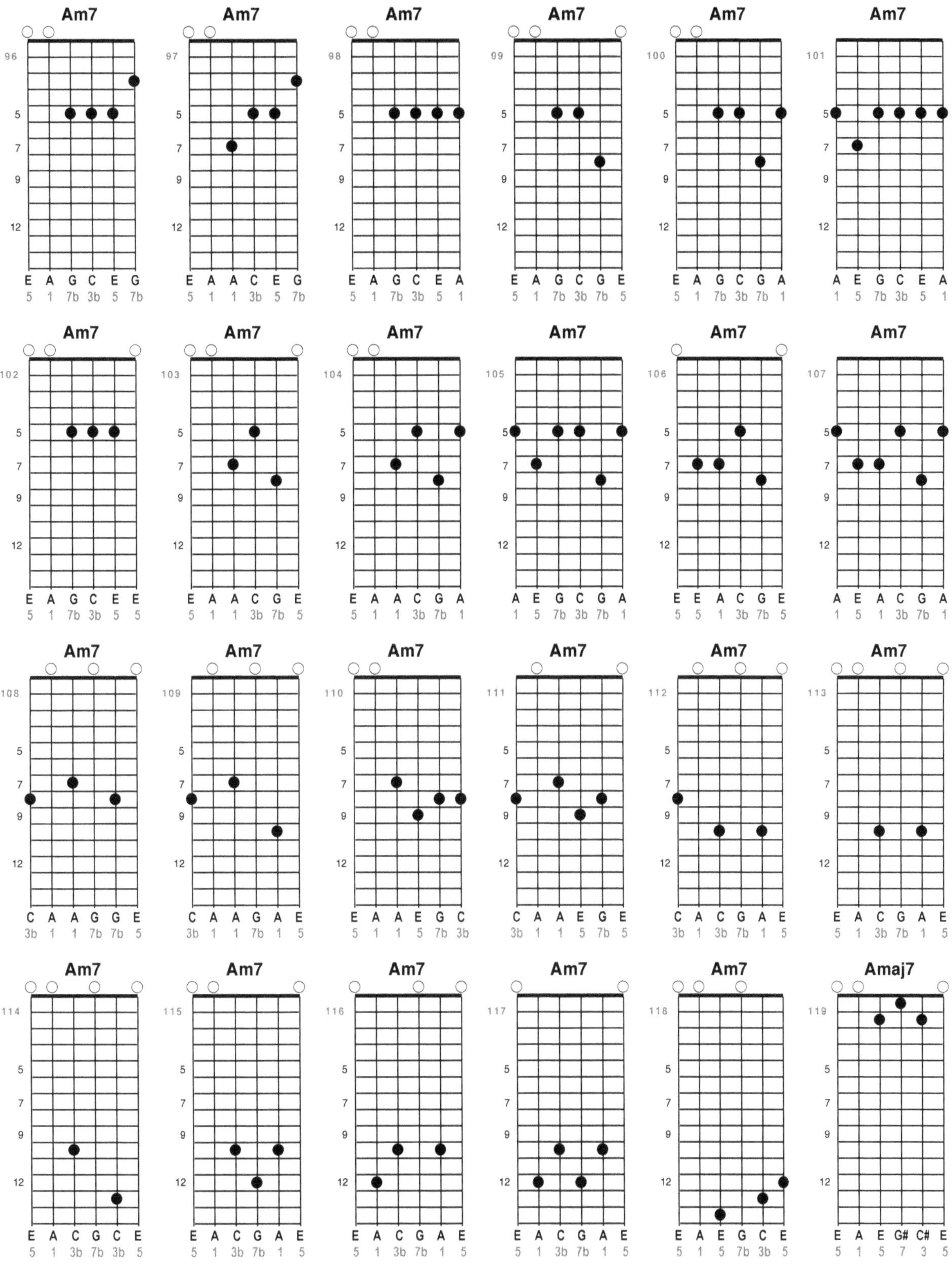
Am7
96
5 7 9 12
E A G C E G
5 1 7b 3b 5 7b
Am7
97
5 7 9 12
E A A C E G
5 1 1 3b 5 7b
Am7
98
5 7 9 12
E A G C E A
5 1 7b 3b 5 1
Am7
99
5 7 9 12
E A G C G E
5 1 7b 3b 7b 5
Am7
100
5 7 9 12
E A G C G A
5 1 7b 3b 7b 1
Am7
101
5 7 9 12
A E G C E A
1 5 7b 3b 5 1
Am7
102
5 7 9 12
E A G C E E
5 1 7b 3b 5 5
Am7
103
5 7 9 12
E A A C G E
5 1 1 3b 7b 5
Am7
104
5 7 9 12
E A A C G A
5 1 1 3b 7b 1
Am7
105
5 7 9 12
A E G C G A
1 5 7b 3b 7b 1
Am7
106
5 7 9 12
E E A C G E
5 5 1 3b 7b 5
Am7
107
5 7 9 12
A E A C G A
1 5 1 3b 7b 1
Am7
108
5 7 9 12
C A A G G E
3b 1 1 7b 7b 5
Am7
109
5 7 9 12
C A A G A E
3b 1 1 7b 1 5
Am7
110
5 7 9 12
E A A E G C
5 1 1 5 7b 3b
Am7
111
5 7 9 12
C A A E G E
3b 1 1 5 7b 5
Am7
112
5 7 9 12
C A C G A E
3b 1 3b 7b 1 5
Am7
113
5 7 9 12
E A C G A E
5 1 3b 7b 1 5
Am7
114
5 7 9 12
E A C G C E
5 1 3b 7b 3b 5
Am7
115
5 7 9 12
E A C G A E
5 1 3b 7b 1 5
Am7
116
5 7 9 12
E A C G A E
5 1 3b 7b 1 5
Am7
117
5 7 9 12
E A C G A E
5 1 3b 7b 1 5
Am7
118
5 7 9 12
E A E G C E
5 1 5 7b 3b 5
Amaj7
119
5 7 9 12
E A E G# C# E
5 1 5 7 3 5

Troubadour Guitar Chords

TUNING: E A D G B E (Standard)

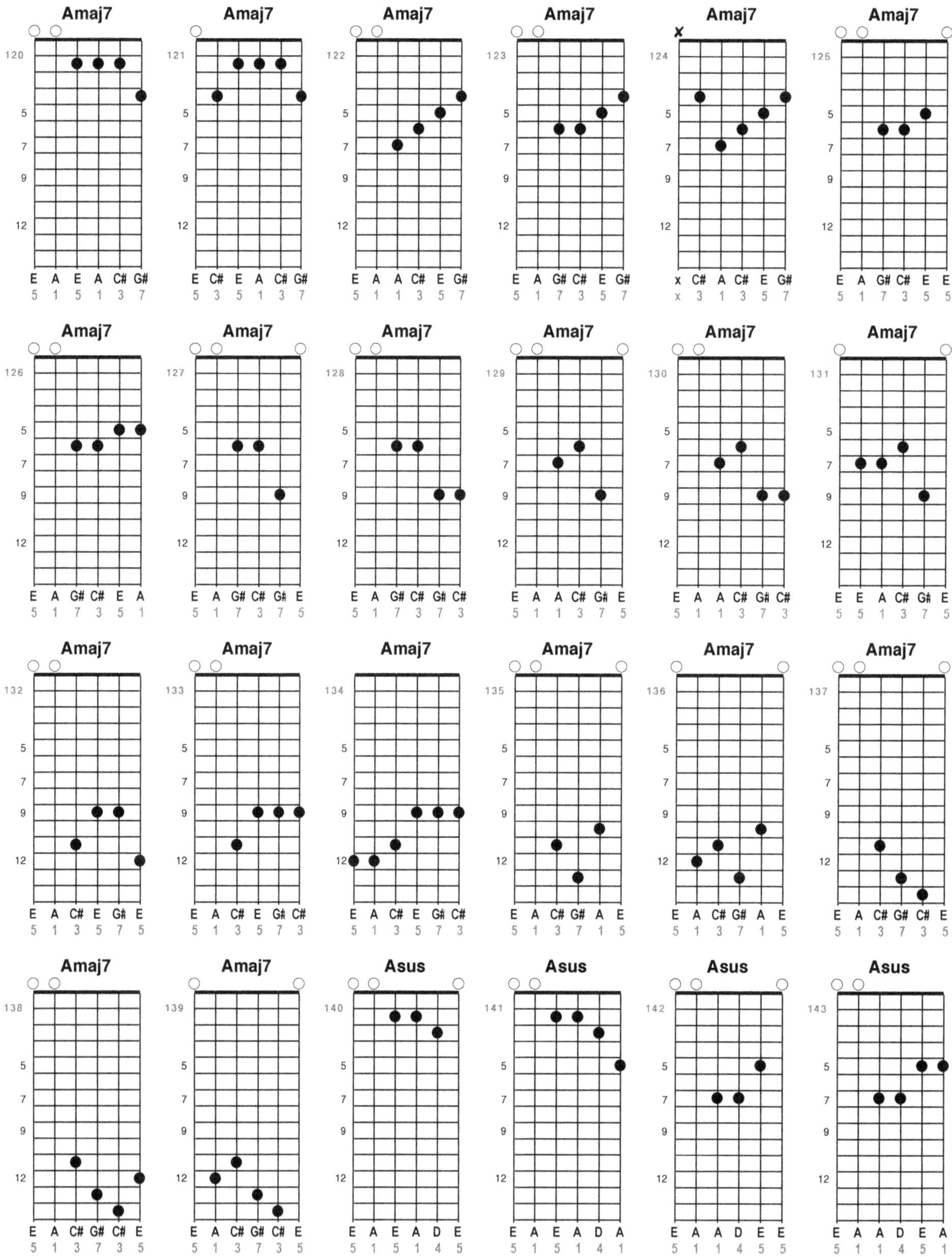
Amaj7
120
E A E A C# G#
5 1 5 1 3 7
Amaj7
121
E C# E A C# G#
5 3 5 1 3 7
Amaj7
122
E A A C# E G#
5 1 1 3 5 7
Amaj7
123
E A G# C# E G#
5 1 7 3 5 7
Amaj7
124
x C# A C# E G#
x 3 1 3 5 7
Amaj7
125
E A G# C# E E
5 1 7 3 5 5
Amaj7
126
E A G# C# E A
5 1 7 3 5 1
Amaj7
127
E A G# C# G# E
5 1 7 3 7 5
Amaj7
128
E A G# C# G# C#
5 1 7 3 7 3
Amaj7
129
E A A C# G# E
5 1 1 3 7 5
Amaj7
130
E A A C# G# C#
5 1 1 3 7 3
Amaj7
131
E E A C# G# E
5 5 1 3 7 5
Amaj7
132
E A C# E G# E
5 1 3 5 7 5
Amaj7
133
E A C# E G# C#
5 1 3 5 7 3
Amaj7
134
E A C# E G# C#
5 1 3 5 7 3
Amaj7
135
E A C# G# A E
5 1 3 7 1 5
Amaj7
136
E A C# G# A E
5 1 3 7 1 5
Amaj7
137
E A C# G# C# E
5 1 3 7 3 5
Amaj7
138
E A C# G# C# E
5 1 3 7 3 5
Amaj7
139
E A C# G# C# E
5 1 3 7 3 5
Asus
140
E A E A D E
5 1 5 1 4 5
Asus
141
E A E A D A
5 1 5 1 4 1
Asus
142
E A A D E E
5 1 1 4 5 5
Asus
143
E A A D E A
5 1 1 4 5 1

TUNING: E A D G B E (Standard)

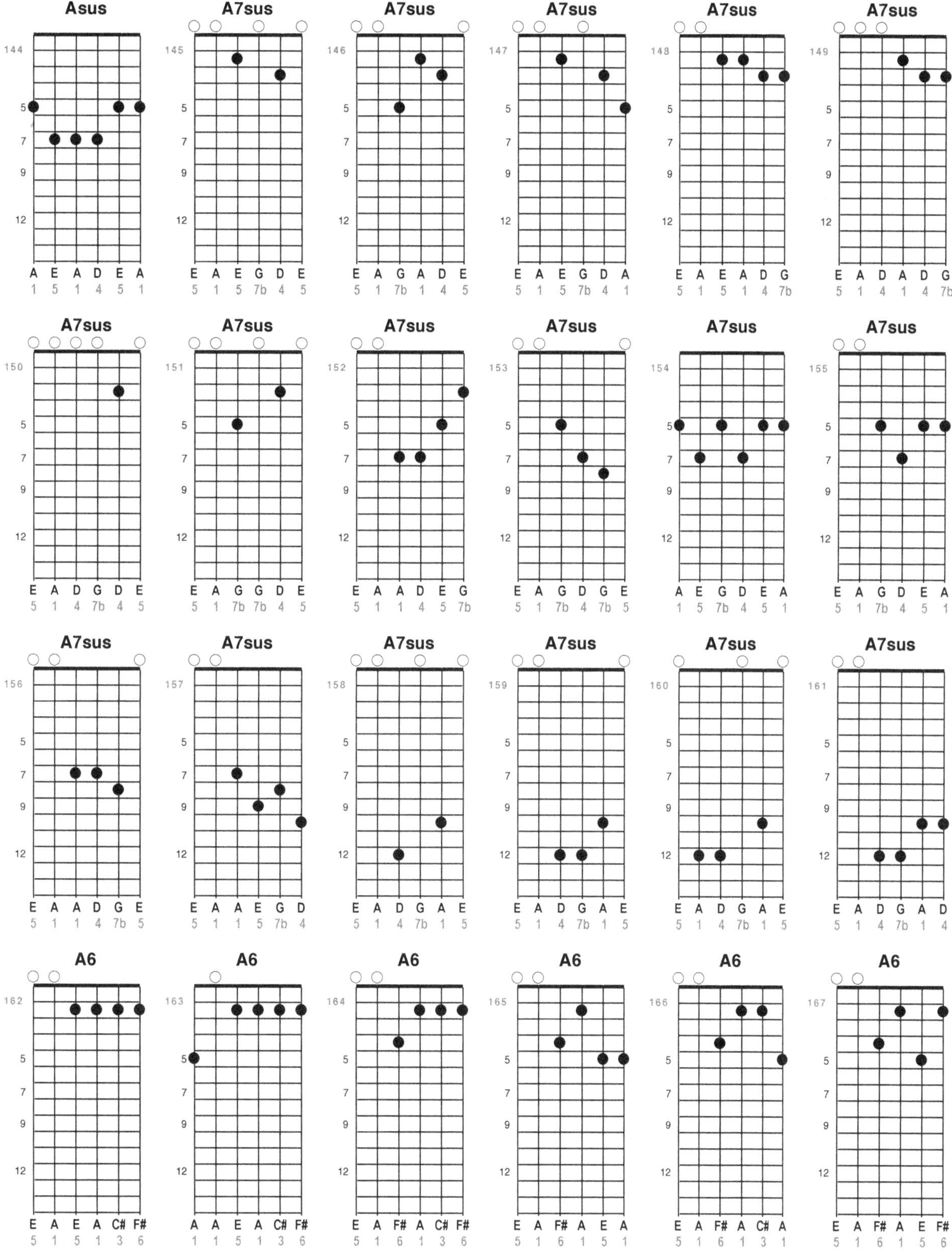
Asus
144
A E A D E A
1 5 1 4 5 1
A7sus
145
E A E G D E
5 1 5 7b 4 5
A7sus
146
E A G A D E
5 1 7b 1 4 5
A7sus
147
E A E G D A
5 1 5 7b 4 1
A7sus
148
E A E A D G
5 1 5 1 4 7b
A7sus
149
E A D A D G
5 1 4 1 4 7b
A7sus
150
E A D G D E
5 1 4 7b 4 5
A7sus
151
E A G G D E
5 1 7b 7b 4 5
A7sus
152
E A A D E G
5 1 1 4 5 7b
A7sus
153
E A G D G E
5 1 7b 4 7b 5
A7sus
154
A E G D E A
1 5 7b 4 5 1
A7sus
155
E A G D E A
5 1 7b 4 5 1
A7sus
156
E A A D G E
5 1 1 4 7b 5
A7sus
157
E A A E G D
5 1 1 5 7b 4
A7sus
158
E A D G A E
5 1 4 7b 1 5
A7sus
159
E A D G A E
5 1 4 7b 1 5
A7sus
160
E A D G A E
5 1 4 7b 1 5
A7sus
161
E A D G A D
5 1 4 7b 1 4
A6
162
E A E A C# F#
5 1 5 1 3 6
A6
163
A A E A C# F#
1 1 5 1 3 6
A6
164
E A F# A C# F#
5 1 6 1 3 6
A6
165
E A F# A E A
5 1 6 1 5 1
A6
166
E A F# A C# A
5 1 6 1 3 1
A6
167
E A F# A E F#
5 1 6 1 5 6
5
7
9
12

Troubadour Guitar Chords

TUNING: E A D G B E (Standard)

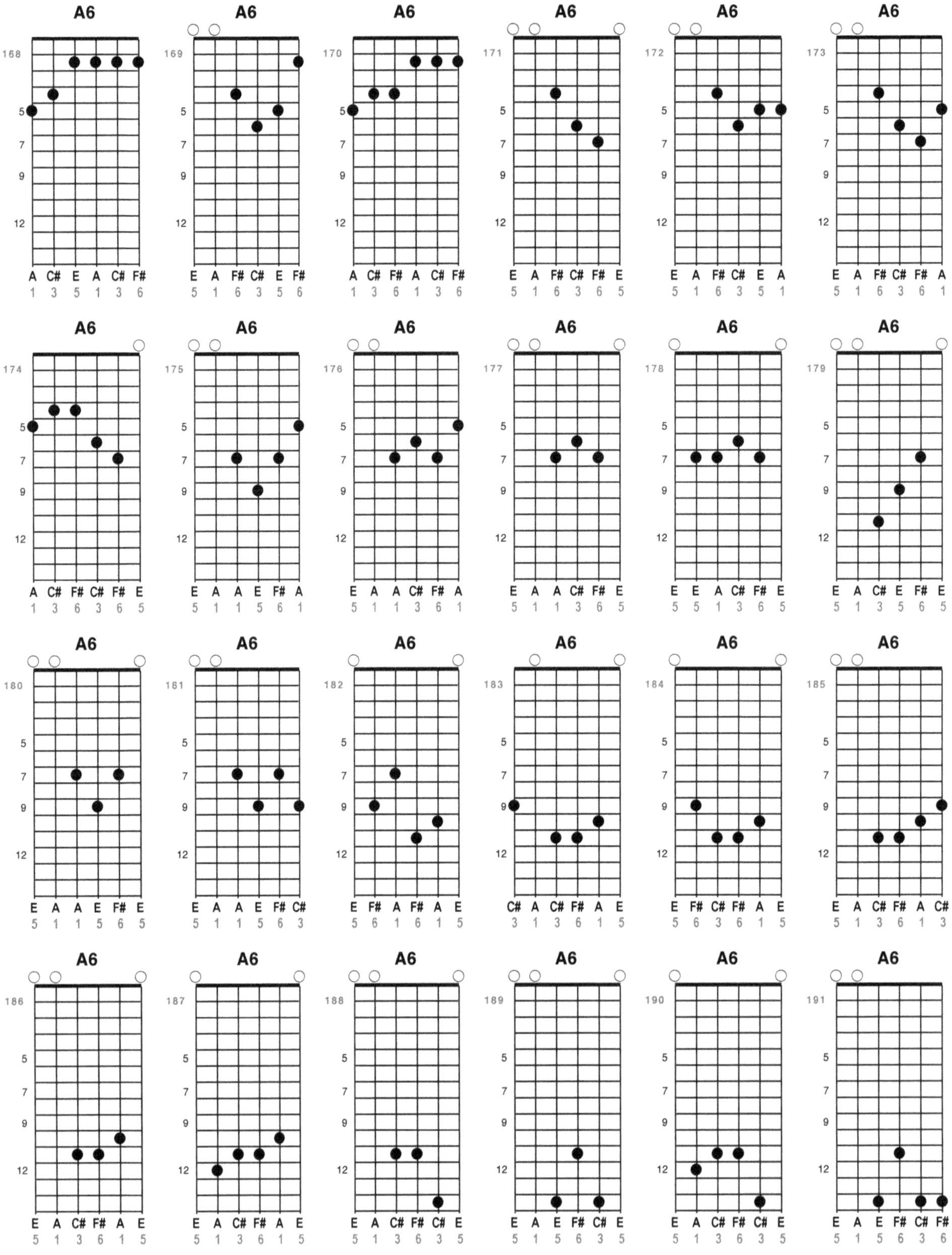
A6
168
169
170
171
172
173
174
175
176
177
178
179
180
181
182
183
184
185
186
187
188
189
190
191

Troubadour Guitar Chords

TUNING: E A D G B E (Standard)

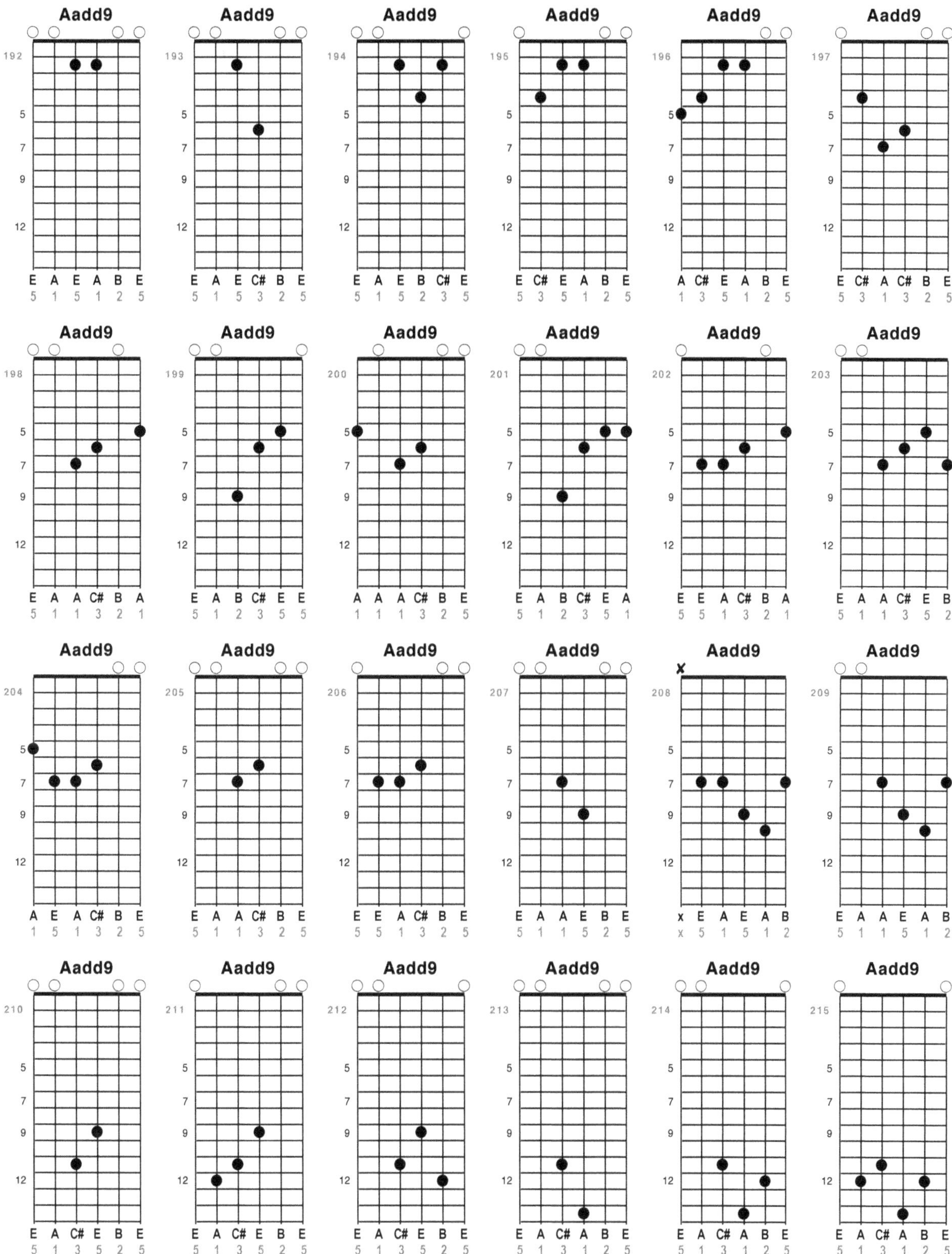

Aadd9
192
5
7
9
12
E A E A B E
5 1 5 1 2 5
Aadd9
193
E A E C# B E
5 1 5 3 2 5
Aadd9
194
E A E B C# E
5 1 5 2 3 5
Aadd9
195
E C# E A B E
5 3 5 1 2 5
Aadd9
196
A C# E A B E
1 3 5 1 2 5
Aadd9
197
E C# A C# B E
5 3 1 3 2 5
Aadd9
198
E A A C# B A
5 1 1 3 2 1
Aadd9
199
E A B C# E E
5 1 2 3 5 5
Aadd9
200
A A A C# B E
1 1 1 3 2 5
Aadd9
201
E A B C# E A
5 1 2 3 5 1
Aadd9
202
E E A C# B A
5 5 1 3 2 1
Aadd9
203
E A A C# E B
5 1 1 3 5 2
Aadd9
204
A E A C# B E
1 5 1 3 2 5
Aadd9
205
E A A C# B E
5 1 1 3 2 5
Aadd9
206
E E A C# B E
5 5 1 3 2 5
Aadd9
207
E A A E B E
5 1 1 5 2 5
Aadd9
208
x E A E A B
x 5 1 5 1 2
Aadd9
209
E A A E A B
5 1 1 5 1 2
Aadd9
210
E A C# E B E
5 1 3 5 2 5
Aadd9
211
E A C# E B E
5 1 3 5 2 5
Aadd9
212
E A C# E B E
5 1 3 5 2 5
Aadd9
213
E A C# A B E
5 1 3 1 2 5
Aadd9
214
E A C# A B E
5 1 3 1 2 5
Aadd9
215
E A C# A B E
5 1 3 1 2 5

TUNING: E A D G B E (Standard)

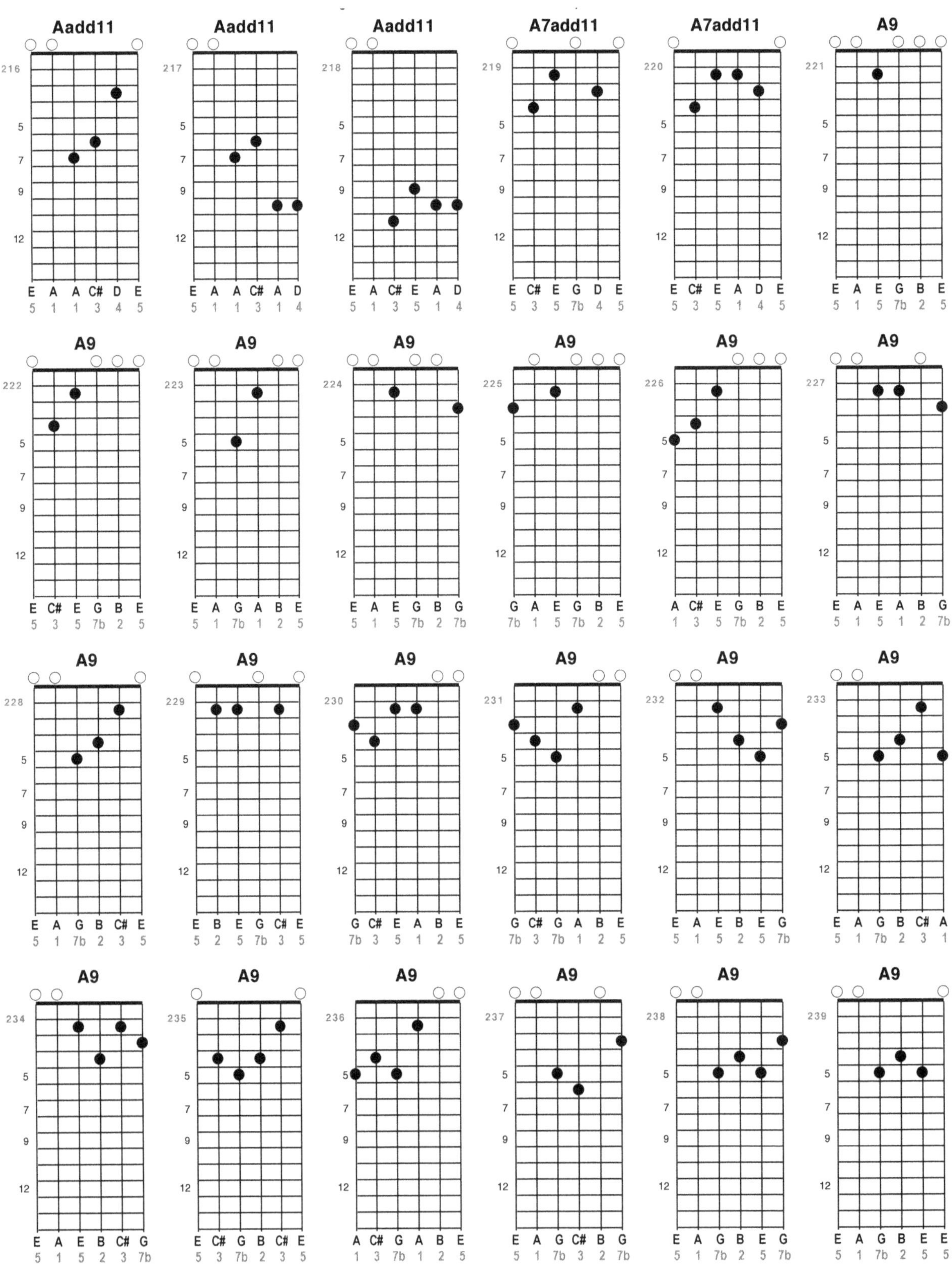

Aadd11
216
E A A C# D E
5 1 1 3 4 5
Aadd11
217
E A A C# A D
5 1 1 3 1 4
Aadd11
218
E A C# E A D
5 1 3 5 1 4
A7add11
219
E C# E G D E
5 3 5 7b 4 5
A7add11
220
E C# E A D E
5 3 5 1 4 5
A9
221
E A E G B E
5 1 5 7b 2 5
A9
222
E C# E G B E
5 3 5 7b 2 5
A9
223
E A G A B E
5 1 7b 1 2 5
A9
224
E A E G B G
5 1 5 7b 2 7b
A9
225
G A E G B E
7b 1 5 7b 2 5
A9
226
A C# E G B E
1 3 5 7b 2 5
A9
227
E A E A B G
5 1 5 1 2 7b
A9
228
E A G B C# E
5 1 7b 2 3 5
A9
229
E B E G C# E
5 2 5 7b 3 5
A9
230
G C# E A B E
7b 3 5 1 2 5
A9
231
G C# G A B E
7b 3 7b 1 2 5
A9
232
E A E B E G
5 1 5 2 5 7b
A9
233
E A G B C# A
5 1 7b 2 3 1
A9
234
E A E B C# G
5 1 5 2 3 7b
A9
235
E C# G B C# E
5 3 7b 2 3 5
A9
236
A C# G A B E
1 3 7b 1 2 5
A9
237
E A G C# B G
5 1 7b 3 2 7b
A9
238
E A G B E G
5 1 7b 2 5 7b
A9
239
E A G B E E
5 1 7b 2 5 5

TUNING: E A D G B E (Standard)

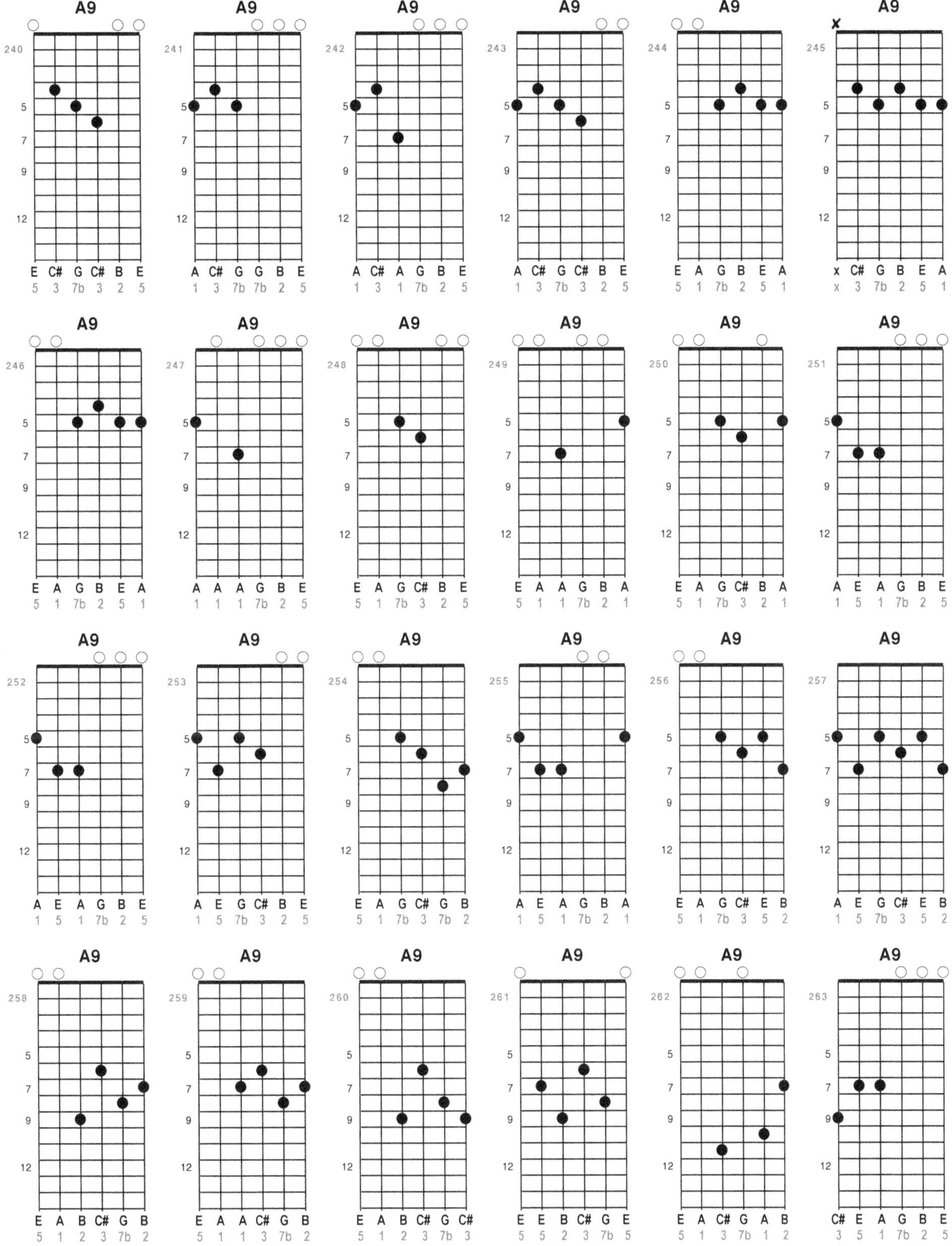

Troubadour Guitar Chords

TUNING: E A D G B E (Standard)

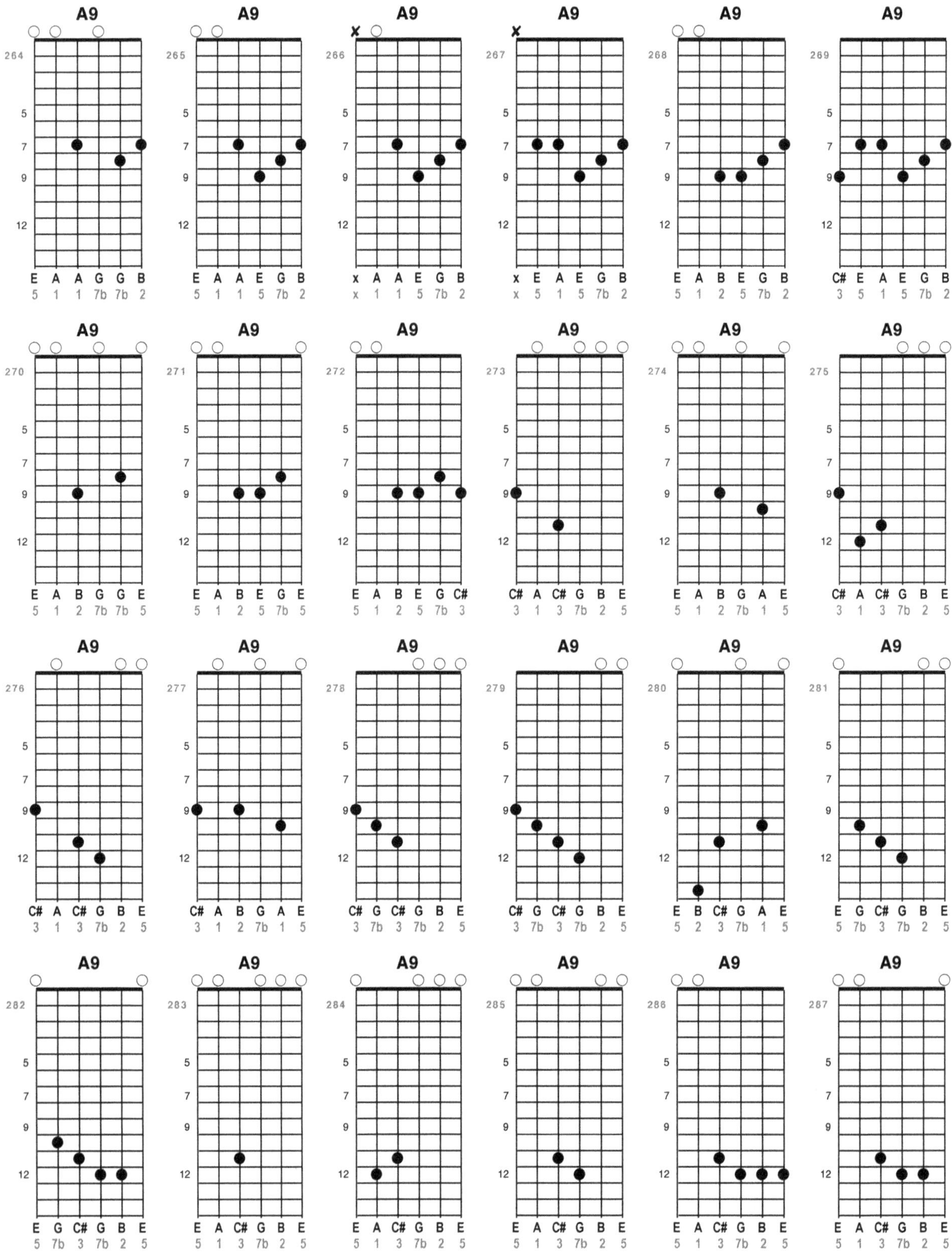

Troubadour Guitar Chords

TUNING: E A D G B E (Standard)

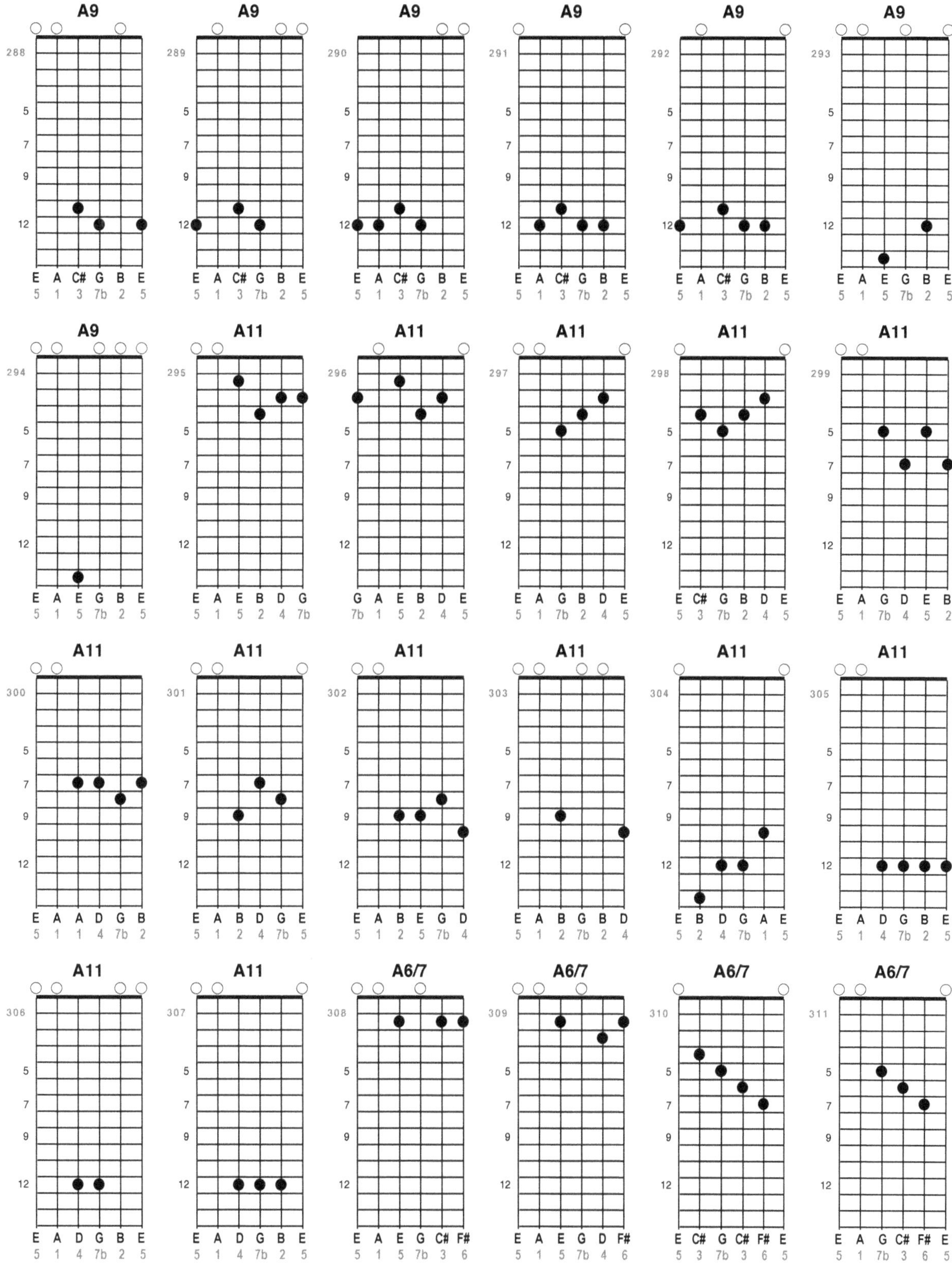

A9
288
E A C# G B E
5 1 3 7b 2 5
A9
289
E A C# G B E
5 1 3 7b 2 5
A9
290
E A C# G B E
5 1 3 7b 2 5
A9
291
E A C# G B E
5 1 3 7b 2 5
A9
292
E A C# G B E
5 1 3 7b 2 5
A9
293
E A E G B E
5 1 5 7b 2 5
A9
294
E A E G B E
5 1 5 7b 2 5
A11
295
E A E B D G
5 1 5 2 4 7b
A11
296
G A E B D E
7b 1 5 2 4 5
A11
297
E A G B D E
5 1 7b 2 4 5
A11
298
E C# G B D E
5 3 7b 2 4 5
A11
299
E A G D E B
5 1 7b 4 5 2
A11
300
E A A D G B
5 1 1 4 7b 2
A11
301
E A B D G E
5 1 2 4 7b 5
A11
302
E A B E G D
5 1 2 5 7b 4
A11
303
E A B G B D
5 1 2 7b 2 4
A11
304
E B D G A E
5 2 4 7b 1 5
A11
305
E A D G B E
5 1 4 7b 2 5
A11
306
E A D G B E
5 1 4 7b 2 5
A11
307
E A D G B E
5 1 4 7b 2 5
A6/7
308
E A E G C# F#
5 1 5 7b 3 6
A6/7
309
E A E G D F#
5 1 5 7b 4 6
A6/7
310
E C# G C# F# E
5 3 7b 3 6 5
A6/7
311
E A G C# F# E
5 1 7b 3 6 5
5
7
9
12

Troubadour Guitar Chords

TUNING: E A D G B E (Standard)

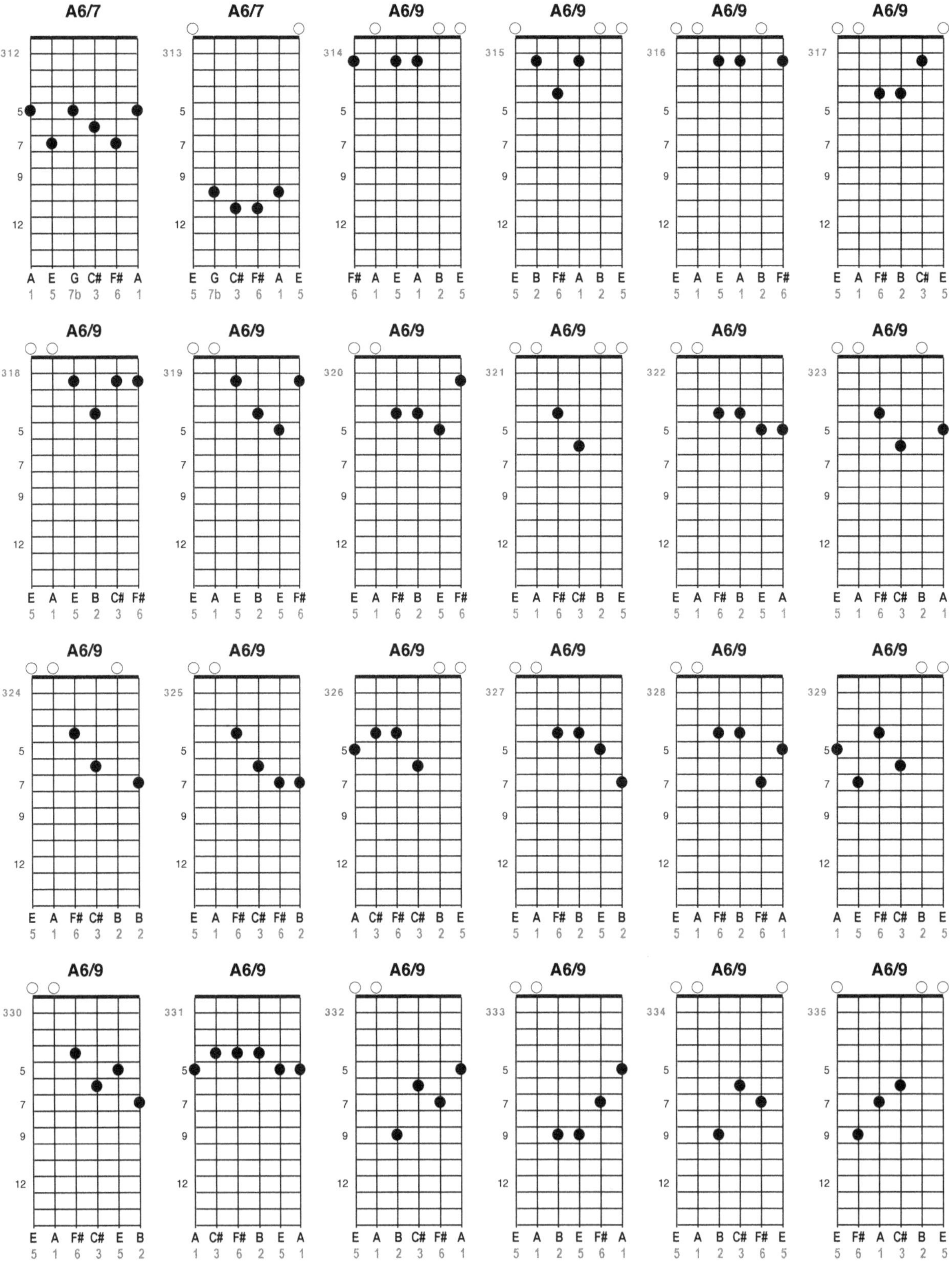
A6/7
312
A E G C# F# A
1 5 7b 3 6 1
A6/7
313
E G C# F# A E
5 7b 3 6 1 5
A6/9
314
F# A E A B E
6 1 5 1 2 5
A6/9
315
E B F# A B E
5 2 6 1 2 5
A6/9
316
E A E A B F#
5 1 5 1 2 6
A6/9
317
E A F# B C# E
5 1 6 2 3 5
A6/9
318
E A E B C# F#
5 1 5 2 3 6
A6/9
319
E A E B E F#
5 1 5 2 5 6
A6/9
320
E A F# B E F#
5 1 6 2 5 6
A6/9
321
E A F# C# B E
5 1 6 3 2 5
A6/9
322
E A F# B E A
5 1 6 2 5 1
A6/9
323
E A F# C# B A
5 1 6 3 2 1
A6/9
324
E A F# C# B B
5 1 6 3 2 2
A6/9
325
E A F# C# F# B
5 1 6 3 6 2
A6/9
326
A C# F# C# B E
1 3 6 3 2 5
A6/9
327
E A F# B E B
5 1 6 2 5 2
A6/9
328
E A F# B F# A
5 1 6 2 6 1
A6/9
329
A E F# C# B E
1 5 6 3 2 5
A6/9
330
E A F# C# E B
5 1 6 3 5 2
A6/9
331
A C# F# B E A
1 3 6 2 5 1
A6/9
332
E A B C# F# A
5 1 2 3 6 1
A6/9
333
E A B E F# A
5 1 2 5 6 1
A6/9
334
E A B C# F# E
5 1 2 3 6 5
A6/9
335
E F# A C# B E
5 6 1 3 2 5

Troubadour Guitar Chords

TUNING: E A D G B E (Standard)

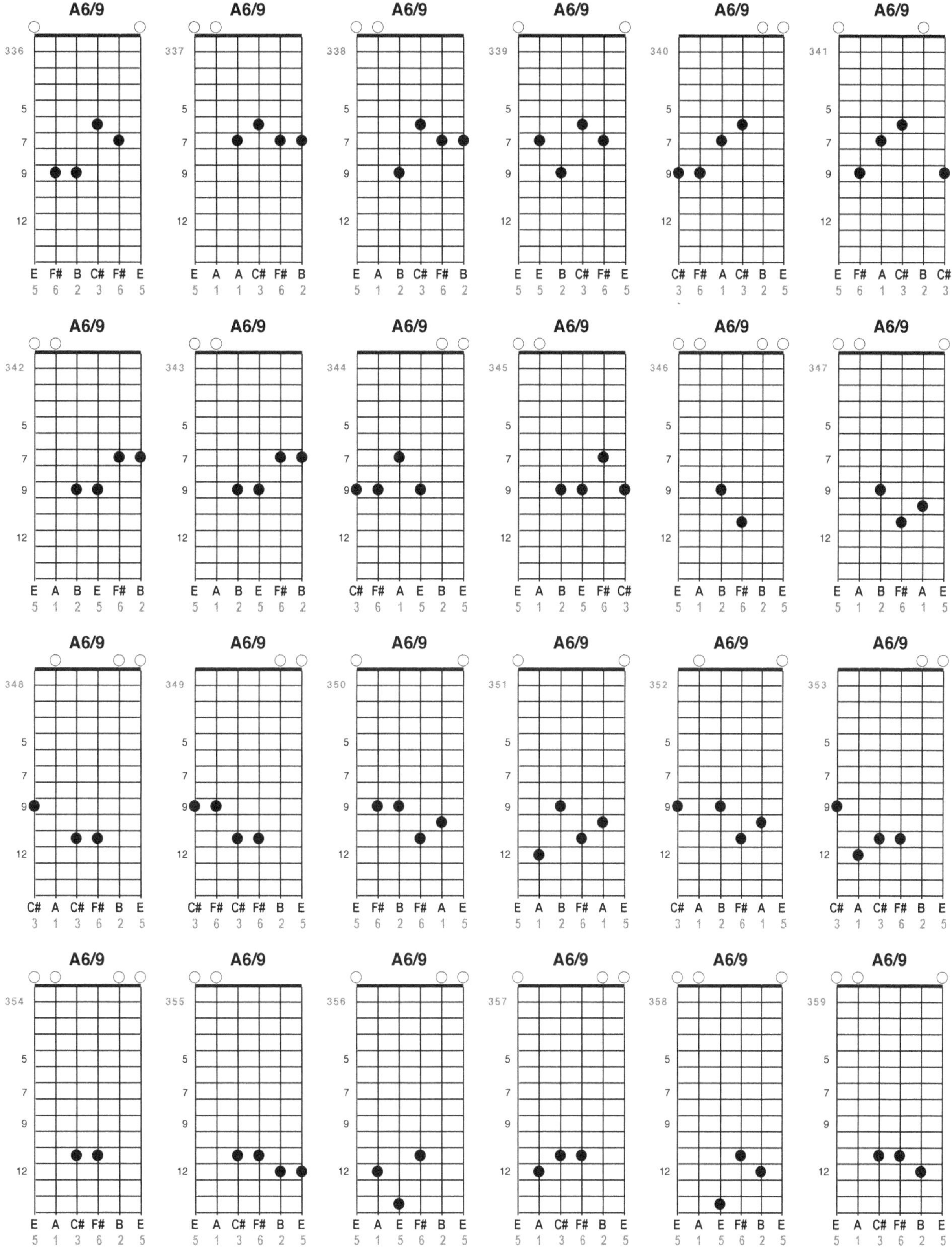

A6/9
336
E F# B C# F# E
5 6 2 3 6 5
A6/9
337
E A A C# F# B
5 1 1 3 6 2
A6/9
338
E A B C# F# B
5 1 2 3 6 2
A6/9
339
E E B C# F# E
5 5 2 3 6 5
A6/9
340
C# F# A C# B E
3 6 1 3 2 5
A6/9
341
E F# A C# B C#
5 6 1 3 2 3
A6/9
342
E A B E F# B
5 1 2 5 6 2
A6/9
343
E A B E F# B
5 1 2 5 6 2
A6/9
344
C# F# A E B E
3 6 1 5 2 5
A6/9
345
E A B E F# C#
5 1 2 5 6 3
A6/9
346
E A B F# B E
5 1 2 6 2 5
A6/9
347
E A B F# A E
5 1 2 6 1 5
A6/9
348
C# A C# F# B E
3 1 3 6 2 5
A6/9
349
C# F# C# F# B E
3 6 3 6 2 5
A6/9
350
E F# B F# A E
5 6 2 6 1 5
A6/9
351
E A B F# A E
5 1 2 6 1 5
A6/9
352
C# A B F# A E
3 1 2 6 1 5
A6/9
353
C# A C# F# B E
3 1 3 6 2 5
A6/9
354
E A C# F# B E
5 1 3 6 2 5
A6/9
355
E A C# F# B E
5 1 3 6 2 5
A6/9
356
E A E F# B E
5 1 5 6 2 5
A6/9
357
E A C# F# B E
5 1 3 6 2 5
A6/9
358
E A E F# B E
5 1 5 6 2 5
A6/9
359
E A C# F# B E
5 1 3 6 2 5

TUNING: E A D G B E (Standard)

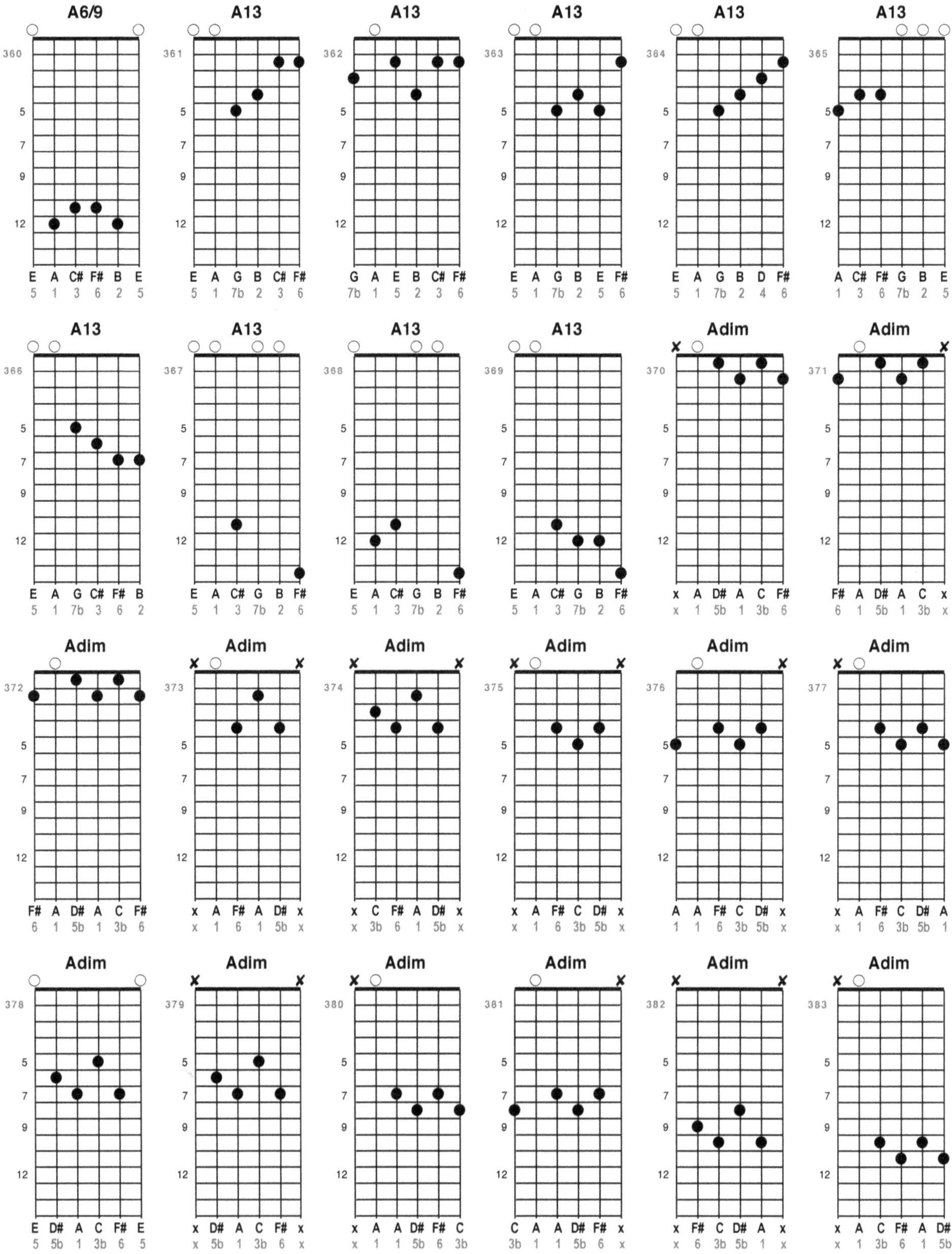

Troubadour Guitar Chords

TUNING: E A D G B E (Standard)

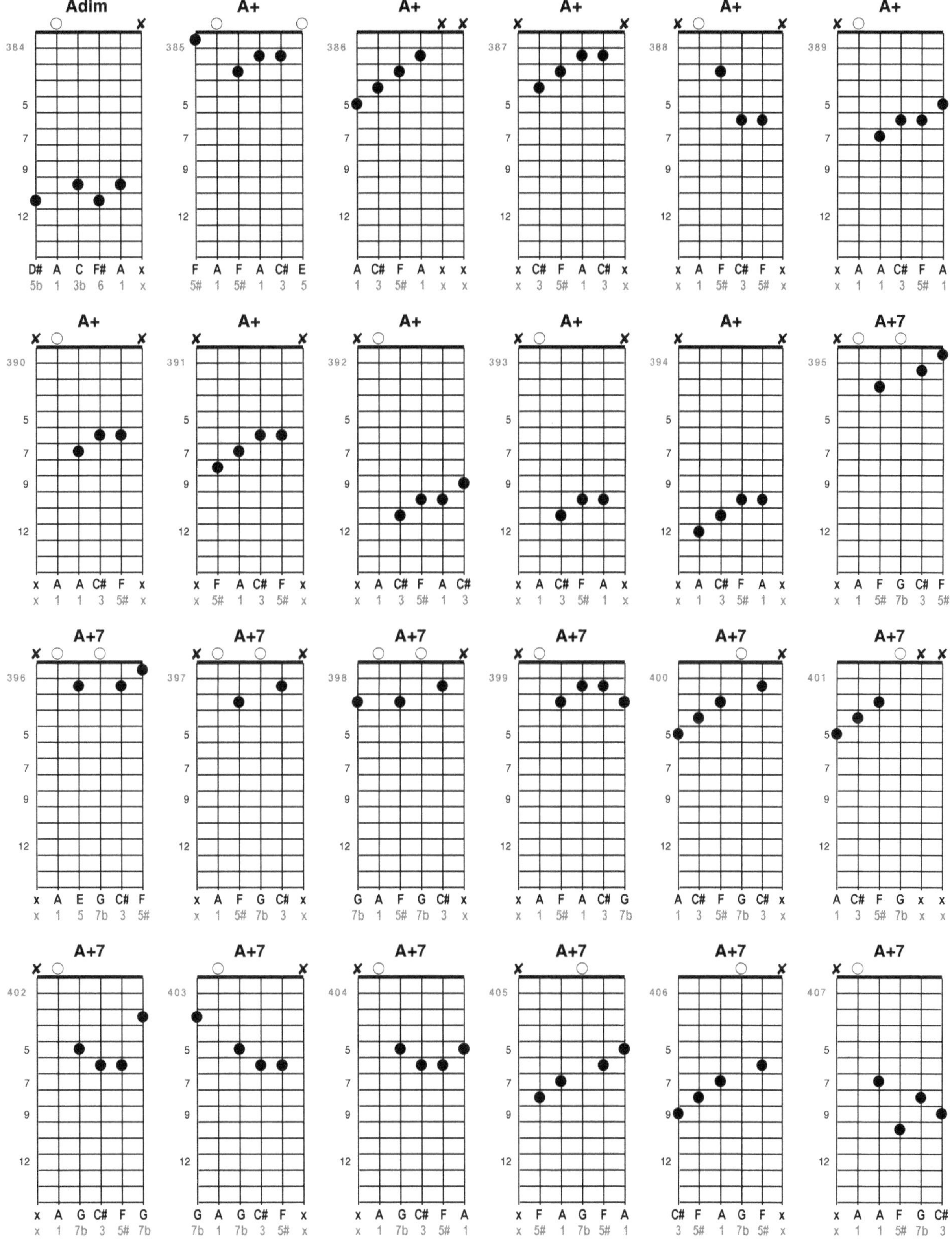

Adim
384
D# A C F# A x
5b 1 3b 6 1 x
A+
385
F A F A C# E
5# 1 5# 1 3 5
A+
386
A C# F A x x
1 3 5# 1 x x
A+
387
x C# F A C# x
x 3 5# 1 3 x
A+
388
x A F C# F x
x 1 5# 3 5# x
A+
389
x A A C# F A
x 1 1 3 5# 1
A+
390
x A A C# F x
x 1 1 3 5# x
A+
391
x F A C# F x
x 5# 1 3 5# x
A+
392
x A C# F A C#
x 1 3 5# 1 3
A+
393
x A C# F A x
x 1 3 5# 1 x
A+
394
x A C# F A x
x 1 3 5# 1 x
A+7
395
x A F G C# F
x 1 5# 7b 3 5#
A+7
396
x A E G C# F
x 1 5 7b 3 5#
A+7
397
x A F G C# x
x 1 5# 7b 3 x
A+7
398
G A F G C# x
7b 1 5# 7b 3 x
A+7
399
x A F A C# G
x 1 5# 1 3 7b
A+7
400
A C# F G C# x
1 3 5# 7b 3 x
A+7
401
A C# F G x x
1 3 5# 7b x x
A+7
402
x A G C# F G
x 1 7b 3 5# 7b
A+7
403
G A G C# F x
7b 1 7b 3 5# x
A+7
404
x A G C# F A
x 1 7b 3 5# 1
A+7
405
x F A G F A
x 5# 1 7b 5# 1
A+7
406
C# F A G F x
3 5# 1 7b 5# x
A+7
407
x A A F G C#
x 1 1 5# 7b 3

TUNING: E A D G B E (Standard)

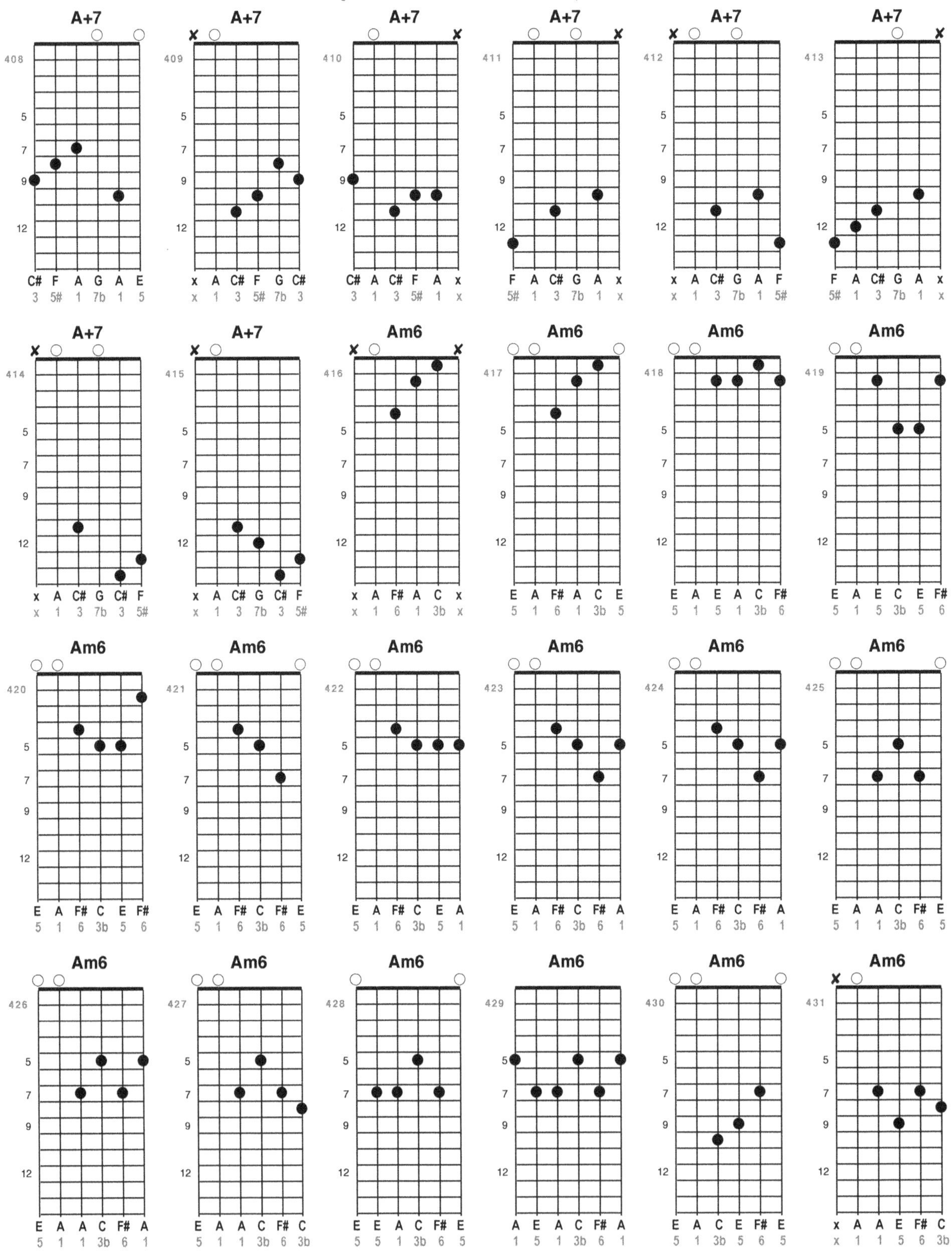
A+7
408
C# F A G A E
3 5# 1 7b 1 5
A+7
409
x A C# F G C#
x 1 3 5# 7b 3
A+7
410
C# A C# F A x
3 1 3 5# 1 x
A+7
411
F A C# G A x
5# 1 3 7b 1 x
A+7
412
x A C# G A F
x 1 3 7b 1 5#
A+7
413
F A C# G A x
5# 1 3 7b 1 x
A+7
414
x A C# G C# F
x 1 3 7b 3 5#
A+7
415
x A C# G C# F
x 1 3 7b 3 5#
Am6
416
x A F# A C x
x 1 6 1 3b x
Am6
417
E A F# A C E
5 1 6 1 3b 5
Am6
418
E A E A C F#
5 1 5 1 3b 6
Am6
419
E A E C E F#
5 1 5 3b 5 6
Am6
420
E A F# C E F#
5 1 6 3b 5 6
Am6
421
E A F# C F# E
5 1 6 3b 6 5
Am6
422
E A F# C E A
5 1 6 3b 5 1
Am6
423
E A F# C F# A
5 1 6 3b 6 1
Am6
424
E A F# C F# A
5 1 6 3b 6 1
Am6
425
E A A C F# E
5 1 1 3b 6 5
Am6
426
E A A C F# A
5 1 1 3b 6 1
Am6
427
E A A C F# C
5 1 1 3b 6 3b
Am6
428
E E A C F# E
5 5 1 3b 6 5
Am6
429
A E A C F# A
1 5 1 3b 6 1
Am6
430
E A C E F# E
5 1 3b 5 6 5
Am6
431
x A A E F# C
x 1 1 5 6 3b

TUNING: E A D G B E (Standard)

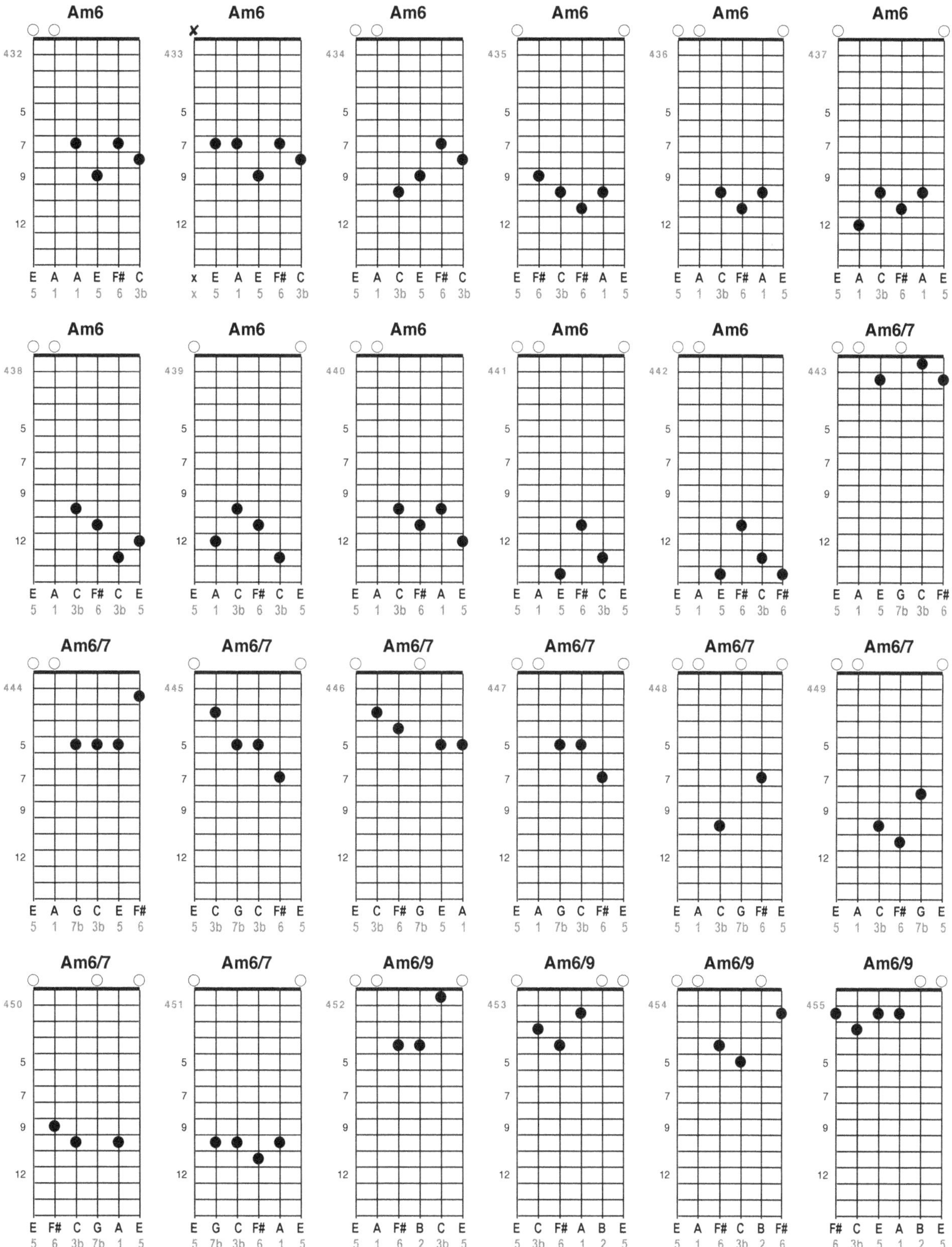
Am6
432
E A A E F# C
5 1 1 5 6 3b
Am6
433
x E A E F# C
x 5 1 5 6 3b
Am6
434
E A C E F# C
5 1 3b 5 6 3b
Am6
435
E F# C F# A E
5 6 3b 6 1 5
Am6
436
E A C F# A E
5 1 3b 6 1 5
Am6
437
E A C F# A E
5 1 3b 6 1 5
Am6
438
E A C F# C E
5 1 3b 6 3b 5
Am6
439
E A C F# C E
5 1 3b 6 3b 5
Am6
440
E A C F# A E
5 1 3b 6 1 5
Am6
441
E A E F# C E
5 1 5 6 3b 5
Am6
442
E A E F# C F#
5 1 5 6 3b 6
Am6/7
443
E A E G C F#
5 1 5 7b 3b 6
Am6/7
444
E A G C E F#
5 1 7b 3b 5 6
Am6/7
445
E C G C F# E
5 3b 7b 3b 6 5
Am6/7
446
E C F# G E A
5 3b 6 7b 5 1
Am6/7
447
E A G C F# E
5 1 7b 3b 6 5
Am6/7
448
E A C G F# E
5 1 3b 7b 6 5
Am6/7
449
E A C F# G E
5 1 3b 6 7b 5
Am6/7
450
E F# C G A E
5 6 3b 7b 1 5
Am6/7
451
E G C F# A E
5 7b 3b 6 1 5
Am6/9
452
E A F# B C E
5 1 6 2 3b 5
Am6/9
453
E C F# A B E
5 3b 6 1 2 5
Am6/9
454
E A F# C B F#
5 1 6 3b 2 6
Am6/9
455
F# C E A B E
6 3b 5 1 2 5

TUNING: E A D G B E (Standard)

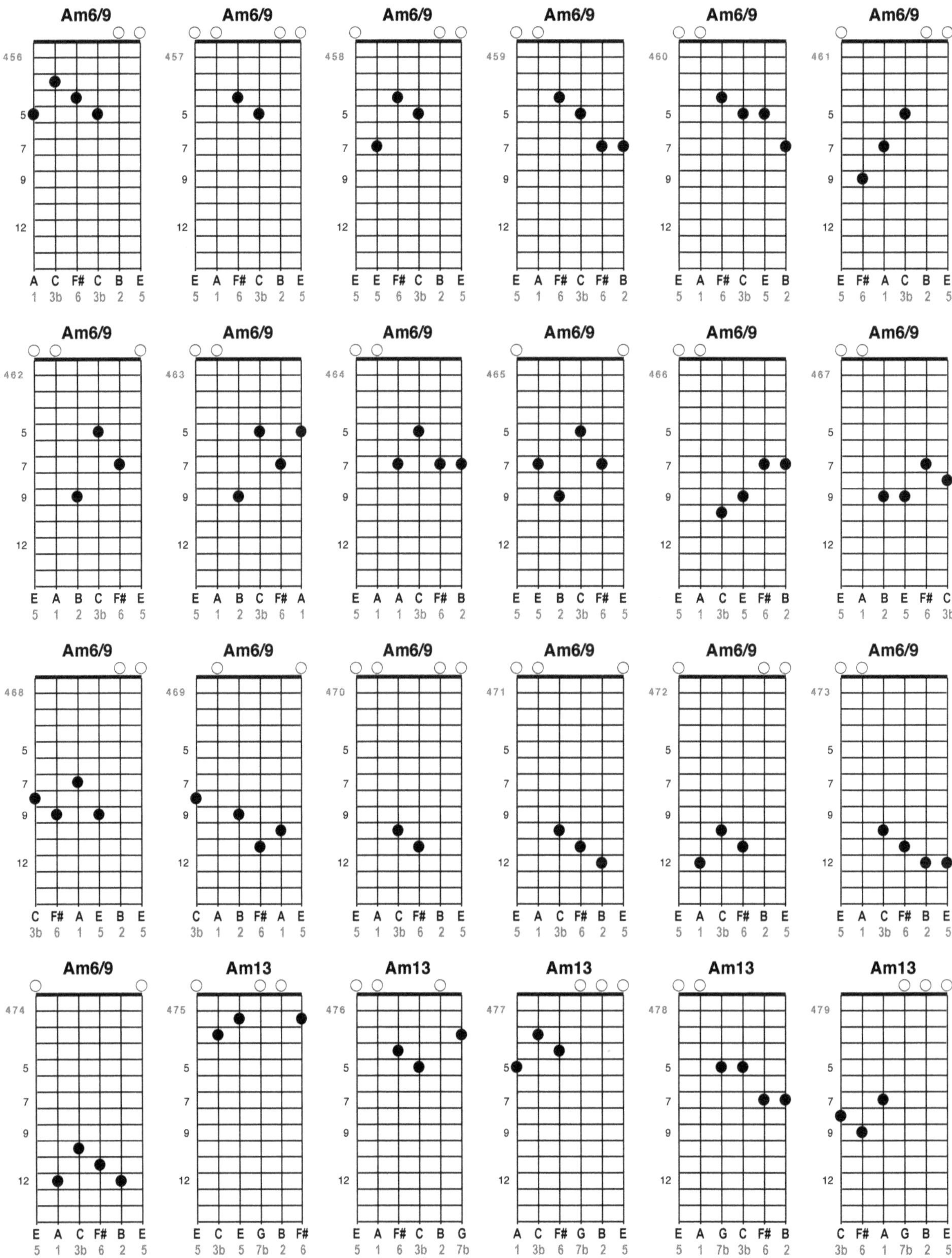

Am6/9 456
A C F# C B E
1 3b 6 3b 2 5

Am6/9 457
E A F# C B E
5 1 6 3b 2 5

Am6/9 458
E E F# C B E
5 5 6 3b 2 5

Am6/9 459
E A F# C F# B
5 1 6 3b 6 2

Am6/9 460
E A F# C E B
5 1 6 3b 5 2

Am6/9 461
E F# A C B E
5 6 1 3b 2 5

Am6/9 462
E A B C F# E
5 1 2 3b 6 5

Am6/9 463
E A B C F# A
5 1 2 3b 6 1

Am6/9 464
E A A C F# B
5 1 1 3b 6 2

Am6/9 465
E E B C F# E
5 5 2 3b 6 5

Am6/9 466
E A C E F# B
5 1 3b 5 6 2

Am6/9 467
E A B E F# C
5 1 2 5 6 3b

Am6/9 468
C F# A E B E
3b 6 1 5 2 5

Am6/9 469
C A B F# A E
3b 1 2 6 1 5

Am6/9 470
E A C F# B E
5 1 3b 6 2 5

Am6/9 471
E A C F# B E
5 1 3b 6 2 5

Am6/9 472
E A C F# B E
5 1 3b 6 2 5

Am6/9 473
E A C F# B E
5 1 3b 6 2 5

Am6/9 474
E A C F# B E
5 1 3b 6 2 5

Am13 475
E C E G B F#
5 3b 5 7b 2 6

Am13 476
E A F# C B G
5 1 6 3b 2 7b

Am13 477
A C F# G B E
1 3b 6 7b 2 5

Am13 478
E A G C F# B
5 1 7b 3b 6 2

Am13 479
C F# A G B E
3b 6 1 7b 2 5

20

Troubadour Guitar Chords

TUNING: E A D G B E (Standard)

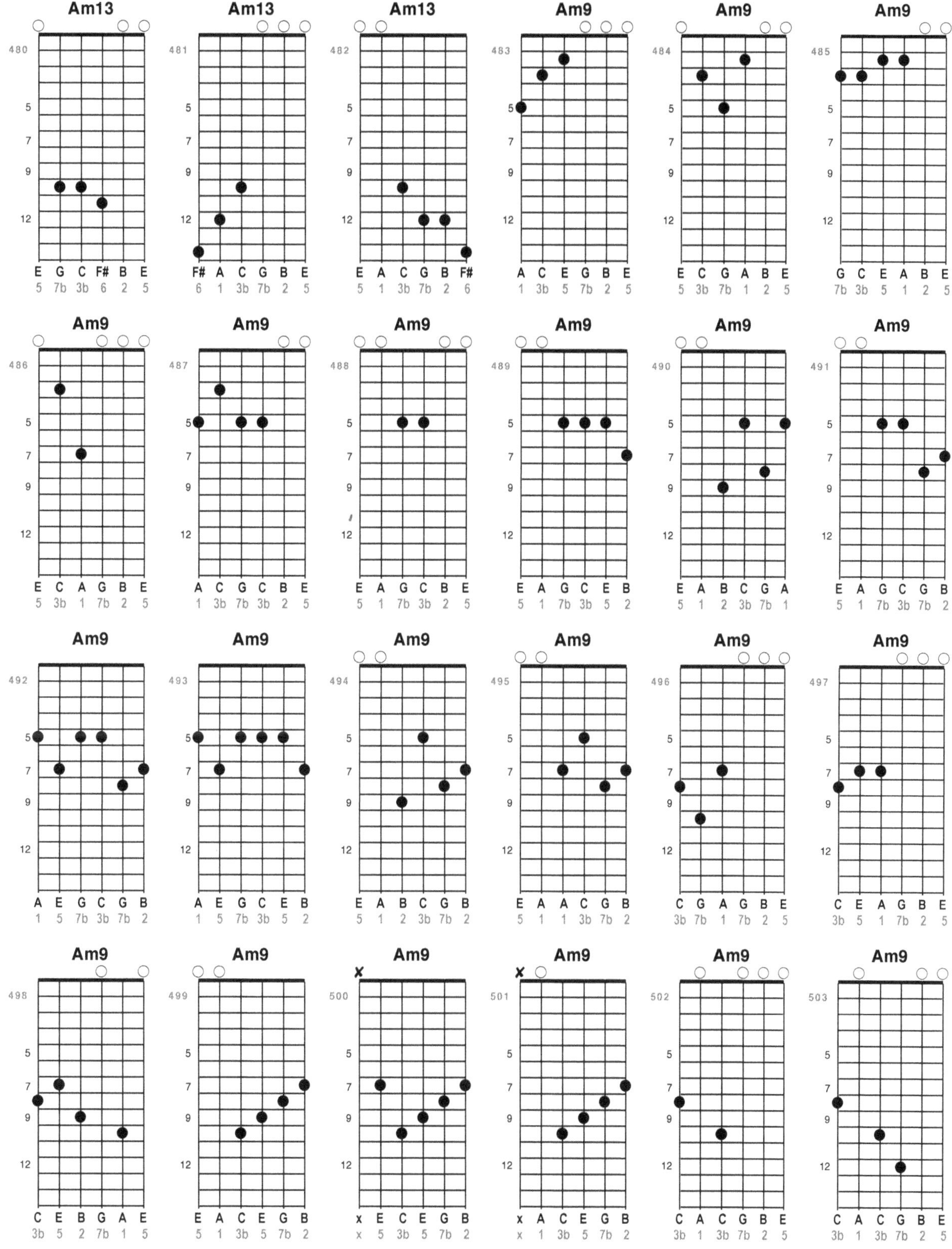

Am13
480
E G C F# B E
5 7b 3b 6 2 5
Am13
481
F# A C G B E
6 1 3b 7b 2 5
Am13
482
E A C G B F#
5 1 3b 7b 2 6
Am9
483
A C E G B E
1 3b 5 7b 2 5
Am9
484
E C G A B E
5 3b 7b 1 2 5
Am9
485
G C E A B E
7b 3b 5 1 2 5
Am9
486
E C A G B E
5 3b 1 7b 2 5
Am9
487
A C G C B E
1 3b 7b 3b 2 5
Am9
488
E A G C B E
5 1 7b 3b 2 5
Am9
489
E A G C E B
5 1 7b 3b 5 2
Am9
490
E A B C G A
5 1 2 3b 7b 1
Am9
491
E A G C G B
5 1 7b 3b 7b 2
Am9
492
A E G C G B
1 5 7b 3b 7b 2
Am9
493
A E G C E B
1 5 7b 3b 5 2
Am9
494
E A B C G B
5 1 2 3b 7b 2
Am9
495
E A A C G B
5 1 1 3b 7b 2
Am9
496
C G A G B E
3b 7b 1 7b 2 5
Am9
497
C E A G B E
3b 5 1 7b 2 5
Am9
498
C E B G A E
3b 5 2 7b 1 5
Am9
499
E A C E G B
5 1 3b 5 7b 2
Am9
500
x E C E G B
x 5 3b 5 7b 2
Am9
501
x A C E G B
x 1 3b 5 7b 2
Am9
502
C A C G B E
3b 1 3b 7b 2 5
Am9
503
C A C G B E
3b 1 3b 7b 2 5

TUNING: E A D G B E (Standard)

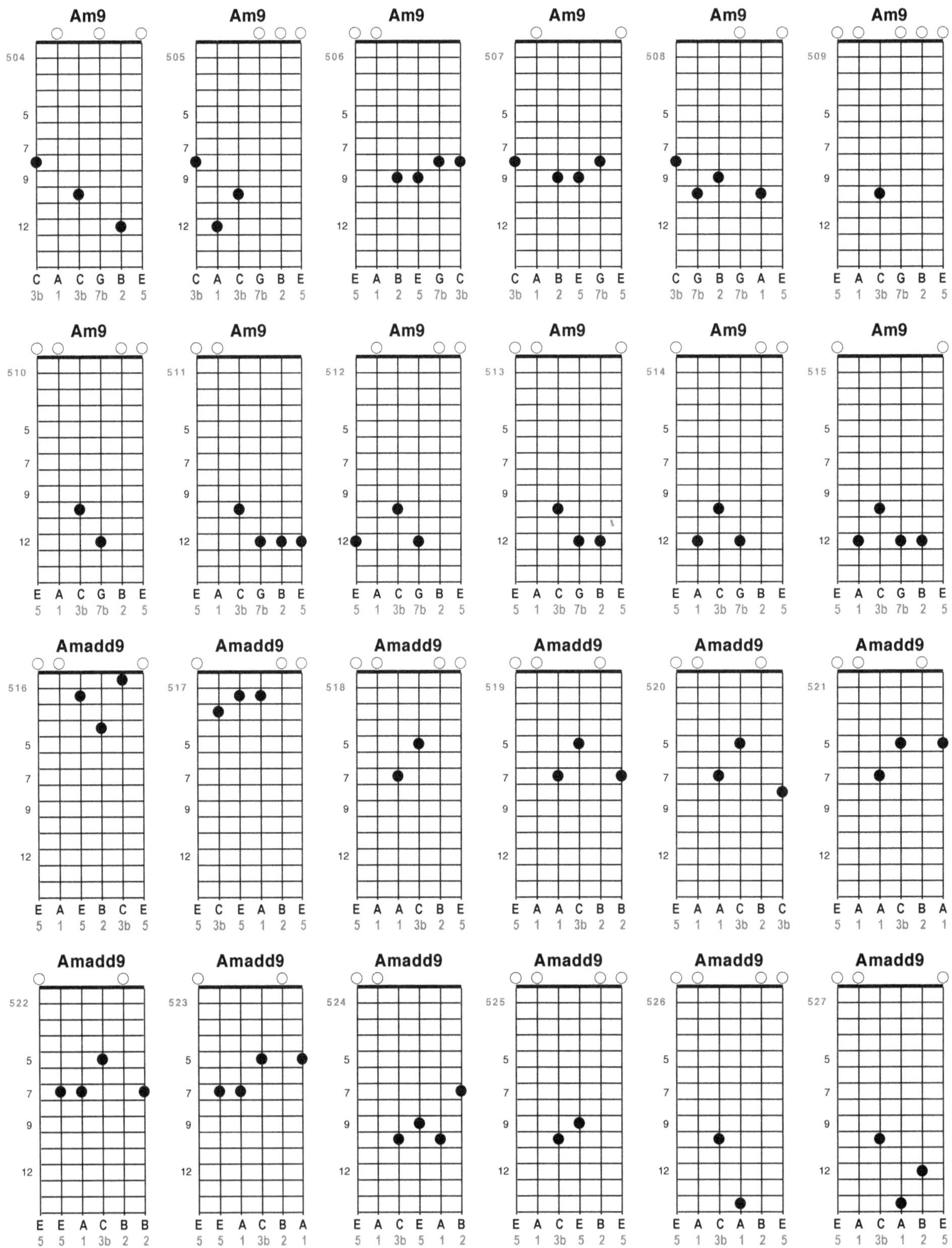
Am9
504
C A C G B E
3b 1 3b 7b 2 5
Am9
505
C A C G B E
3b 1 3b 7b 2 5
Am9
506
E A B E G C
5 1 2 5 7b 3b
Am9
507
C A B E G E
3b 1 2 5 7b 5
Am9
508
C G B G A E
3b 7b 2 7b 1 5
Am9
509
E A C G B E
5 1 3b 7b 2 5
Am9
510
E A C G B E
5 1 3b 7b 2 5
Am9
511
E A C G B E
5 1 3b 7b 2 5
Am9
512
E A C G B E
5 1 3b 7b 2 5
Am9
513
E A C G B E
5 1 3b 7b 2 5
Am9
514
E A C G B E
5 1 3b 7b 2 5
Am9
515
E A C G B E
5 1 3b 7b 2 5
Amadd9
516
E A E B C E
5 1 5 2 3b 5
Amadd9
517
E C E A B E
5 3b 5 1 2 5
Amadd9
518
E A A C B E
5 1 1 3b 2 5
Amadd9
519
E A A C B B
5 1 1 3b 2 2
Amadd9
520
E A A C B C
5 1 1 3b 2 3b
Amadd9
521
E A A C B A
5 1 1 3b 2 1
Amadd9
522
E E A C B B
5 5 1 3b 2 2
Amadd9
523
E E A C B A
5 5 1 3b 2 1
Amadd9
524
E A C E A B
5 1 3b 5 1 2
Amadd9
525
E A C E B E
5 1 3b 5 2 5
Amadd9
526
E A C A B E
5 1 3b 1 2 5
Amadd9
527
E A C A B E
5 1 3b 1 2 5

TUNING: E A D G B E (Standard)

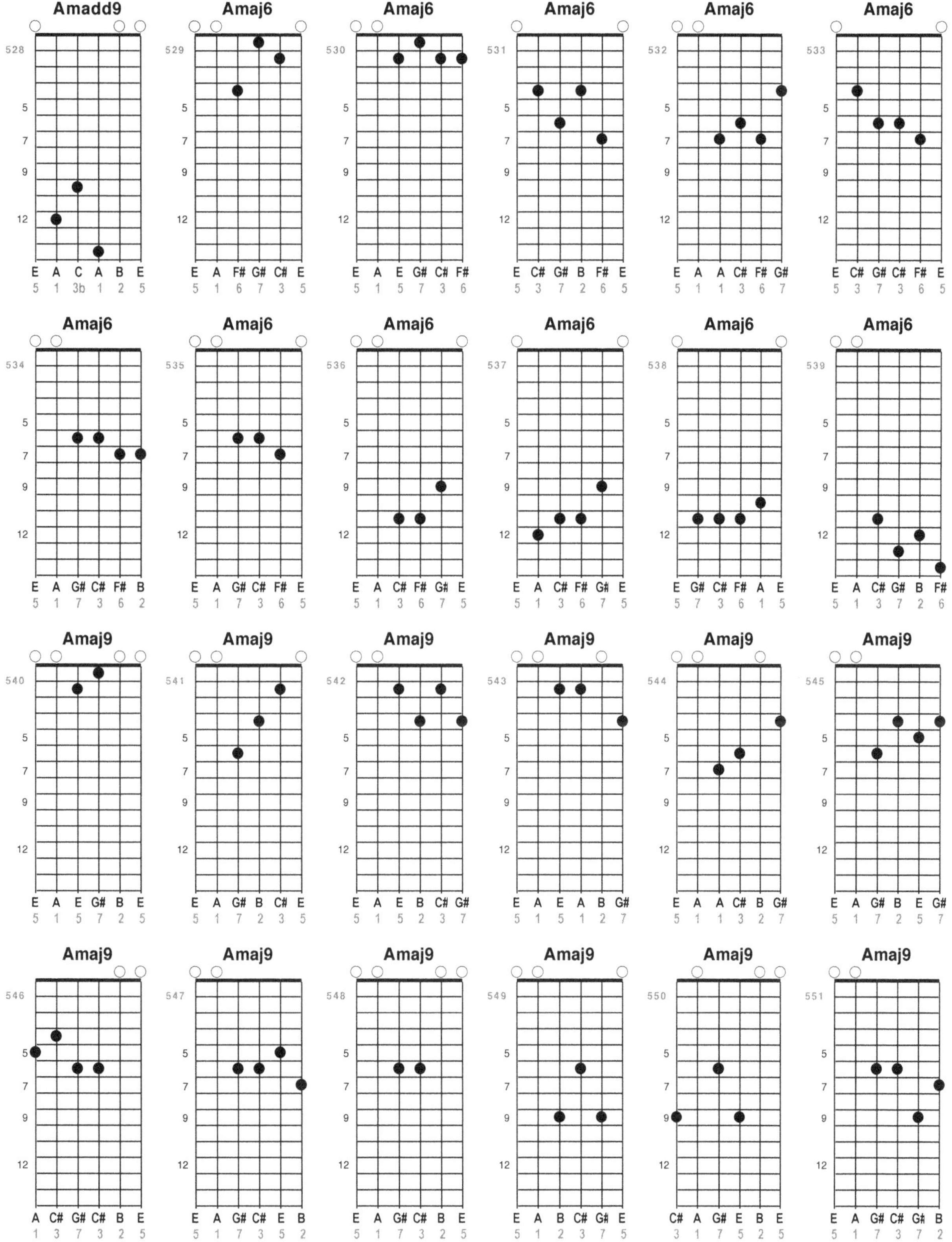
Amadd9
528
5 7 9 12
E A C A B E
5 1 3b 1 2 5
Amaj6
529
5 7 9 12
E A F# G# C# E
5 1 6 7 3 5
Amaj6
530
5 7 9 12
E A E G# C# F#
5 1 5 7 3 6
Amaj6
531
5 7 9 12
E C# G# B F# E
5 3 7 2 6 5
Amaj6
532
5 7 9 12
E A A C# F# G#
5 1 1 3 6 7
Amaj6
533
5 7 9 12
E C# G# C# F# E
5 3 7 3 6 5
Amaj6
534
5 7 9 12
E A G# C# F# B
5 1 7 3 6 2
Amaj6
535
5 7 9 12
E A G# C# F# E
5 1 7 3 6 5
Amaj6
536
5 7 9 12
E A C# F# G# E
5 1 3 6 7 5
Amaj6
537
5 7 9 12
E A C# F# G# E
5 1 3 6 7 5
Amaj6
538
5 7 9 12
E G# C# F# A E
5 7 3 6 1 5
Amaj6
539
5 7 9 12
E A C# G# B F#
5 1 3 7 2 6
Amaj9
540
5 7 9 12
E A E G# B E
5 1 5 7 2 5
Amaj9
541
5 7 9 12
E A G# B C# E
5 1 7 2 3 5
Amaj9
542
5 7 9 12
E A E B C# G#
5 1 5 2 3 7
Amaj9
543
5 7 9 12
E A E A B G#
5 1 5 1 2 7
Amaj9
544
5 7 9 12
E A A C# B G#
5 1 1 3 2 7
Amaj9
545
5 7 9 12
E A G# B E G#
5 1 7 2 5 7
Amaj9
546
5 7 9 12
A C# G# C# B E
1 3 7 3 2 5
Amaj9
547
5 7 9 12
E A G# C# E B
5 1 7 3 5 2
Amaj9
548
5 7 9 12
E A G# C# B E
5 1 7 3 2 5
Amaj9
549
5 7 9 12
E A B C# G# E
5 1 2 3 7 5
Amaj9
550
5 7 9 12
C# A G# E B E
3 1 7 5 2 5
Amaj9
551
5 7 9 12
E A G# C# G# B
5 1 7 3 7 2

Troubadour Guitar Chords

TUNING: E A D G B E (Standard)

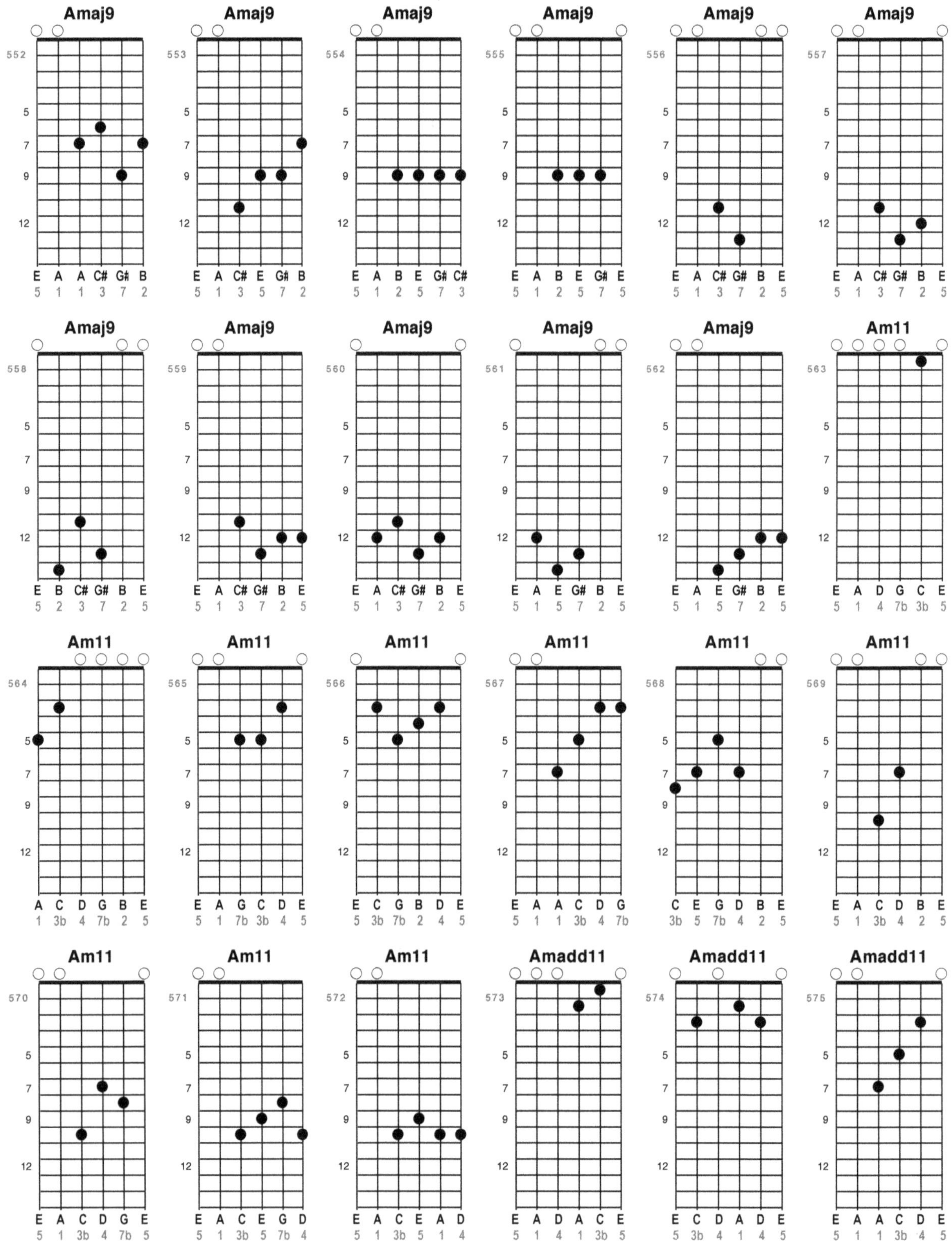

Amaj9
552
E A A C# G# B
5 1 1 3 7 2
Amaj9
553
E A C# E G# B
5 1 3 5 7 2
Amaj9
554
E A B E G# C#
5 1 2 5 7 3
Amaj9
555
E A B E G# E
5 1 2 5 7 5
Amaj9
556
E A C# G# B E
5 1 3 7 2 5
Amaj9
557
E A C# G# B E
5 1 3 7 2 5
Amaj9
558
E B C# G# B E
5 2 3 7 2 5
Amaj9
559
E A C# G# B E
5 1 3 7 2 5
Amaj9
560
E A C# G# B E
5 1 3 7 2 5
Amaj9
561
E A E G# B E
5 1 5 7 2 5
Amaj9
562
E A E G# B E
5 1 5 7 2 5
Am11
563
E A D G C E
5 1 4 7b 3b 5
Am11
564
A C D G B E
1 3b 4 7b 2 5
Am11
565
E A G C D E
5 1 7b 3b 4 5
Am11
566
E C G B D E
5 3b 7b 2 4 5
Am11
567
E A A C D G
5 1 1 3b 4 7b
Am11
568
C E G D B E
3b 5 7b 4 2 5
Am11
569
E A C D B E
5 1 3b 4 2 5
Am11
570
E A C D G E
5 1 3b 4 7b 5
Am11
571
E A C E G D
5 1 3b 5 7b 4
Am11
572
E A C E A D
5 1 3b 5 1 4
Amadd11
573
E A D A C E
5 1 4 1 3b 5
Amadd11
574
E C D A D E
5 3b 4 1 4 5
Amadd11
575
E A A C D E
5 1 1 3b 4 5

TUNING: E A D G B E (Standard)

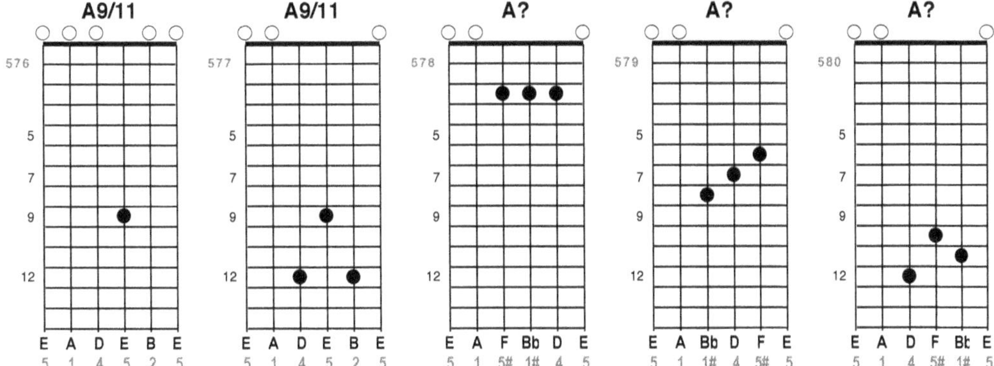
A9/11
576
E A D E B E
5 1 4 5 2 5
A9/11
577
E A D E B E
5 1 4 5 2 5
A?
578
E A F Bb D E
5 1 5# 1# 4 5
A?
579
E A Bb D F E
5 1 1# 4 5# 5
A?
580
E A D F Bt E
5 1 4 5# 1# 5

OPEN VS. CLOSED CHORDS

An area of confusion in guitar chords is the use of movable closed position shapes, which make sense for people playing lead guitar, and open-string voicings, which are favored by solo guitar troubadour types. The open-string chords are usually unique to a particular key, they involve most of the strings, and are not movable to other keys. The closed-position shapes are often just smaller blocks of strings that don't make sense for a campfire strummer. Most books of guitar chords just show a few shapes, and move them up and down the neck, seemingly giving you thousands of chords, but actually ignoring all the open-voiced chords.

Tom Principato's ***Open String Guitar Chords*** book has a lot of excellent open-string voicings, but does not include even the basic barre chords that everybody plays. I chose to include the kinds of open-voiced and also barre chords that troubadours regularly use.

Troubadour Guitar Chords

TUNING: E A D G B E (Standard)

A# Bb

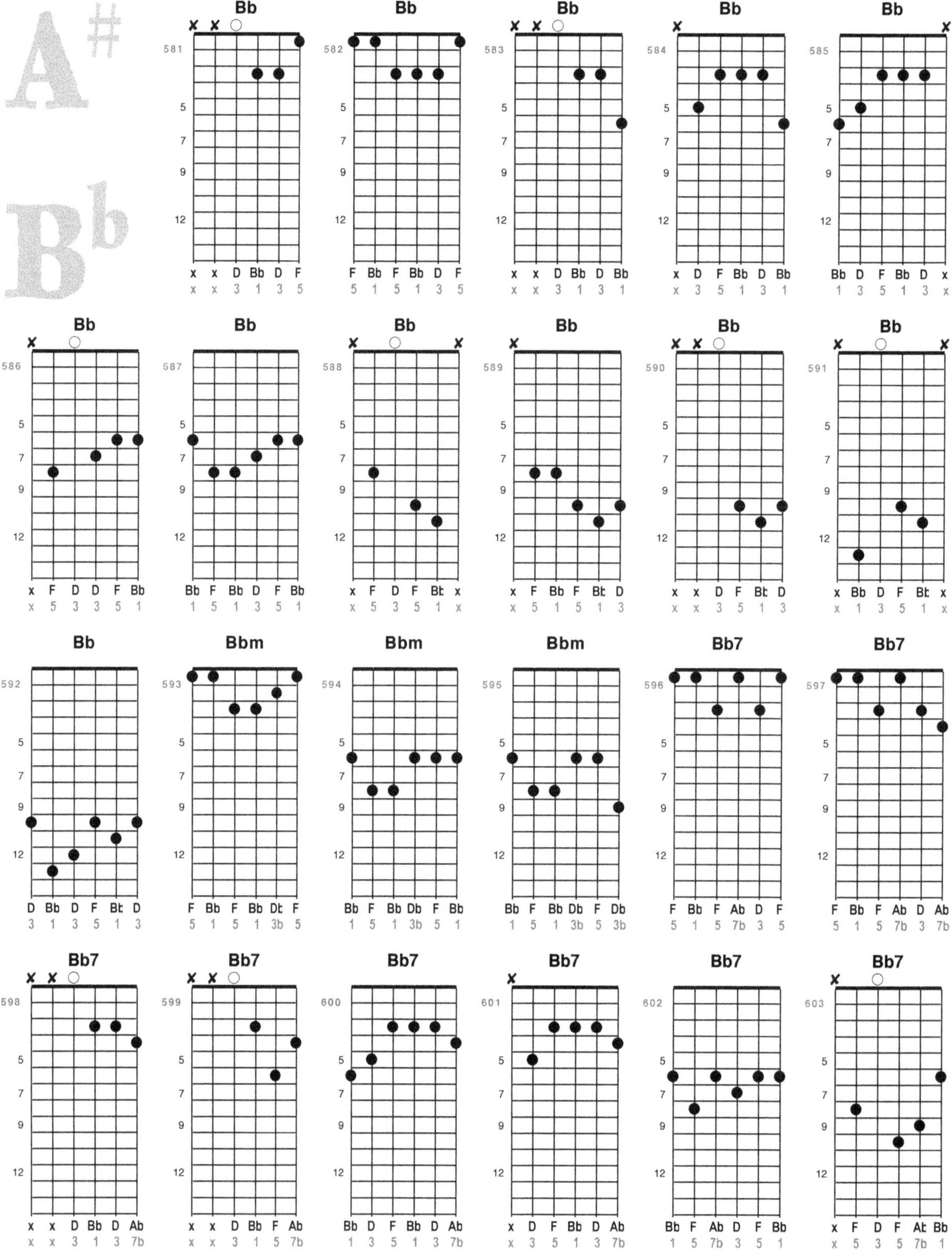

TUNING: E A D G B E (Standard)

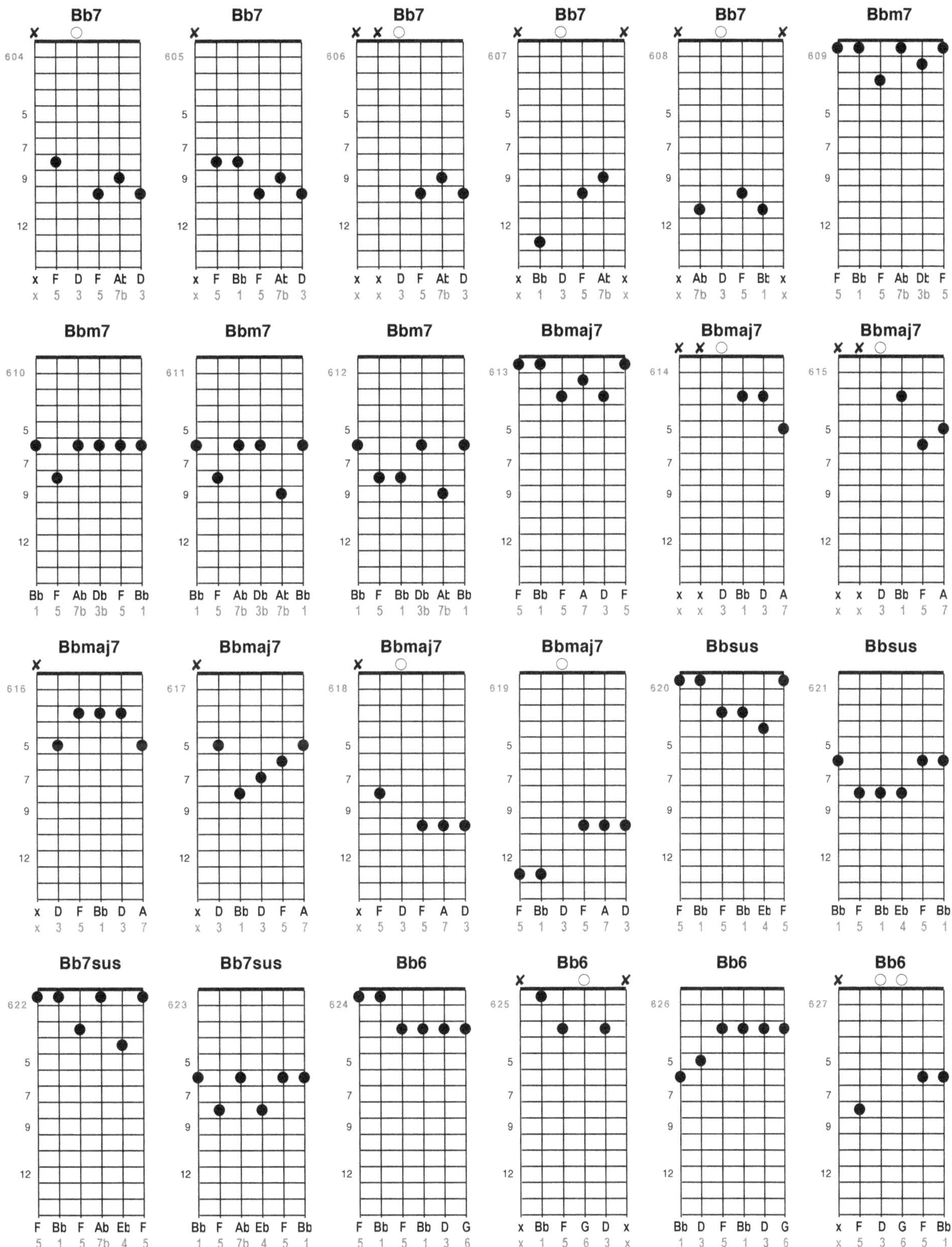
Bb7
604
x F D F Ab D
x 5 3 5 7b 3
Bb7
605
x F Bb F Ab D
x 5 1 5 7b 3
Bb7
606
x x D F Ab D
x x 3 5 7b 3
Bb7
607
x Bb D F Ab x
x 1 3 5 7b x
Bb7
608
x Ab D F Bb x
x 7b 3 5 1 x
Bbm7
609
F Bb F Ab Db F
5 1 5 7b 3b 5
Bbm7
610
Bb F Ab Db F Bb
1 5 7b 3b 5 1
Bbm7
611
Bb F Ab Db Ab Bb
1 5 7b 3b 7b 1
Bbm7
612
Bb F Bb Db Ab Bb
1 5 1 3b 7b 1
Bbmaj7
613
F Bb F A D F
5 1 5 7 3 5
Bbmaj7
614
x x D Bb D A
x x 3 1 3 7
Bbmaj7
615
x x D Bb F A
x x 3 1 5 7
Bbmaj7
616
x D F Bb D A
x 3 5 1 3 7
Bbmaj7
617
x D Bb D F A
x 3 1 3 5 7
Bbmaj7
618
x F D F A D
x 5 3 5 7 3
Bbmaj7
619
F Bb D F A D
5 1 3 5 7 3
Bbsus
620
F Bb F Bb Eb F
5 1 5 1 4 5
Bbsus
621
Bb F Bb Eb F Bb
1 5 1 4 5 1
Bb7sus
622
F Bb F Ab Eb F
5 1 5 7b 4 5
Bb7sus
623
Bb F Ab Eb F Bb
1 5 7b 4 5 1
Bb6
624
F Bb F Bb D G
5 1 5 1 3 6
Bb6
625
x Bb F G D x
x 1 5 6 3 x
Bb6
626
Bb D F Bb D G
1 3 5 1 3 6
Bb6
627
x F D G F Bb
x 5 3 6 5 1

TUNING: E A D G B E (Standard)

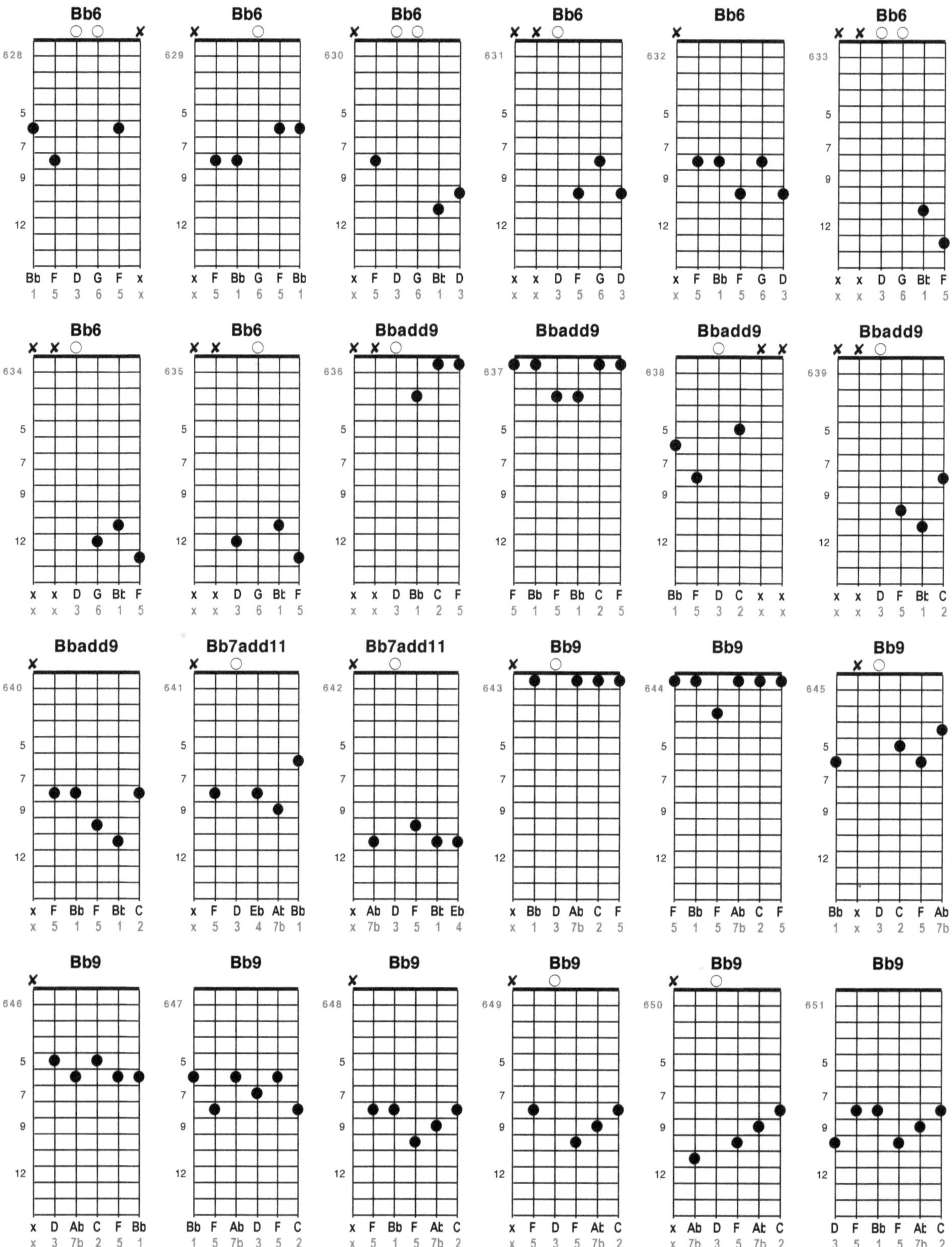
Bb6
628
Bb F D G F x
1 5 3 6 5 x
Bb6
629
x F Bb G F Bb
x 5 1 6 5 1
Bb6
630
x F D G Bb D
x 5 3 6 1 3
Bb6
631
x x D F G D
x x 3 5 6 3
Bb6
632
x F Bb F G D
x 5 1 5 6 3
Bb6
633
x x D G Bb F
x x 3 6 1 5
Bb6
634
x x D G Bb F
x x 3 6 1 5
Bb6
635
x x D G Bb F
x x 3 6 1 5
Bbadd9
636
x x D Bb C F
x x 3 1 2 5
Bbadd9
637
F Bb F Bb C F
5 1 5 1 2 5
Bbadd9
638
Bb F D C x x
1 5 3 2 x x
Bbadd9
639
x x D F Bb C
x x 3 5 1 2
Bbadd9
640
x F Bb F Bb C
x 5 1 5 1 2
Bb7add11
641
x F D Eb Ab Bb
x 5 3 4 7b 1
Bb7add11
642
x Ab D F Bb Eb
x 7b 3 5 1 4
Bb9
643
x Bb D Ab C F
x 1 3 7b 2 5
Bb9
644
F Bb F Ab C F
5 1 5 7b 2 5
Bb9
645
Bb x D C F Ab
1 x 3 2 5 7b
Bb9
646
x D Ab C F Bb
x 3 7b 2 5 1
Bb9
647
Bb F Ab D F C
1 5 7b 3 5 2
Bb9
648
x F Bb F Ab C
x 5 1 5 7b 2
Bb9
649
x F D F Ab C
x 5 3 5 7b 2
Bb9
650
x Ab D F Ab C
x 7b 3 5 7b 2
Bb9
651
D F Bb F Ab C
3 5 1 5 7b 2

TUNING: E A D G B E (Standard)

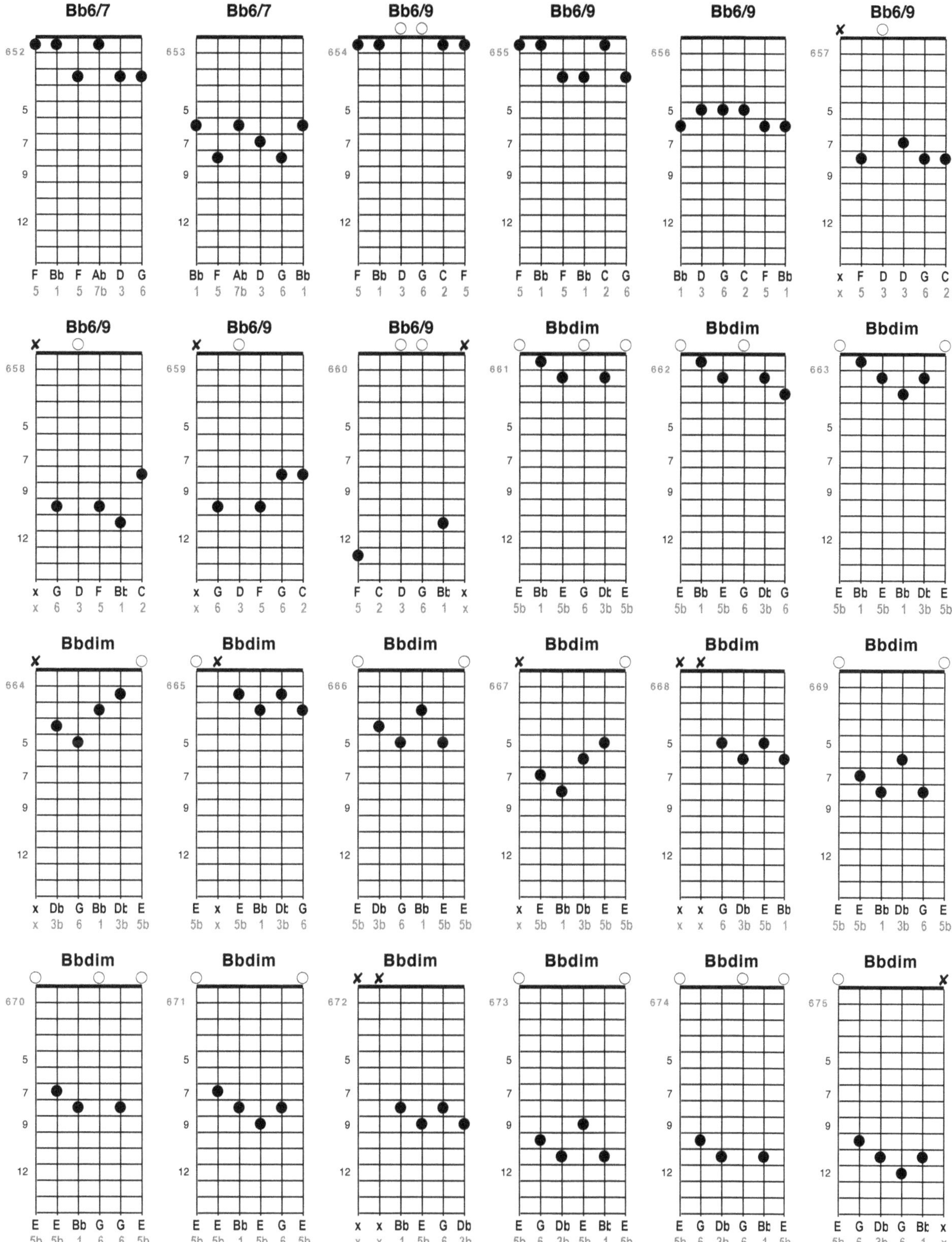
Bb6/7
652
F Bb F Ab D G
5 1 5 7b 3 6
Bb6/7
653
Bb F Ab D G Bb
1 5 7b 3 6 1
Bb6/9
654
F Bb D G C F
5 1 3 6 2 5
Bb6/9
655
F Bb F Bb C G
5 1 5 1 2 6
Bb6/9
656
Bb D G C F Bb
1 3 6 2 5 1
Bb6/9
657
x F D D G C
x 5 3 3 6 2
Bb6/9
658
x G D F Bb C
x 6 3 5 1 2
Bb6/9
659
x G D F G C
x 6 3 5 6 2
Bb6/9
660
F C D G Bb x
5 2 3 6 1 x
Bbdim
661
E Bb E G Db E
5b 1 5b 6 3b 5b
Bbdim
662
E Bb E G Db G
5b 1 5b 6 3b 6
Bbdim
663
E Bb E Bb Db E
5b 1 5b 1 3b 5b
Bbdim
664
x Db G Bb Db E
x 3b 6 1 3b 5b
Bbdim
665
E x E Bb Db G
5b x 5b 1 3b 6
Bbdim
666
E Db G Bb E E
5b 3b 6 1 5b 5b
Bbdim
667
x E Bb Db E E
x 5b 1 3b 5b 5b
Bbdim
668
x x G Db E Bb
x x 6 3b 5b 1
Bbdim
669
E E Bb Db G E
5b 5b 1 3b 6 5b
Bbdim
670
E E Bb G G E
5b 5b 1 6 6 5b
Bbdim
671
E E Bb E G E
5b 5b 1 5b 6 5b
Bbdim
672
x x Bb E G Db
x x 1 5b 6 3b
Bbdim
673
E G Db E Bb E
5b 6 3b 5b 1 5b
Bbdim
674
E G Db G Bb E
5b 6 3b 6 1 5b
Bbdim
675
E G Db G Bb x
5b 6 3b 6 1 x

TUNING: E A D G B E (Standard)

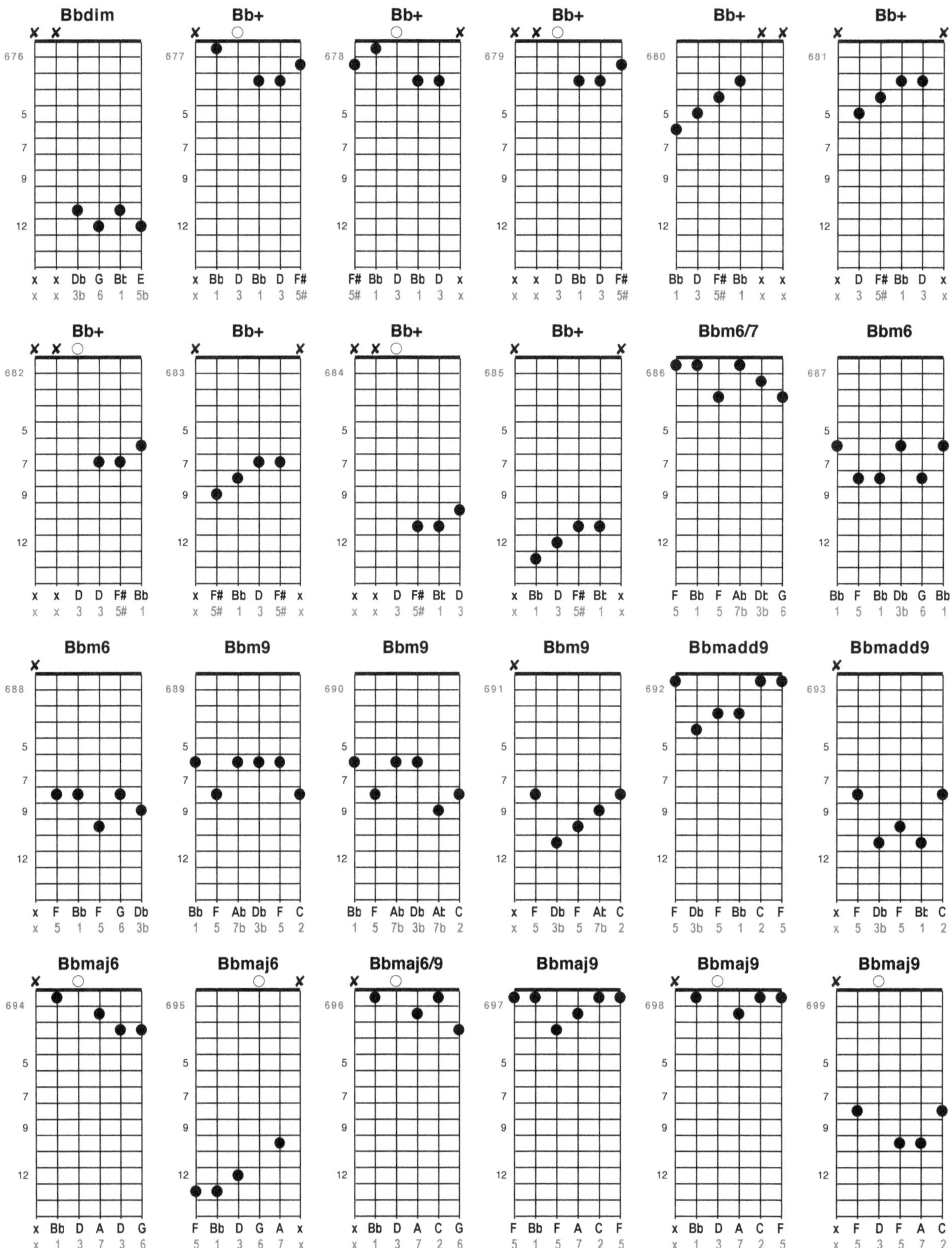

Bbdim (676)
x x Db G Bb E
x x 3b 6 1 5b

Bb+ (677)
x Bb D Bb D F#
x 1 3 1 3 5#

Bb+ (678)
F# Bb D Bb D x
5# 1 3 1 3 x

Bb+ (679)
x x D Bb D F#
x x 3 1 3 5#

Bb+ (680)
Bb D F# Bb x x
1 3 5# 1 x x

Bb+ (681)
x D F# Bb D x
x 3 5# 1 3 x

Bb+ (682)
x x D D F# Bb
x x 3 3 5# 1

Bb+ (683)
x F# Bb D F# x
x 5# 1 3 5# x

Bb+ (684)
x x D F# Bb D
x x 3 5# 1 3

Bb+ (685)
x Bb D F# Bb x
x 1 3 5# 1 x

Bbm6/7 (686)
F Bb F Ab Db G
5 1 5 7b 3b 6

Bbm6 (687)
Bb F Bb Db G Bb
1 5 1 3b 6 1

Bbm6 (688)
x F Bb F G Db
x 5 1 5 6 3b

Bbm9 (689)
Bb F Ab Db F C
1 5 7b 3b 5 2

Bbm9 (690)
Bb F Ab Db Ab C
1 5 7b 3b 7b 2

Bbm9 (691)
x F Db F Ab C
x 5 3b 5 7b 2

Bbmadd9 (692)
F Db F Bb C F
5 3b 5 1 2 5

Bbmadd9 (693)
x F Db F Bb C
x 5 3b 5 1 2

Bbmaj6 (694)
x Bb D A D G
x 1 3 7 3 6

Bbmaj6 (695)
F Bb D G A x
5 1 3 6 7 x

Bbmaj6/9 (696)
x Bb D A C G
x 1 3 7 2 6

Bbmaj9 (697)
F Bb F A C F
5 1 5 7 2 5

Bbmaj9 (698)
x Bb D A C F
x 1 3 7 2 5

Bbmaj9 (699)
x F D F A C
x 5 3 5 7 2

Troubadour Guitar Chords

TUNING: E A D G B E (Standard)

B

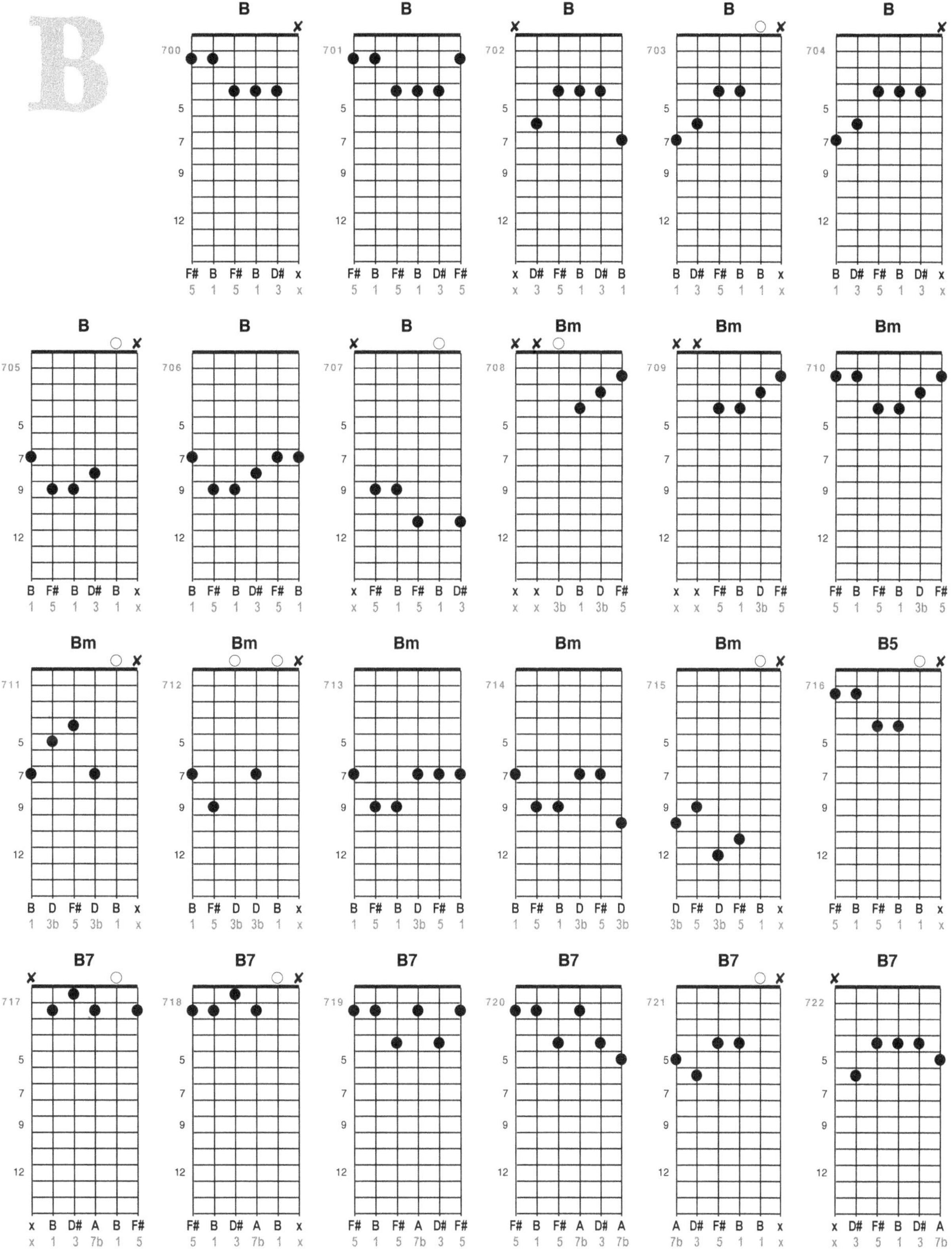

B
700
F# B F# B D# x
5 1 5 1 3 x
B
701
F# B F# B D# F#
5 1 5 1 3 5
B
702
x D# F# B D# B
x 3 5 1 3 1
B
703
B D# F# B B x
1 3 5 1 1 x
B
704
B D# F# B D# x
1 3 5 1 3 x
B
705
B F# B D# B x
1 5 1 3 1 x
B
706
B F# B D# F# B
1 5 1 3 5 1
B
707
x F# B F# B D#
x 5 1 5 1 3
Bm
708
x x D B D F#
x x 3b 1 3b 5
Bm
709
x x F# B D F#
x x 5 1 3b 5
Bm
710
F# B F# B D F#
5 1 5 1 3b 5
Bm
711
B D F# D B x
1 3b 5 3b 1 x
Bm
712
B F# D D B x
1 5 3b 3b 1 x
Bm
713
B F# B D F# B
1 5 1 3b 5 1
Bm
714
B F# B D F# D
1 5 1 3b 5 3b
Bm
715
D F# D F# B x
3b 5 3b 5 1 x
B5
716
F# B F# B B x
5 1 5 1 1 x
B7
717
x B D# A B F#
x 1 3 7b 1 5
B7
718
F# B D# A B x
5 1 3 7b 1 x
B7
719
F# B F# A D# F#
5 1 5 7b 3 5
B7
720
F# B F# A D# A
5 1 5 7b 3 7b
B7
721
A D# F# B B x
7b 3 5 1 1 x
B7
722
x D# F# B D# A
x 3 5 1 3 7b

Troubadour Guitar Chords

TUNING: E A D G B E (Standard)

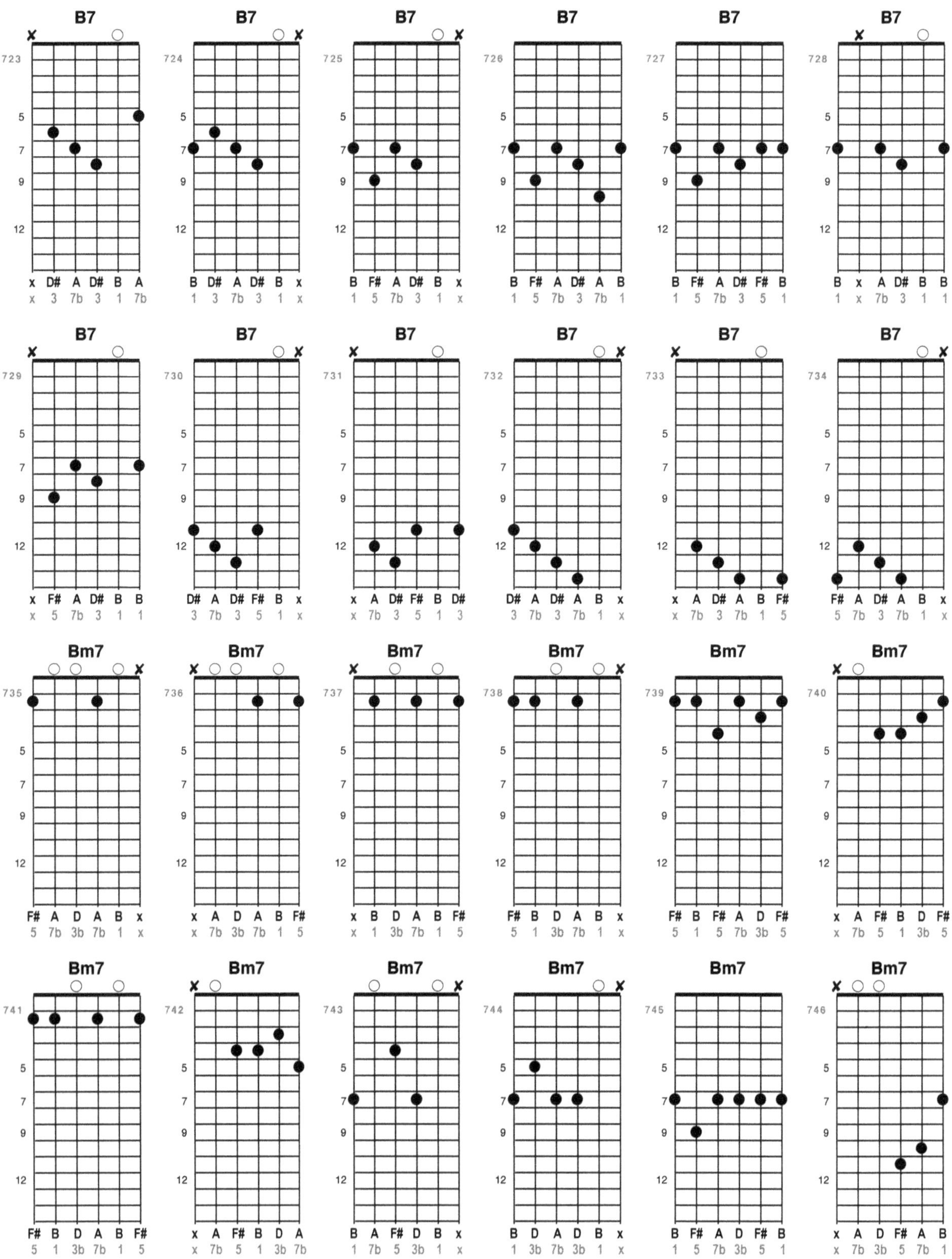

TUNING: E A D G B E (Standard)

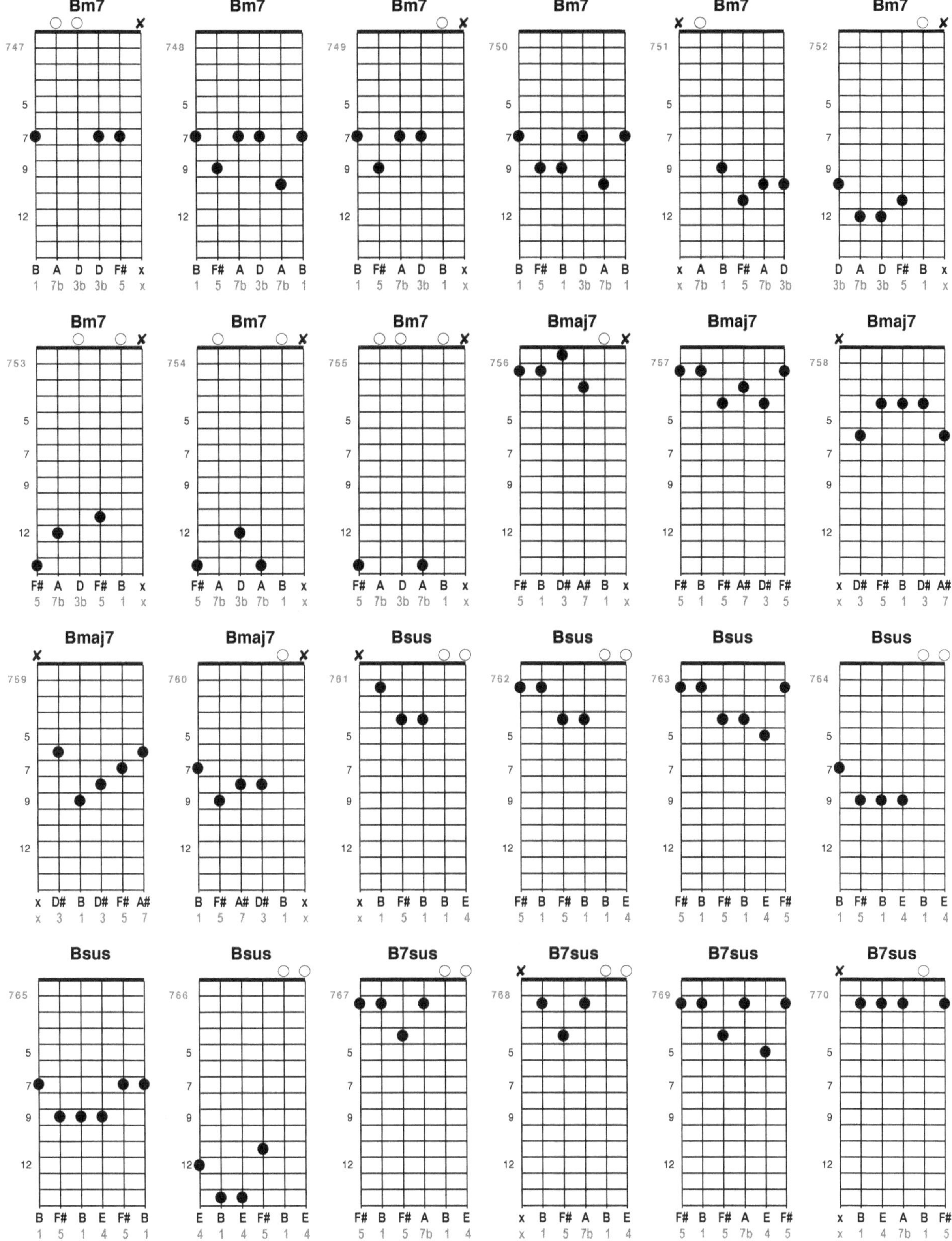

Bm7
747
B A D D F# x
1 7b 3b 3b 5 x
Bm7
748
B F# A D A B
1 5 7b 3b 7b 1
Bm7
749
B F# A D B x
1 5 7b 3b 1 x
Bm7
750
B F# B D A B
1 5 1 3b 7b 1
Bm7
751
x A B F# A D
x 7b 1 5 7b 3b
Bm7
752
D A D F# B x
3b 7b 3b 5 1 x
Bm7
753
F# A D F# B x
5 7b 3b 5 1 x
Bm7
754
F# A D A B x
5 7b 3b 7b 1 x
Bm7
755
F# A D A B x
5 7b 3b 7b 1 x
Bmaj7
756
F# B D# A# B x
5 1 3 7 1 x
Bmaj7
757
F# B F# A# D# F#
5 1 5 7 3 5
Bmaj7
758
x D# F# B D# A#
x 3 5 1 3 7
Bmaj7
759
x D# B D# F# A#
x 3 1 3 5 7
Bmaj7
760
B F# A# D# B x
1 5 7 3 1 x
Bsus
761
x B F# B B E
x 1 5 1 1 4
Bsus
762
F# B F# B B E
5 1 5 1 1 4
Bsus
763
F# B F# B E F#
5 1 5 1 4 5
Bsus
764
B F# B E B E
1 5 1 4 1 4
Bsus
765
B F# B E F# B
1 5 1 4 5 1
Bsus
766
E B E F# B E
4 1 4 5 1 4
B7sus
767
F# B F# A B E
5 1 5 7b 1 4
B7sus
768
x B F# A B E
x 1 5 7b 1 4
B7sus
769
F# B F# A E F#
5 1 5 7b 4 5
B7sus
770
x B E A B F#
x 1 4 7b 1 5

TUNING: E A D G B E (Standard)

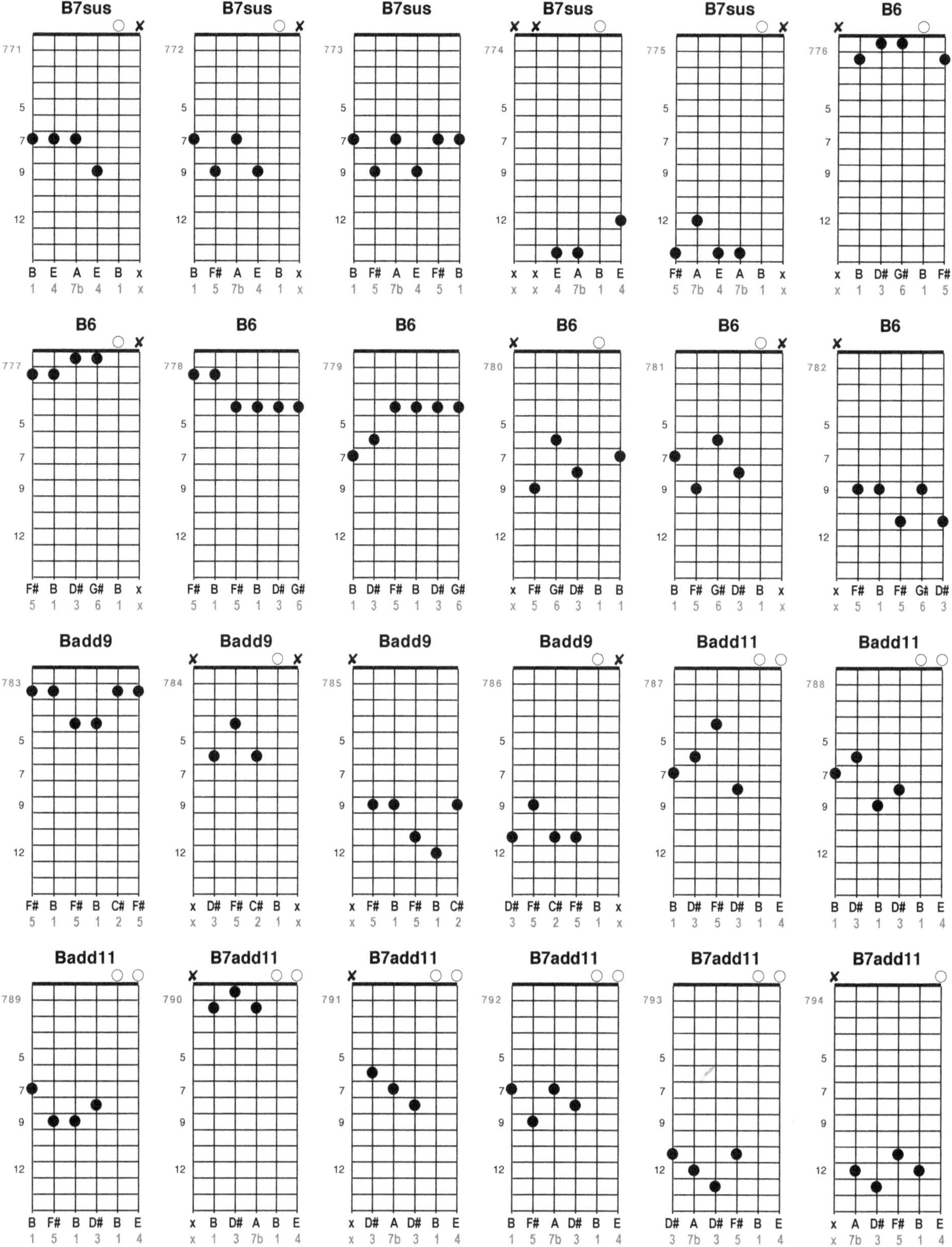
B7sus
771
B E A E B x
1 4 7b 4 1 x
B7sus
772
B F# A E B x
1 5 7b 4 1 x
B7sus
773
B F# A E F# B
1 5 7b 4 5 1
B7sus
774
x x E A B E
x x 4 7b 1 4
B7sus
775
F# A E A B x
5 7b 4 7b 1 x
B6
776
x B D# G# B F#
x 1 3 6 1 5
B6
777
F# B D# G# B x
5 1 3 6 1 x
B6
778
F# B F# B D# G#
5 1 5 1 3 6
B6
779
B D# F# B D# G#
1 3 5 1 3 6
B6
780
x F# G# D# B B
x 5 6 3 1 1
B6
781
B F# G# D# B x
1 5 6 3 1 x
B6
782
x F# B F# G# D#
x 5 1 5 6 3
Badd9
783
F# B F# B C# F#
5 1 5 1 2 5
Badd9
784
x D# F# C# B x
x 3 5 2 1 x
Badd9
785
x F# B F# B C#
x 5 1 5 1 2
Badd9
786
D# F# C# F# B x
3 5 2 5 1 x
Badd11
787
B D# F# D# B E
1 3 5 3 1 4
Badd11
788
B D# B D# B E
1 3 1 3 1 4
Badd11
789
B F# B D# B E
1 5 1 3 1 4
B7add11
790
x B D# A B E
x 1 3 7b 1 4
B7add11
791
x D# A D# B E
x 3 7b 3 1 4
B7add11
792
B F# A D# B E
1 5 7b 3 1 4
B7add11
793
D# A D# F# B E
3 7b 3 5 1 4
B7add11
794
x A D# F# B E
x 7b 3 5 1 4

TUNING: E A D G B E (Standard)

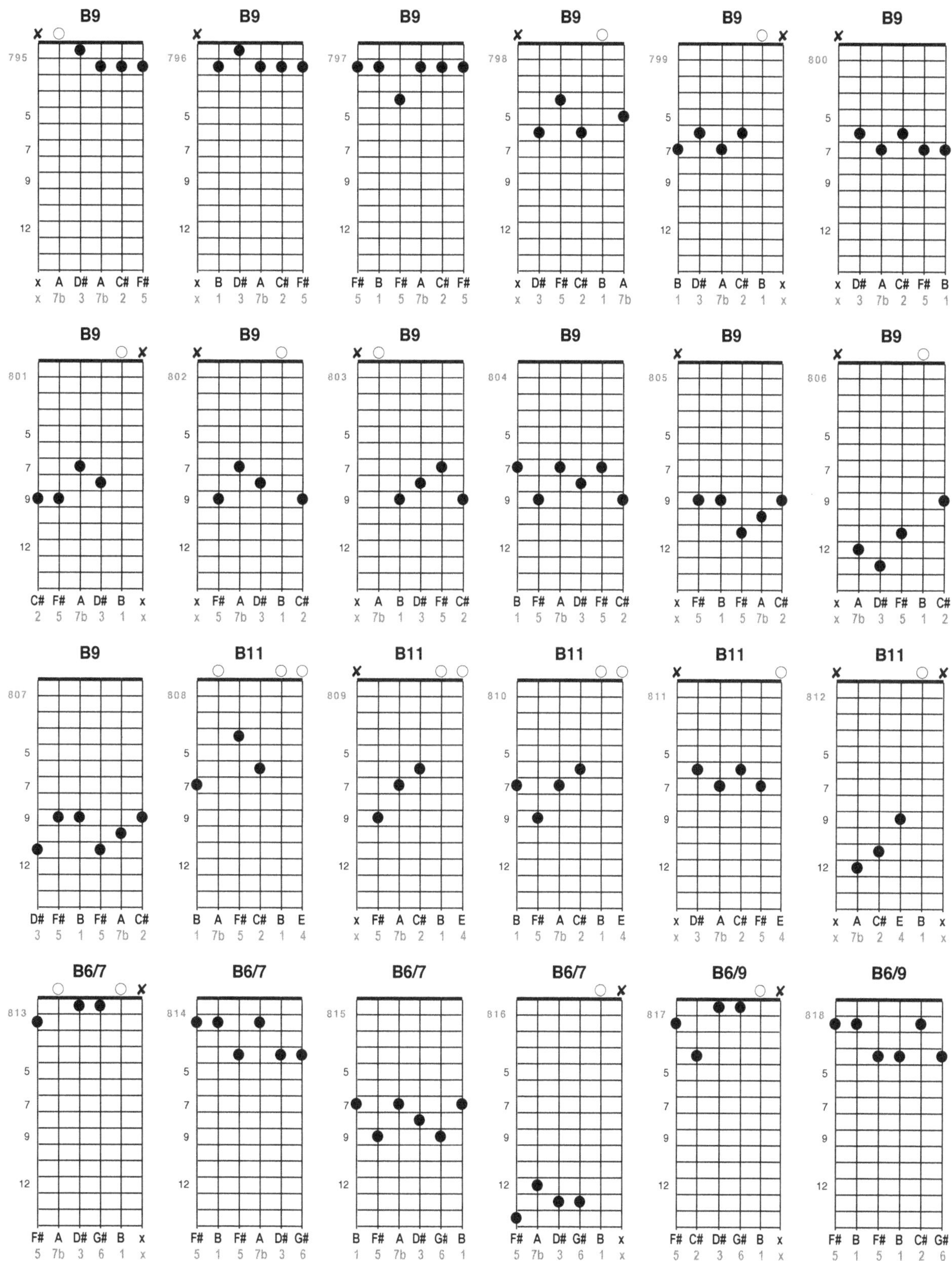
B9
795
x A D# A C# F#
x 7b 3 7b 2 5
B9
796
x B D# A C# F#
x 1 3 7b 2 5
B9
797
F# B F# A C# F#
5 1 5 7b 2 5
B9
798
x D# F# C# B A
x 3 5 2 1 7b
B9
799
B D# A C# B x
1 3 7b 2 1 x
B9
800
x D# A C# F# B
x 3 7b 2 5 1
B9
801
C# F# A D# B x
2 5 7b 3 1 x
B9
802
x F# A D# B C#
x 5 7b 3 1 2
B9
803
x A B D# F# C#
x 7b 1 3 5 2
B9
804
B F# A D# F# C#
1 5 7b 3 5 2
B9
805
x F# B F# A C#
x 5 1 5 7b 2
B9
806
x A D# F# B C#
x 7b 3 5 1 2
B9
807
D# F# B F# A C#
3 5 1 5 7b 2
B11
808
B A F# C# B E
1 7b 5 2 1 4
B11
809
x F# A C# B E
x 5 7b 2 1 4
B11
810
B F# A C# B E
1 5 7b 2 1 4
B11
811
x D# A C# F# E
x 3 7b 2 5 4
B11
812
x A C# E B x
x 7b 2 4 1 x
B6/7
813
F# A D# G# B x
5 7b 3 6 1 x
B6/7
814
F# B F# A D# G#
5 1 5 7b 3 6
B6/7
815
B F# A D# G# B
1 5 7b 3 6 1
B6/7
816
F# A D# G# B x
5 7b 3 6 1 x
B6/9
817
F# C# D# G# B x
5 2 3 6 1 x
B6/9
818
F# B F# B C# G#
5 1 5 1 2 6

TUNING: E A D G B E (Standard)

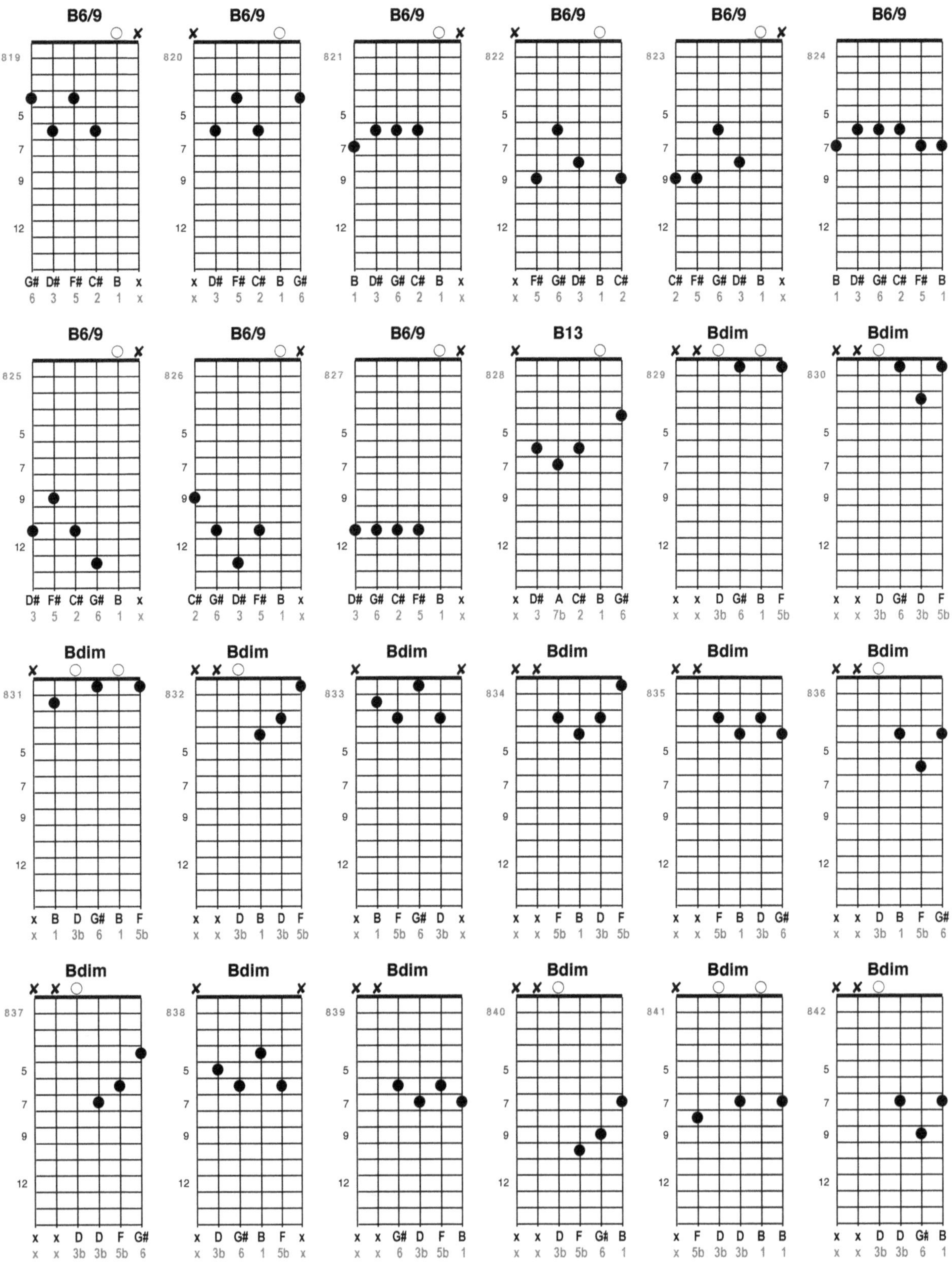

B6/9
819
G# D# F# C# B x
6 3 5 2 1 x
B6/9
820
x D# F# C# B G#
x 3 5 2 1 6
B6/9
821
B D# G# C# B x
1 3 6 2 1 x
B6/9
822
x F# G# D# B C#
x 5 6 3 1 2
B6/9
823
C# F# G# D# B x
2 5 6 3 1 x
B6/9
824
B D# G# C# F# B
1 3 6 2 5 1
B6/9
825
D# F# C# G# B x
3 5 2 6 1 x
B6/9
826
C# G# D# F# B x
2 6 3 5 1 x
B6/9
827
D# G# C# F# B x
3 6 2 5 1 x
B13
828
x D# A C# B G#
x 3 7b 2 1 6
Bdim
829
x x D G# B F
x x 3b 6 1 5b
Bdim
830
x x D G# D F
x x 3b 6 3b 5b
Bdim
831
x B D G# B F
x 1 3b 6 1 5b
Bdim
832
x x D B D F
x x 3b 1 3b 5b
Bdim
833
x B F G# D x
x 1 5b 6 3b x
Bdim
834
x x F B D F
x x 5b 1 3b 5b
Bdim
835
x x F B D G#
x x 5b 1 3b 6
Bdim
836
x x D B F G#
x x 3b 1 5b 6
Bdim
837
x x D D F G#
x x 3b 3b 5b 6
Bdim
838
x D G# B F x
x 3b 6 1 5b x
Bdim
839
x x G# D F B
x x 6 3b 5b 1
Bdim
840
x x D F G# B
x x 3b 5b 6 1
Bdim
841
x F D D B B
x 5b 3b 3b 1 1
Bdim
842
x x D D G# B
x x 3b 3b 6 1

TUNING: E A D G B E (Standard)

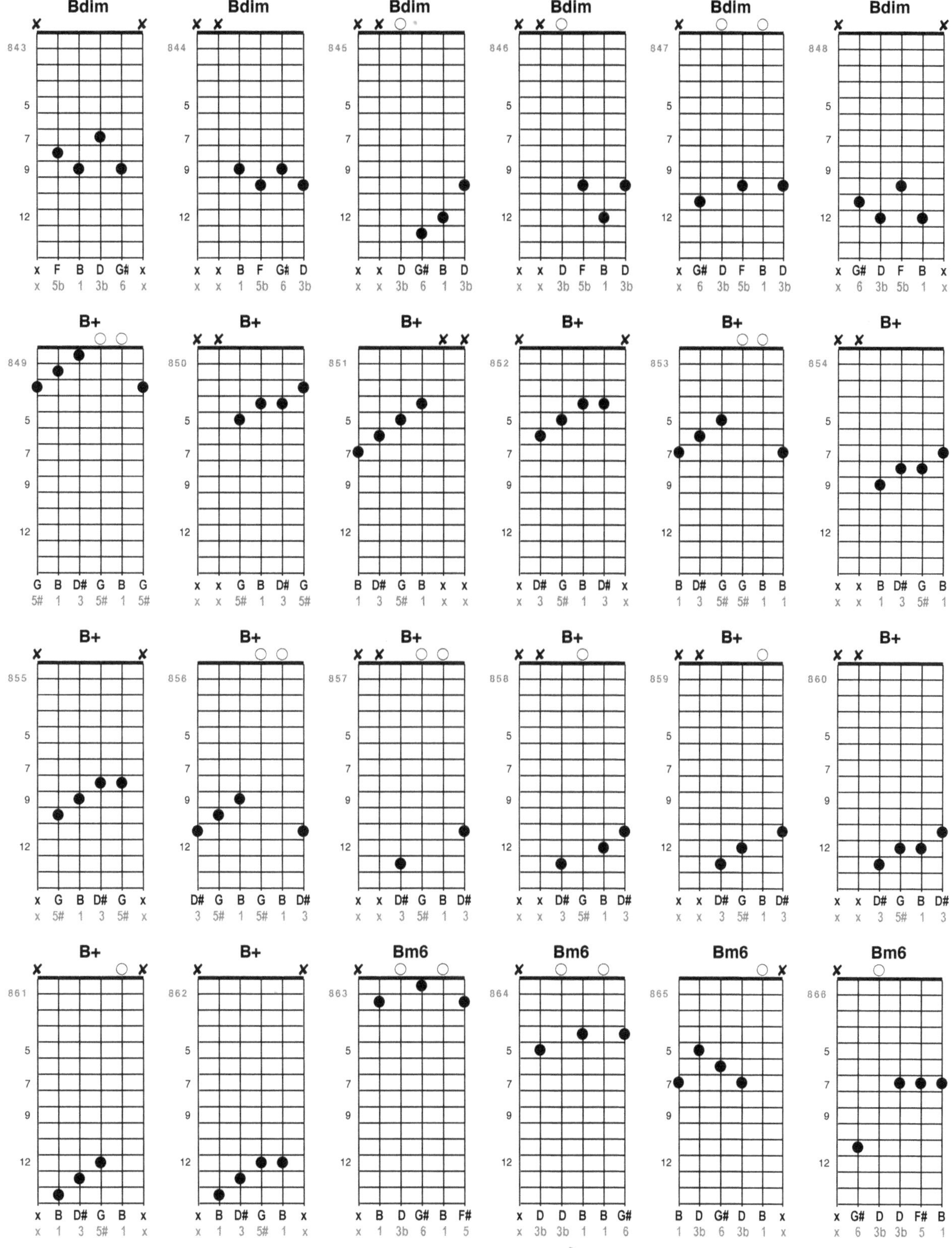
Bdim
843
x F B D G# x
x 5b 1 3b 6 x
Bdim
844
x x B F G# D
x x 1 5b 6 3b
Bdim
845
x x D G# B D
x x 3b 6 1 3b
Bdim
846
x x D F B D
x x 3b 5b 1 3b
Bdim
847
x G# D F B D
x 6 3b 5b 1 3b
Bdim
848
x G# D F B x
x 6 3b 5b 1 x
B+
849
G B D# G B G
5# 1 3 5# 1 5#
B+
850
x x G B D# G
x x 5# 1 3 5#
B+
851
B D# G B x x
1 3 5# 1 x x
B+
852
x D# G B D# x
x 3 5# 1 3 x
B+
853
B D# G G B B
1 3 5# 5# 1 1
B+
854
x x B D# G B
x x 1 3 5# 1
B+
855
x G B D# G x
x 5# 1 3 5# x
B+
856
D# G B G B D#
3 5# 1 5# 1 3
B+
857
x x D# G B D#
x x 3 5# 1 3
B+
858
x x D# G B D#
x x 3 5# 1 3
B+
859
x x D# G B D#
x x 3 5# 1 3
B+
860
x x D# G B D#
x x 3 5# 1 3
B+
861
x B D# G B x
x 1 3 5# 1 x
B+
862
x B D# G B x
x 1 3 5# 1 x
Bm6
863
x B D G# B F#
x 1 3b 6 1 5
Bm6
864
x D D B B G#
x 3b 3b 1 1 6
Bm6
865
B D G# D B x
1 3b 6 3b 1 x
Bm6
866
x G# D D F# B
x 6 3b 3b 5 1

TUNING: E A D G B E (Standard)

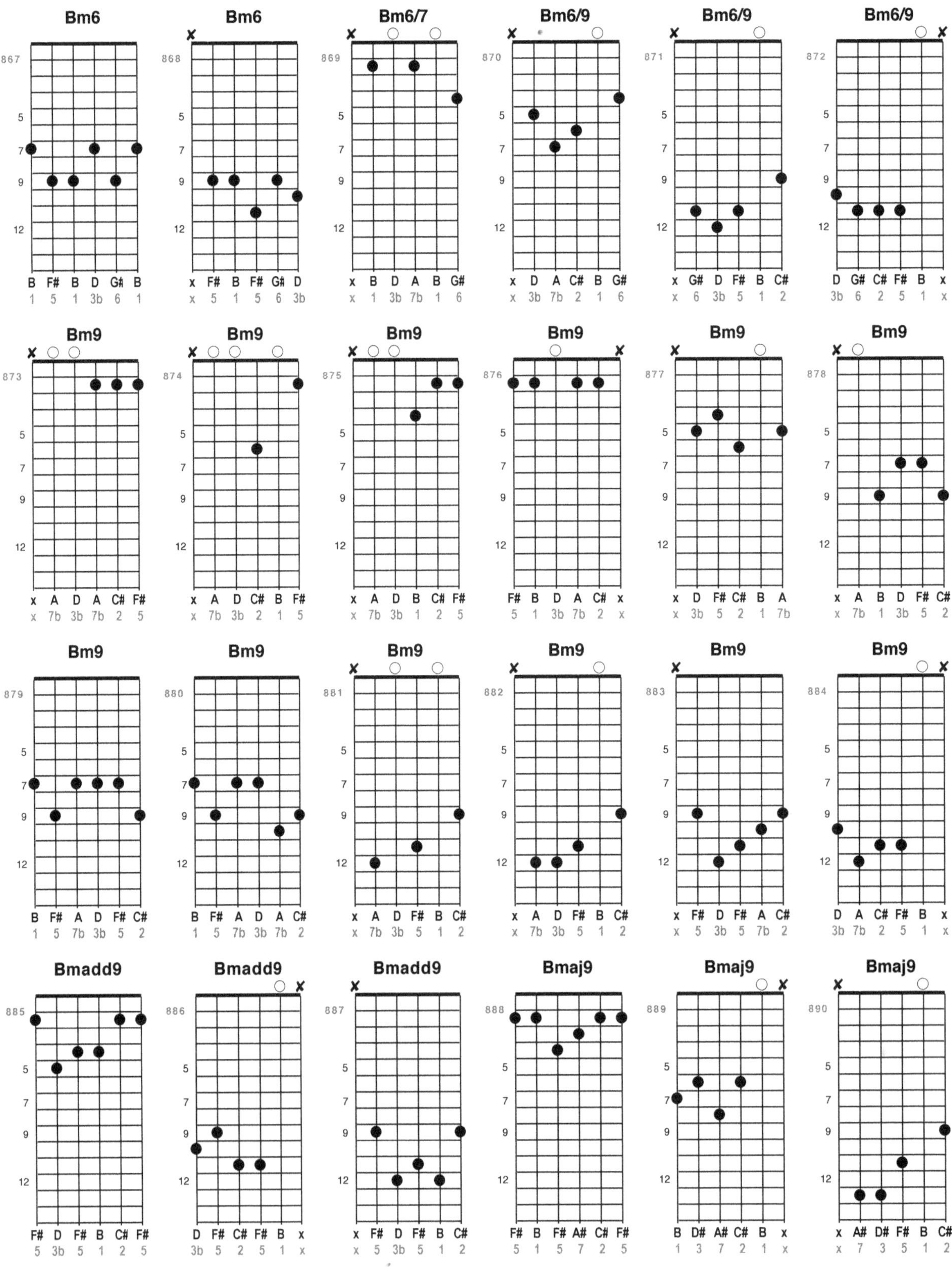
Bm6
867
B F# B D G# B
1 5 1 3b 6 1
Bm6
868
x F# B F# G# D
x 5 1 5 6 3b
Bm6/7
869
x B D A B G#
x 1 3b 7b 1 6
Bm6/9
870
x D A C# B G#
x 3b 7b 2 1 6
Bm6/9
871
x G# D F# B C#
x 6 3b 5 1 2
Bm6/9
872
D G# C# F# B x
3b 6 2 5 1 x
Bm9
873
x A D A C# F#
x 7b 3b 7b 2 5
Bm9
874
x A D C# B F#
x 7b 3b 2 1 5
Bm9
875
x A D B C# F#
x 7b 3b 1 2 5
Bm9
876
F# B D A C# x
5 1 3b 7b 2 x
Bm9
877
x D F# C# B A
x 3b 5 2 1 7b
Bm9
878
x A B D F# C#
x 7b 1 3b 5 2
Bm9
879
B F# A D F# C#
1 5 7b 3b 5 2
Bm9
880
B F# A D A C#
1 5 7b 3b 7b 2
Bm9
881
x A D F# B C#
x 7b 3b 5 1 2
Bm9
882
x A D F# B C#
x 7b 3b 5 1 2
Bm9
883
x F# D F# A C#
x 5 3b 5 7b 2
Bm9
884
D A C# F# B x
3b 7b 2 5 1 x
Bmadd9
885
F# D F# B C# F#
5 3b 5 1 2 5
Bmadd9
886
D F# C# F# B x
3b 5 2 5 1 x
Bmadd9
887
x F# D F# B C#
x 5 3b 5 1 2
Bmaj9
888
F# B F# A# C# F#
5 1 5 7 2 5
Bmaj9
889
B D# A# C# B x
1 3 7 2 1 x
Bmaj9
890
x A# D# F# B C#
x 7 3 5 1 2

TUNING: E A D G B E (Standard)

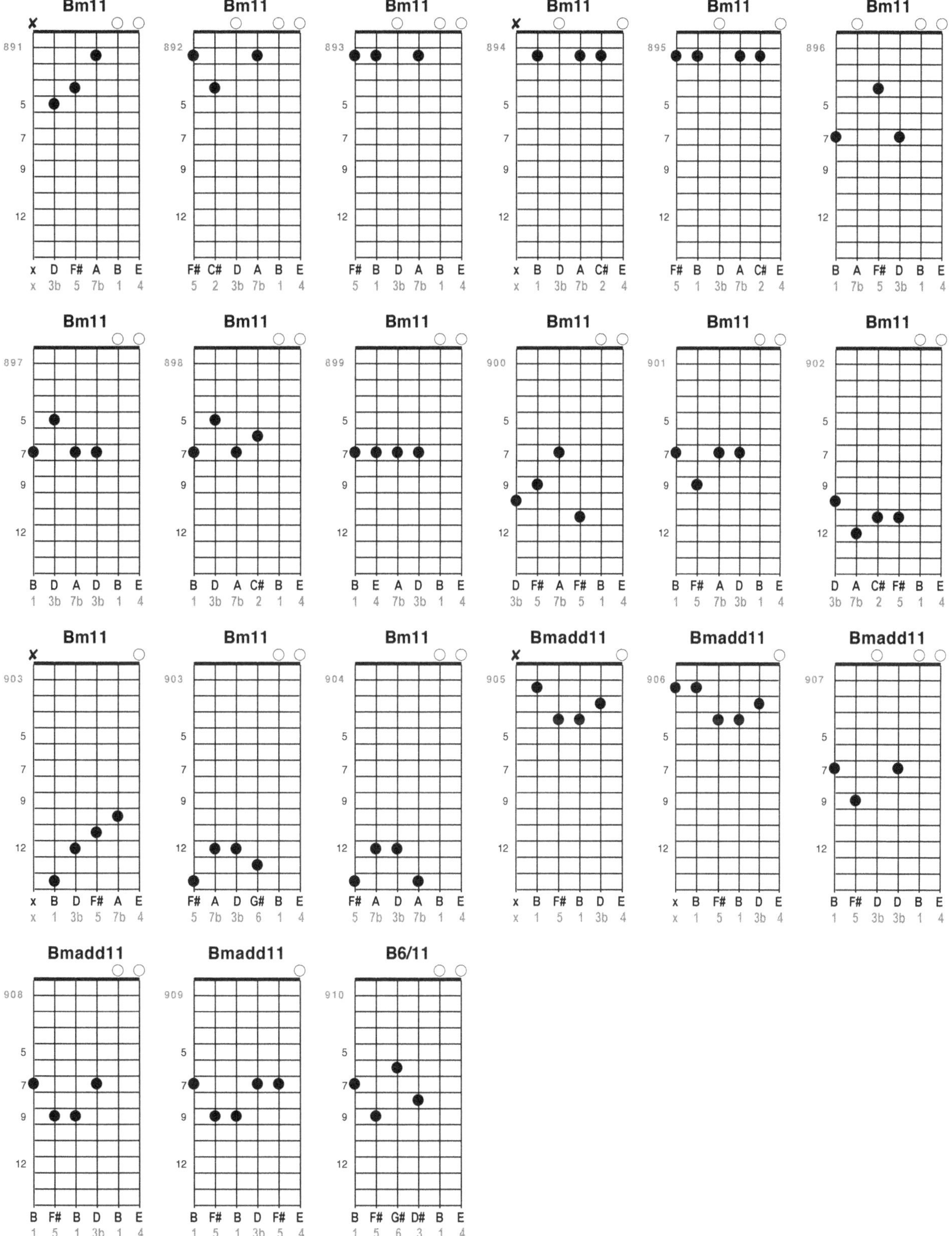

Bm11 · 891
x D F# A B E
x 3b 5 7b 1 4

Bm11 · 892
F# C# D A B E
5 2 3b 7b 1 4

Bm11 · 893
F# B D A B E
5 1 3b 7b 1 4

Bm11 · 894
x B D A C# E
x 1 3b 7b 2 4

Bm11 · 895
F# B D A C# E
5 1 3b 7b 2 4

Bm11 · 896
B A F# D B E
1 7b 5 3b 1 4

Bm11 · 897
B D A D B E
1 3b 7b 3b 1 4

Bm11 · 898
B D A C# B E
1 3b 7b 2 1 4

Bm11 · 899
B E A D B E
1 4 7b 3b 1 4

Bm11 · 900
D F# A F# B E
3b 5 7b 5 1 4

Bm11 · 901
B F# A D B E
1 5 7b 3b 1 4

Bm11 · 902
D A C# F# B E
3b 7b 2 5 1 4

Bm11 · 903
x B D F# A E
x 1 3b 5 7b 4

Bm11 · 903
F# A D G# B E
5 7b 3b 6 1 4

Bm11 · 904
F# A D A B E
5 7b 3b 7b 1 4

Bmadd11 · 905
x B F# B D E
x 1 5 1 3b 4

Bmadd11 · 906
x B F# B D E
x 1 5 1 3b 4

Bmadd11 · 907
B F# D D B E
1 5 3b 3b 1 4

Bmadd11 · 908
B F# B D B E
1 5 1 3b 1 4

Bmadd11 · 909
B F# B D F# E
1 5 1 3b 5 4

B6/11 · 910
B F# G# D# B E
1 5 6 3 1 4

Troubadour Guitar Chords

TUNING: E A D G B E (Standard)

C

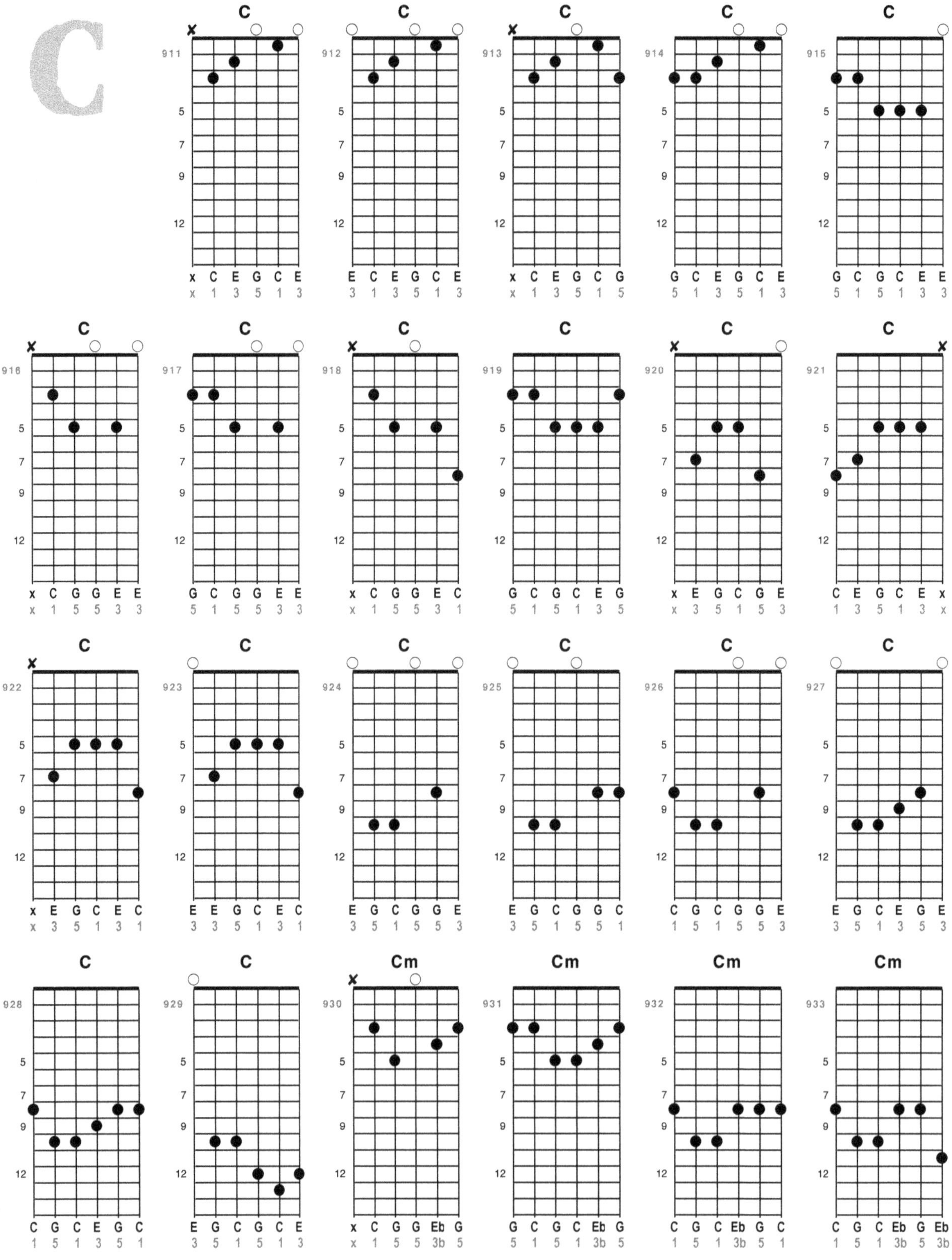

C
911
x C E G C E
x 1 3 5 1 3
C
912
E C E G C E
3 1 3 5 1 3
C
913
x C E G C G
x 1 3 5 1 5
C
914
G C E G C E
5 1 3 5 1 3
C
915
G C G C E E
5 1 5 1 3 3
C
916
x C G G E E
x 1 5 5 3 3
C
917
G C G G E E
5 1 5 5 3 3
C
918
x C G G E C
x 1 5 5 3 1
C
919
G C G C E G
5 1 5 1 3 5
C
920
x E G C G E
x 3 5 1 5 3
C
921
C E G C E x
1 3 5 1 3 x
C
922
x E G C E C
x 3 5 1 3 1
C
923
E E G C E C
3 3 5 1 3 1
C
924
E G C G G E
3 5 1 5 5 3
C
925
E G C G G C
3 5 1 5 5 1
C
926
C G C G G E
1 5 1 5 5 3
C
927
E G C E G E
3 5 1 3 5 3
C
928
C G C E G C
1 5 1 3 5 1
C
929
E G C G C E
3 5 1 5 1 3
Cm
930
x C G G Eb G
x 1 5 5 3b 5
Cm
931
G C G C Eb G
5 1 5 1 3b 5
Cm
932
C G C Eb G C
1 5 1 3b 5 1
Cm
933
C G C Eb G Eb
1 5 1 3b 5 3b

Troubadour Guitar Chords

TUNING: E A D G B E (Standard)

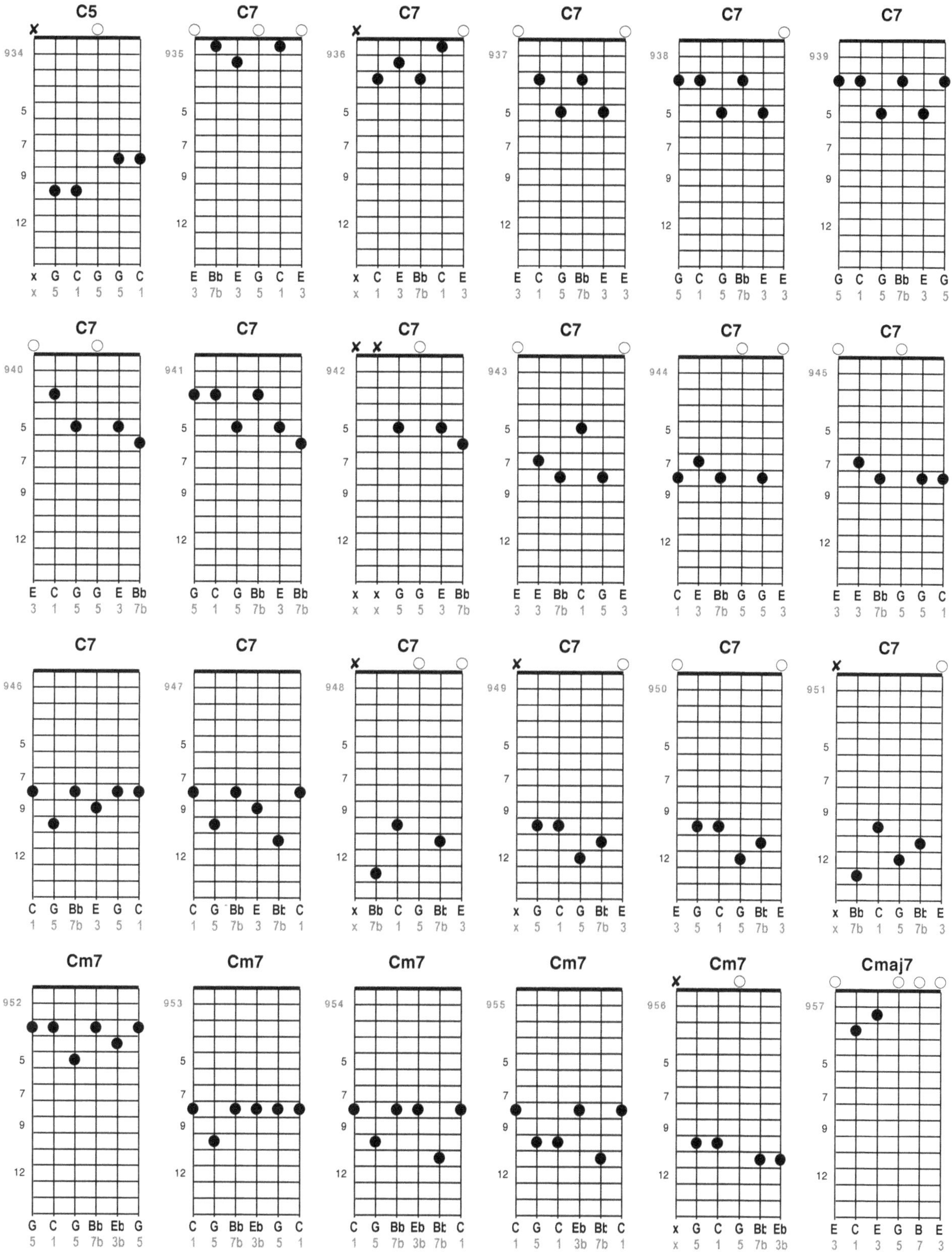

C5
934
x G C G G C
x 5 1 5 5 1
C7
935
E Bb E G C E
3 7b 3 5 1 3
C7
936
x C E Bb C E
x 1 3 7b 1 3
C7
937
E C G Bb E E
3 1 5 7b 3 3
C7
938
G C G Bb E E
5 1 5 7b 3 3
C7
939
G C G Bb E G
5 1 5 7b 3 5
C7
940
E C G G E Bb
3 1 5 5 3 7b
C7
941
G C G Bb E Bb
5 1 5 7b 3 7b
C7
942
x x G G E Bb
x x 5 5 3 7b
C7
943
E E Bb C G E
3 3 7b 1 5 3
C7
944
C E Bb G G E
1 3 7b 5 5 3
C7
945
E E Bb G G C
3 3 7b 5 5 1
C7
946
C G Bb E G C
1 5 7b 3 5 1
C7
947
C G Bb E Bb C
1 5 7b 3 7b 1
C7
948
x Bb C G Bb E
x 7b 1 5 7b 3
C7
949
x G C G Bb E
x 5 1 5 7b 3
C7
950
E G C G Bb E
3 5 1 5 7b 3
C7
951
x Bb C G Bb E
x 7b 1 5 7b 3
Cm7
952
G C G Bb Eb G
5 1 5 7b 3b 5
Cm7
953
C G Bb Eb G C
1 5 7b 3b 5 1
Cm7
954
C G Bb Eb Bb C
1 5 7b 3b 7b 1
Cm7
955
C G C Eb Bb C
1 5 1 3b 7b 1
Cm7
956
x G C G Bb Eb
x 5 1 5 7b 3b
Cmaj7
957
E C E G B E
3 1 3 5 7 3

Troubadour Guitar Chords

TUNING: E A D G B E (Standard)

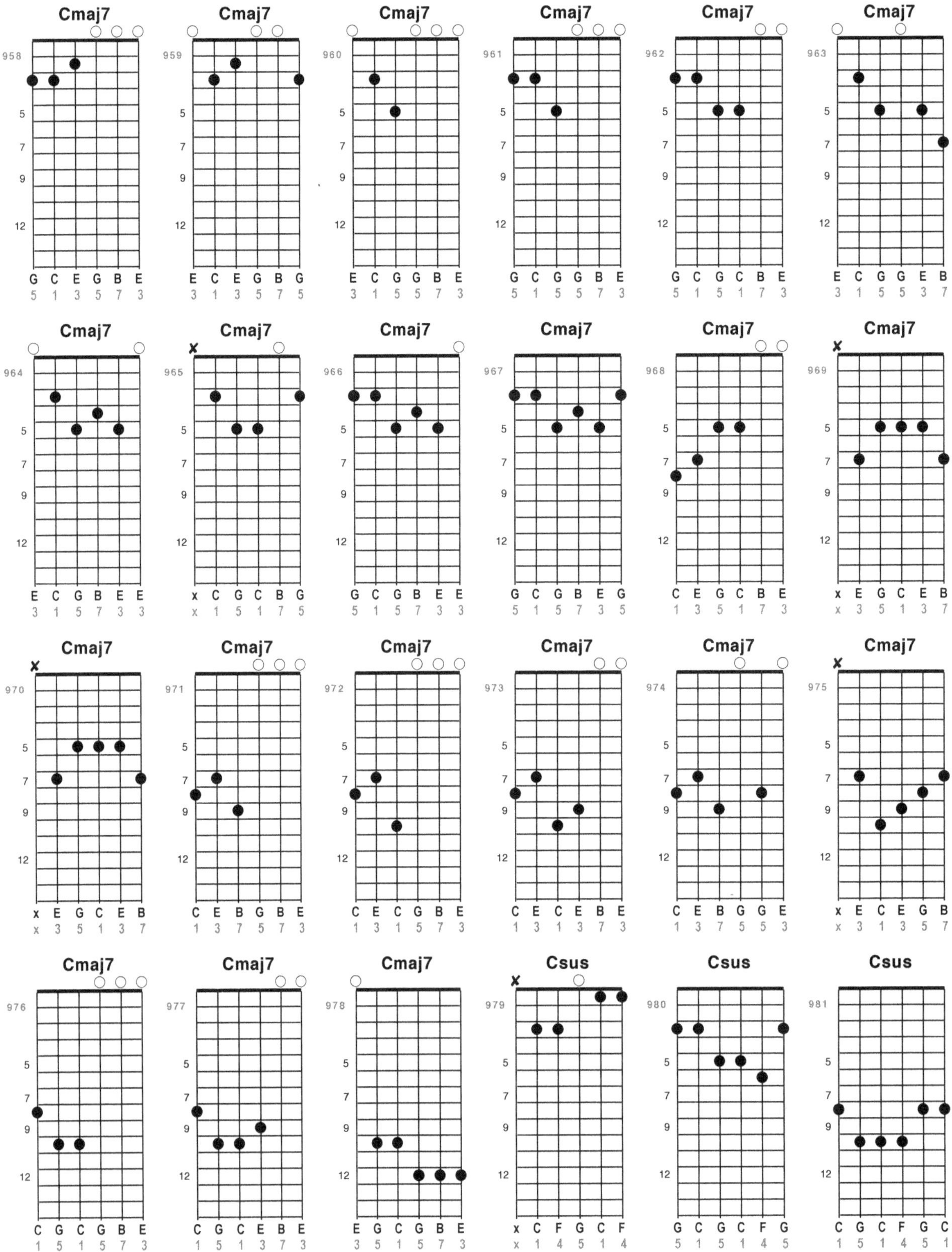

Cmaj7	Cmaj7	Cmaj7	Cmaj7	Cmaj7	Cmaj7
958	959	960	961	962	963
G C E G B E	E C E G B G	E C G G B E	G C G G B E	G C G C B E	E C G G E B
5 1 3 5 7 3	3 1 3 5 7 5	3 1 5 5 7 3	5 1 5 5 7 3	5 1 5 1 7 3	3 1 5 5 3 7

Cmaj7	Cmaj7	Cmaj7	Cmaj7	Cmaj7	Cmaj7
964	965	966	967	968	969
E C G B E E	x C G C B G	G C G B E E	G C G B E G	C E G C B E	x E G C E B
3 1 5 7 3 3	x 1 5 1 7 5	5 1 5 7 3 3	5 1 5 7 3 5	1 3 5 1 7 3	x 3 5 1 3 7

Cmaj7	Cmaj7	Cmaj7	Cmaj7	Cmaj7	Cmaj7
970	971	972	973	974	975
x E G C E B	C E B G B E	C E C G B E	C E C E B E	C E B G G E	x E C E G B
x 3 5 1 3 7	1 3 7 5 7 3	1 3 1 5 7 3	1 3 1 3 7 3	1 3 7 5 5 3	x 3 1 3 5 7

Cmaj7	Cmaj7	Cmaj7	Csus	Csus	Csus
976	977	978	979	980	981
C G C G B E	C G C E B E	E G C G B E	x C F G C F	G C G C F G	C G C F G C
1 5 1 5 7 3	1 5 1 3 7 3	3 5 1 5 7 3	x 1 4 5 1 4	5 1 5 1 4 5	1 5 1 4 5 1

Troubadour Guitar Chords

TUNING: E A D G B E (Standard)

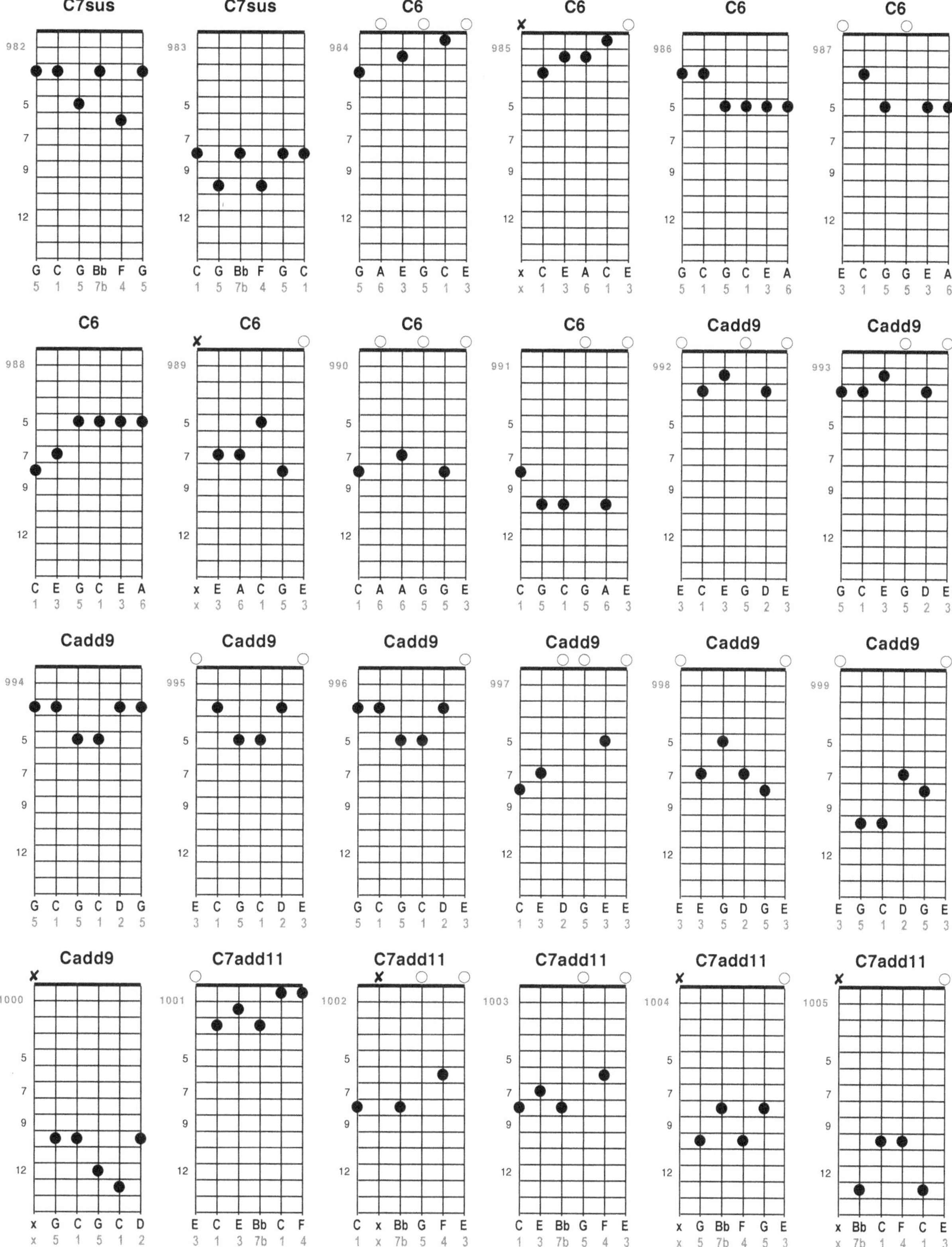

C7sus
982
G C G Bb F G
5 1 5 7b 4 5
C7sus
983
C G Bb F G C
1 5 7b 4 5 1
C6
984
G A E G C E
5 6 3 5 1 3
C6
985
x C E A C E
x 1 3 6 1 3
C6
986
G C G C E A
5 1 5 1 3 6
C6
987
E C G G E A
3 1 5 5 3 6
C6
988
C E G C E A
1 3 5 1 3 6
C6
989
x E A C G E
x 3 6 1 5 3
C6
990
C A A G G E
1 6 6 5 5 3
C6
991
C G C G A E
1 5 1 5 6 3
Cadd9
992
E C E G D E
3 1 3 5 2 3
Cadd9
993
G C E G D E
5 1 3 5 2 3
Cadd9
994
G C G C D G
5 1 5 1 2 5
Cadd9
995
E C G C D E
3 1 5 1 2 3
Cadd9
996
G C G C D E
5 1 5 1 2 3
Cadd9
997
C E D G E E
1 3 2 5 3 3
Cadd9
998
E E G D G E
3 3 5 2 5 3
Cadd9
999
E G C D G E
3 5 1 2 5 3
Cadd9
1000
x G C G C D
x 5 1 5 1 2
C7add11
1001
E C E Bb C F
3 1 3 7b 1 4
C7add11
1002
C x Bb G F E
1 x 7b 5 4 3
C7add11
1003
C E Bb G F E
1 3 7b 5 4 3
C7add11
1004
x G Bb F G E
x 5 7b 4 5 3
C7add11
1005
x Bb C F C E
x 7b 1 4 1 3

TUNING: E A D G B E (Standard)

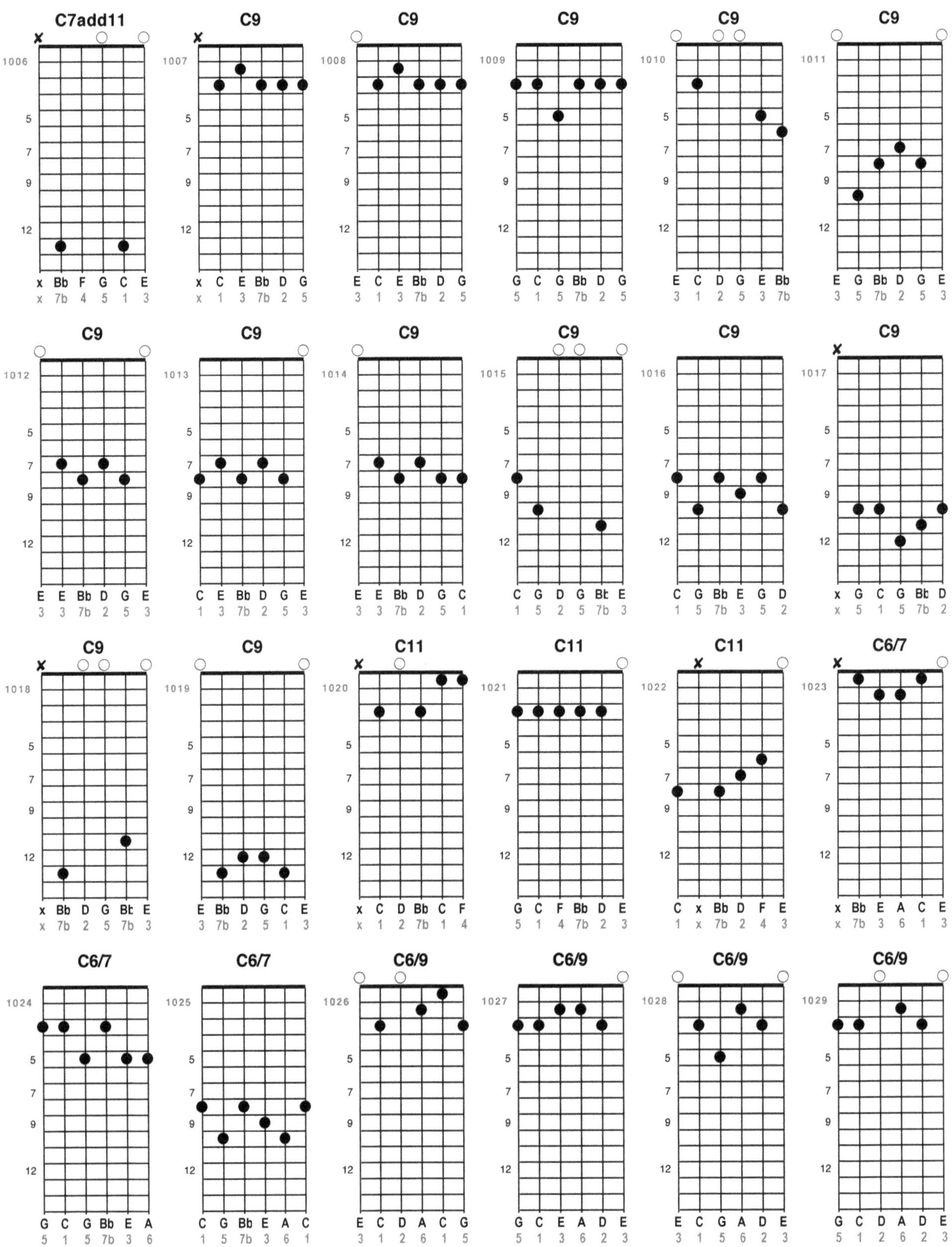

C7add11 — 1006
x x Bb F G C E
x 7b 4 5 1 3

C9 — 1007
x C E Bb D G
x 1 3 7b 2 5

C9 — 1008
E C E Bb D G
3 1 3 7b 2 5

C9 — 1009
G C G Bb D G
5 1 5 7b 2 5

C9 — 1010
E C D G E Bb
3 1 2 5 3 7b

C9 — 1011
E G Bb D G E
3 5 7b 2 5 3

C9 — 1012
E E Bb D G E
3 3 7b 2 5 3

C9 — 1013
C E Bb D G E
1 3 7b 2 5 3

C9 — 1014
E E Bb D G C
3 3 7b 2 5 1

C9 — 1015
C G D G Bb E
1 5 2 5 7b 3

C9 — 1016
C G Bb E G D
1 5 7b 3 5 2

C9 — 1017
x G C G Bb D
x 5 1 5 7b 2

C9 — 1018
x Bb D G Bb E
x 7b 2 5 7b 3

C9 — 1019
E Bb D G C E
3 7b 2 5 1 3

C11 — 1020
x C D Bb C F
x 1 2 7b 1 4

C11 — 1021
G C F Bb D E
5 1 4 7b 2 3

C11 — 1022
C x Bb D F E
1 x 7b 2 4 3

C6/7 — 1023
x Bb E A C E
x 7b 3 6 1 3

C6/7 — 1024
G C G Bb E A
5 1 5 7b 3 6

C6/7 — 1025
C G Bb E A C
1 5 7b 3 6 1

C6/9 — 1026
E C D A C G
3 1 2 6 1 5

C6/9 — 1027
G C E A D E
5 1 3 6 2 3

C6/9 — 1028
E C G A D E
3 1 5 6 2 3

C6/9 — 1029
G C D A D E
5 1 2 6 2 3

TUNING: E A D G B E (Standard)

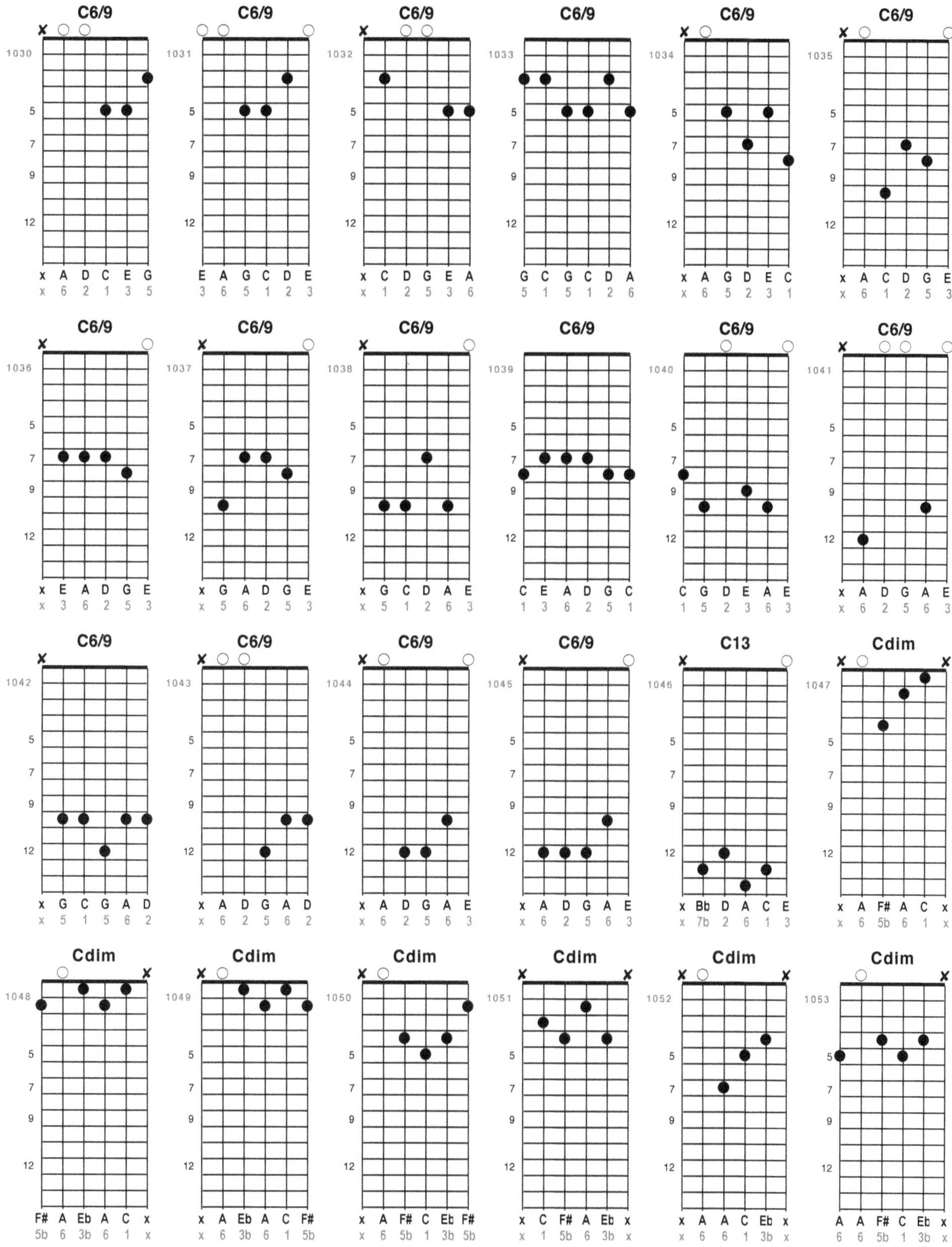
C6/9
1030
x A D C E G
x 6 2 1 3 5
C6/9
1031
E A G C D E
3 6 5 1 2 3
C6/9
1032
x C D G E A
x 1 2 5 3 6
C6/9
1033
G C G C D A
5 1 5 1 2 6
C6/9
1034
x A G D E C
x 6 5 2 3 1
C6/9
1035
x A C D G E
x 6 1 2 5 3
C6/9
1036
x E A D G E
x 3 6 2 5 3
C6/9
1037
x G A D G E
x 5 6 2 5 3
C6/9
1038
x G C D A E
x 5 1 2 6 3
C6/9
1039
C E A D G C
1 3 6 2 5 1
C6/9
1040
C G D E A E
1 5 2 3 6 3
C6/9
1041
x A D G A E
x 6 2 5 6 3
C6/9
1042
x G C G A D
x 5 1 5 6 2
C6/9
1043
x A D G A D
x 6 2 5 6 2
C6/9
1044
x A D G A E
x 6 2 5 6 3
C6/9
1045
x A D G A E
x 6 2 5 6 3
C13
1046
x Bb D A C E
x 7b 2 6 1 3
Cdim
1047
x A F# A C x
x 6 5b 6 1 x
Cdim
1048
F# A Eb A C x
5b 6 3b 6 1 x
Cdim
1049
x A Eb A C F#
x 6 3b 6 1 5b
Cdim
1050
x A F# C Eb F#
x 6 5b 1 3b 5b
Cdim
1051
x C F# A Eb x
x 1 5b 6 3b x
Cdim
1052
x A A C Eb x
x 6 6 1 3b x
Cdim
1053
A A F# C Eb x
6 6 5b 1 3b x

TUNING: E A D G B E (Standard)

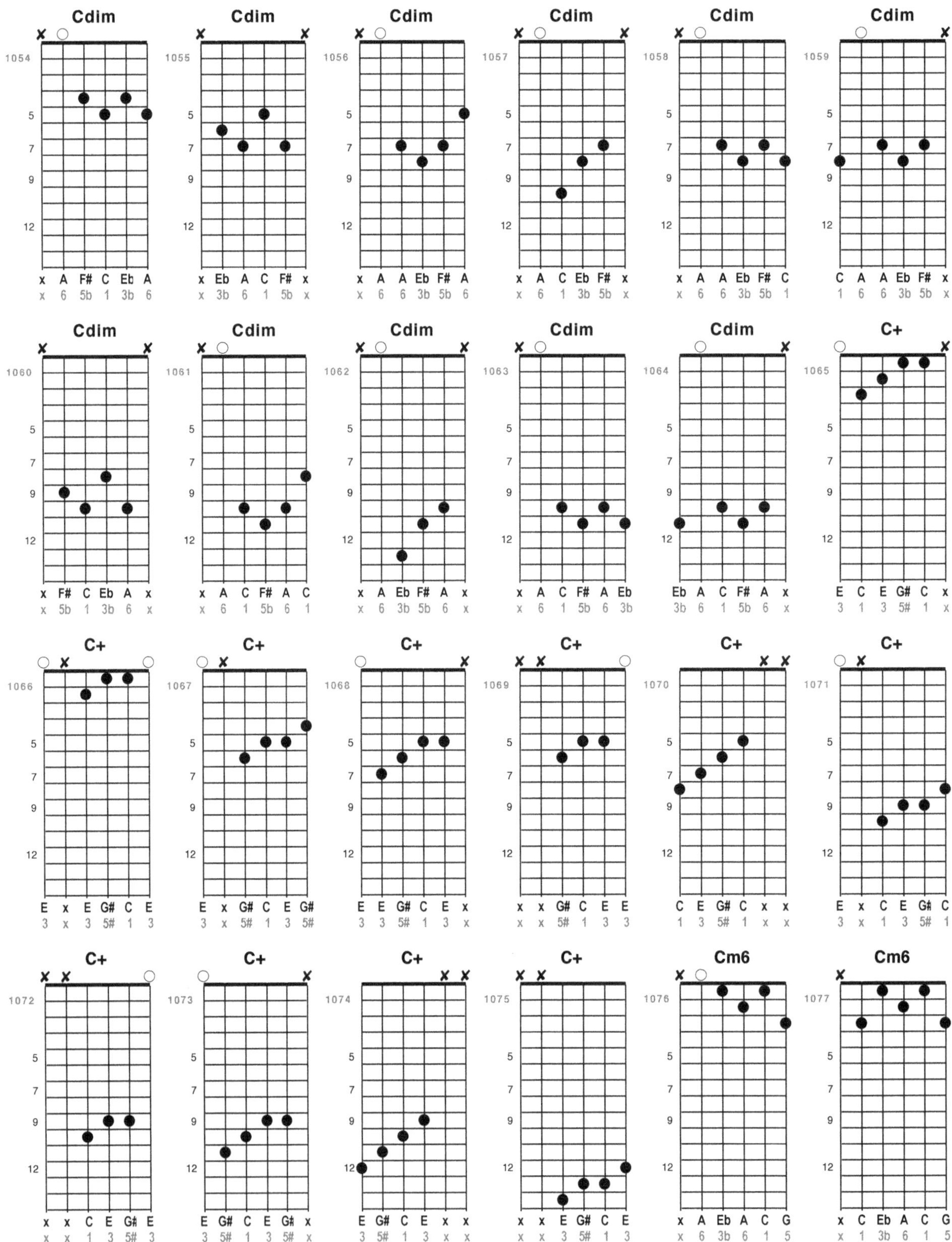
Cdim
1054
x A F# C Eb A
x 6 5b 1 3b 6
Cdim
1055
x Eb A C F# x
x 3b 6 1 5b x
Cdim
1056
x A A Eb F# A
x 6 6 3b 5b 6
Cdim
1057
x A C Eb F# x
x 6 1 3b 5b x
Cdim
1058
x A A Eb F# C
x 6 6 3b 5b 1
Cdim
1059
C A A Eb F# x
1 6 6 3b 5b x
Cdim
1060
x F# C Eb A x
x 5b 1 3b 6 x
Cdim
1061
x A C F# A C
x 6 1 5b 6 1
Cdim
1062
x A Eb F# A x
x 6 3b 5b 6 x
Cdim
1063
x A C F# A Eb
x 6 1 5b 6 3b
Cdim
1064
Eb A C F# A x
3b 6 1 5b 6 x
C+
1065
E C E G# C x
3 1 3 5# 1 x
C+
1066
E x E G# C E
3 x 3 5# 1 3
C+
1067
E x G# C E G#
3 x 5# 1 3 5#
C+
1068
E E G# C E x
3 3 5# 1 3 x
C+
1069
x x G# C E E
x x 5# 1 3 3
C+
1070
C E G# C x x
1 3 5# 1 x x
C+
1071
E x C E G# C
3 x 1 3 5# 1
C+
1072
x x C E G# E
x x 1 3 5# 3
C+
1073
E G# C E G# x
3 5# 1 3 5# x
C+
1074
E G# C E x x
3 5# 1 3 x x
C+
1075
x x E G# C E
x x 3 5# 1 3
Cm6
1076
x A Eb A C G
x 6 3b 6 1 5
Cm6
1077
x C Eb A C G
x 1 3b 6 1 5

TUNING: E A D G B E (Standard)

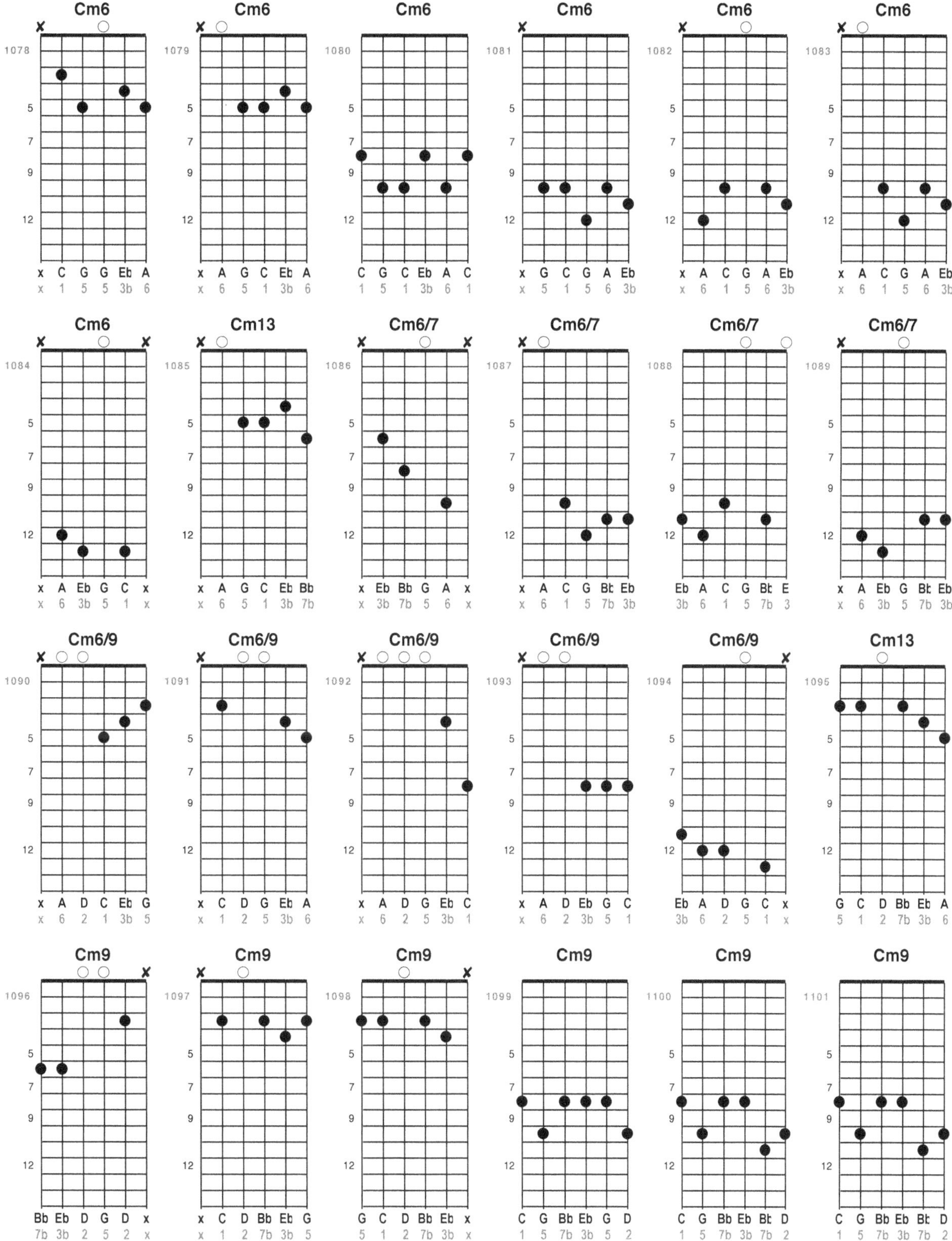
1078 Cm6
x C G G Eb A
x 1 5 5 3b 6
1079 Cm6
x A G C Eb A
x 6 5 1 3b 6
1080 Cm6
C G C Eb A C
1 5 1 3b 6 1
1081 Cm6
x G C G A Eb
x 5 1 5 6 3b
1082 Cm6
x A C G A Eb
x 6 1 5 6 3b
1083 Cm6
x A C G A Eb
x 6 1 5 6 3b
1084 Cm6
x A Eb G C x
x 6 3b 5 1 x
1085 Cm13
x A G C Eb Bb
x 6 5 1 3b 7b
1086 Cm6/7
x Eb Bb G A x
x 3b 7b 5 6 x
1087 Cm6/7
x A C G Bb Eb
x 6 1 5 7b 3b
1088 Cm6/7
Eb A C G Bb E
3b 6 1 5 7b 3
1089 Cm6/7
x A Eb G Bb Eb
x 6 3b 5 7b 3b
1090 Cm6/9
x A D C Eb G
x 6 2 1 3b 5
1091 Cm6/9
x C D G Eb A
x 1 2 5 3b 6
1092 Cm6/9
x A D G Eb C
x 6 2 5 3b 1
1093 Cm6/9
x A D Eb G C
x 6 2 3b 5 1
1094 Cm6/9
Eb A D G C x
3b 6 2 5 1 x
1095 Cm13
G C D Bb Eb A
5 1 2 7b 3b 6
1096 Cm9
Bb Eb D G D x
7b 3b 2 5 2 x
1097 Cm9
x C D Bb Eb G
x 1 2 7b 3b 5
1098 Cm9
G C D Bb Eb x
5 1 2 7b 3b x
1099 Cm9
C G Bb Eb G D
1 5 7b 3b 5 2
1100 Cm9
C G Bb Eb Bb D
1 5 7b 3b 7b 2
1101 Cm9
C G Bb Eb Bb D
1 5 7b 3b 7b 2

TUNING: E A D G B E (Standard)

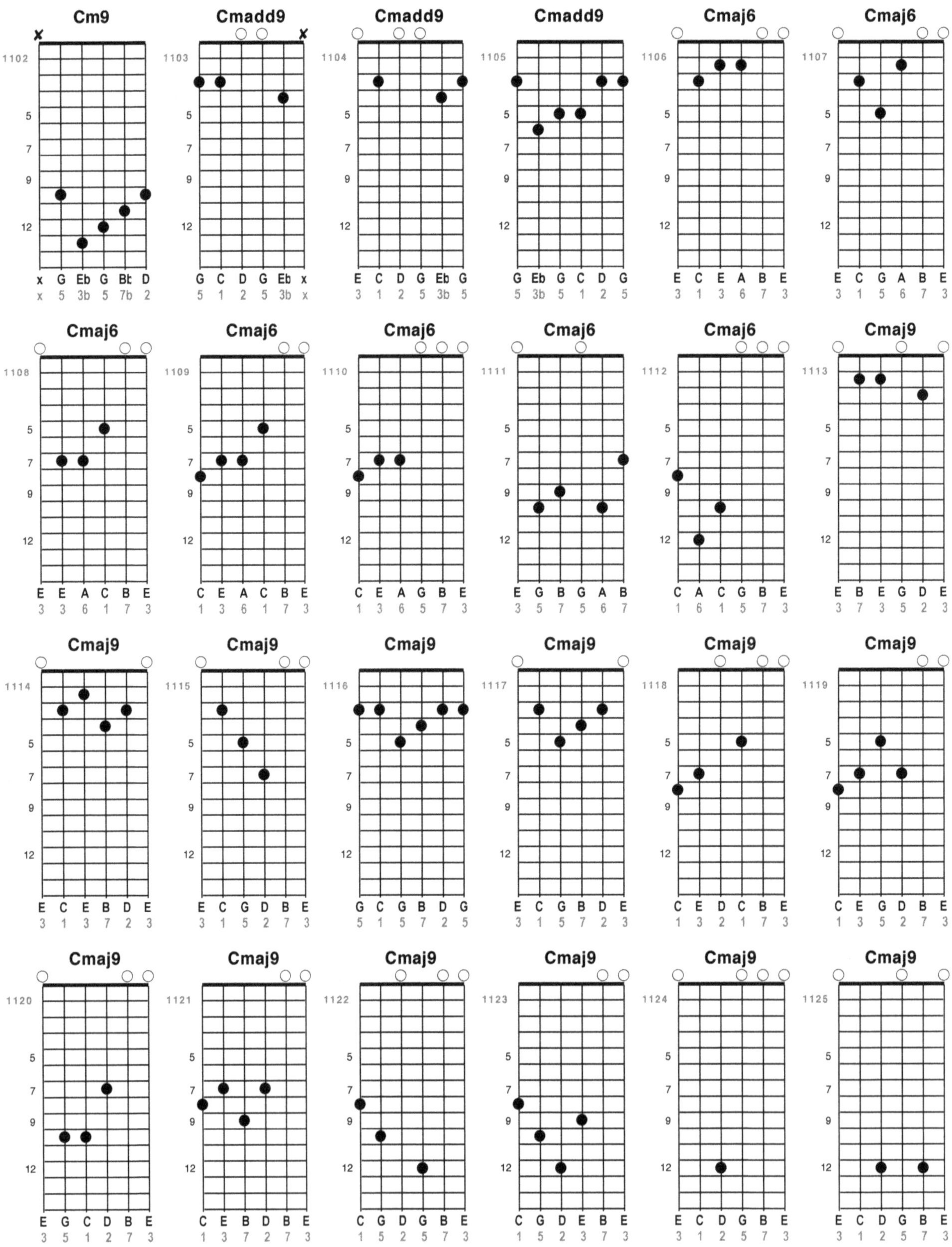
Cm9
1102
x G Eb G Bb D
x 5 3b 5 7b 2
Cmadd9
1103
G C D G Eb x
5 1 2 5 3b x
Cmadd9
1104
E C D G Eb G
3 1 2 5 3b 5
Cmadd9
1105
G Eb G C D G
5 3b 5 1 2 5
Cmaj6
1106
E C E A B E
3 1 3 6 7 3
Cmaj6
1107
E C G A B E
3 1 5 6 7 3
Cmaj6
1108
E E A C B E
3 3 6 1 7 3
Cmaj6
1109
C E A C B E
1 3 6 1 7 3
Cmaj6
1110
C E A G B E
1 3 6 5 7 3
Cmaj6
1111
E G B G A B
3 5 7 5 6 7
Cmaj6
1112
C A C G B E
1 6 1 5 7 3
Cmaj9
1113
E B E G D E
3 7 3 5 2 3
Cmaj9
1114
E C E B D E
3 1 3 7 2 3
Cmaj9
1115
E C G D B E
3 1 5 2 7 3
Cmaj9
1116
G C G B D G
5 1 5 7 2 5
Cmaj9
1117
E C G B D E
3 1 5 7 2 3
Cmaj9
1118
C E D C B E
1 3 2 1 7 3
Cmaj9
1119
C E G D B E
1 3 5 2 7 3
Cmaj9
1120
E G C D B E
3 5 1 2 7 3
Cmaj9
1121
C E B D B E
1 3 7 2 7 3
Cmaj9
1122
C G D G B E
1 5 2 5 7 3
Cmaj9
1123
C G D E B E
1 5 2 3 7 3
Cmaj9
1124
E C D G B E
3 1 2 5 7 3
Cmaj9
1125
E C D G B E
3 1 2 5 7 3

TUNING: E A D G B E (Standard)

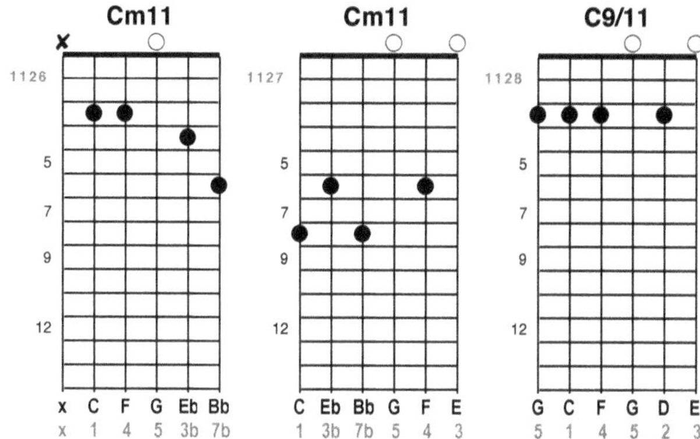
Cm11
1126
5
7
9
12
x C F G Eb Bb
x 1 4 5 3b 7b
Cm11
1127
5
7
9
12
C Eb Bb G F E
1 3b 7b 5 4 3
C9/11
1128
5
7
9
12
G C F G D E
5 1 4 5 2 3

TUNING: E A D G B E (Standard)

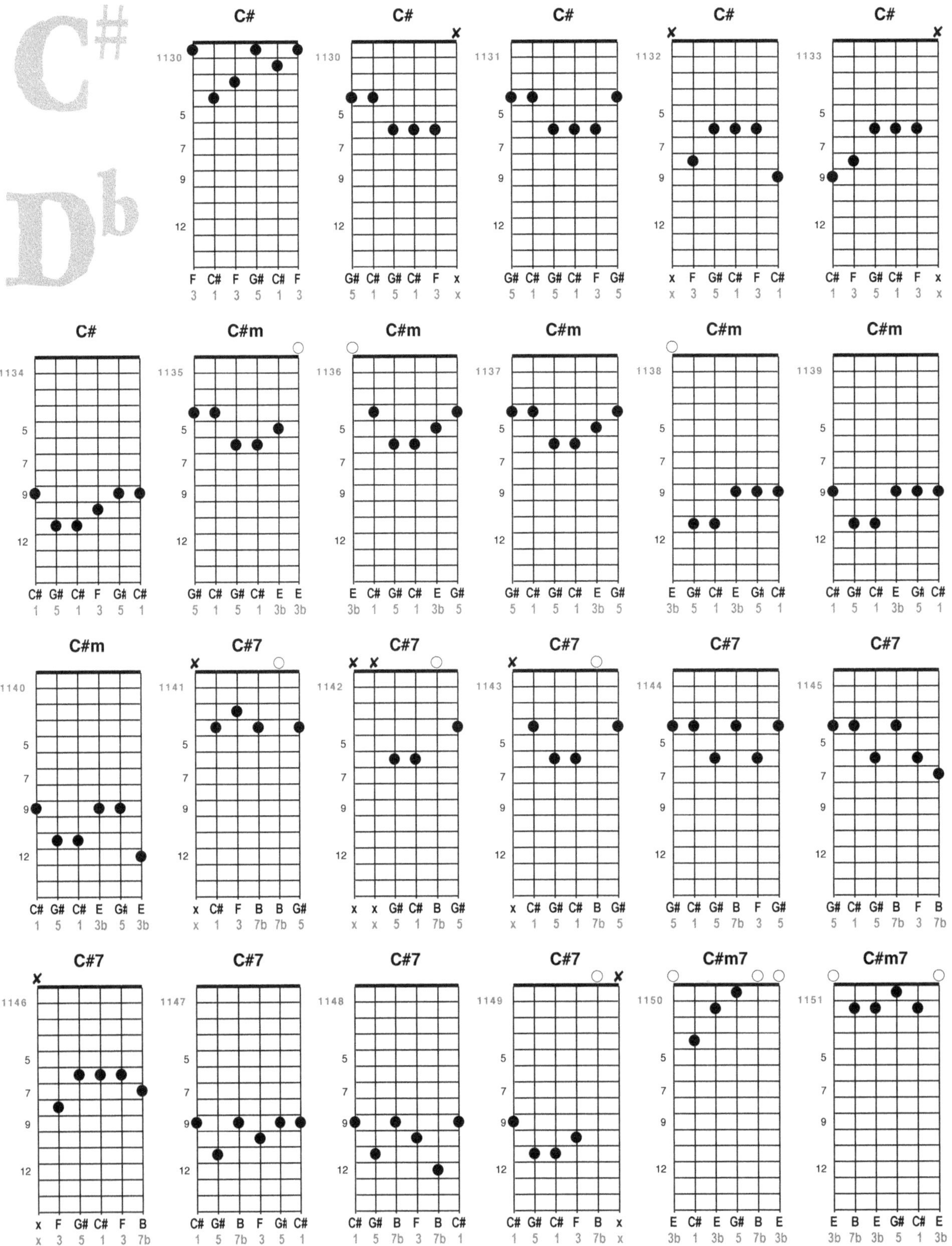
C#
D♭
C#
1130
5
7
9
12
F C# F G# C# F
3 1 3 5 1 3
C#
1130
G# C# G# C# F x
5 1 5 1 3 x
C#
1131
G# C# G# C# F G#
5 1 5 1 3 5
C#
1132
x F G# C# F C#
x 3 5 1 3 1
C#
1133
C# F G# C# F x
1 3 5 1 3 x
C#
1134
C# G# C# F G# C#
1 5 1 3 5 1
C#m
1135
G# C# G# C# E E
5 1 5 1 3b 3b
C#m
1136
E C# G# C# E G#
3b 1 5 1 3b 5
C#m
1137
G# C# G# C# E G#
5 1 5 1 3b 5
C#m
1138
E G# C# E G# C#
3b 5 1 3b 5 1
C#m
1139
C# G# C# E G# C#
1 5 1 3b 5 1
C#m
1140
C# G# C# E G# E
1 5 1 3b 5 3b
C#7
1141
x C# F B B G#
x 1 3 7b 7b 5
C#7
1142
x x G# C# B G#
x x 5 1 7b 5
C#7
1143
x C# G# C# B G#
x 1 5 1 7b 5
C#7
1144
G# C# G# B F G#
5 1 5 7b 3 5
C#7
1145
G# C# G# B F B
5 1 5 7b 3 7b
C#7
1146
x F G# C# F B
x 3 5 1 3 7b
C#7
1147
C# G# B F G# C#
1 5 7b 3 5 1
C#7
1148
C# G# B F B C#
1 5 7b 3 7b 1
C#7
1149
C# G# C# F B x
1 5 1 3 7b x
C#m7
1150
E C# E G# B E
3b 1 3b 5 7b 3b
C#m7
1151
E B E G# C# E
3b 7b 3b 5 1 3b

Troubadour Guitar Chords

TUNING: E A D G B E (Standard)

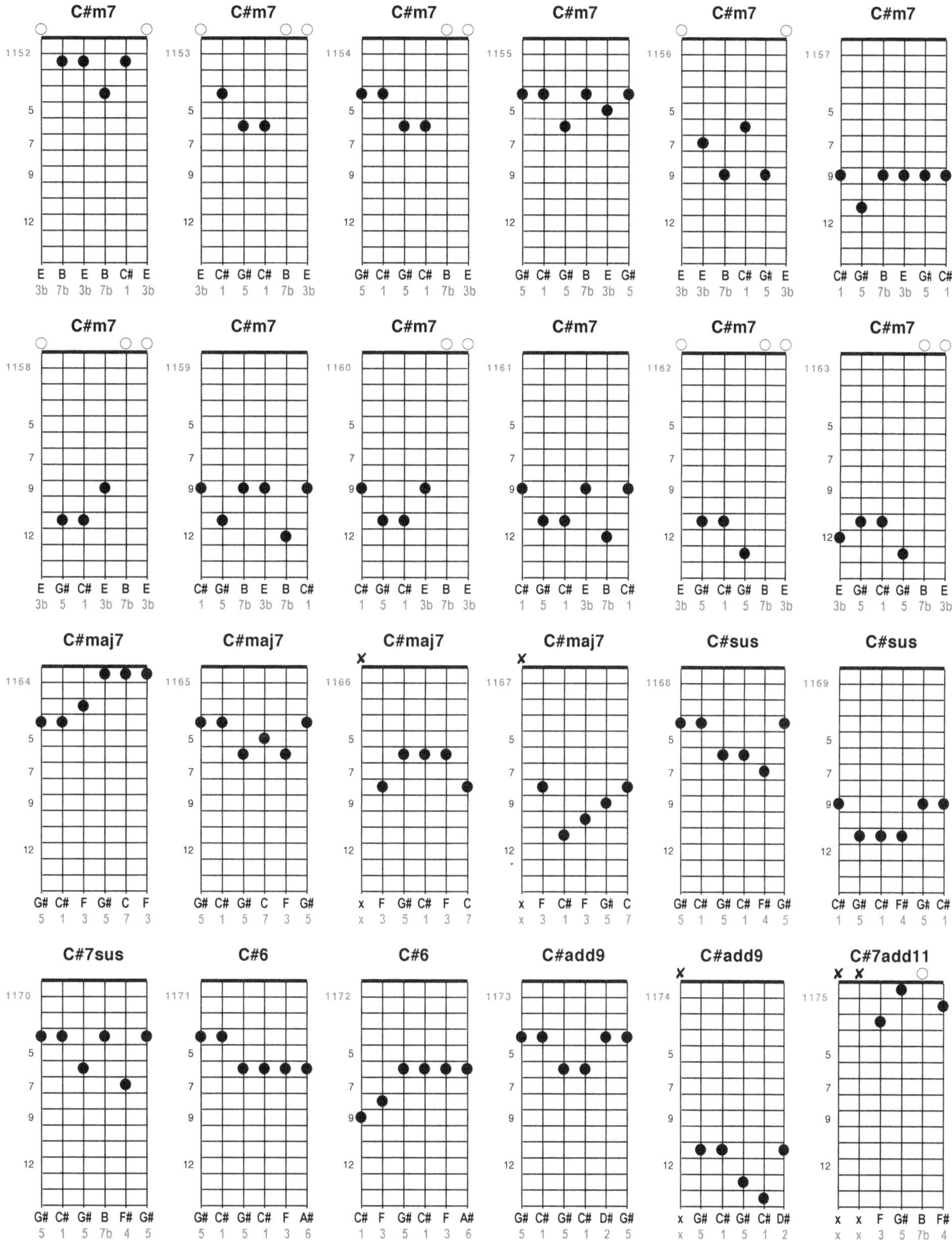

C#m7
1152
E B E B C# E
3b 7b 3b 7b 1 3b
C#m7
1153
E C# G# C# B E
3b 1 5 1 7b 3b
C#m7
1154
G# C# G# C# B E
5 1 5 1 7b 3b
C#m7
1155
G# C# G# B E G#
5 1 5 7b 3b 5
C#m7
1156
E E B C# G# E
3b 3b 7b 1 5 3b
C#m7
1157
C# G# B E G# C#
1 5 7b 3b 5 1
C#m7
1158
E G# C# E B E
3b 5 1 3b 7b 3b
C#m7
1159
C# G# B E B C#
1 5 7b 3b 7b 1
C#m7
1160
C# G# C# E B E
1 5 1 3b 7b 3b
C#m7
1161
C# G# C# E B C#
1 5 1 3b 7b 1
C#m7
1162
E G# C# G# B E
3b 5 1 5 7b 3b
C#m7
1163
E G# C# G# B E
3b 5 1 5 7b 3b
C#maj7
1164
G# C# F G# C F
5 1 3 5 7 3
C#maj7
1165
G# C# G# C F G#
5 1 5 7 3 5
C#maj7
1166
x F G# C# F C
x 3 5 1 3 7
C#maj7
1167
x F C# F G# C
x 3 1 3 5 7
C#sus
1168
G# C# G# C# F# G#
5 1 5 1 4 5
C#sus
1169
C# G# C# F# G# C#
1 5 1 4 5 1
C#7sus
1170
G# C# G# B F# G#
5 1 5 7b 4 5
C#6
1171
G# C# G# C# F A#
5 1 5 1 3 6
C#6
1172
C# F G# C# F A#
1 3 5 1 3 6
C#add9
1173
G# C# G# C# D# G#
5 1 5 1 2 5
C#add9
1174
x G# C# G# C# D#
x 5 1 5 1 2
C#7add11
1175
x x F G# B F#
x x 3 5 7b 4

TUNING: E A D G B E (Standard)

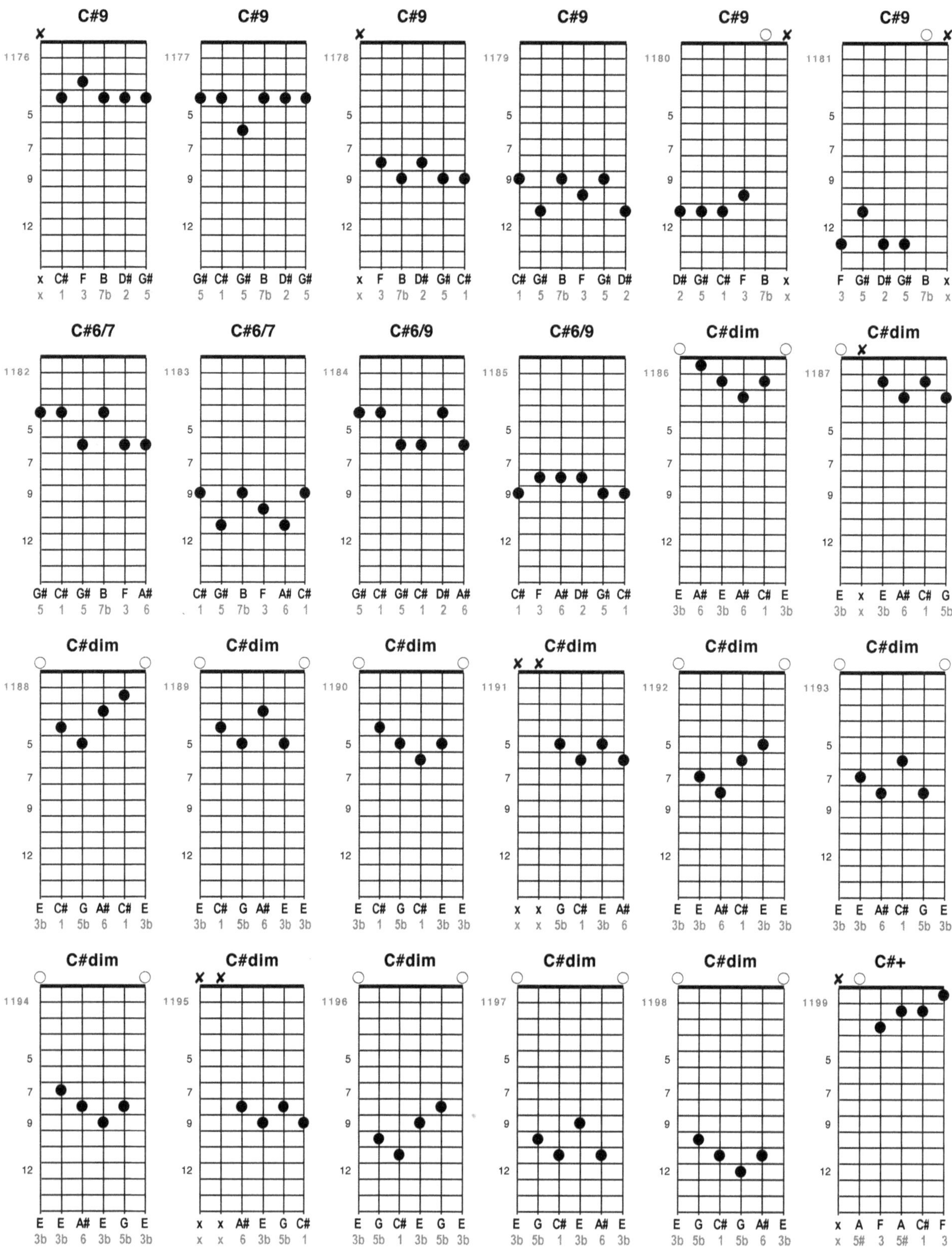
C#9
1176
x C# F B D# G#
x 1 3 7b 2 5
C#9
1177
G# C# G# B D# G#
5 1 5 7b 2 5
C#9
1178
x F B D# G# C#
x 3 7b 2 5 1
C#9
1179
C# G# B F G# D#
1 5 7b 3 5 2
C#9
1180
D# G# C# F B x
2 5 1 3 7b x
C#9
1181
F G# D# G# B x
3 5 2 5 7b x
C#6/7
1182
G# C# G# B F A#
5 1 5 7b 3 6
C#6/7
1183
C# G# B F A# C#
1 5 7b 3 6 1
C#6/9
1184
G# C# G# C# D# A#
5 1 5 1 2 6
C#6/9
1185
C# F A# D# G# C#
1 3 6 2 5 1
C#dim
1186
E A# E A# C# E
3b 6 3b 6 1 3b
C#dim
1187
E x E A# C# G
3b x 3b 6 1 5b
C#dim
1188
E C# G A# C# E
3b 1 5b 6 1 3b
C#dim
1189
E C# G A# E E
3b 1 5b 6 3b 3b
C#dim
1190
E C# G C# E E
3b 1 5b 1 3b 3b
C#dim
1191
x x G C# E A#
x x 5b 1 3b 6
C#dim
1192
E E A# C# E E
3b 3b 6 1 3b 3b
C#dim
1193
E E A# C# G E
3b 3b 6 1 5b 3b
C#dim
1194
E E A# E G E
3b 3b 6 3b 5b 3b
C#dim
1195
x x A# E G C#
x x 6 3b 5b 1
C#dim
1196
E G C# E G E
3b 5b 1 3b 5b 3b
C#dim
1197
E G C# E A# E
3b 5b 1 3b 6 3b
C#dim
1198
E G C# G A# E
3b 5b 1 5b 6 3b
C#+
1199
x A F A C# F
x 5# 3 5# 1 3

TUNING: E A D G B E (Standard)

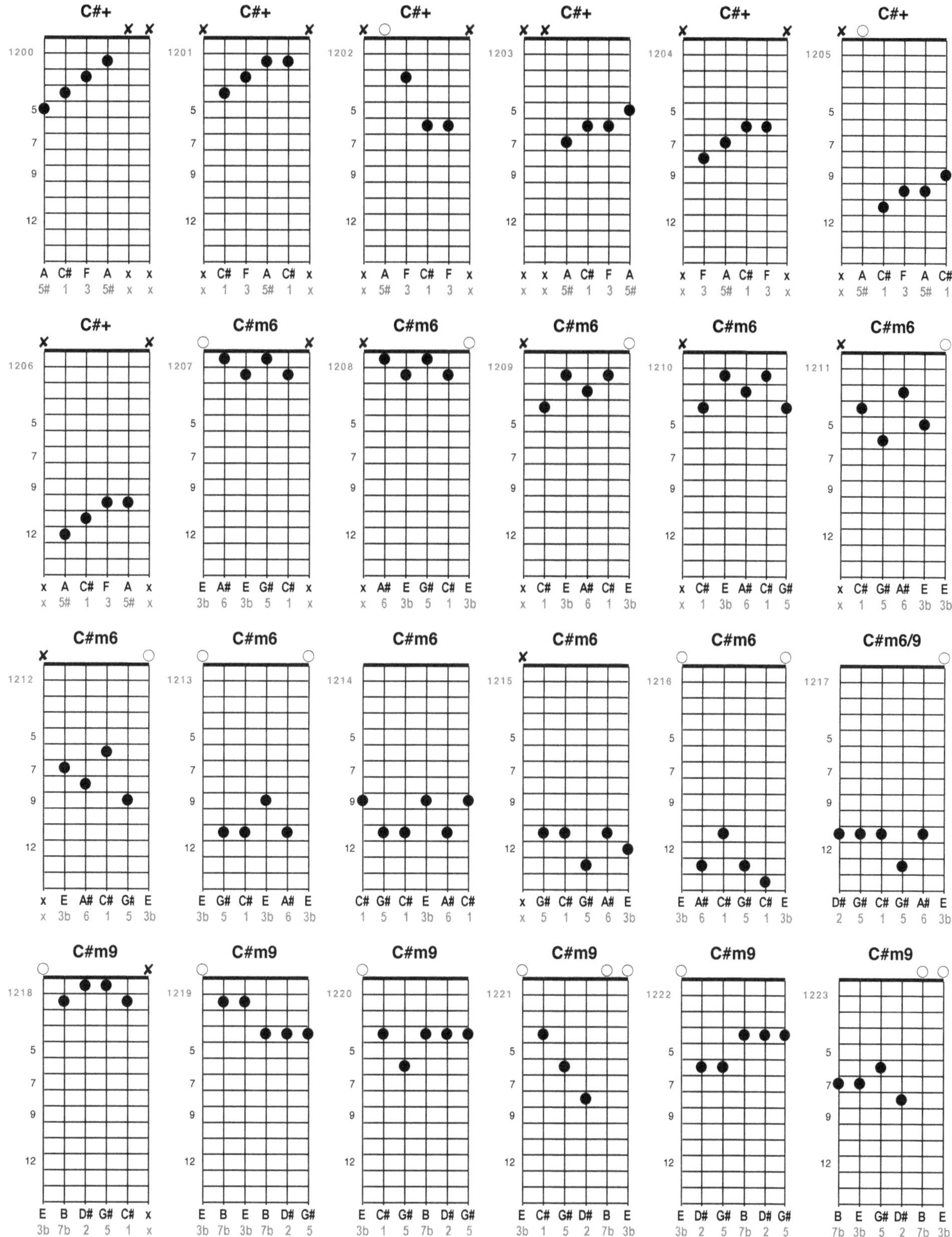
C#+
1200
A C# F A x x
5# 1 3 5# x x
C#+
1201
x C# F A C# x
x 1 3 5# 1 x
C#+
1202
x A F C# F x
x 5# 3 1 3 x
C#+
1203
x x A C# F A
x x 5# 1 3 5#
C#+
1204
x F A C# F x
x 3 5# 1 3 x
C#+
1205
x A C# F A C#
x 5# 1 3 5# 1
C#+
1206
x A C# F A x
x 5# 1 3 5# x
C#m6
1207
E A# E G# C# x
3b 6 3b 5 1 x
C#m6
1208
x A# E G# C# E
x 6 3b 5 1 3b
C#m6
1209
x C# E A# C# E
x 1 3b 6 1 3b
C#m6
1210
x C# E A# C# G#
x 1 3b 6 1 5
C#m6
1211
x C# G# A# E E
x 1 5 6 3b 3b
C#m6
1212
x E A# C# G# E
x 3b 6 1 5 3b
C#m6
1213
E G# C# E A# E
3b 5 1 3b 6 3b
C#m6
1214
C# G# C# E A# C#
1 5 1 3b 6 1
C#m6
1215
x G# C# G# A# E
x 5 1 5 6 3b
C#m6
1216
E A# C# G# C# E
3b 6 1 5 1 3b
C#m6/9
1217
D# G# C# G# A# E
2 5 1 5 6 3b
C#m9
1218
E B D# G# C# x
3b 7b 2 5 1 x
C#m9
1219
E B E B D# G#
3b 7b 3b 7b 2 5
C#m9
1220
E C# G# B D# G#
3b 1 5 7b 2 5
C#m9
1221
E C# G# D# B E
3b 1 5 2 7b 3b
C#m9
1222
E D# G# B D# G#
3b 2 5 7b 2 5
C#m9
1223
B E G# D# B E
7b 3b 5 2 7b 3b

TUNING: E A D G B E (Standard)

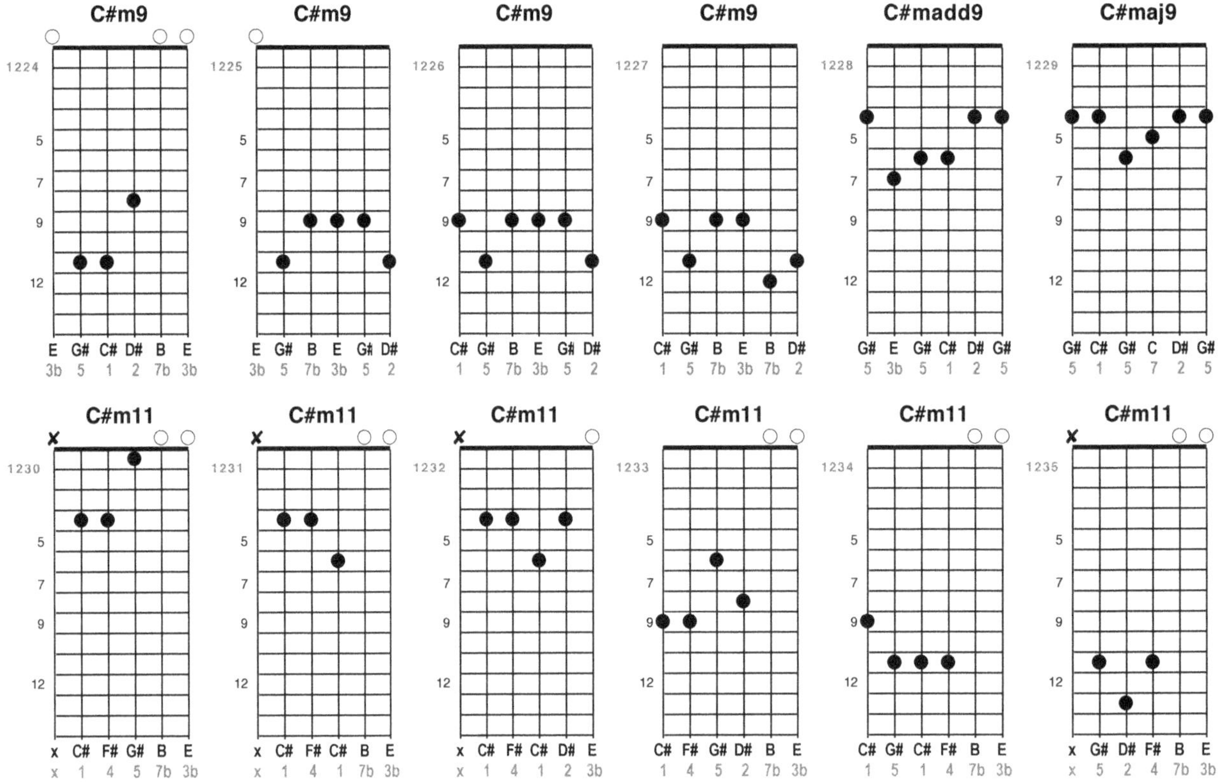
C#m9
1224
5 7 9 12
E G# C# D# B E
3b 5 1 2 7b 3b
C#m9
1225
5 7 9 12
E G# B E G# D#
3b 5 7b 3b 5 2
C#m9
1226
5 7 9 12
C# G# B E G# D#
1 5 7b 3b 5 2
C#m9
1227
5 7 9 12
C# G# B E B D#
1 5 7b 3b 7b 2
C#madd9
1228
5 7 9 12
G# E G# C# D# G#
5 3b 5 1 2 5
C#maj9
1229
5 7 9 12
G# C# G# C D# G#
5 1 5 7 2 5
C#m11
1230
5 7 9 12
x C# F# G# B E
x 1 4 5 7b 3b
C#m11
1231
5 7 9 12
x C# F# C# B E
x 1 4 1 7b 3b
C#m11
1232
5 7 9 12
x C# F# C# D# E
x 1 4 1 2 3b
C#m11
1233
5 7 9 12
C# F# G# D# B E
1 4 5 2 7b 3b
C#m11
1234
5 7 9 12
C# G# C# F# B E
1 5 1 4 7b 3b
C#m11
1235
5 7 9 12
x G# D# F# B E
x 5 2 4 7b 3b

Troubadour Guitar Chords

TUNING: E A D G B E (Standard)

D

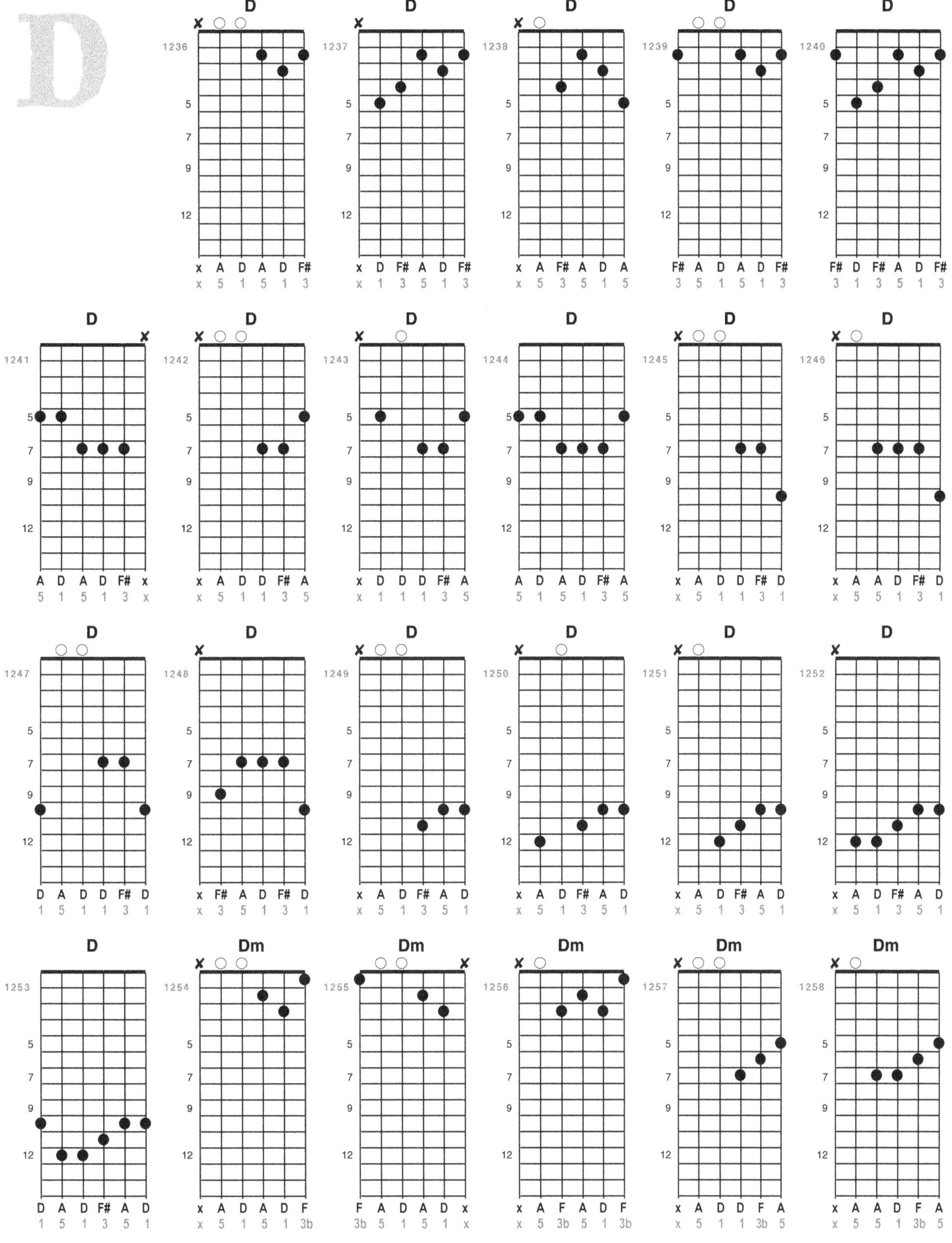

Troubadour Guitar Chords

TUNING: E A D G B E (Standard)

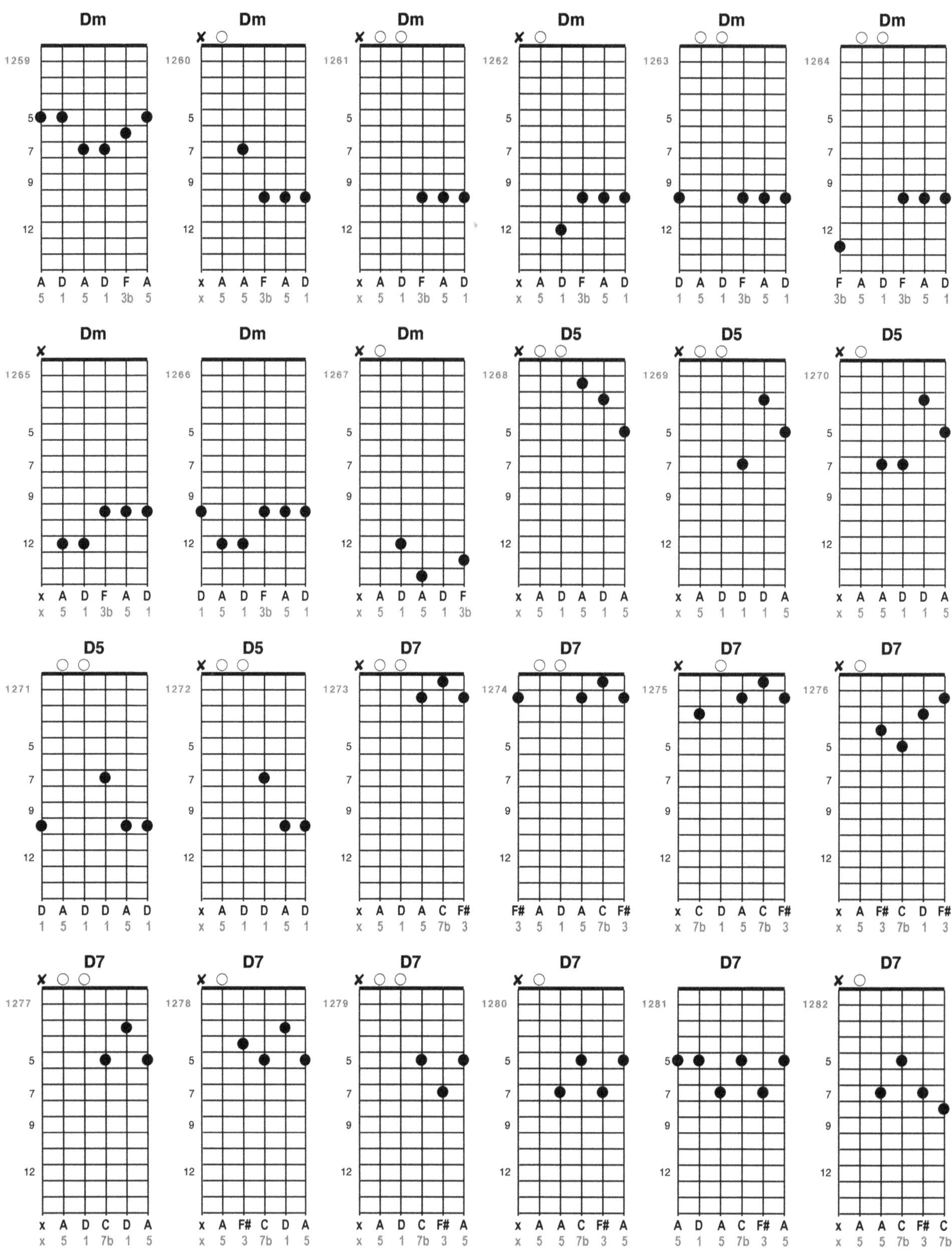

Dm 1259
A D A D F A
5 1 5 1 3b 5
Dm 1260
x A A F A D
x 5 5 3b 5 1
Dm 1261
x A D F A D
x 5 1 3b 5 1
Dm 1262
x A D F A D
x 5 1 3b 5 1
Dm 1263
D A D F A D
1 5 1 3b 5 1
Dm 1264
F A D F A D
3b 5 1 3b 5 1
Dm 1265
x A D F A D
x 5 1 3b 5 1
Dm 1266
D A D F A D
1 5 1 3b 5 1
Dm 1267
x A D A D F
x 5 1 5 1 3b
D5 1268
x A D A D A
x 5 1 5 1 5
D5 1269
x A D D D A
x 5 1 1 1 5
D5 1270
x A A D D A
x 5 5 1 1 5
D5 1271
D A D D A D
1 5 1 1 5 1
D5 1272
x A D D A D
x 5 1 1 5 1
D7 1273
x A D A C F#
x 5 1 5 7b 3
D7 1274
F# A D A C F#
3 5 1 5 7b 3
D7 1275
x C D A C F#
x 7b 1 5 7b 3
D7 1276
x A F# C D F#
x 5 3 7b 1 3
D7 1277
x A D C D A
x 5 1 7b 1 5
D7 1278
x A F# C D A
x 5 3 7b 1 5
D7 1279
x A D C F# A
x 5 1 7b 3 5
D7 1280
x A A C F# A
x 5 5 7b 3 5
D7 1281
A D A C F# A
5 1 5 7b 3 5
D7 1282
x A A C F# C
x 5 5 7b 3 7b

Troubadour Guitar Chords

TUNING: E A D G B E (Standard)

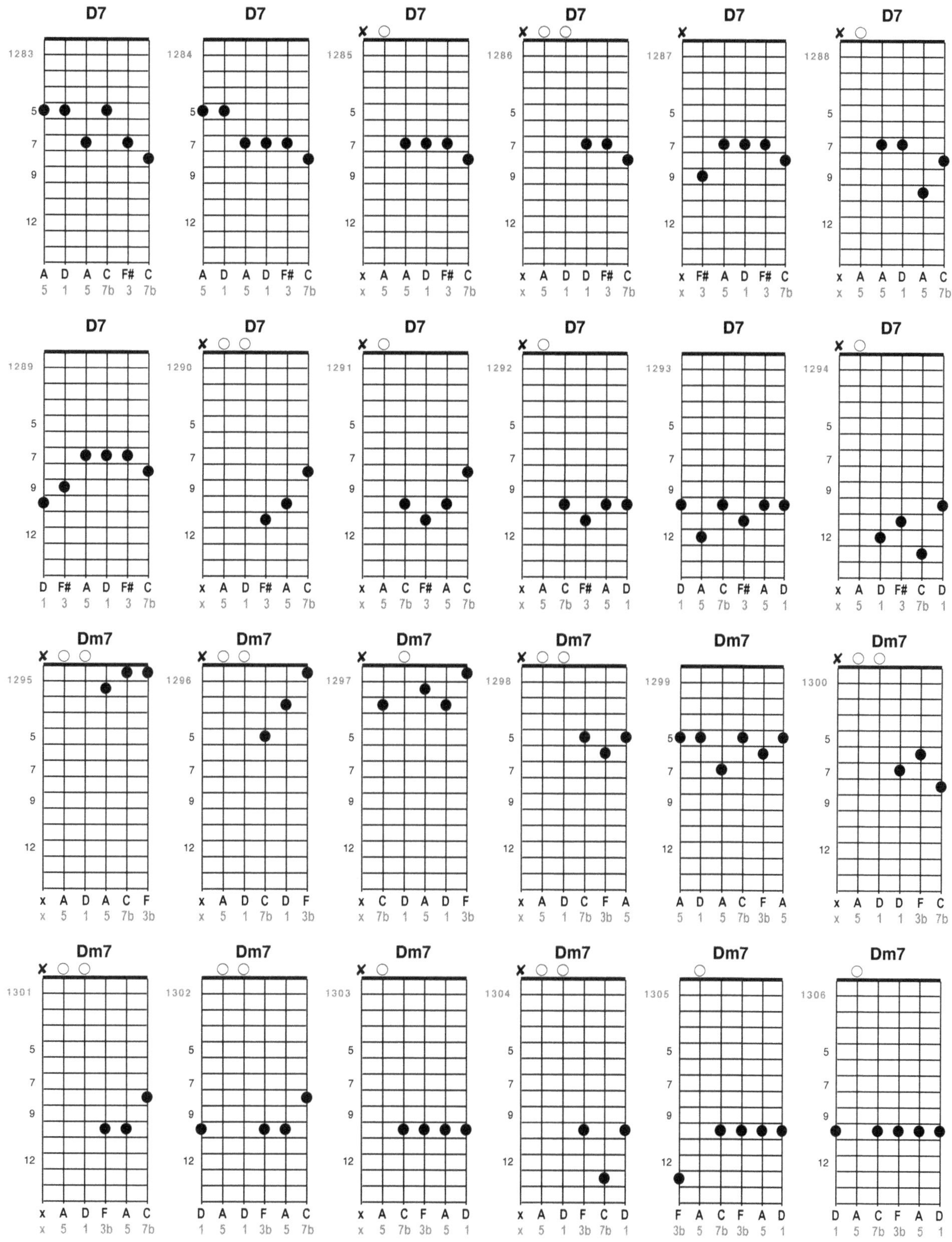

D7
1283
A D A C F# C
5 1 5 7b 3 7b
D7
1284
A D A D F# C
5 1 5 1 3 7b
D7
1285
x A A D F# C
x 5 5 1 3 7b
D7
1286
x A D D F# C
x 5 1 1 3 7b
D7
1287
x F# A D F# C
x 3 5 1 3 7b
D7
1288
x A A D A C
x 5 5 1 5 7b
D7
1289
D F# A D F# C
1 3 5 1 3 7b
D7
1290
x A D F# A C
x 5 1 3 5 7b
D7
1291
x A C F# A C
x 5 7b 3 5 7b
D7
1292
x A C F# A D
x 5 7b 3 5 1
D7
1293
D A C F# A D
1 5 7b 3 5 1
D7
1294
x A D F# C D
x 5 1 3 7b 1
Dm7
1295
x A D A C F
x 5 1 5 7b 3b
Dm7
1296
x A D C D F
x 5 1 7b 1 3b
Dm7
1297
x C D A D F
x 7b 1 5 1 3b
Dm7
1298
x A D C F A
x 5 1 7b 3b 5
Dm7
1299
A D A C F A
5 1 5 7b 3b 5
Dm7
1300
x A D D F C
x 5 1 1 3b 7b
Dm7
1301
x A D F A C
x 5 1 3b 5 7b
Dm7
1302
D A D F A C
1 5 1 3b 5 7b
Dm7
1303
x A C F A D
x 5 7b 3b 5 1
Dm7
1304
x A D F C D
x 5 1 3b 7b 1
Dm7
1305
F A C F A D
3b 5 7b 3b 5 1
Dm7
1306
D A C F A D
1 5 7b 3b 5 1

TUNING: E A D G B E (Standard)

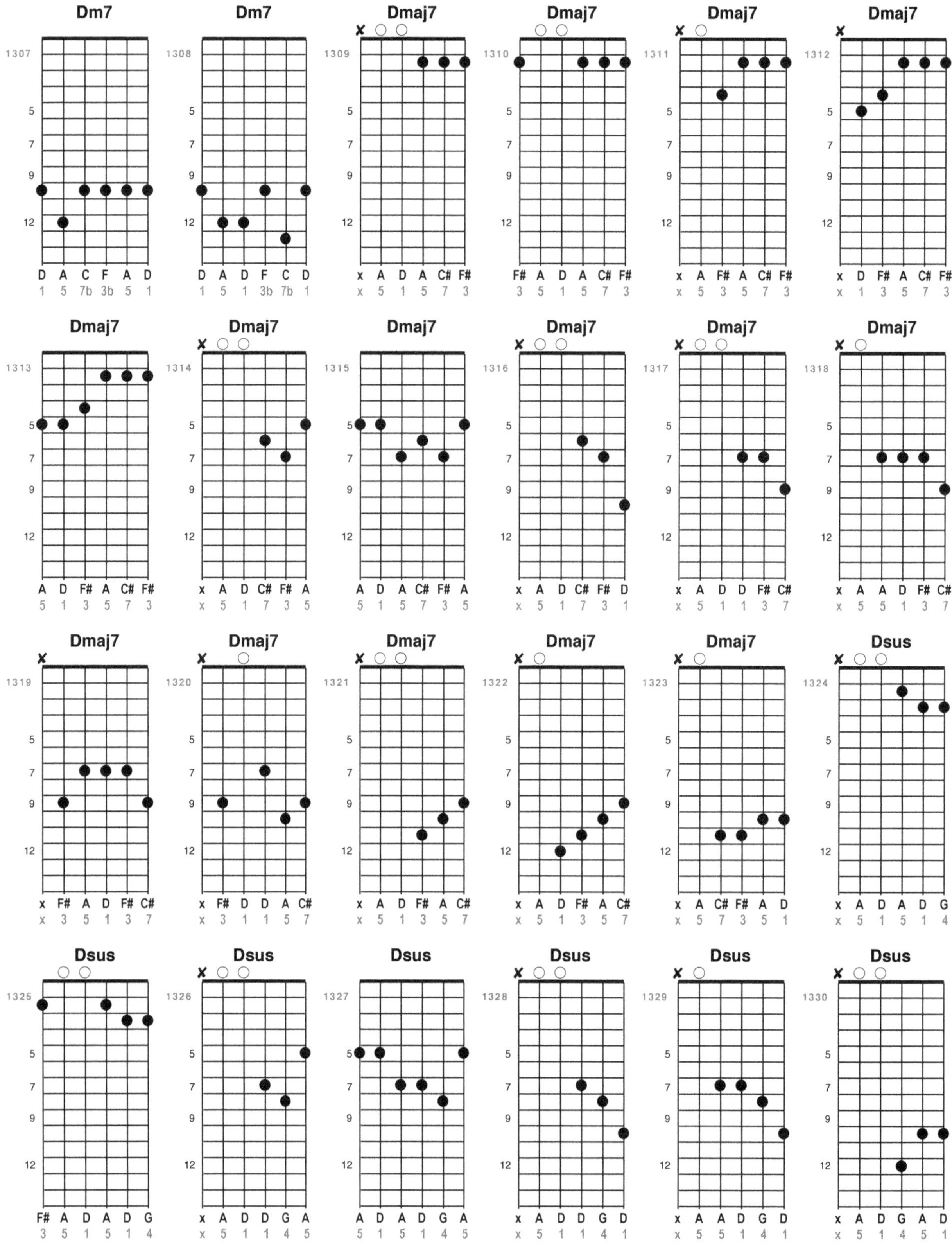
Dm7
1307
D A C F A D
1 5 7b 3b 5 1
Dm7
1308
D A D F C D
1 5 1 3b 7b 1
Dmaj7
1309
x A D A C# F#
x 5 1 5 7 3
Dmaj7
1310
F# A D A C# F#
3 5 1 5 7 3
Dmaj7
1311
x A F# A C# F#
x 5 3 5 7 3
Dmaj7
1312
x D F# A C# F#
x 1 3 5 7 3
Dmaj7
1313
A D F# A C# F#
5 1 3 5 7 3
Dmaj7
1314
x A D C# F# A
x 5 1 7 3 5
Dmaj7
1315
A D A C# F# A
5 1 5 7 3 5
Dmaj7
1316
x A D C# F# D
x 5 1 7 3 1
Dmaj7
1317
x A D D F# C#
x 5 1 1 3 7
Dmaj7
1318
x A A D F# C#
x 5 5 1 3 7
Dmaj7
1319
x F# A D F# C#
x 3 5 1 3 7
Dmaj7
1320
x F# D D A C#
x 3 1 1 5 7
Dmaj7
1321
x A D F# A C#
x 5 1 3 5 7
Dmaj7
1322
x A D F# A C#
x 5 1 3 5 7
Dmaj7
1323
x A C# F# A D
x 5 7 3 5 1
Dsus
1324
x A D A D G
x 5 1 5 1 4
Dsus
1325
F# A D A D G
3 5 1 5 1 4
Dsus
1326
x A D D G A
x 5 1 1 4 5
Dsus
1327
A D A D G A
5 1 5 1 4 5
Dsus
1328
x A D D G D
x 5 1 1 4 1
Dsus
1329
x A A D G D
x 5 5 1 4 1
Dsus
1330
x A D G A D
x 5 1 4 5 1

TUNING: E A D G B E (Standard)

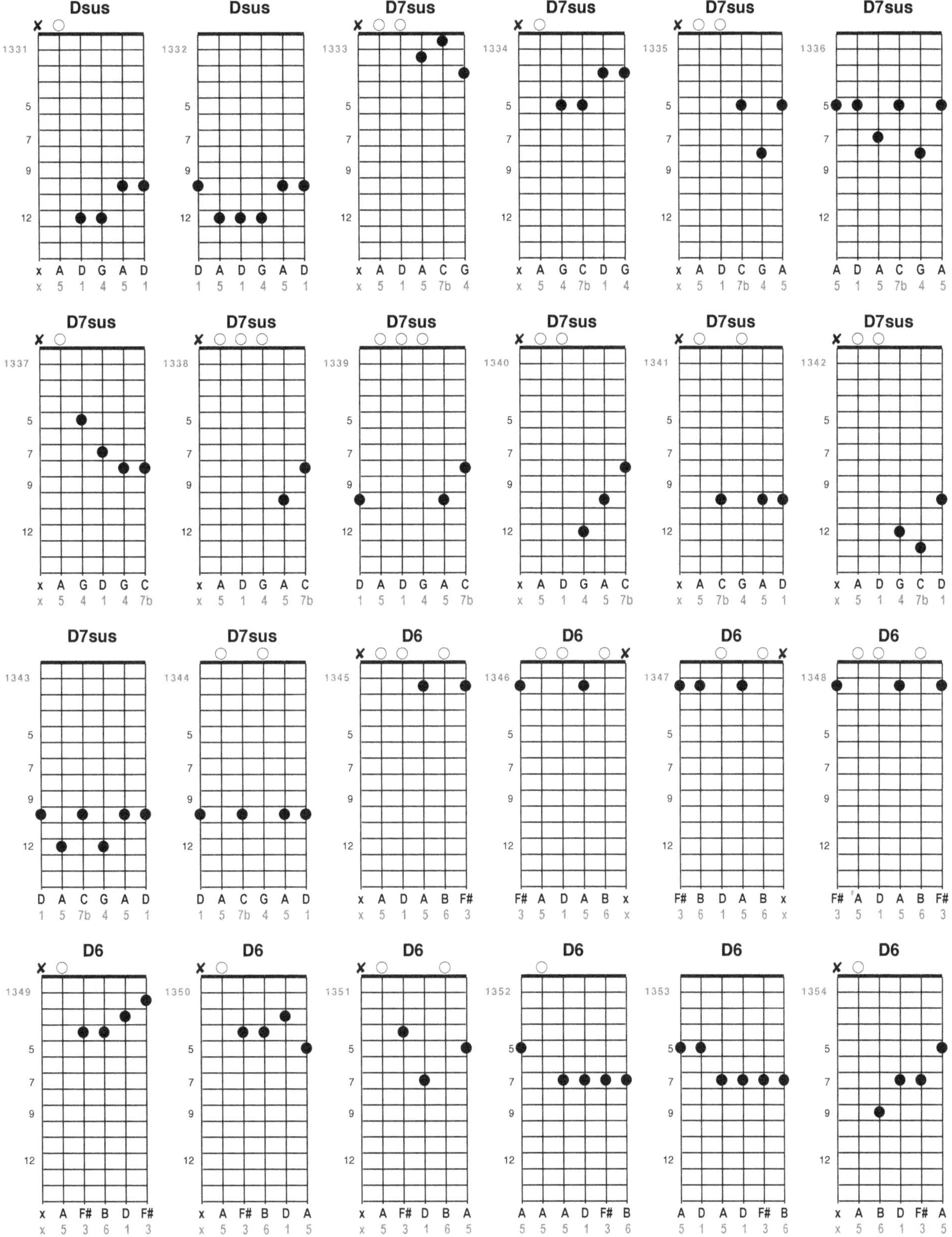
Dsus
1331
x A D G A D
x 5 1 4 5 1
Dsus
1332
D A D G A D
1 5 1 4 5 1
D7sus
1333
x A D A C G
x 5 1 5 7b 4
D7sus
1334
x A G C D G
x 5 4 7b 1 4
D7sus
1335
x A D C G A
x 5 1 7b 4 5
D7sus
1336
A D A C G A
5 1 5 7b 4 5
D7sus
1337
x A G D G C
x 5 4 1 4 7b
D7sus
1338
x A D G A C
x 5 1 4 5 7b
D7sus
1339
D A D G A C
1 5 1 4 5 7b
D7sus
1340
x A D G A C
x 5 1 4 5 7b
D7sus
1341
x A C G A D
x 5 7b 4 5 1
D7sus
1342
x A D G C D
x 5 1 4 7b 1
D7sus
1343
D A C G A D
1 5 7b 4 5 1
D7sus
1344
D A C G A D
1 5 7b 4 5 1
D6
1345
x A D A B F#
x 5 1 5 6 3
D6
1346
F# A D A B x
3 5 1 5 6 x
D6
1347
F# B D A B x
3 6 1 5 6 x
D6
1348
F# A D A B F#
3 5 1 5 6 3
D6
1349
x A F# B D F#
x 5 3 6 1 3
D6
1350
x A F# B D A
x 5 3 6 1 5
D6
1351
x A F# D B A
x 5 3 1 6 5
D6
1352
A A A D F# B
5 5 5 1 3 6
D6
1353
A D A D F# B
5 1 5 1 3 6
D6
1354
x A B D F# A
x 5 6 1 3 5

TUNING: E A D G B E (Standard)

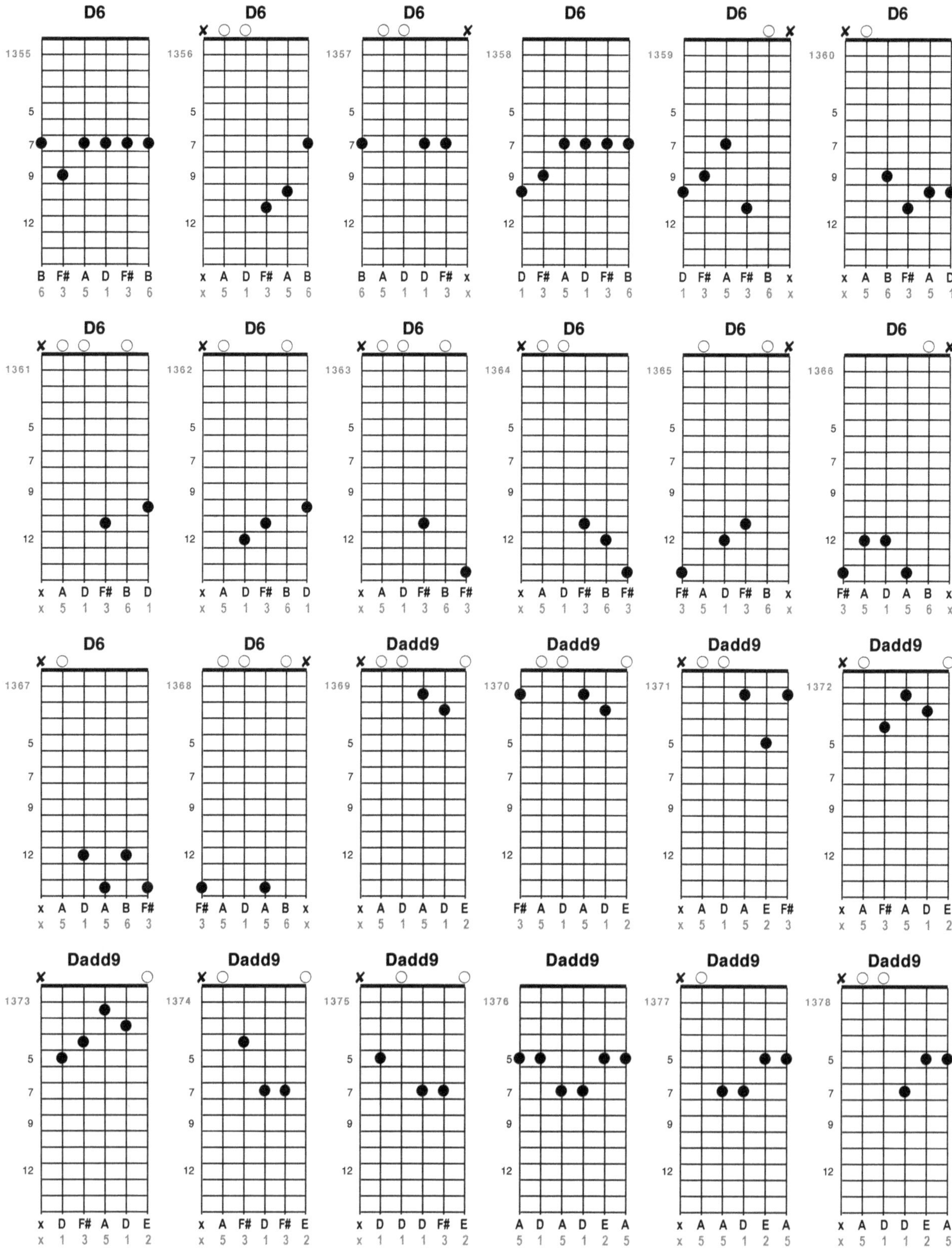
D6
1355
B F# A D F# B
6 3 5 1 3 6
D6
1356
x A D F# A B
x 5 1 3 5 6
D6
1357
B A D D F# x
6 5 1 1 3 x
D6
1358
D F# A D F# B
1 3 5 1 3 6
D6
1359
D F# A F# B x
1 3 5 3 6 x
D6
1360
x A B F# A D
x 5 6 3 5 1
D6
1361
x A D F# B D
x 5 1 3 6 1
D6
1362
x A D F# B D
x 5 1 3 6 1
D6
1363
x A D F# B F#
x 5 1 3 6 3
D6
1364
x A D F# B F#
x 5 1 3 6 3
D6
1365
F# A D F# B x
3 5 1 3 6 x
D6
1366
F# A D A B x
3 5 1 5 6 x
D6
1367
x A D A B F#
x 5 1 5 6 3
D6
1368
F# A D A B x
3 5 1 5 6 x
Dadd9
1369
x A D A D E
x 5 1 5 1 2
Dadd9
1370
F# A D A D E
3 5 1 5 1 2
Dadd9
1371
x A D A E F#
x 5 1 5 2 3
Dadd9
1372
x A F# A D E
x 5 3 5 1 2
Dadd9
1373
x D F# A D E
x 1 3 5 1 2
Dadd9
1374
x A F# D F# E
x 5 3 1 3 2
Dadd9
1375
x D D D F# E
x 1 1 1 3 2
Dadd9
1376
A D A D E A
5 1 5 1 2 5
Dadd9
1377
x A A D E A
x 5 5 1 2 5
Dadd9
1378
x A D D E A
x 5 1 1 2 5

TUNING: E A D G B E (Standard)

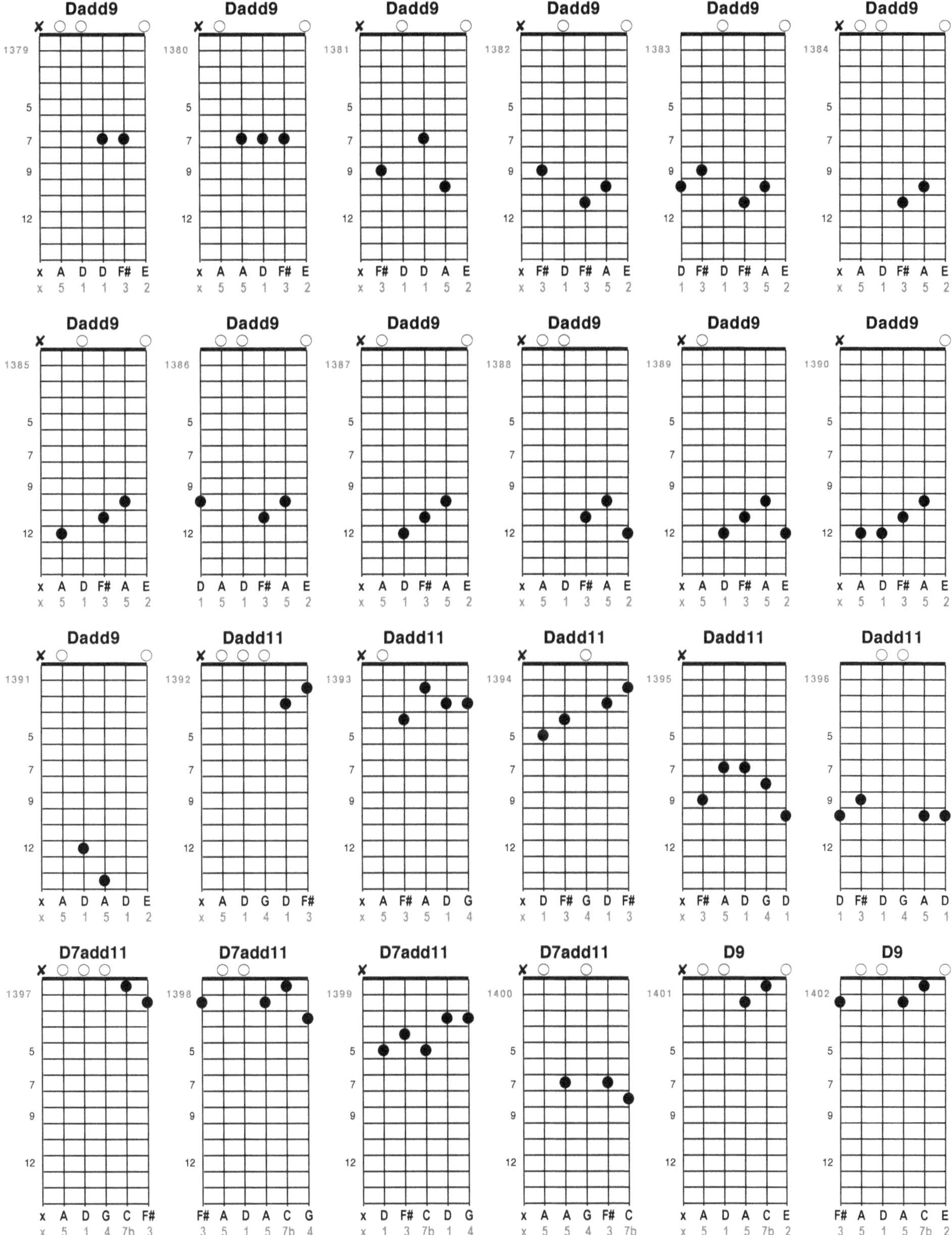

Dadd9	Dadd9	Dadd9	Dadd9	Dadd9	Dadd9
1379	1380	1381	1382	1383	1384
x A D D F# E	x A A D F# E	x F# D D A E	x F# D F# A E	D F# D F# A E	x A D F# A E
x 5 1 1 3 2	x 5 5 1 3 2	x 3 1 1 5 2	x 3 1 3 5 2	1 3 1 3 5 2	x 5 1 3 5 2

Dadd9	Dadd9	Dadd9	Dadd9	Dadd9	Dadd9
1385	1386	1387	1388	1389	1390
x A D F# A E	D A D F# A E	x A D F# A E	x A D F# A E	x A D F# A E	x A D F# A E
x 5 1 3 5 2	1 5 1 3 5 2	x 5 1 3 5 2	x 5 1 3 5 2	x 5 1 3 5 2	x 5 1 3 5 2

Dadd9	Dadd11	Dadd11	Dadd11	Dadd11	Dadd11
1391	1392	1393	1394	1395	1396
x A D A D E	x A D G D F#	x A F# A D G	x D F# G D F#	x F# A D G D	D F# D G A D
x 5 1 5 1 2	x 5 1 4 1 3	x 5 3 5 1 4	x 1 3 4 1 3	x 3 5 1 4 1	1 3 1 4 5 1

D7add11	D7add11	D7add11	D7add11	D9	D9
1397	1398	1399	1400	1401	1402
x A D G C F#	F# A D A C G	x D F# C D G	x A A G F# C	x A D A C E	F# A D A C E
x 5 1 4 7b 3	3 5 1 5 7b 4	x 1 3 7b 1 4	x 5 5 4 3 7b	x 5 1 5 7b 2	3 5 1 5 7b 2

61

Troubadour Guitar Chords

TUNING: E A D G B E (Standard)

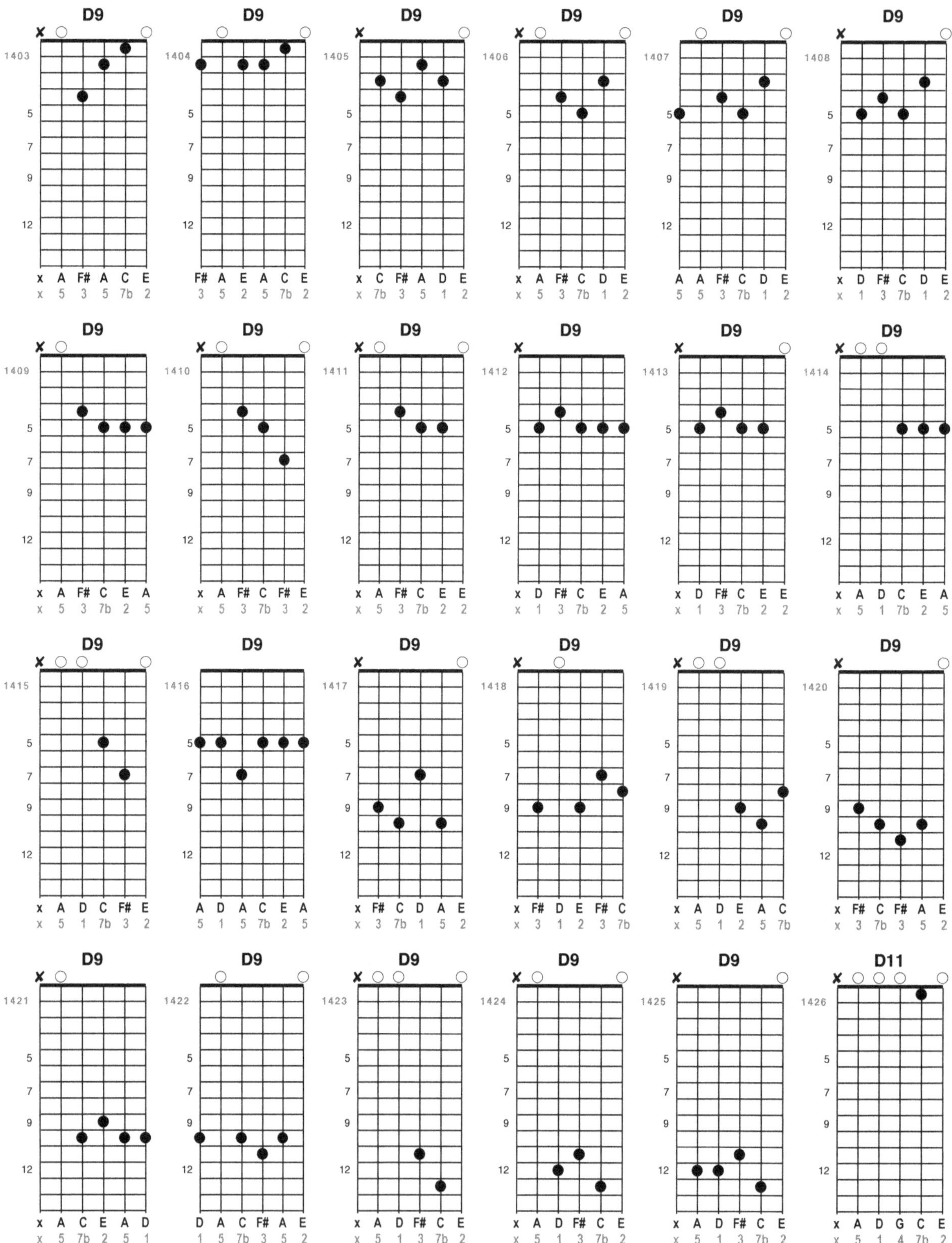
D9
1403
5 7 9 12
x A F# A C E
x 5 3 5 7b 2
D9
1404
5 7 9 12
F# A E A C E
3 5 2 5 7b 2
D9
1405
5 7 9 12
x C F# A D E
x 7b 3 5 1 2
D9
1406
5 7 9 12
x A F# C D E
x 5 3 7b 1 2
D9
1407
5 7 9 12
A A F# C D E
5 5 3 7b 1 2
D9
1408
5 7 9 12
x D F# C D E
x 1 3 7b 1 2
D9
1409
5 7 9 12
x A F# C E A
x 5 3 7b 2 5
D9
1410
5 7 9 12
x A F# C F# E
x 5 3 7b 3 2
D9
1411
5 7 9 12
x A F# C E E
x 5 3 7b 2 2
D9
1412
5 7 9 12
x D F# C E A
x 1 3 7b 2 5
D9
1413
5 7 9 12
x D F# C E E
x 1 3 7b 2 2
D9
1414
5 7 9 12
x A D C E A
x 5 1 7b 2 5
D9
1415
5 7 9 12
x A D C F# E
x 5 1 7b 3 2
D9
1416
5 7 9 12
A D A C E A
5 1 5 7b 2 5
D9
1417
5 7 9 12
x F# C D A E
x 3 7b 1 5 2
D9
1418
5 7 9 12
x F# D E F# C
x 3 1 2 3 7b
D9
1419
5 7 9 12
x A D E A C
x 5 1 2 5 7b
D9
1420
5 7 9 12
x F# C F# A E
x 3 7b 3 5 2
D9
1421
5 7 9 12
x A C E A D
x 5 7b 2 5 1
D9
1422
5 7 9 12
D A C F# A E
1 5 7b 3 5 2
D9
1423
5 7 9 12
x A D F# C E
x 5 1 3 7b 2
D9
1424
5 7 9 12
x A D F# C E
x 5 1 3 7b 2
D9
1425
5 7 9 12
x A D F# C E
x 5 1 3 7b 2
D11
1426
5 7 9 12
x A D G C E
x 5 1 4 7b 2

Troubadour Guitar Chords

TUNING: E A D G B E (Standard)

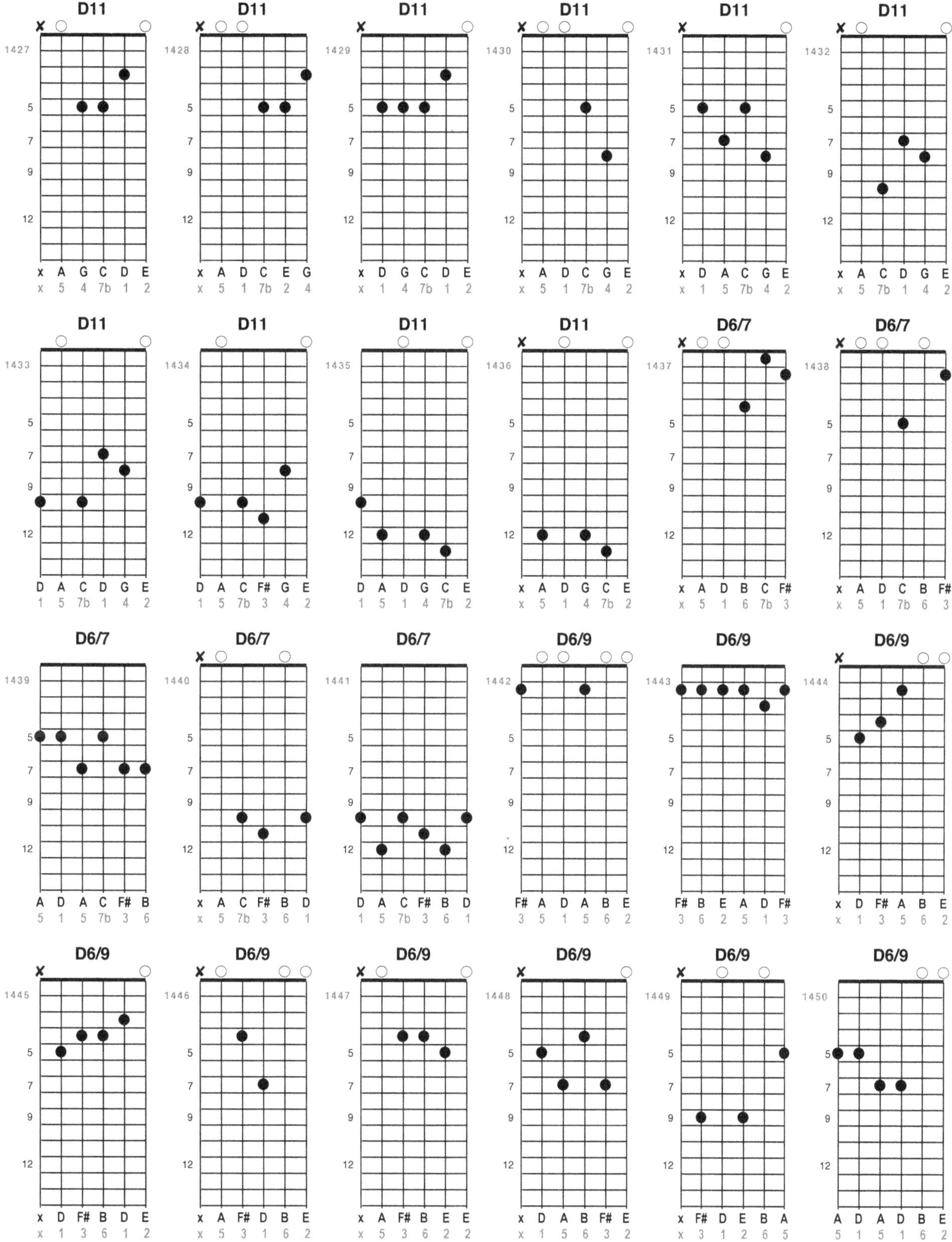

D11
1427
x A G C D E
x 5 4 7b 1 2
D11
1428
x A D C E G
x 5 1 7b 2 4
D11
1429
x D G C D E
x 1 4 7b 1 2
D11
1430
x A D C G E
x 5 1 7b 4 2
D11
1431
x D A C G E
x 1 5 7b 4 2
D11
1432
x A C D G E
x 5 7b 1 4 2
D11
1433
D A C D G E
1 5 7b 1 4 2
D11
1434
D A C F# G E
1 5 7b 3 4 2
D11
1435
D A D G C E
1 5 1 4 7b 2
D11
1436
x A D G C E
x 5 1 4 7b 2
D6/7
1437
x A D B C F#
x 5 1 6 7b 3
D6/7
1438
x A D C B F#
x 5 1 7b 6 3
D6/7
1439
A D A C F# B
5 1 5 7b 3 6
D6/7
1440
x A C F# B D
x 5 7b 3 6 1
D6/7
1441
D A C F# B D
1 5 7b 3 6 1
D6/9
1442
F# A D A B E
3 5 1 5 6 2
D6/9
1443
F# B E A D F#
3 6 2 5 1 3
D6/9
1444
x D F# A B E
x 1 3 5 6 2
D6/9
1445
x D F# B D E
x 1 3 6 1 2
D6/9
1446
x A F# D B E
x 5 3 1 6 2
D6/9
1447
x A F# B E E
x 5 3 6 2 2
D6/9
1448
x D A B F# E
x 1 5 6 3 2
D6/9
1449
x F# D E B A
x 3 1 2 6 5
D6/9
1450
A D A D B E
5 1 5 1 6 2

TUNING: E A D G B E (Standard)

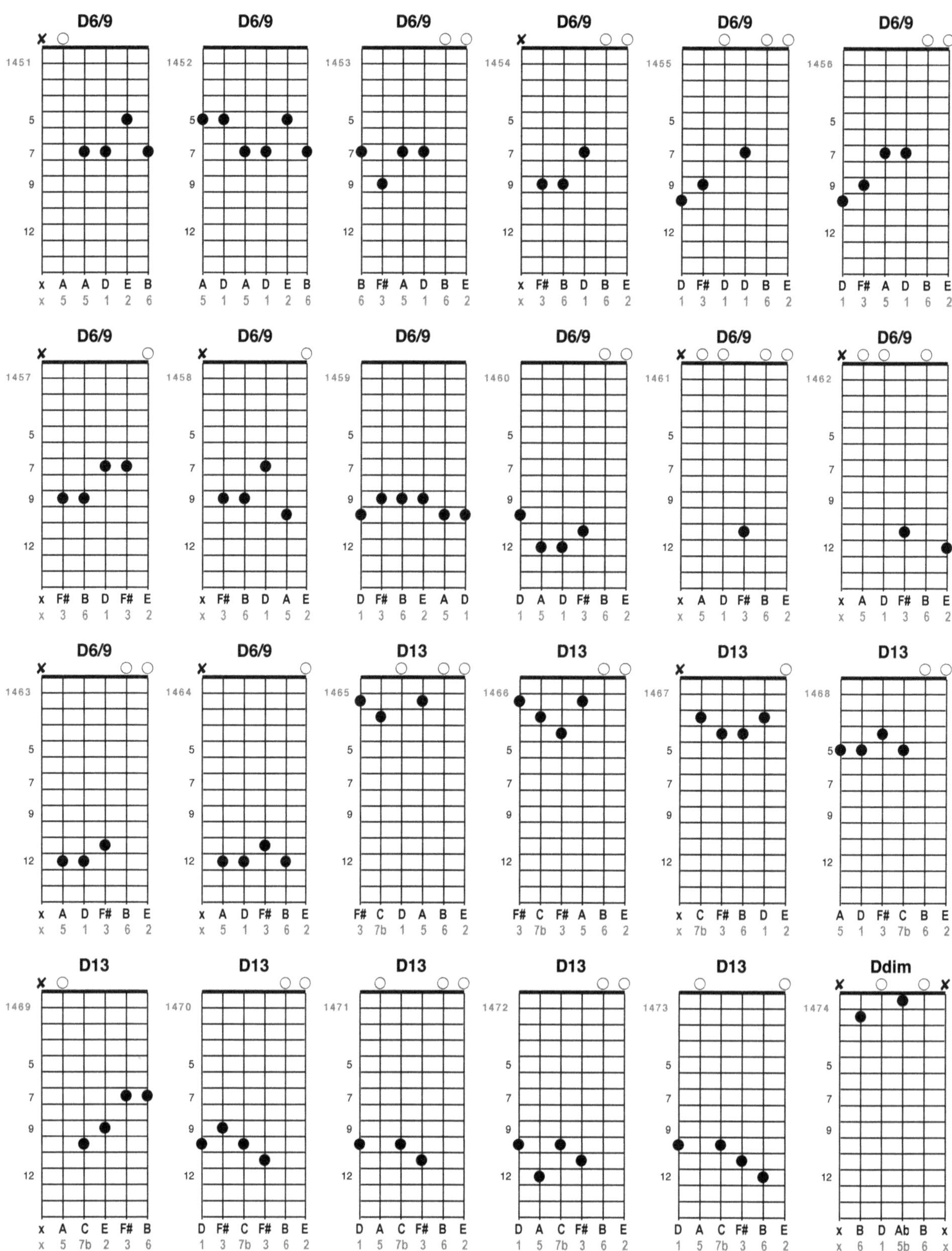
1451 D6/9
x A A D E B
x 5 5 1 2 6
1452 D6/9
A D A D E B
5 1 5 1 2 6
1453 D6/9
B F# A D B E
6 3 5 1 6 2
1454 D6/9
x F# B D B E
x 3 6 1 6 2
1455 D6/9
D F# D D B E
1 3 1 1 6 2
1456 D6/9
D F# A D B E
1 3 5 1 6 2
1457 D6/9
x F# B D F# E
x 3 6 1 3 2
1458 D6/9
x F# B D A E
x 3 6 1 5 2
1459 D6/9
D F# B E A D
1 3 6 2 5 1
1460 D6/9
D A D F# B E
1 5 1 3 6 2
1461 D6/9
x A D F# B E
x 5 1 3 6 2
1462 D6/9
x A D F# B E
x 5 1 3 6 2
1463 D6/9
x A D F# B E
x 5 1 3 6 2
1464 D6/9
x A D F# B E
x 5 1 3 6 2
1465 D13
F# C D A B E
3 7b 1 5 6 2
1466 D13
F# C F# A B E
3 7b 3 5 6 2
1467 D13
x C F# B D E
x 7b 3 6 1 2
1468 D13
A D F# C B E
5 1 3 7b 6 2
1469 D13
x A C E F# B
x 5 7b 2 3 6
1470 D13
D F# C F# B E
1 3 7b 3 6 2
1471 D13
D A C F# B E
1 5 7b 3 6 2
1472 D13
D A C F# B E
1 5 7b 3 6 2
1473 D13
D A C F# B E
1 5 7b 3 6 2
1474 Ddim
x B D Ab B x
x 6 1 5b 6 x

TUNING: E A D G B E (Standard)

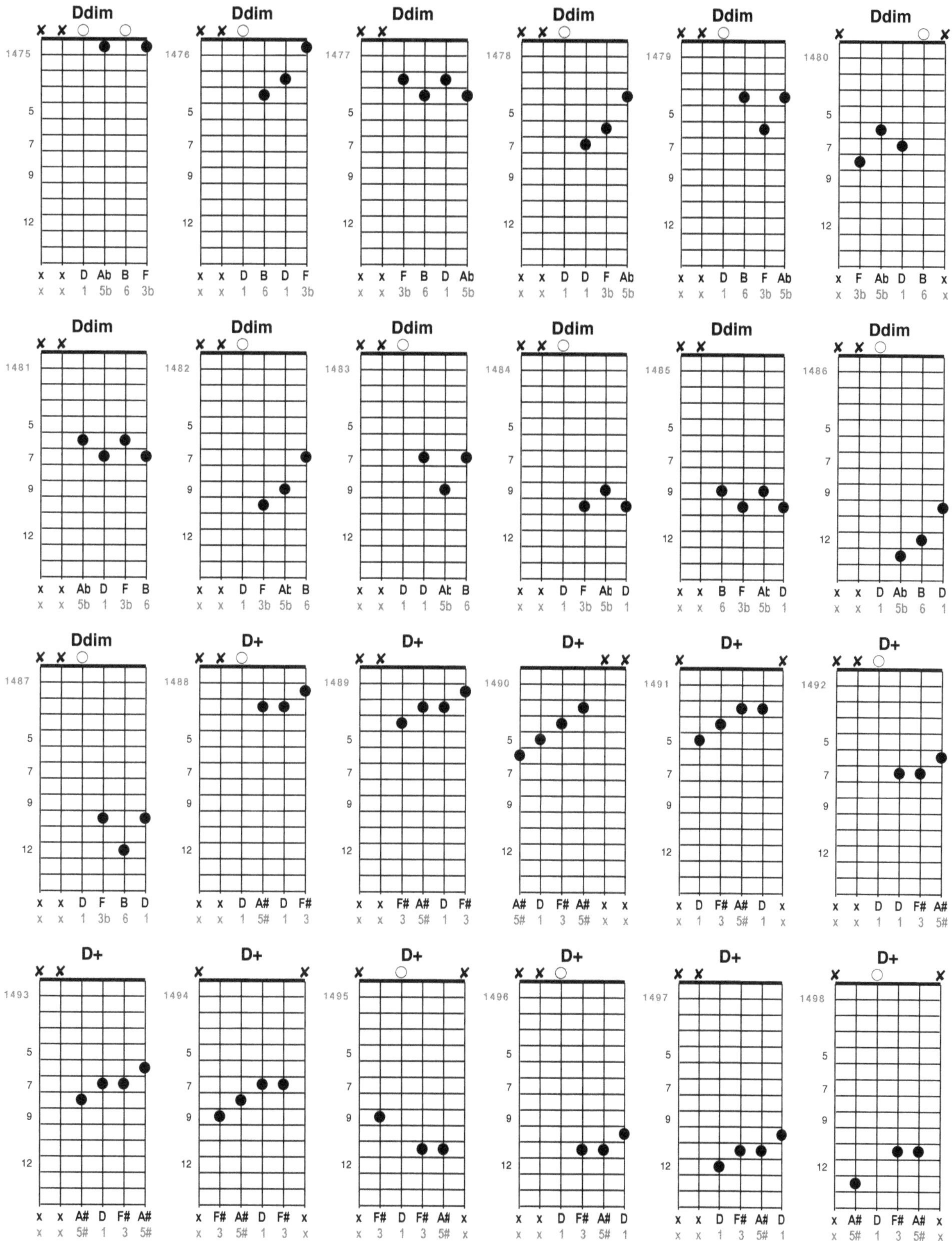
Ddim
1475
x x D Ab B F
x x 1 5b 6 3b
Ddim
1476
x x D B D F
x x 1 6 1 3b
Ddim
1477
x x F B D Ab
x x 3b 6 1 5b
Ddim
1478
x x D D F Ab
x x 1 1 3b 5b
Ddim
1479
x x D B F Ab
x x 1 6 3b 5b
Ddim
1480
x F Ab D B x
x 3b 5b 1 6 x
Ddim
1481
x x Ab D F B
x x 5b 1 3b 6
Ddim
1482
x x D F Ab B
x x 1 3b 5b 6
Ddim
1483
x x D D Ab B
x x 1 1 5b 6
Ddim
1484
x x D F Ab D
x x 1 3b 5b 1
Ddim
1485
x x B F Ab D
x x 6 3b 5b 1
Ddim
1486
x x D Ab B D
x x 1 5b 6 1
Ddim
1487
x x D F B D
x x 1 3b 6 1
D+
1488
x x D A# D F#
x x 1 5# 1 3
D+
1489
x x F# A# D F#
x x 3 5# 1 3
D+
1490
A# D F# A# x x
5# 1 3 5# x x
D+
1491
x D F# A# D x
x 1 3 5# 1 x
D+
1492
x x D D F# A#
x x 1 1 3 5#
D+
1493
x x A# D F# A#
x x 5# 1 3 5#
D+
1494
x F# A# D F# x
x 3 5# 1 3 x
D+
1495
x F# D F# A# x
x 3 1 3 5# x
D+
1496
x x D F# A# D
x x 1 3 5# 1
D+
1497
x x D F# A# D
x x 1 3 5# 1
D+
1498
x A# D F# A# x
x 5# 1 3 5# x

TUNING: E A D G B E (Standard)

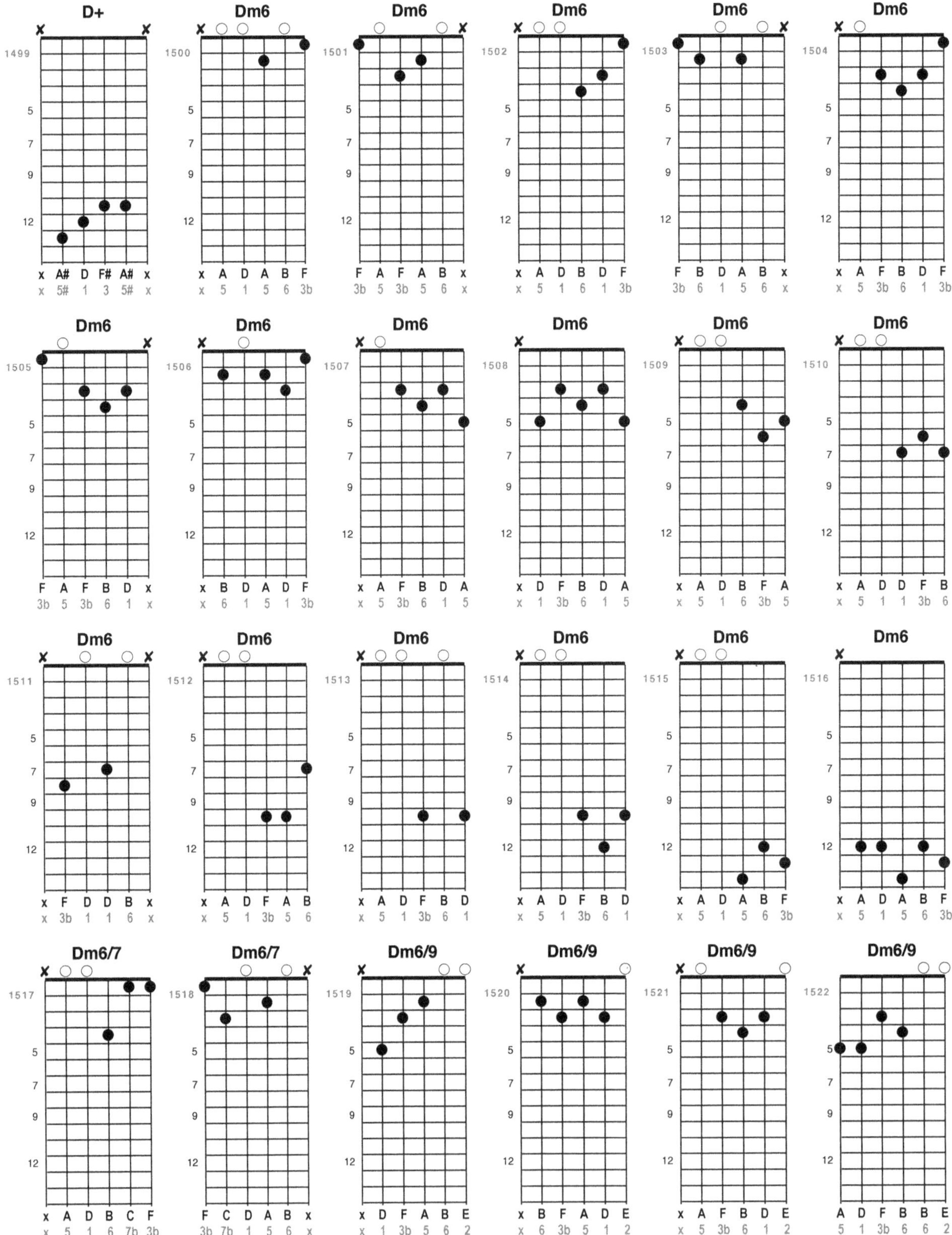
D+
1499
x A# D F# A# x
x 5# 1 3 5# x
Dm6
1500
x A D A B F
x 5 1 5 6 3b
Dm6
1501
F A F A B x
3b 5 3b 5 6 x
Dm6
1502
x A D B D F
x 5 1 6 1 3b
Dm6
1503
F B D A B x
3b 6 1 5 6 x
Dm6
1504
x A F B D F
x 5 3b 6 1 3b
Dm6
1505
F A F B D x
3b 5 3b 6 1 x
Dm6
1506
x B D A D F
x 6 1 5 1 3b
Dm6
1507
x A F B D A
x 5 3b 6 1 5
Dm6
1508
x D F B D A
x 1 3b 6 1 5
Dm6
1509
x A D B F A
x 5 1 6 3b 5
Dm6
1510
x A D D F B
x 5 1 1 3b 6
Dm6
1511
x F D D B x
x 3b 1 1 6 x
Dm6
1512
x A D F A B
x 5 1 3b 5 6
Dm6
1513
x A D F B D
x 5 1 3b 6 1
Dm6
1514
x A D F B D
x 5 1 3b 6 1
Dm6
1515
x A D A B F
x 5 1 5 6 3b
Dm6
1516
x A D A B F
x 5 1 5 6 3b
Dm6/7
1517
x A D B C F
x 5 1 6 7b 3b
Dm6/7
1518
F C D A B x
3b 7b 1 5 6 x
Dm6/9
1519
x D F A B E
x 1 3b 5 6 2
Dm6/9
1520
x B F A D E
x 6 3b 5 1 2
Dm6/9
1521
x A F B D E
x 5 3b 6 1 2
Dm6/9
1522
A D F B B E
5 1 3b 6 6 2

TUNING: E A D G B E (Standard)

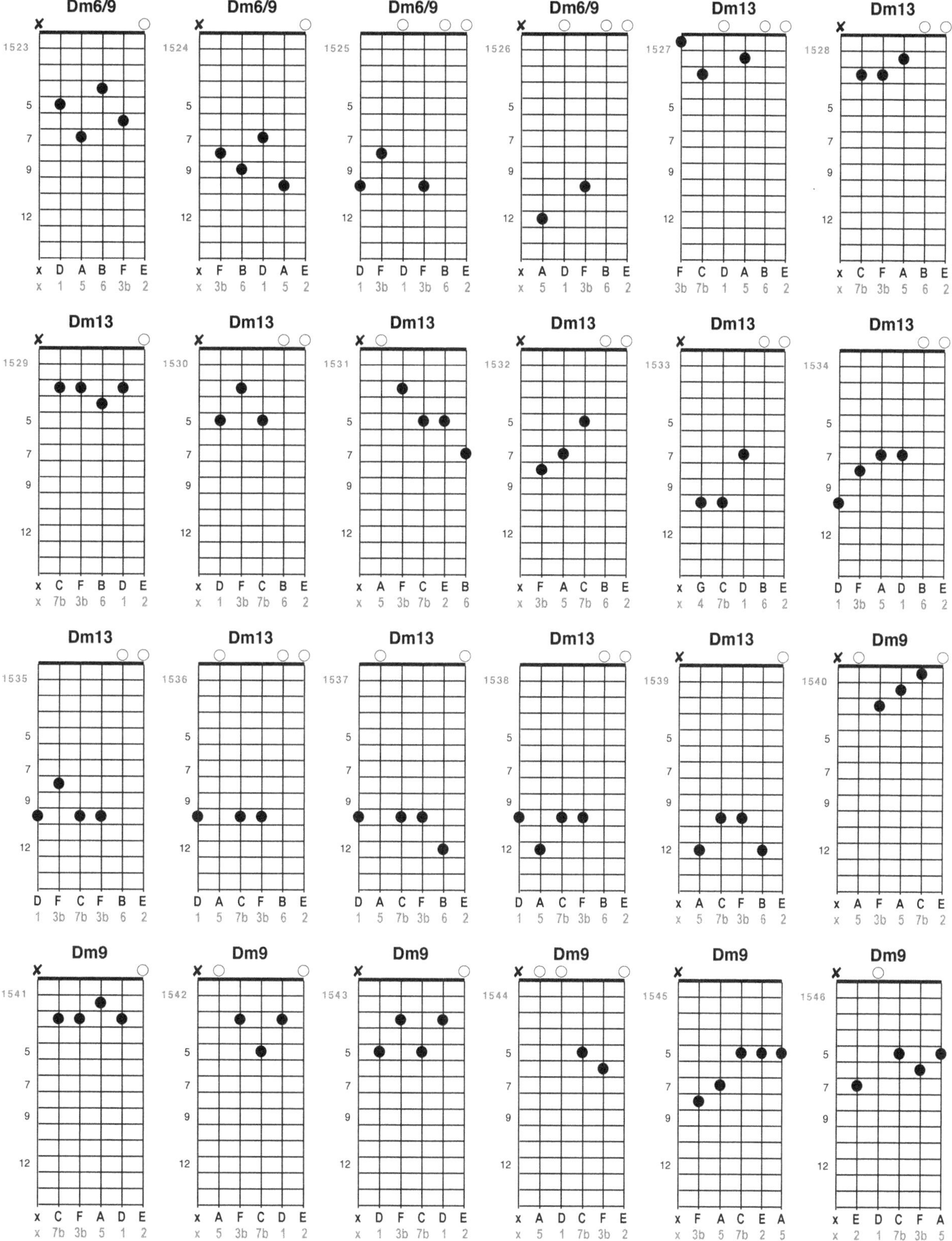
1523 Dm6/9
x D A B F E
x 1 5 6 3b 2
1524 Dm6/9
x F B D A E
x 3b 6 1 5 2
1525 Dm6/9
D F D F B E
1 3b 1 3b 6 2
1526 Dm6/9
x A D F B E
x 5 1 3b 6 2
1527 Dm13
F C D A B E
3b 7b 1 5 6 2
1528 Dm13
x C F A B E
x 7b 3b 5 6 2
1529 Dm13
x C F B D E
x 7b 3b 6 1 2
1530 Dm13
x D F C B E
x 1 3b 7b 6 2
1531 Dm13
x A F C E B
x 5 3b 7b 2 6
1532 Dm13
x F A C B E
x 3b 5 7b 6 2
1533 Dm13
x G C D B E
x 4 7b 1 6 2
1534 Dm13
D F A D B E
1 3b 5 1 6 2
1535 Dm13
D F C F B E
1 3b 7b 3b 6 2
1536 Dm13
D A C F B E
1 5 7b 3b 6 2
1537 Dm13
D A C F B E
1 5 7b 3b 6 2
1538 Dm13
D A C F B E
1 5 7b 3b 6 2
1539 Dm13
x A C F B E
x 5 7b 3b 6 2
1540 Dm9
x A F A C E
x 5 3b 5 7b 2
1541 Dm9
x C F A D E
x 7b 3b 5 1 2
1542 Dm9
x A F C D E
x 5 3b 7b 1 2
1543 Dm9
x D F C D E
x 1 3b 7b 1 2
1544 Dm9
x A D C F E
x 5 1 7b 3b 2
1545 Dm9
x F A C E A
x 3b 5 7b 2 5
1546 Dm9
x E D C F A
x 2 1 7b 3b 5

TUNING: E A D G B E (Standard)

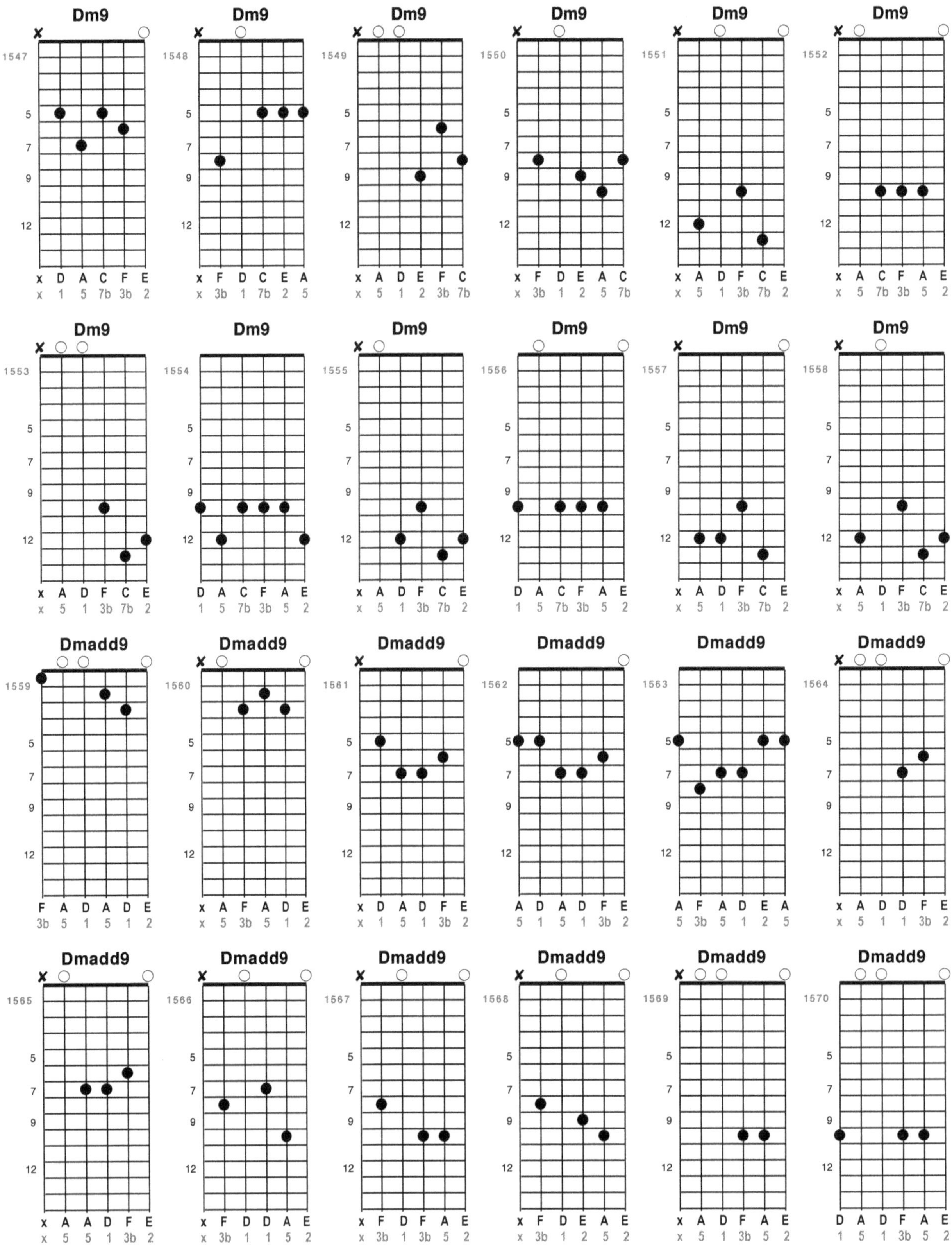
Dm9
1547
x D A C F E
x 1 5 7b 3b 2
Dm9
1548
x F D C E A
x 3b 1 7b 2 5
Dm9
1549
x A D E F C
x 5 1 2 3b 7b
Dm9
1550
x F D E A C
x 3b 1 2 5 7b
Dm9
1551
x A D F C E
x 5 1 3b 7b 2
Dm9
1552
x A C F A E
x 5 7b 3b 5 2
Dm9
1553
x A D F C E
x 5 1 3b 7b 2
Dm9
1554
D A C F A E
1 5 7b 3b 5 2
Dm9
1555
x A D F C E
x 5 1 3b 7b 2
Dm9
1556
D A C F A E
1 5 7b 3b 5 2
Dm9
1557
x A D F C E
x 5 1 3b 7b 2
Dm9
1558
x A D F C E
x 5 1 3b 7b 2
Dmadd9
1559
F A D A D E
3b 5 1 5 1 2
Dmadd9
1560
x A F A D E
x 5 3b 5 1 2
Dmadd9
1561
x D A D F E
x 1 5 1 3b 2
Dmadd9
1562
A D A D F E
5 1 5 1 3b 2
Dmadd9
1563
A F A D E A
5 3b 5 1 2 5
Dmadd9
1564
x A D D F E
x 5 1 1 3b 2
Dmadd9
1565
x A A D F E
x 5 5 1 3b 2
Dmadd9
1566
x F D D A E
x 3b 1 1 5 2
Dmadd9
1567
x F D F A E
x 3b 1 3b 5 2
Dmadd9
1568
x F D E A E
x 3b 1 2 5 2
Dmadd9
1569
x A D F A E
x 5 1 3b 5 2
Dmadd9
1570
D A D F A E
1 5 1 3b 5 2

TUNING: E A D G B E (Standard)

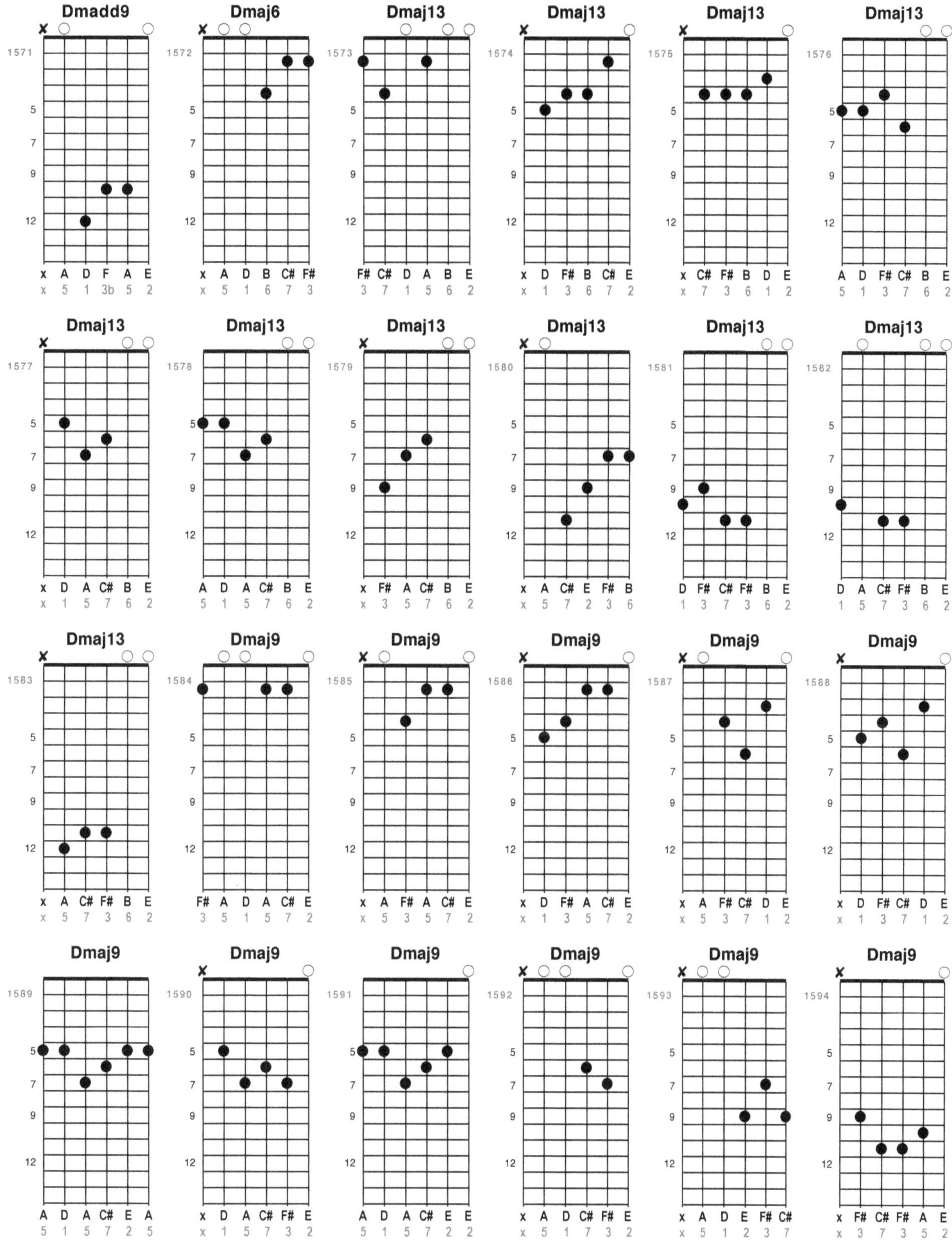
Dmadd9
1571
x A D F A E
x 5 1 3b 5 2
Dmaj6
1572
x A D B C# F#
x 5 1 6 7 3
Dmaj13
1573
F# C# D A B E
3 7 1 5 6 2
Dmaj13
1574
x D F# B C# E
x 1 3 6 7 2
Dmaj13
1575
x C# F# B D E
x 7 3 6 1 2
Dmaj13
1576
A D F# C# B E
5 1 3 7 6 2
Dmaj13
1577
x D A C# B E
x 1 5 7 6 2
Dmaj13
1578
A D A C# B E
5 1 5 7 6 2
Dmaj13
1579
x F# A C# B E
x 3 5 7 6 2
Dmaj13
1580
x A C# E F# B
x 5 7 2 3 6
Dmaj13
1581
D F# C# F# B E
1 3 7 3 6 2
Dmaj13
1582
D A C# F# B E
1 5 7 3 6 2
Dmaj13
1583
x A C# F# B E
x 5 7 3 6 2
Dmaj9
1584
F# A D A C# E
3 5 1 5 7 2
Dmaj9
1585
x A F# A C# E
x 5 3 5 7 2
Dmaj9
1586
x D F# A C# E
x 1 3 5 7 2
Dmaj9
1587
x A F# C# D E
x 5 3 7 1 2
Dmaj9
1588
x D F# C# D E
x 1 3 7 1 2
Dmaj9
1589
A D A C# E A
5 1 5 7 2 5
Dmaj9
1590
x D A C# F# E
x 1 5 7 3 2
Dmaj9
1591
A D A C# E E
5 1 5 7 2 2
Dmaj9
1592
x A D C# F# E
x 5 1 7 3 2
Dmaj9
1593
x A D E F# C#
x 5 1 2 3 7
Dmaj9
1594
x F# C# F# A E
x 3 7 3 5 2

TUNING: E A D G B E (Standard)

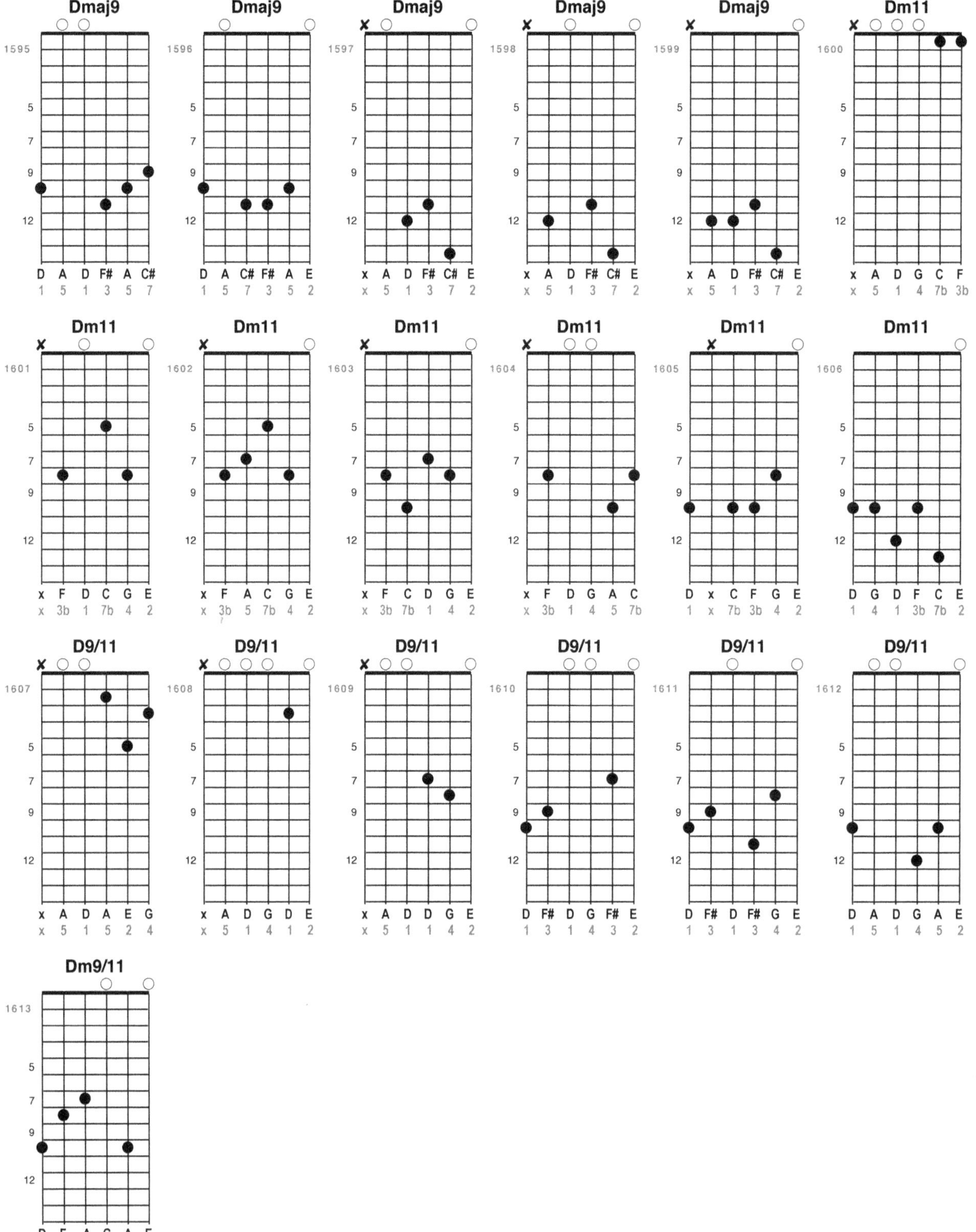
Dmaj9
1595
D A D F# A C#
1 5 1 3 5 7
Dmaj9
1596
D A C# F# A E
1 5 7 3 5 2
Dmaj9
1597
x A D F# C# E
x 5 1 3 7 2
Dmaj9
1598
x A D F# C# E
x 5 1 3 7 2
Dmaj9
1599
x A D F# C# E
x 5 1 3 7 2
Dm11
1600
x A D G C F
x 5 1 4 7b 3b
Dm11
1601
x F D C G E
x 3b 1 7b 4 2
Dm11
1602
x F A C G E
x 3b 5 7b 4 2
Dm11
1603
x F C D G E
x 3b 7b 1 4 2
Dm11
1604
x F D G A C
x 3b 1 4 5 7b
Dm11
1605
D x C F G E
1 x 7b 3b 4 2
Dm11
1606
D G D F C E
1 4 1 3b 7b 2
D9/11
1607
x A D A E G
x 5 1 5 2 4
D9/11
1608
x A D G D E
x 5 1 4 1 2
D9/11
1609
x A D D G E
x 5 1 1 4 2
D9/11
1610
D F# D G F# E
1 3 1 4 3 2
D9/11
1611
D F# D F# G E
1 3 1 3 4 2
D9/11
1612
D A D G A E
1 5 1 4 5 2
Dm9/11
1613
D F A G A E
1 3b 5 4 5 2

TUNING: E A D G B E (Standard)

D# Eb

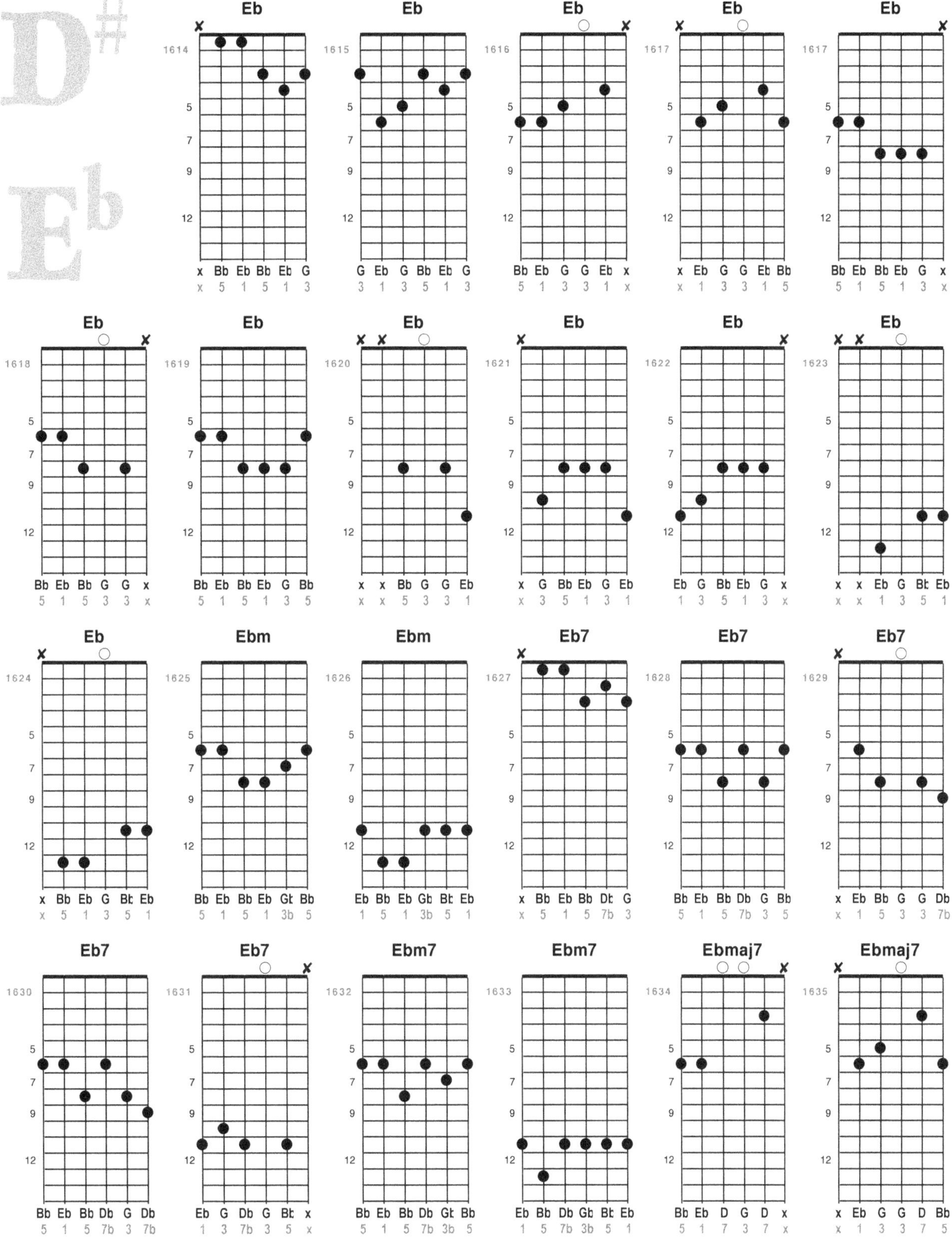

TUNING: E A D G B E (Standard)

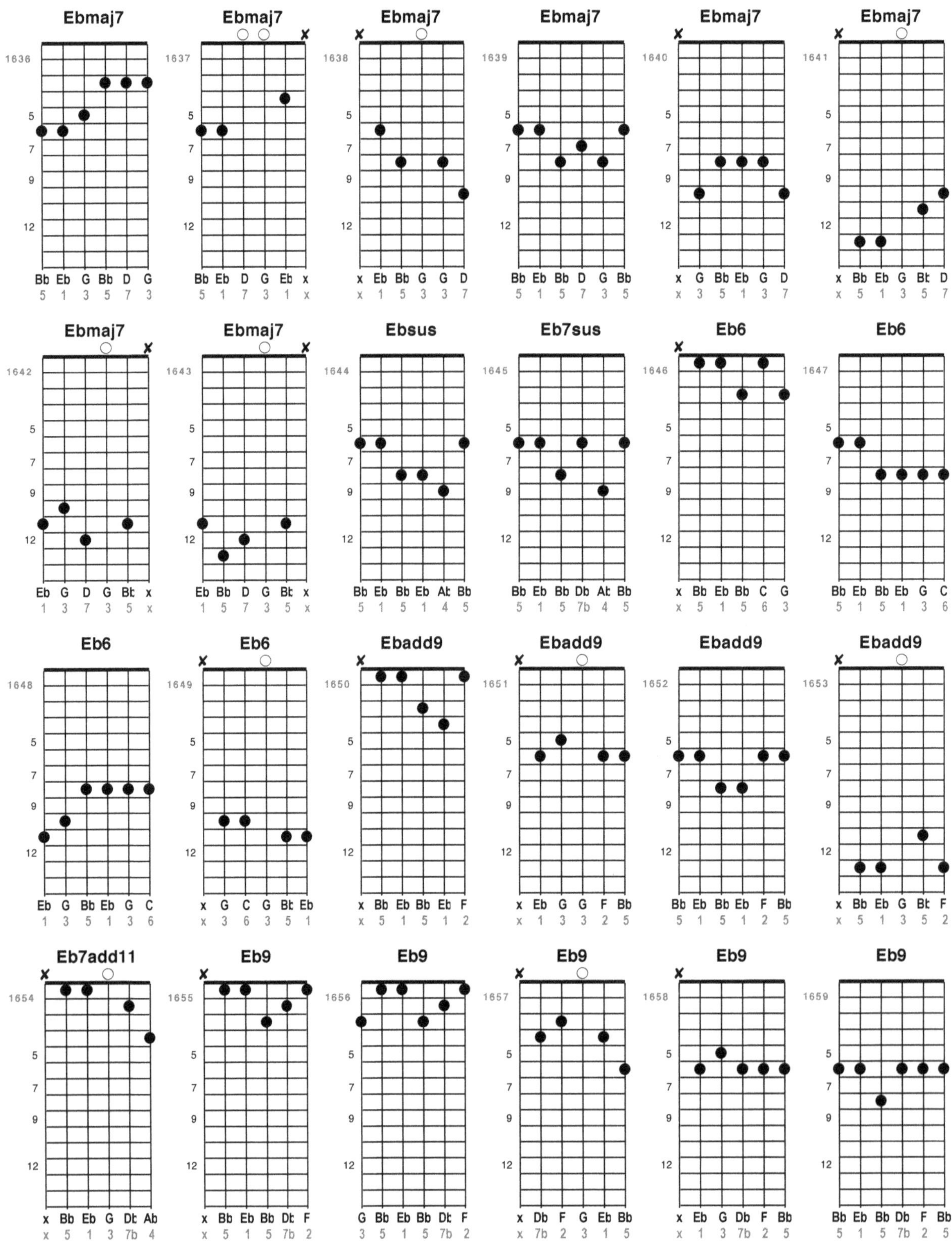

Ebmaj7
1636
Bb Eb G Bb D G
5 1 3 5 7 3
Ebmaj7
1637
Bb Eb D G Eb x
5 1 7 3 1 x
Ebmaj7
1638
x Eb Bb G G D
x 1 5 3 3 7
Ebmaj7
1639
Bb Eb Bb D G Bb
5 1 5 7 3 5
Ebmaj7
1640
x G Bb Eb G D
x 3 5 1 3 7
Ebmaj7
1641
x Bb Eb G Bb D
x 5 1 3 5 7
Ebmaj7
1642
Eb G D G Bb x
1 3 7 3 5 x
Ebmaj7
1643
Eb Bb D G Bb x
1 5 7 3 5 x
Ebsus
1644
Bb Eb Bb Eb Ab Bb
5 1 5 1 4 5
Eb7sus
1645
Bb Eb Bb Db Ab Bb
5 1 5 7b 4 5
Eb6
1646
x Bb Eb Bb C G
x 5 1 5 6 3
Eb6
1647
Bb Eb Bb Eb G C
5 1 5 1 3 6
Eb6
1648
Eb G Bb Eb G C
1 3 5 1 3 6
Eb6
1649
x G C G Bb Eb
x 3 6 3 5 1
Ebadd9
1650
x Bb Eb Bb Eb F
x 5 1 5 1 2
Ebadd9
1651
x Eb G G F Bb
x 1 3 3 2 5
Ebadd9
1652
Bb Eb Bb Eb F Bb
5 1 5 1 2 5
Ebadd9
1653
x Bb Eb G Bb F
x 5 1 3 5 2
Eb7add11
1654
x Bb Eb G Db Ab
x 5 1 3 7b 4
Eb9
1655
x Bb Eb Bb Db F
x 5 1 5 7b 2
Eb9
1656
G Bb Eb Bb Db F
3 5 1 5 7b 2
Eb9
1657
x Db F G Eb Bb
x 7b 2 3 1 5
Eb9
1658
x Eb G Db F Bb
x 1 3 7b 2 5
Eb9
1659
Bb Eb Bb Db F Bb
5 1 5 7b 2 5

TUNING: E A D G B E (Standard)

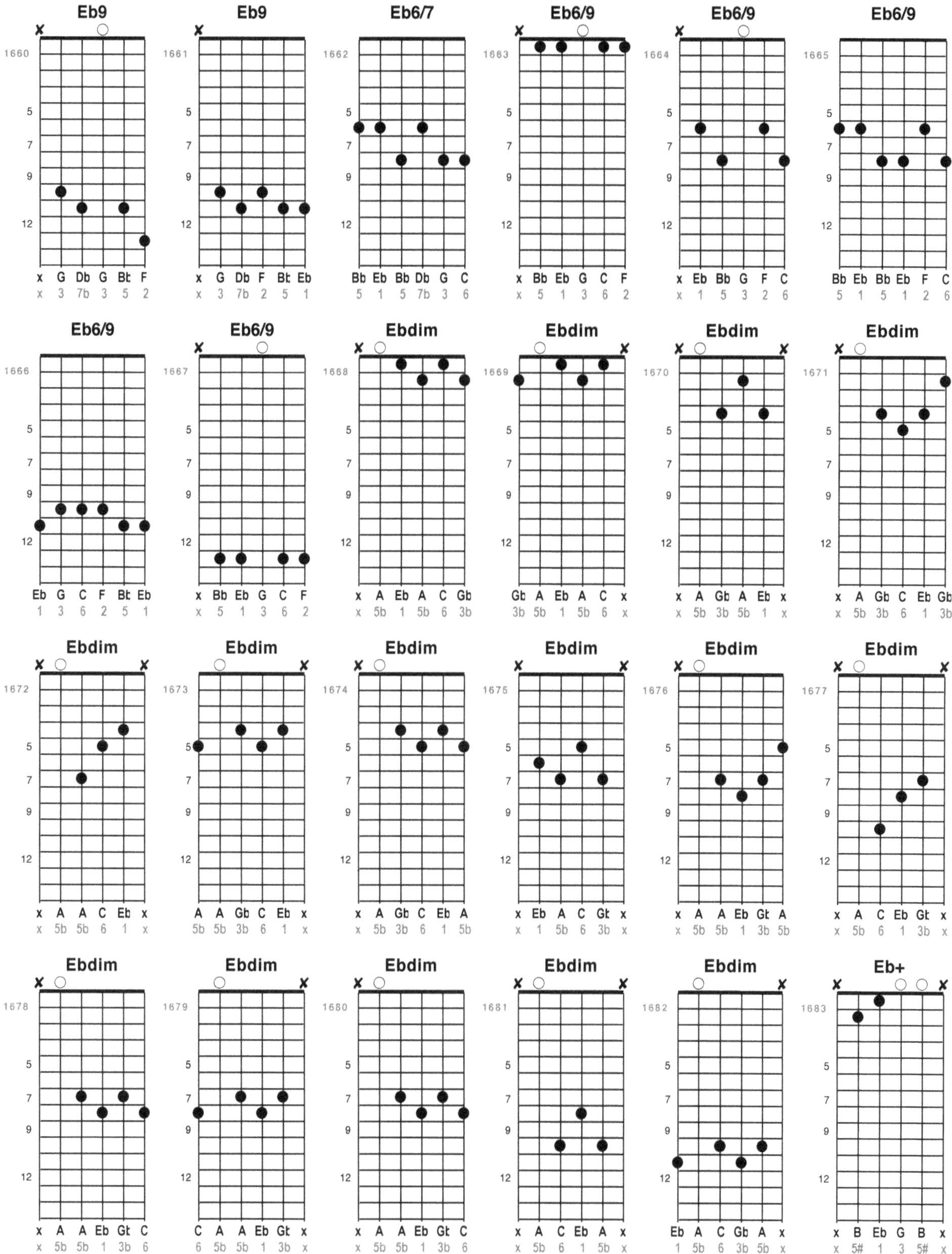
Eb9
1660
x G Db G Bt F
x 3 7b 3 5 2
Eb9
1661
x G Db F Bt Eb
x 3 7b 2 5 1
Eb6/7
1662
Bb Eb Bb Db G C
5 1 5 7b 3 6
Eb6/9
1663
x Bb Eb G C F
x 5 1 3 6 2
Eb6/9
1664
x Eb Bb G F C
x 1 5 3 2 6
Eb6/9
1665
Bb Eb Bb Eb F C
5 1 5 1 2 6
Eb6/9
1666
Eb G C F Bt Eb
1 3 6 2 5 1
Eb6/9
1667
x Bb Eb G C F
x 5 1 3 6 2
Ebdim
1668
x A Eb A C Gb
x 5b 1 5b 6 3b
Ebdim
1669
Gb A Eb A C x
3b 5b 1 5b 6 x
Ebdim
1670
x A Gb A Eb x
x 5b 3b 5b 1 x
Ebdim
1671
x A Gb C Eb Gb
x 5b 3b 6 1 3b
Ebdim
1672
x A A C Eb x
x 5b 5b 6 1 x
Ebdim
1673
A A Gb C Eb x
5b 5b 3b 6 1 x
Ebdim
1674
x A Gb C Eb A
x 5b 3b 6 1 5b
Ebdim
1675
x Eb A C Gt x
x 1 5b 6 3b x
Ebdim
1676
x A A Eb Gt A
x 5b 5b 1 3b 5b
Ebdim
1677
x A C Eb Gt x
x 5b 6 1 3b x
Ebdim
1678
x A A Eb Gt C
x 5b 5b 1 3b 6
Ebdim
1679
C A A Eb Gt x
6 5b 5b 1 3b x
Ebdim
1680
x A A Eb Gt C
x 5b 5b 1 3b 6
Ebdim
1681
x A C Eb A x
x 5b 6 1 5b x
Ebdim
1682
Eb A C Gb A x
1 5b 6 3b 5b x
Eb+
1683
x B Eb G B x
x 5# 1 3 5# x

TUNING: E A D G B E (Standard)

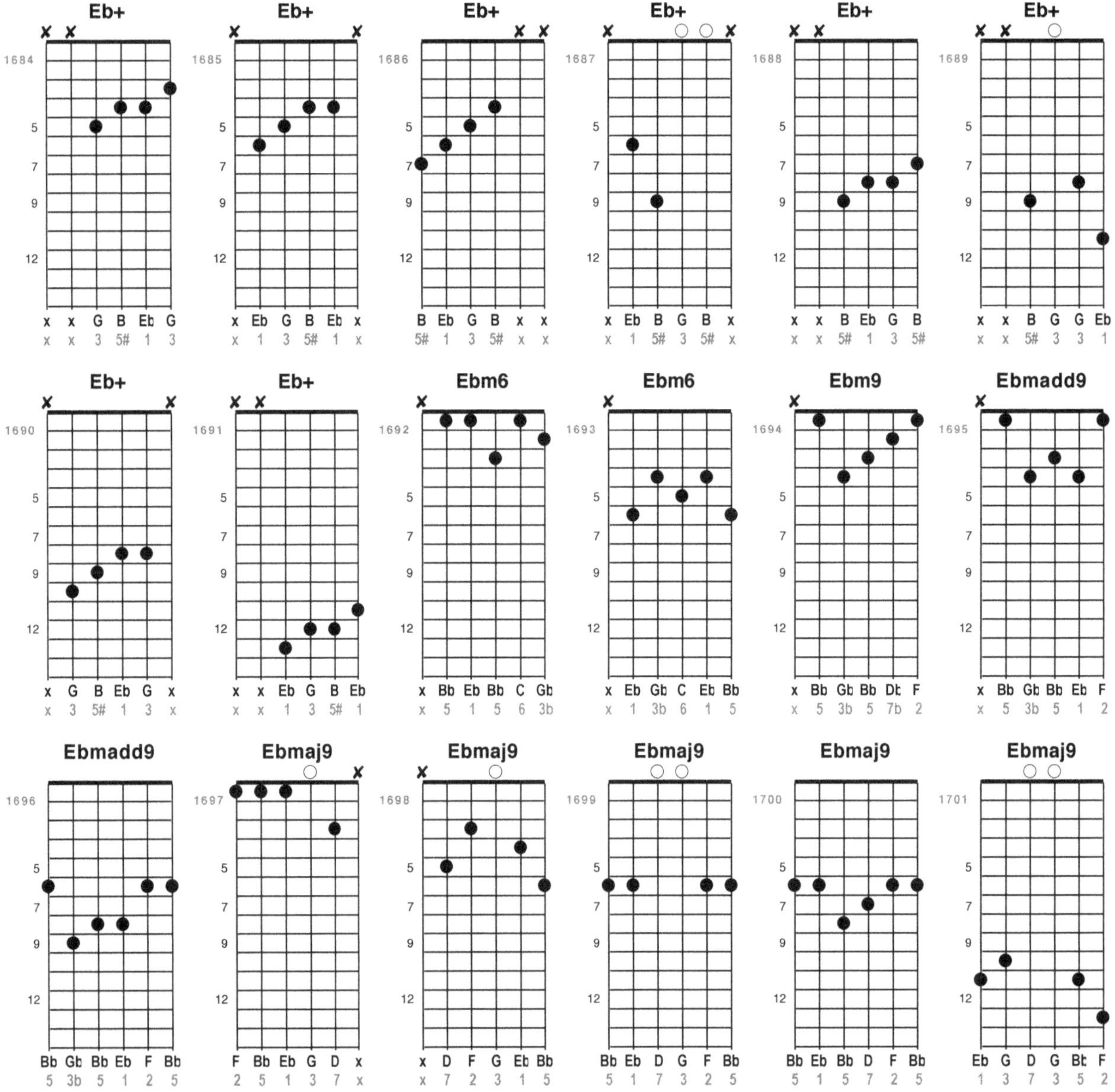
Eb+
1684
x x G B Eb G
x x 3 5# 1 3
Eb+
1685
x Eb G B Eb x
x 1 3 5# 1 x
Eb+
1686
B Eb G B x x
5# 1 3 5# x x
Eb+
1687
x Eb B G B x
x 1 5# 3 5# x
Eb+
1688
x x B Eb G B
x x 5# 1 3 5#
Eb+
1689
x x B G G Eb
x x 5# 3 3 1
Eb+
1690
x G B Eb G x
x 3 5# 1 3 x
Eb+
1691
x x Eb G B Eb
x x 1 3 5# 1
Ebm6
1692
x Bb Eb Bb C Gb
x 5 1 5 6 3b
Ebm6
1693
x Eb Gb C Eb Bb
x 1 3b 6 1 5
Ebm9
1694
x Bb Gb Bb Db F
x 5 3b 5 7b 2
Ebmadd9
1695
x Bb Gb Bb Eb F
x 5 3b 5 1 2
Ebmadd9
1696
Bb Gb Bb Eb F Bb
5 3b 5 1 2 5
Ebmaj9
1697
F Bb Eb G D x
2 5 1 3 7 x
Ebmaj9
1698
x D F G Eb Bb
x 7 2 3 1 5
Ebmaj9
1699
Bb Eb D G F Bb
5 1 7 3 2 5
Ebmaj9
1700
Bb Eb Bb D F Bb
5 1 5 7 2 5
Ebmaj9
1701
Eb G D G Bb F
1 3 7 3 5 2

Troubadour Guitar Chords

TUNING: E A D G B E (Standard)

E

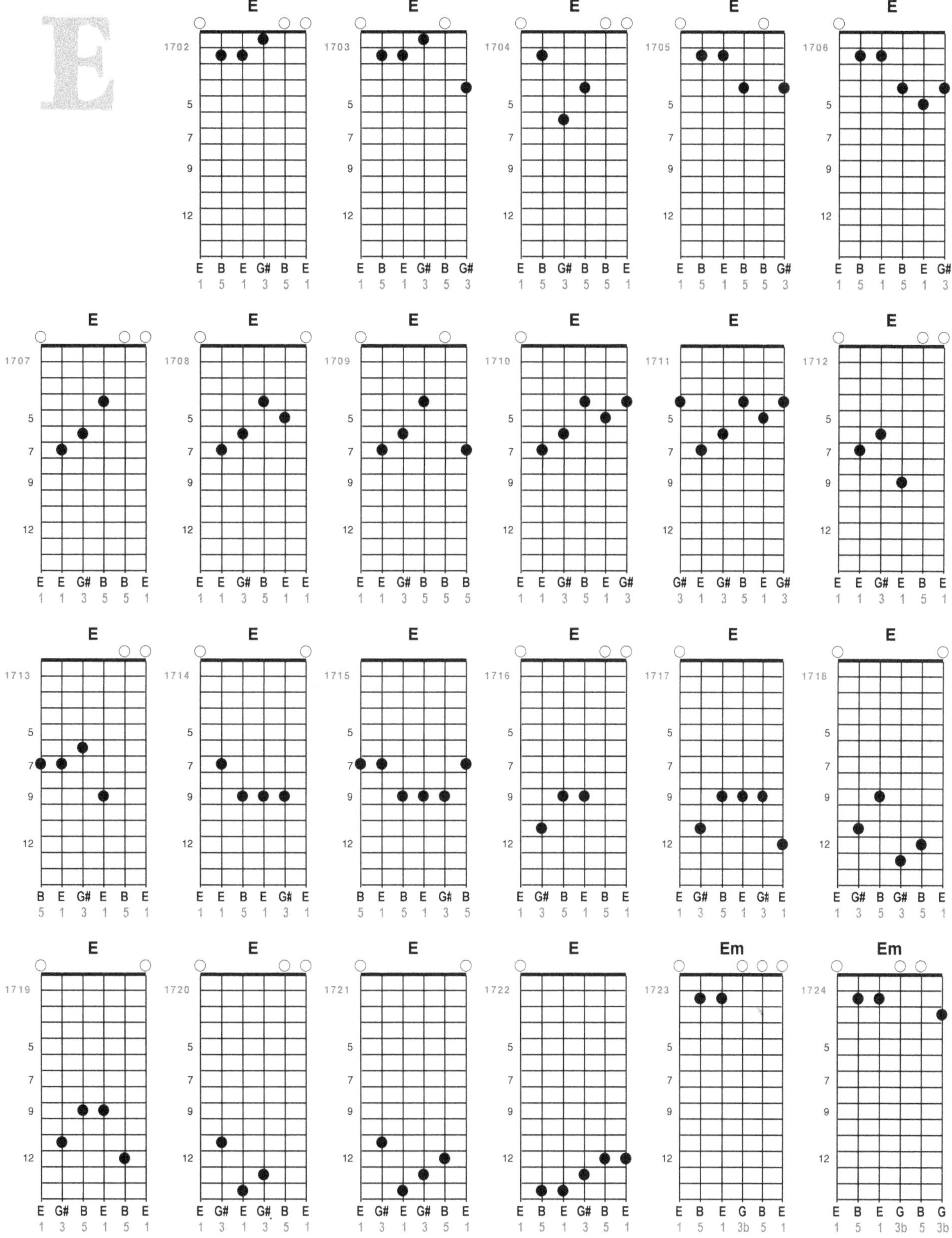
E
1702
E B E G# B E
1 5 1 3 5 1
E
1703
E B E G# B G#
1 5 1 3 5 3
E
1704
E B G# B B E
1 5 3 5 5 1
E
1705
E B E B B G#
1 5 1 5 5 3
E
1706
E B E B E G#
1 5 1 5 1 3
E
1707
E E G# B B E
1 1 3 5 5 1
E
1708
E E G# B E E
1 1 3 5 1 1
E
1709
E E G# B B B
1 1 3 5 5 5
E
1710
E E G# B E G#
1 1 3 5 1 3
E
1711
G# E G# B E G#
3 1 3 5 1 3
E
1712
E E G# E B E
1 1 3 1 5 1
E
1713
B E G# E B E
5 1 3 1 5 1
E
1714
E E B E G# E
1 1 5 1 3 1
E
1715
B E B E G# B
5 1 5 1 3 5
E
1716
E G# B E B E
1 3 5 1 5 1
E
1717
E G# B E G# E
1 3 5 1 3 1
E
1718
E G# B G# B E
1 3 5 3 5 1
E
1719
E G# B E B E
1 3 5 1 5 1
E
1720
E G# E G# B E
1 3 1 3 5 1
E
1721
E G# E G# B E
1 3 1 3 5 1
E
1722
E B E G# B E
1 5 1 3 5 1
Em
1723
E B E G B E
1 5 1 3b 5 1
Em
1724
E B E G B G
1 5 1 3b 5 3b

TUNING: E A D G B E (Standard)

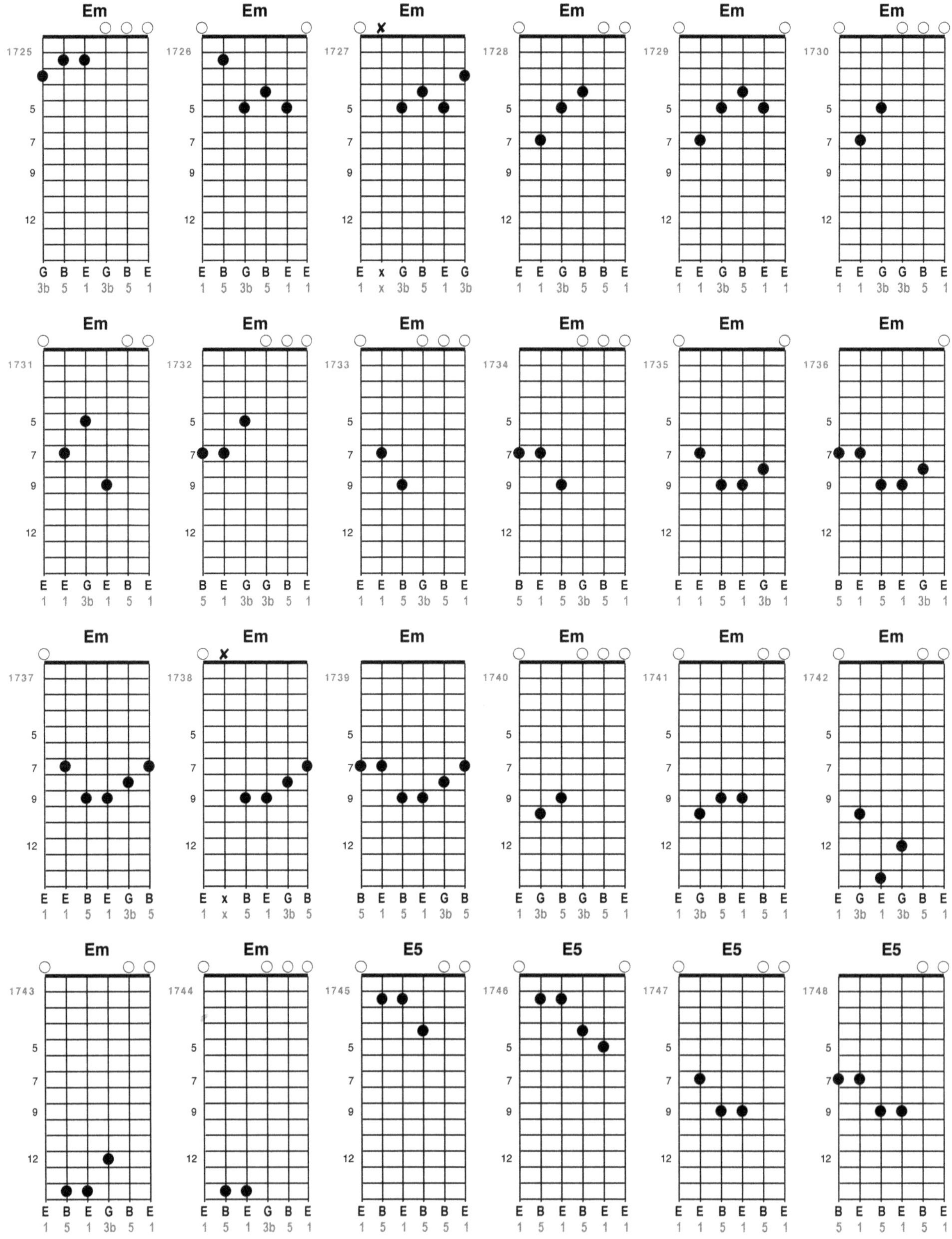
Em
1725
G B E G B E
3b 5 1 3b 5 1
Em
1726
E B G B E E
1 5 3b 5 1 1
Em
1727
E x G B E G
1 x 3b 5 1 3b
Em
1728
E E G B B E
1 1 3b 5 5 1
Em
1729
E E G B E E
1 1 3b 5 1 1
Em
1730
E E G G B E
1 1 3b 3b 5 1
Em
1731
E E G E B E
1 1 3b 1 5 1
Em
1732
B E G G B E
5 1 3b 3b 5 1
Em
1733
E E B G B E
1 1 5 3b 5 1
Em
1734
B E B G B E
5 1 5 3b 5 1
Em
1735
E E B E G E
1 1 5 1 3b 1
Em
1736
B E B E G E
5 1 5 1 3b 1
Em
1737
E E B E G B
1 1 5 1 3b 5
Em
1738
E x B E G B
1 x 5 1 3b 5
Em
1739
B E B E G B
5 1 5 1 3b 5
Em
1740
E G B G B E
1 3b 5 3b 5 1
Em
1741
E G B E B E
1 3b 5 1 5 1
Em
1742
E G E G B E
1 3b 1 3b 5 1
Em
1743
E B E G B E
1 5 1 3b 5 1
Em
1744
E B E G B E
1 5 1 3b 5 1
E5
1745
E B E B B E
1 5 1 5 5 1
E5
1746
E B E B E E
1 5 1 5 1 1
E5
1747
E E B E B E
1 1 5 1 5 1
E5
1748
B E B E B E
5 1 5 1 5 1

TUNING: E A D G B E (Standard)

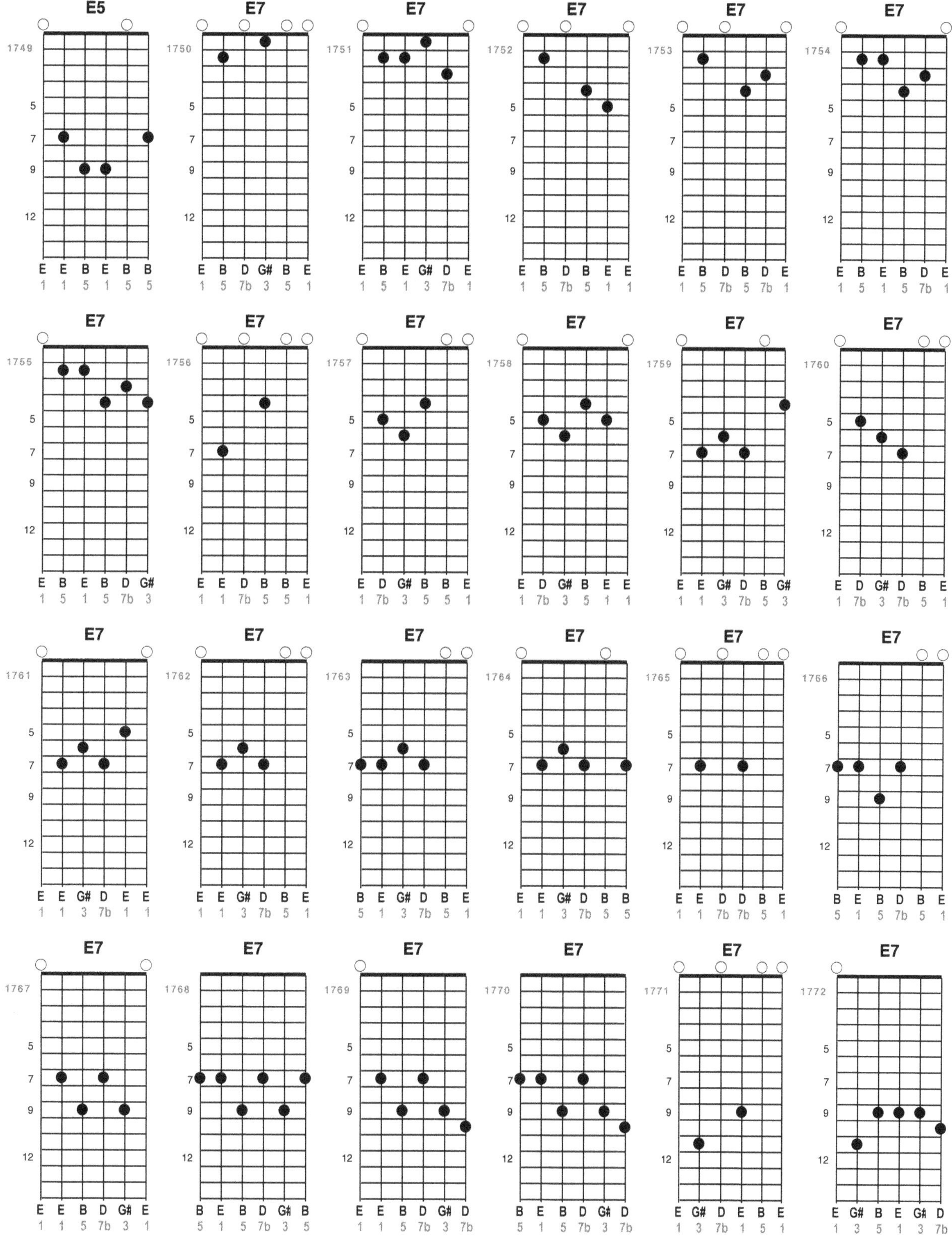

E5	E7	E7	E7	E7	E7
1749	1750	1751	1752	1753	1754

E5 — E E B E B B / 1 1 5 1 5 5
E7 — E B D G# B E / 1 5 7b 3 5 1
E7 — E B E G# D E / 1 5 1 3 7b 1
E7 — E B D B E E / 1 5 7b 5 1 1
E7 — E B D B D E / 1 5 7b 5 7b 1
E7 — E B E B D E / 1 5 1 5 7b 1

E7	E7	E7	E7	E7	E7
1755	1756	1757	1758	1759	1760

E7 — E B E B D G# / 1 5 1 5 7b 3
E7 — E E D B B E / 1 1 7b 5 5 1
E7 — E D G# B B E / 1 7b 3 5 5 1
E7 — E D G# B E E / 1 7b 3 5 1 1
E7 — E E G# D B G# / 1 1 3 7b 5 3
E7 — E D G# D B E / 1 7b 3 7b 5 1

E7	E7	E7	E7	E7	E7
1761	1762	1763	1764	1765	1766

E7 — E E G# D E E / 1 1 3 7b 1 1
E7 — E E G# D B E / 1 1 3 7b 5 1
E7 — B E G# D B E / 5 1 3 7b 5 1
E7 — E E G# D B B / 1 1 3 7b 5 5
E7 — E E D D B E / 1 1 7b 7b 5 1
E7 — B E B D B E / 5 1 5 7b 5 1

E7	E7	E7	E7	E7	E7
1767	1768	1769	1770	1771	1772

E7 — E E B D G# E / 1 1 5 7b 3 1
E7 — B E B D G# B / 5 1 5 7b 3 5
E7 — E E B D G# D / 1 1 5 7b 3 7b
E7 — B E B D G# D / 5 1 5 7b 3 7b
E7 — E G# D E B E / 1 3 7b 1 5 1
E7 — E G# B E G# D / 1 3 5 1 3 7b

Troubadour Guitar Chords

TUNING: E A D G B E (Standard)

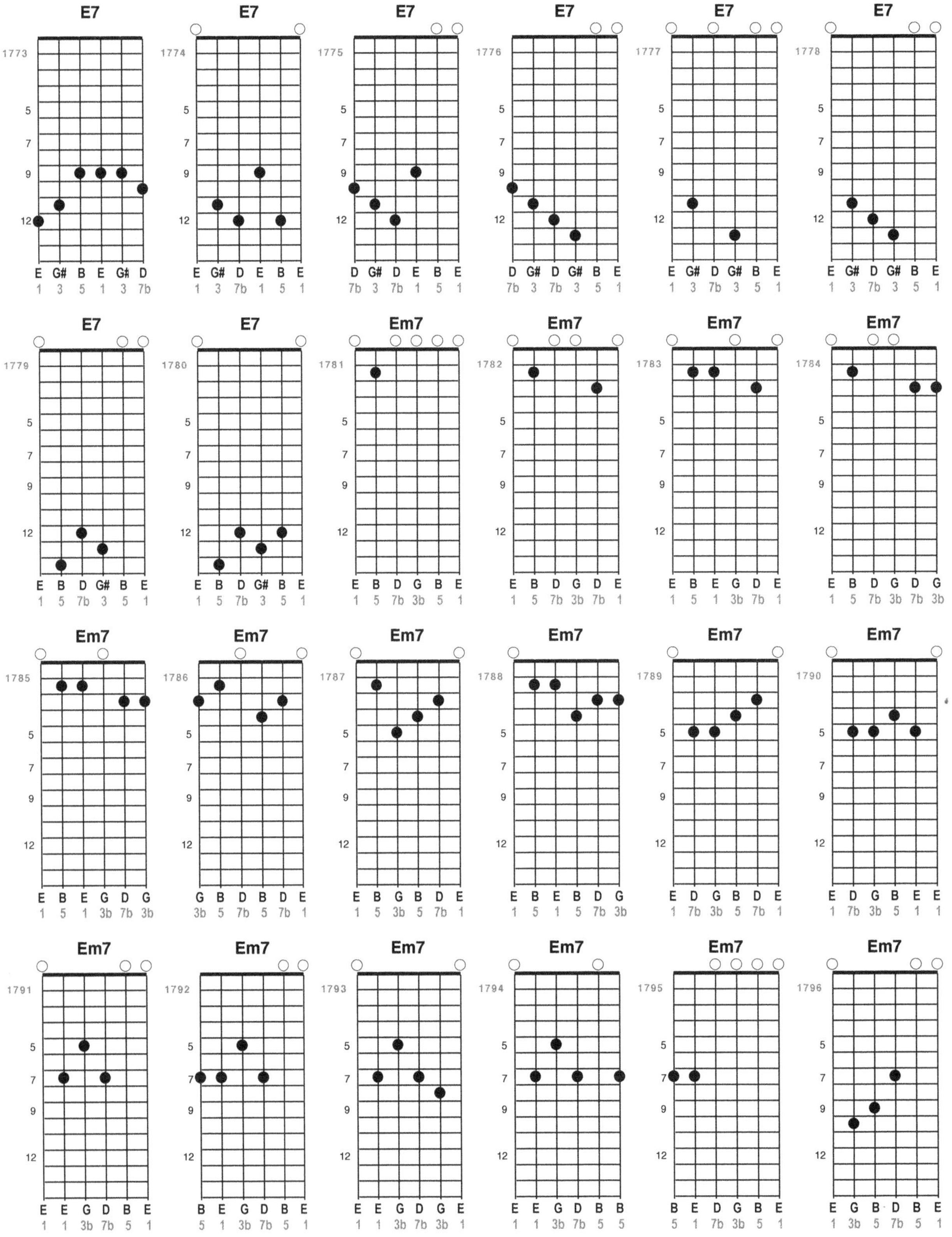

E7
1773
E G# B E G# D
1 3 5 1 3 7b
E7
1774
E G# D E B E
1 3 7b 1 5 1
E7
1775
D G# D E B E
7b 3 7b 1 5 1
E7
1776
D G# D G# B E
7b 3 7b 3 5 1
E7
1777
E G# D G# B E
1 3 7b 3 5 1
E7
1778
E G# D G# B E
1 3 7b 3 5 1
E7
1779
E B D G# B E
1 5 7b 3 5 1
E7
1780
E B D G# B E
1 5 7b 3 5 1
Em7
1781
E B D G B E
1 5 7b 3b 5 1
Em7
1782
E B D G D E
1 5 7b 3b 7b 1
Em7
1783
E B E G D E
1 5 1 3b 7b 1
Em7
1784
E B D G D G
1 5 7b 3b 7b 3b
Em7
1785
E B E G D G
1 5 1 3b 7b 3b
Em7
1786
G B D B D E
3b 5 7b 5 7b 1
Em7
1787
E B G B D E
1 5 3b 5 7b 1
Em7
1788
E B E B D G
1 5 1 5 7b 3b
Em7
1789
E D G B D E
1 7b 3b 5 7b 1
Em7
1790
E D G B E E
1 7b 3b 5 1 1
Em7
1791
E E G D B E
1 1 3b 7b 5 1
Em7
1792
B E G D B E
5 1 3b 7b 5 1
Em7
1793
E E G D G E
1 1 3b 7b 3b 1
Em7
1794
E E G D B B
1 1 3b 7b 5 5
Em7
1795
B E D G B E
5 1 7b 3b 5 1
Em7
1796
E G B D B E
1 3b 5 7b 5 1

Troubadour Guitar Chords

TUNING: E A D G B E (Standard)

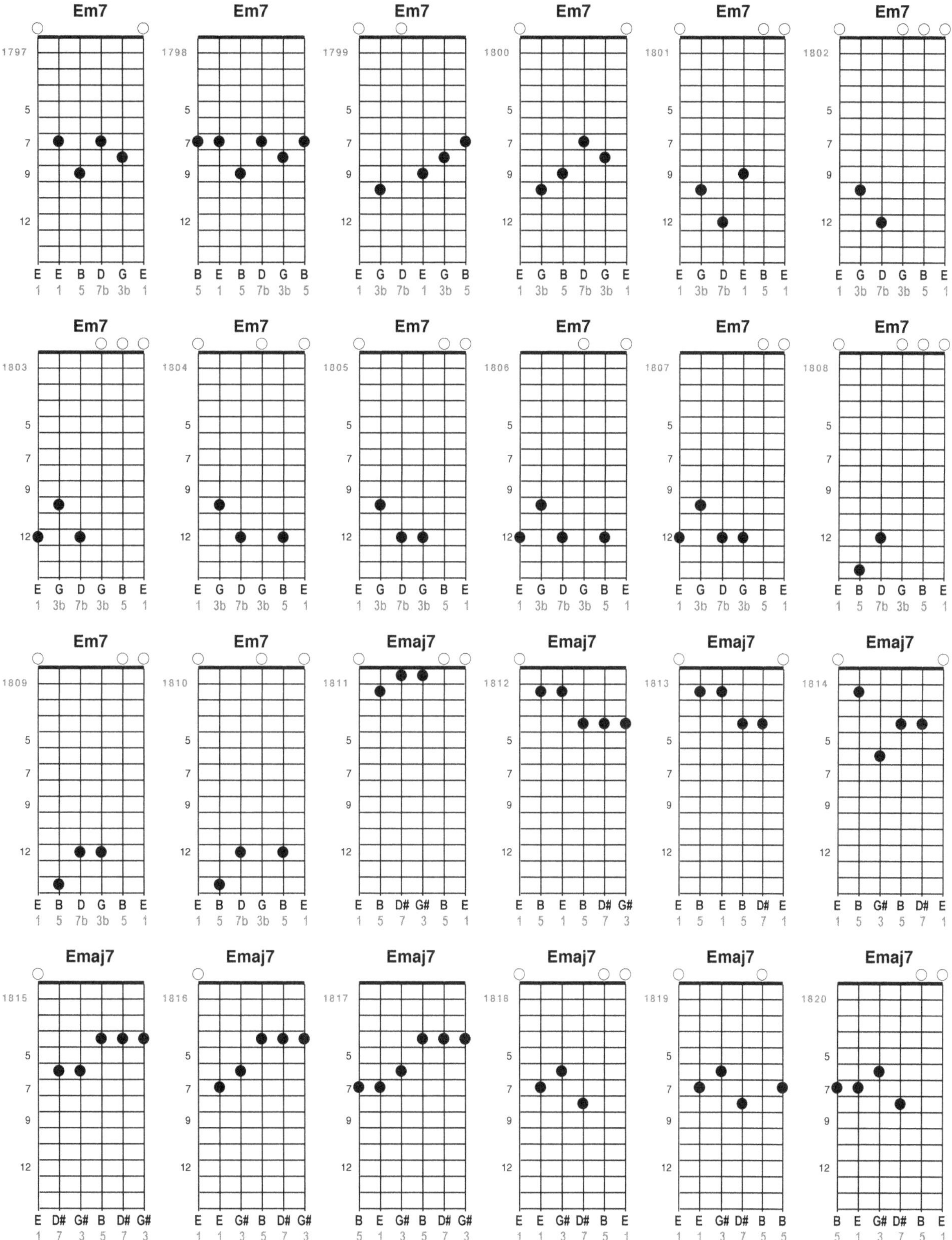
1797 Em7
E E B D G E
1 1 5 7b 3b 1
1798 Em7
B E B D G B
5 1 5 7b 3b 5
1799 Em7
E G D E G B
1 3b 7b 1 3b 5
1800 Em7
E G B D G E
1 3b 5 7b 3b 1
1801 Em7
E G D E B E
1 3b 7b 1 5 1
1802 Em7
E G D G B E
1 3b 7b 3b 5 1
1803 Em7
E G D G B E
1 3b 7b 3b 5 1
1804 Em7
E G D G B E
1 3b 7b 3b 5 1
1805 Em7
E G D G B E
1 3b 7b 3b 5 1
1806 Em7
E G D G B E
1 3b 7b 3b 5 1
1807 Em7
E G D G B E
1 3b 7b 3b 5 1
1808 Em7
E B D G B E
1 5 7b 3b 5 1
1809 Em7
E B D G B E
1 5 7b 3b 5 1
1810 Em7
E B D G B E
1 5 7b 3b 5 1
1811 Emaj7
E B D# G# B E
1 5 7 3 5 1
1812 Emaj7
E B E B D# G#
1 5 1 5 7 3
1813 Emaj7
E B E B D# E
1 5 1 5 7 1
1814 Emaj7
E B G# B D# E
1 5 3 5 7 1
1815 Emaj7
E D# G# B D# G#
1 7 3 5 7 3
1816 Emaj7
E E G# B D# G#
1 1 3 5 7 3
1817 Emaj7
B E G# B D# G#
5 1 3 5 7 3
1818 Emaj7
E E G# D# B E
1 1 3 7 5 1
1819 Emaj7
E E G# D# B B
1 1 3 7 5 5
1820 Emaj7
B E G# D# B E
5 1 3 7 5 1

Troubadour Guitar Chords

TUNING: E A D G B E (Standard)

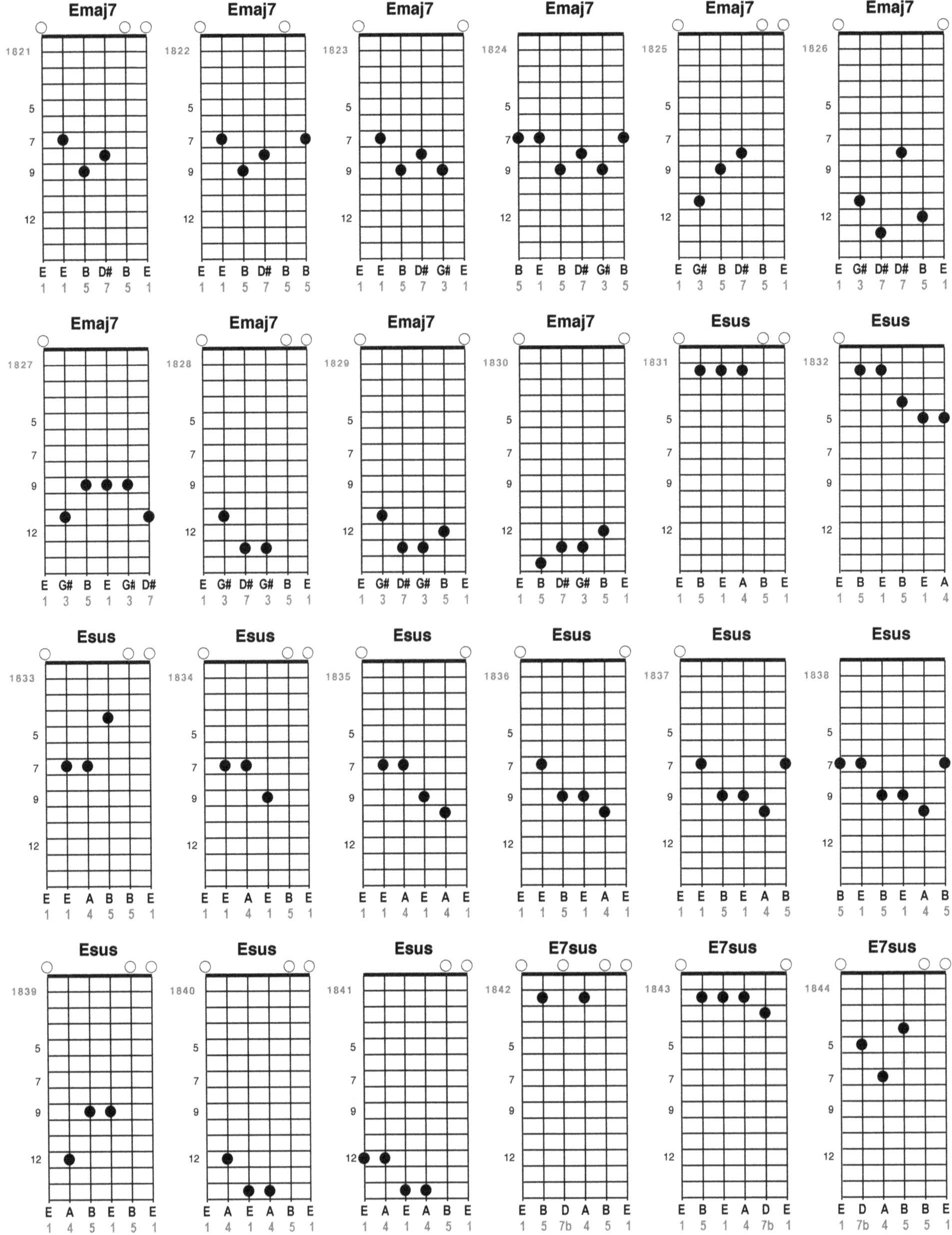
Emaj7
1821
5
7
9
12
E E B D# B E
1 1 5 7 5 1
Emaj7
1822
E E B D# B B
1 1 5 7 5 5
Emaj7
1823
E E B D# G# E
1 1 5 7 3 1
Emaj7
1824
B E B D# G# B
5 1 5 7 3 5
Emaj7
1825
E G# B D# B E
1 3 5 7 5 1
Emaj7
1826
E G# D# D# B E
1 3 7 7 5 1
Emaj7
1827
E G# B E G# D#
1 3 5 1 3 7
Emaj7
1828
E G# D# G# B E
1 3 7 3 5 1
Emaj7
1829
E G# D# G# B E
1 3 7 3 5 1
Emaj7
1830
E B D# G# B E
1 5 7 3 5 1
Esus
1831
E B E A B E
1 5 1 4 5 1
Esus
1832
E B E B E A
1 5 1 5 1 4
Esus
1833
E E A B B E
1 1 4 5 5 1
Esus
1834
E E A E B E
1 1 4 1 5 1
Esus
1835
E E A E A E
1 1 4 1 4 1
Esus
1836
E E B E A E
1 1 5 1 4 1
Esus
1837
E E B E A B
1 1 5 1 4 5
Esus
1838
B E B E A B
5 1 5 1 4 5
Esus
1839
E A B E B E
1 4 5 1 5 1
Esus
1840
E A E A B E
1 4 1 4 5 1
Esus
1841
E A E A B E
1 4 1 4 5 1
E7sus
1842
E B D A B E
1 5 7b 4 5 1
E7sus
1843
E B E A D E
1 5 1 4 7b 1
E7sus
1844
E D A B B E
1 7b 4 5 5 1

Troubadour Guitar Chords

TUNING: E A D G B E (Standard)

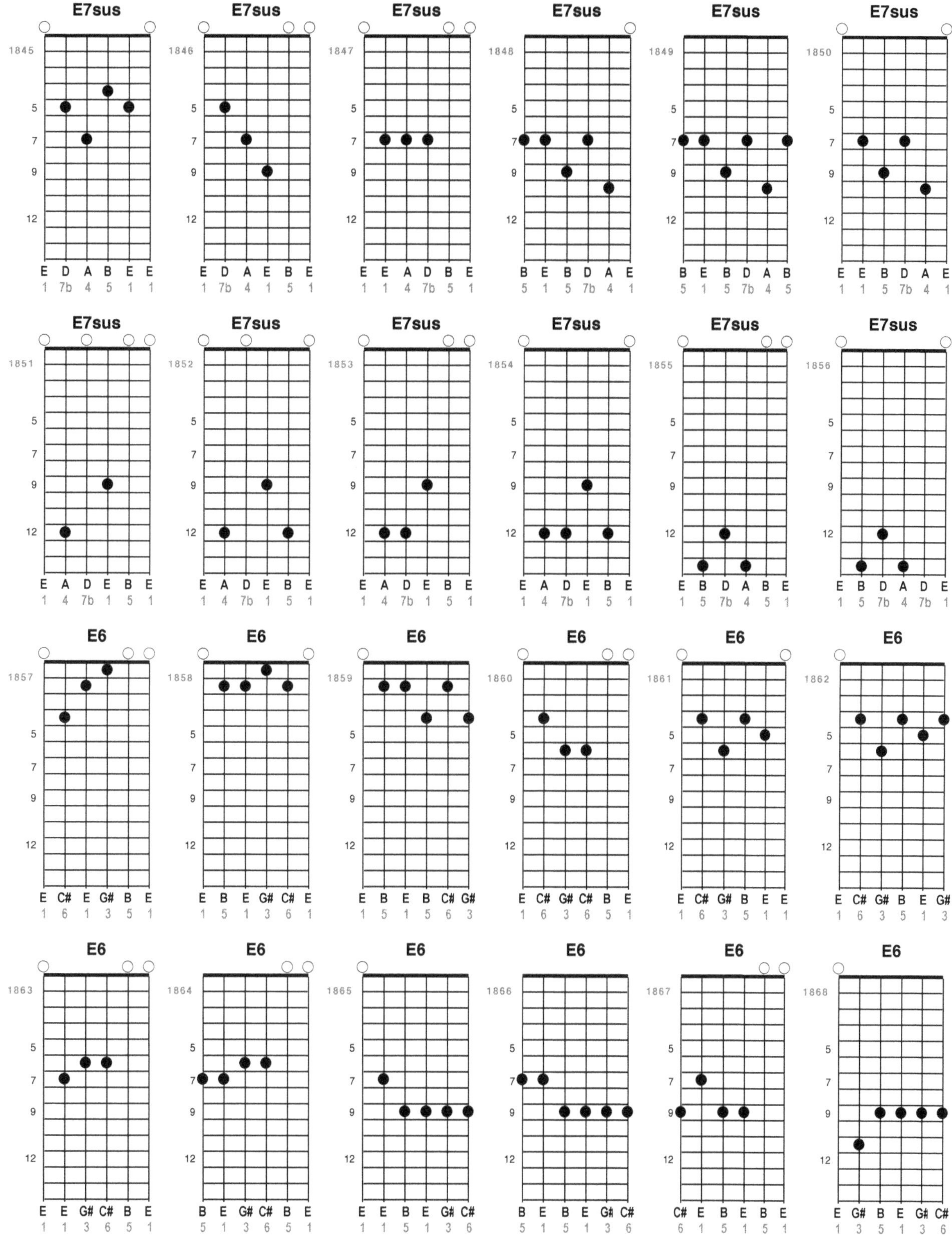
E7sus
1845
E D A B E E
1 7b 4 5 1 1
E7sus
1846
E D A E B E
1 7b 4 1 5 1
E7sus
1847
E E A D B E
1 1 4 7b 5 1
E7sus
1848
B E B D A E
5 1 5 7b 4 1
E7sus
1849
B E B D A B
5 1 5 7b 4 5
E7sus
1850
E E B D A E
1 1 5 7b 4 1
E7sus
1851
E A D E B E
1 4 7b 1 5 1
E7sus
1852
E A D E B E
1 4 7b 1 5 1
E7sus
1853
E A D E B E
1 4 7b 1 5 1
E7sus
1854
E A D E B E
1 4 7b 1 5 1
E7sus
1855
E B D A B E
1 5 7b 4 5 1
E7sus
1856
E B D A D E
1 5 7b 4 7b 1
E6
1857
E C# E G# B E
1 6 1 3 5 1
E6
1858
E B E G# C# E
1 5 1 3 6 1
E6
1859
E B E B C# G#
1 5 1 5 6 3
E6
1860
E C# G# C# B E
1 6 3 6 5 1
E6
1861
E C# G# B E E
1 6 3 5 1 1
E6
1862
E C# G# B E G#
1 6 3 5 1 3
E6
1863
E E G# C# B E
1 1 3 6 5 1
E6
1864
B E G# C# B E
5 1 3 6 5 1
E6
1865
E E B E G# C#
1 1 5 1 3 6
E6
1866
B E B E G# C#
5 1 5 1 3 6
E6
1867
C# E B E B E
6 1 5 1 5 1
E6
1868
E G# B E G# C#
1 3 5 1 3 6

TUNING: E A D G B E (Standard)

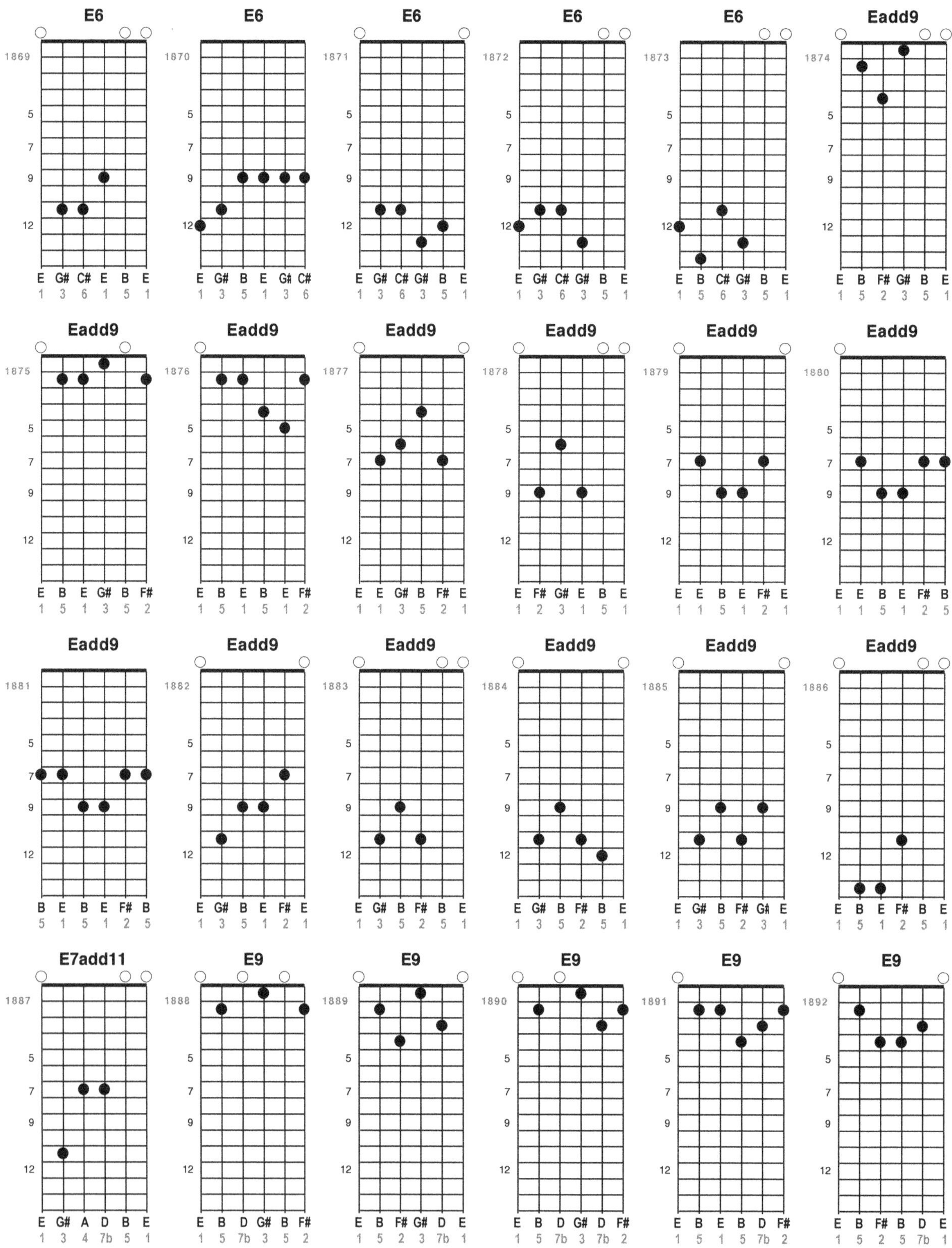
E6
1869
E G# C# E B E
1 3 6 1 5 1
E6
1870
E G# B E G# C#
1 3 5 1 3 6
E6
1871
E G# C# G# B E
1 3 6 3 5 1
E6
1872
E G# C# G# B E
1 3 6 3 5 1
E6
1873
E B C# G# B E
1 5 6 3 5 1
Eadd9
1874
E B F# G# B E
1 5 2 3 5 1
Eadd9
1875
E B E G# B F#
1 5 1 3 5 2
Eadd9
1876
E B E B E F#
1 5 1 5 1 2
Eadd9
1877
E E G# B F# E
1 1 3 5 2 1
Eadd9
1878
E F# G# E B E
1 2 3 1 5 1
Eadd9
1879
E E B E F# E
1 1 5 1 2 1
Eadd9
1880
E E B E F# B
1 1 5 1 2 5
Eadd9
1881
B E B E F# B
5 1 5 1 2 5
Eadd9
1882
E G# B E F# E
1 3 5 1 2 1
Eadd9
1883
E G# B F# B E
1 3 5 2 5 1
Eadd9
1884
E G# B F# B E
1 3 5 2 5 1
Eadd9
1885
E G# B F# G# E
1 3 5 2 3 1
Eadd9
1886
E B E F# B E
1 5 1 2 5 1
E7add11
1887
E G# A D B E
1 3 4 7b 5 1
E9
1888
E B D G# B F#
1 5 7b 3 5 2
E9
1889
E B F# G# D E
1 5 2 3 7b 1
E9
1890
E B D G# D F#
1 5 7b 3 7b 2
E9
1891
E B E B D F#
1 5 1 5 7b 2
E9
1892
E B F# B D E
1 5 2 5 7b 1

TUNING: E A D G B E (Standard)

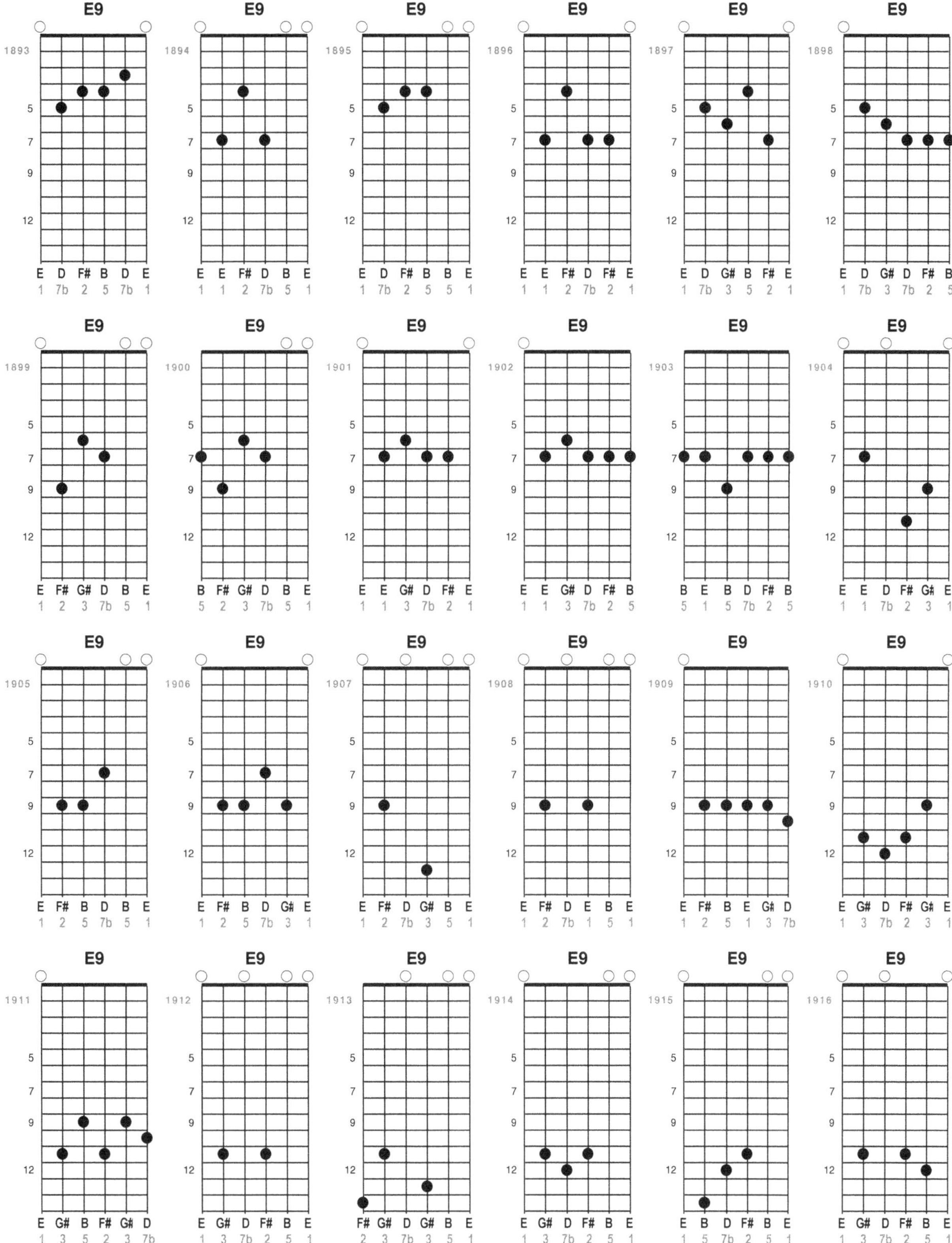
E9
1893
E D F# B D E
1 7b 2 5 7b 1
E9
1894
E E F# D B E
1 1 2 7b 5 1
E9
1895
E D F# B B E
1 7b 2 5 5 1
E9
1896
E E F# D F# E
1 1 2 7b 2 1
E9
1897
E D G# B F# E
1 7b 3 5 2 1
E9
1898
E D G# D F# B
1 7b 3 7b 2 5
E9
1899
E F# G# D B E
1 2 3 7b 5 1
E9
1900
B F# G# D B E
5 2 3 7b 5 1
E9
1901
E E G# D F# E
1 1 3 7b 2 1
E9
1902
E E G# D F# B
1 1 3 7b 2 5
E9
1903
B E B D F# B
5 1 5 7b 2 5
E9
1904
E E D F# G# E
1 1 7b 2 3 1
E9
1905
E F# B D B E
1 2 5 7b 5 1
E9
1906
E F# B D G# E
1 2 5 7b 3 1
E9
1907
E F# D G# B E
1 2 7b 3 5 1
E9
1908
E F# D E B E
1 2 7b 1 5 1
E9
1909
E F# B E G# D
1 2 5 1 3 7b
E9
1910
E G# D F# G# E
1 3 7b 2 3 1
E9
1911
E G# B F# G# D
1 3 5 2 3 7b
E9
1912
E G# D F# B E
1 3 7b 2 5 1
E9
1913
F# G# D G# B E
2 3 7b 3 5 1
E9
1914
E G# D F# B E
1 3 7b 2 5 1
E9
1915
E B D F# B E
1 5 7b 2 5 1
E9
1916
E G# D F# B E
1 3 7b 2 5 1

TUNING: E A D G B E (Standard)

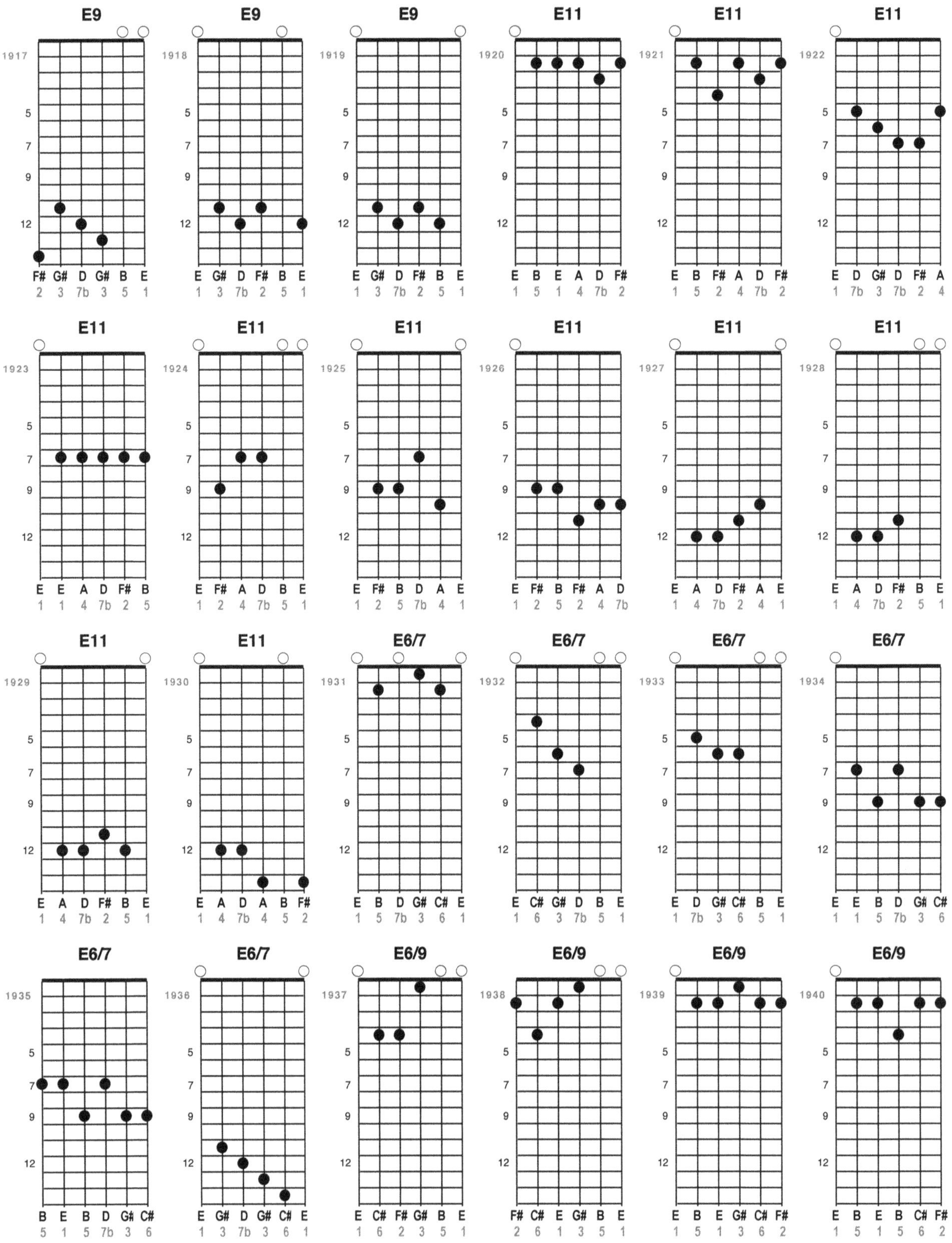

TUNING: E A D G B E (Standard)

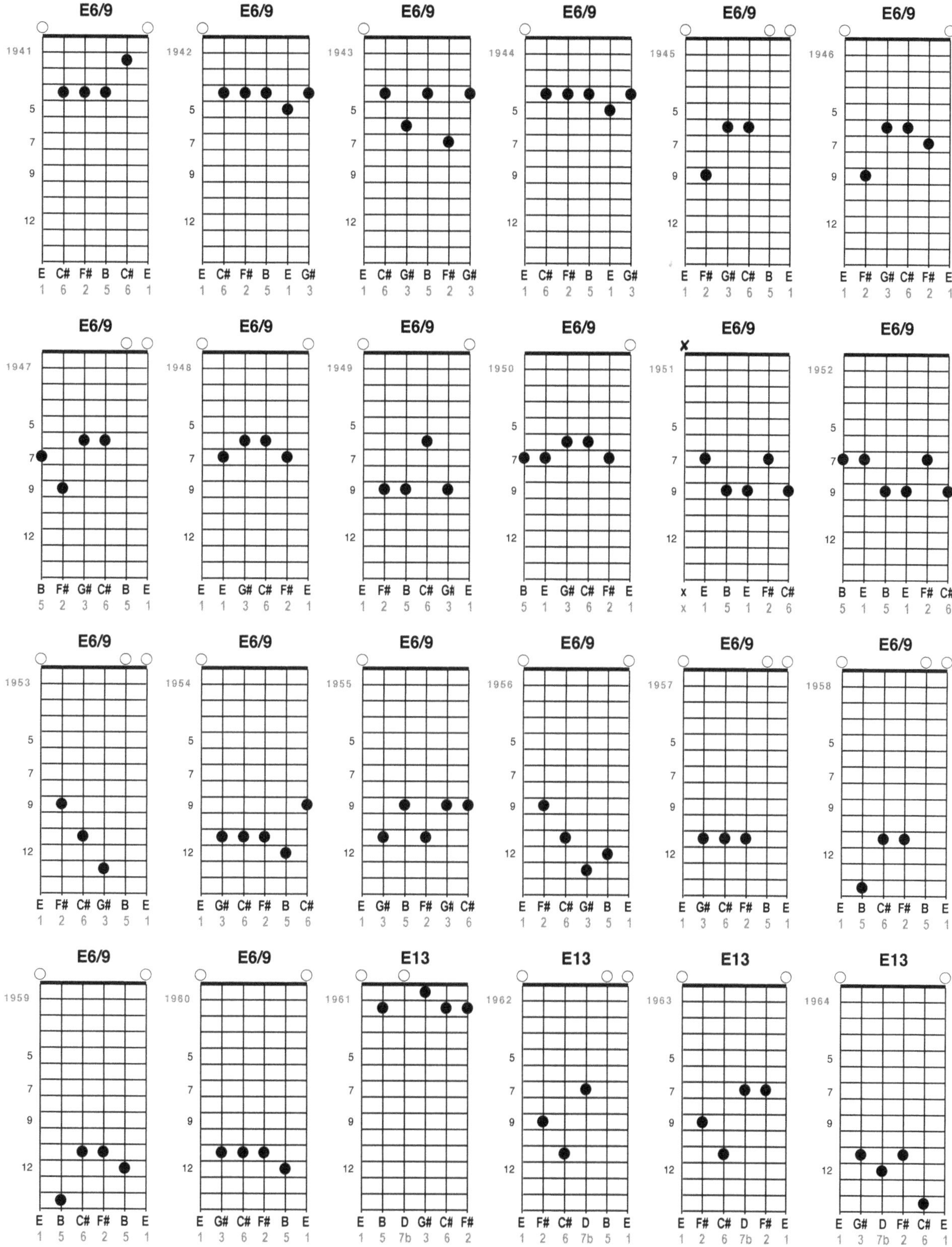
E6/9
1941
E C# F# B C# E
1 6 2 5 6 1
E6/9
1942
E C# F# B E G#
1 6 2 5 1 3
E6/9
1943
E C# G# B F# G#
1 6 3 5 2 3
E6/9
1944
E C# F# B E G#
1 6 2 5 1 3
E6/9
1945
E F# G# C# B E
1 2 3 6 5 1
E6/9
1946
E F# G# C# F# E
1 2 3 6 2 1
E6/9
1947
B F# G# C# B E
5 2 3 6 5 1
E6/9
1948
E E G# C# F# E
1 1 3 6 2 1
E6/9
1949
E F# B C# G# E
1 2 5 6 3 1
E6/9
1950
B E G# C# F# E
5 1 3 6 2 1
E6/9
1951
x E B E F# C#
x 1 5 1 2 6
E6/9
1952
B E B E F# C#
5 1 5 1 2 6
E6/9
1953
E F# C# G# B E
1 2 6 3 5 1
E6/9
1954
E G# C# F# B C#
1 3 6 2 5 6
E6/9
1955
E G# B F# G# C#
1 3 5 2 3 6
E6/9
1956
E F# C# G# B E
1 2 6 3 5 1
E6/9
1957
E G# C# F# B E
1 3 6 2 5 1
E6/9
1958
E B C# F# B E
1 5 6 2 5 1
E6/9
1959
E B C# F# B E
1 5 6 2 5 1
E6/9
1960
E G# C# F# B E
1 3 6 2 5 1
E13
1961
E B D G# C# F#
1 5 7b 3 6 2
E13
1962
E F# C# D B E
1 2 6 7b 5 1
E13
1963
E F# C# D F# E
1 2 6 7b 2 1
E13
1964
E G# D F# C# E
1 3 7b 2 6 1

Troubadour Guitar Chords

TUNING: E A D G B E (Standard)

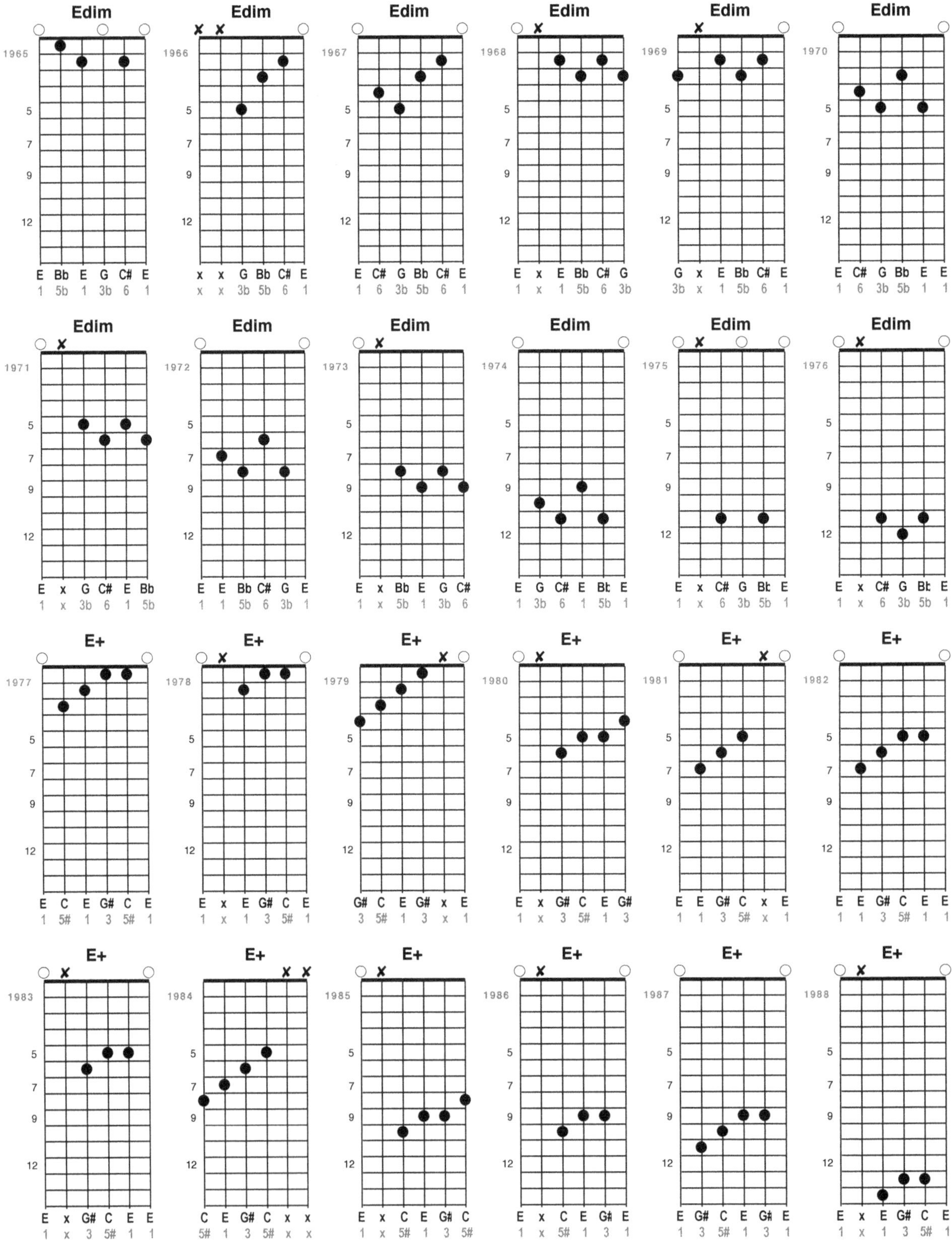
1965 Edim E Bb E G C# E 1 5b 1 3b 6 1
1966 Edim x x G Bb C# E x x 3b 5b 6 1
1967 Edim E C# G Bb C# E 1 6 3b 5b 6 1
1968 Edim E x E Bb C# G 1 x 1 5b 6 3b
1969 Edim G x E Bb C# E 3b x 1 5b 6 1
1970 Edim E C# G Bb E E 1 6 3b 5b 1 1
1971 Edim E x G C# E Bb 1 x 3b 6 1 5b
1972 Edim E E Bb C# G E 1 1 5b 6 3b 1
1973 Edim E x Bb E G C# 1 x 5b 1 3b 6
1974 Edim E G C# E Bb E 1 3b 6 1 5b 1
1975 Edim E x C# G Bb E 1 x 6 3b 5b 1
1976 Edim E x C# G Bb E 1 x 6 3b 5b 1
1977 E+ E C E G# C E 1 5# 1 3 5# 1
1978 E+ E x E G# C E 1 x 1 3 5# 1
1979 E+ G# C E G# x E 3 5# 1 3 x 1
1980 E+ E x G# C E G# 1 x 3 5# 1 3
1981 E+ E E G# C x E 1 1 3 5# x 1
1982 E+ E E G# C E E 1 1 3 5# 1 1
1983 E+ E x G# C E E 1 x 3 5# 1 1
1984 E+ C E G# C x x 5# 1 3 5# x x
1985 E+ E x C E G# C 1 x 5# 1 3 5#
1986 E+ E x C E G# E 1 x 5# 1 3 1
1987 E+ E G# C E G# E 1 3 5# 1 3 1
1988 E+ E x E G# C E 1 x 1 3 5# 1

TUNING: E A D G B E (Standard)

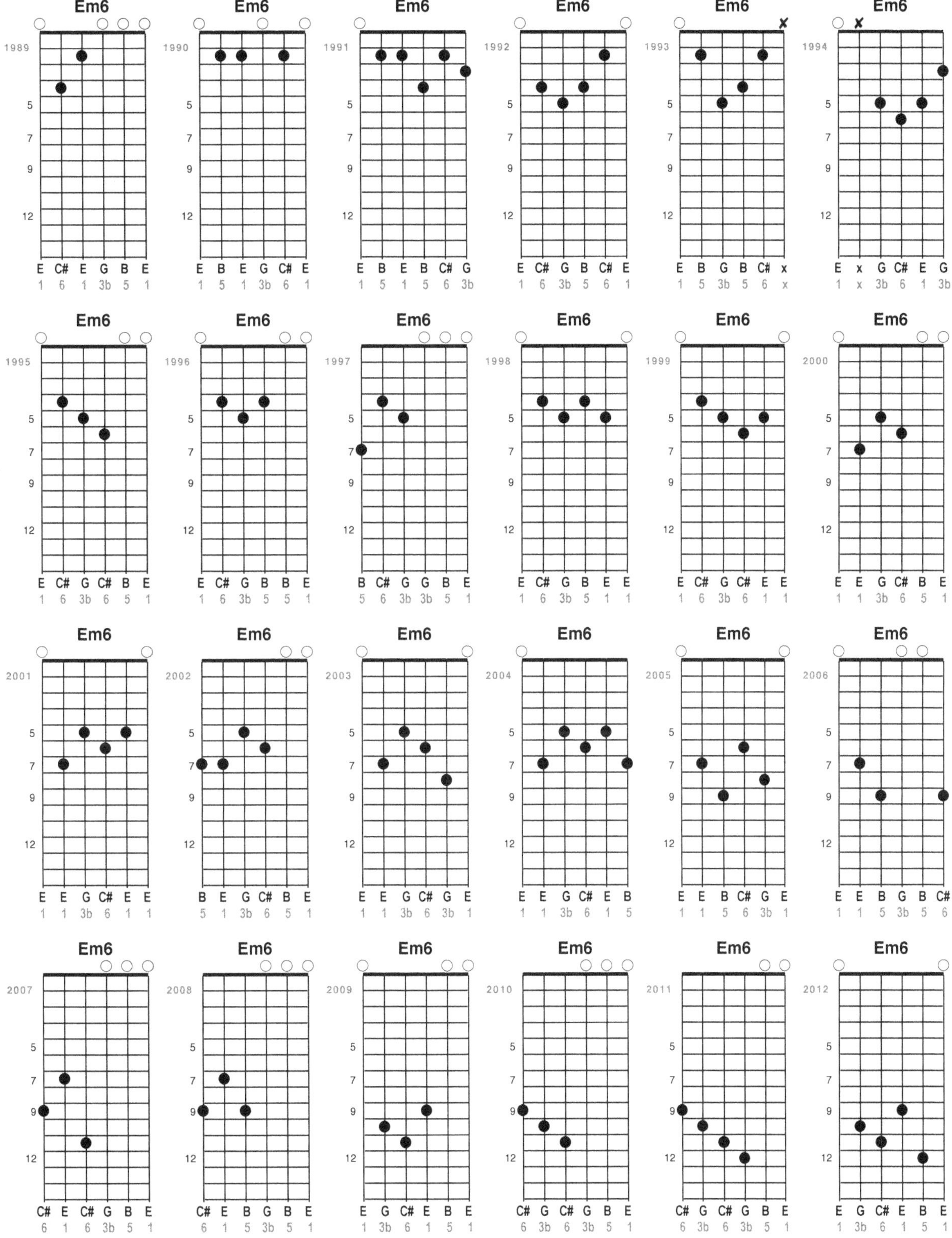

TUNING: E A D G B E (Standard)

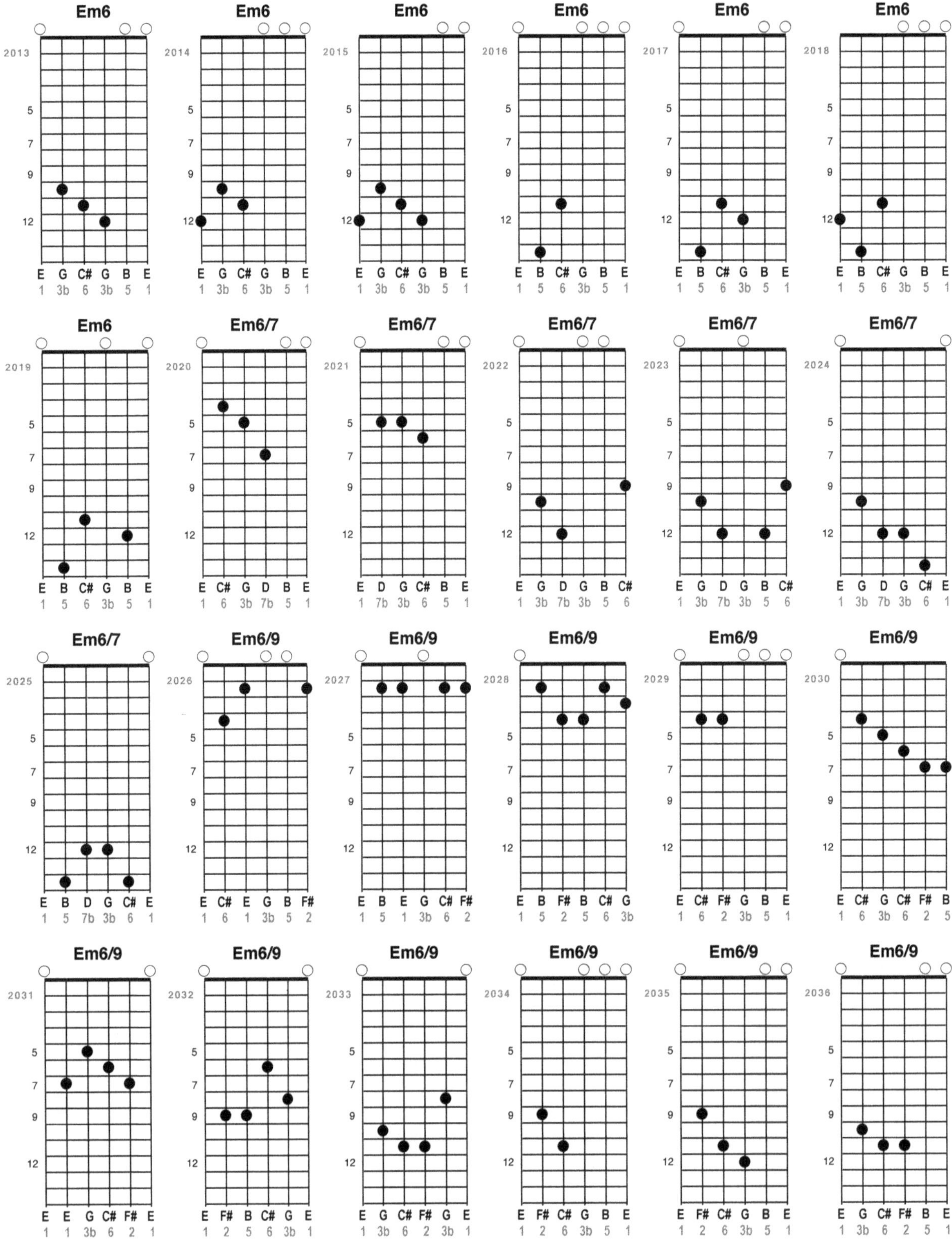

Troubadour Guitar Chords

TUNING: E A D G B E (Standard)

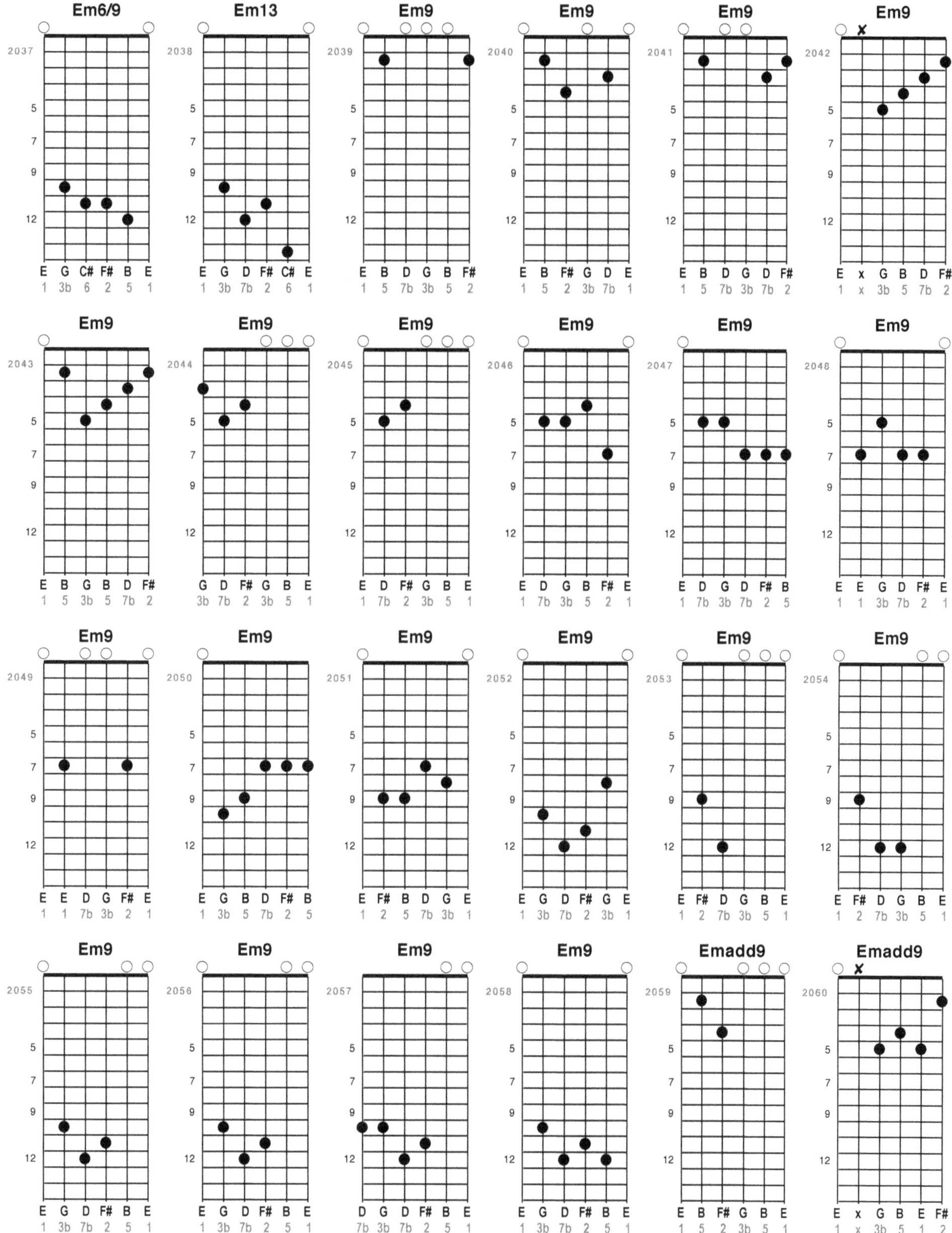

2037 Em6/9
E G C# F# B E
1 3b 6 2 5 1
2038 Em13
E G D F# C# E
1 3b 7b 2 6 1
2039 Em9
E B D G B F#
1 5 7b 3b 5 2
2040 Em9
E B F# G D E
1 5 2 3b 7b 1
2041 Em9
E B D G D F#
1 5 7b 3b 7b 2
2042 Em9
E x G B D F#
1 x 3b 5 7b 2
2043 Em9
E B G B D F#
1 5 3b 5 7b 2
2044 Em9
G D F# G B E
3b 7b 2 3b 5 1
2045 Em9
E D F# G B E
1 7b 2 3b 5 1
2046 Em9
E D G B F# E
1 7b 3b 5 2 1
2047 Em9
E D G D F# B
1 7b 3b 7b 2 5
2048 Em9
E E G D F# E
1 1 3b 7b 2 1
2049 Em9
E E D G F# E
1 1 7b 3b 2 1
2050 Em9
E G B D F# B
1 3b 5 7b 2 5
2051 Em9
E F# B D G E
1 2 5 7b 3b 1
2052 Em9
E G D F# G E
1 3b 7b 2 3b 1
2053 Em9
E F# D G B E
1 2 7b 3b 5 1
2054 Em9
E F# D G B E
1 2 7b 3b 5 1
2055 Em9
E G D F# B E
1 3b 7b 2 5 1
2056 Em9
E G D F# B E
1 3b 7b 2 5 1
2057 Em9
D G D F# B E
7b 3b 7b 2 5 1
2058 Em9
E G D F# B E
1 3b 7b 2 5 1
2059 Emadd9
E B F# G B E
1 5 2 3b 5 1
2060 Emadd9
E x G B E F#
1 x 3b 5 1 2

TUNING: E A D G B E (Standard)

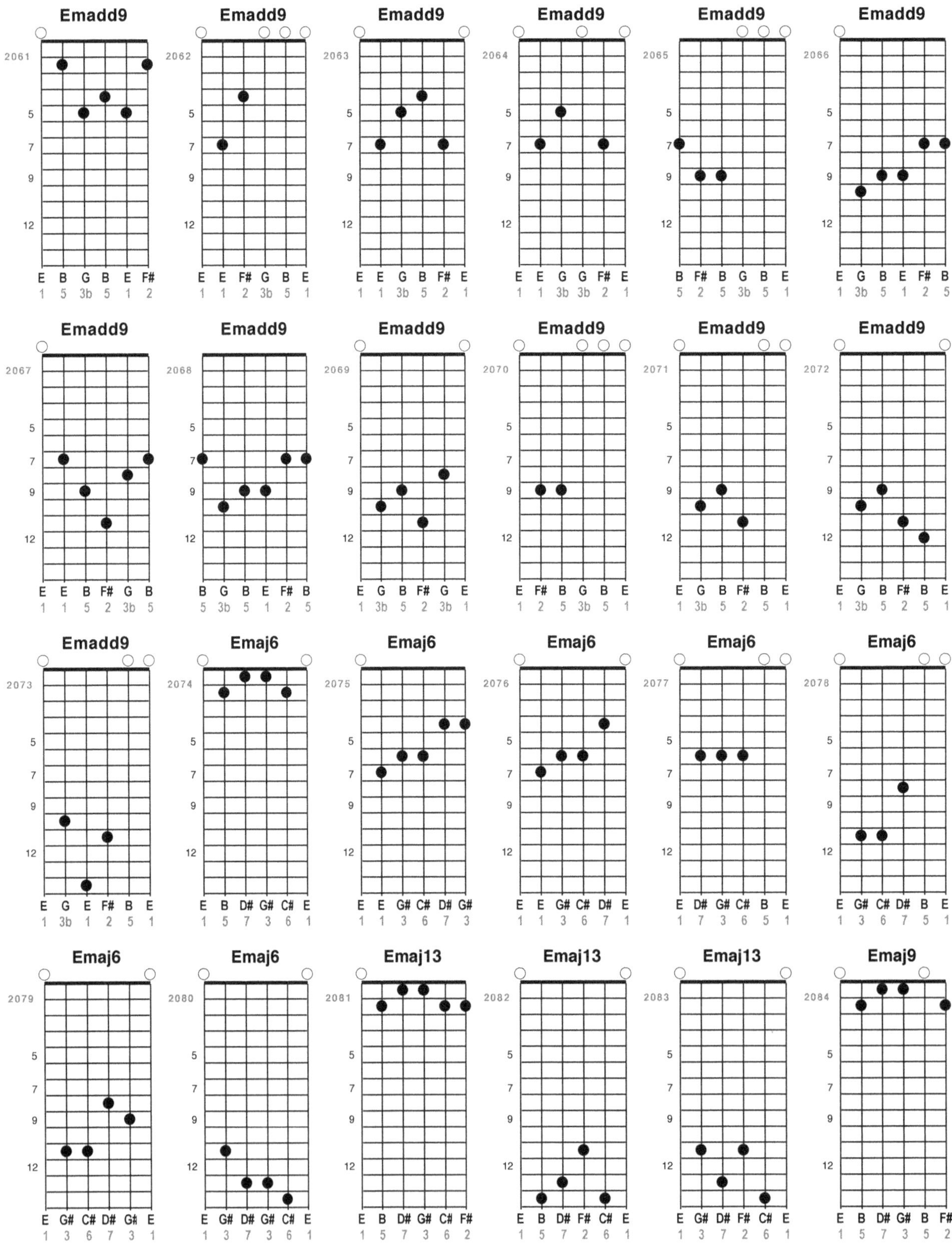
Emadd9 2061 E B G B E F# 1 5 3b 5 1 2
Emadd9 2062 E E F# G B E 1 1 2 3b 5 1
Emadd9 2063 E E G B F# E 1 1 3b 5 2 1
Emadd9 2064 E E G G F# E 1 1 3b 3b 2 1
Emadd9 2065 B F# B G B E 5 2 5 3b 5 1
Emadd9 2066 E G B E F# B 1 3b 5 1 2 5
Emadd9 2067 E E B F# G B 1 1 5 2 3b 5
Emadd9 2068 B G B E F# B 5 3b 5 1 2 5
Emadd9 2069 E G B F# G E 1 3b 5 2 3b 1
Emadd9 2070 E F# B G B E 1 2 5 3b 5 1
Emadd9 2071 E G B F# B E 1 3b 5 2 5 1
Emadd9 2072 E G B F# B E 1 3b 5 2 5 1
Emadd9 2073 E G E F# B E 1 3b 1 2 5 1
Emaj6 2074 E B D# G# C# E 1 5 7 3 6 1
Emaj6 2075 E E G# C# D# G# 1 1 3 6 7 3
Emaj6 2076 E E G# C# D# E 1 1 3 6 7 1
Emaj6 2077 E D# G# C# B E 1 7 3 6 5 1
Emaj6 2078 E G# C# D# B E 1 3 6 7 5 1
Emaj6 2079 E G# C# D# G# E 1 3 6 7 3 1
Emaj6 2080 E G# D# G# C# E 1 3 7 3 6 1
Emaj13 2081 E B D# G# C# F# 1 5 7 3 6 2
Emaj13 2082 E B D# F# C# E 1 5 7 2 6 1
Emaj13 2083 E G# D# F# C# E 1 3 7 2 6 1
Emaj9 2084 E B D# G# B F# 1 5 7 3 5 2

TUNING: E A D G B E (Standard)

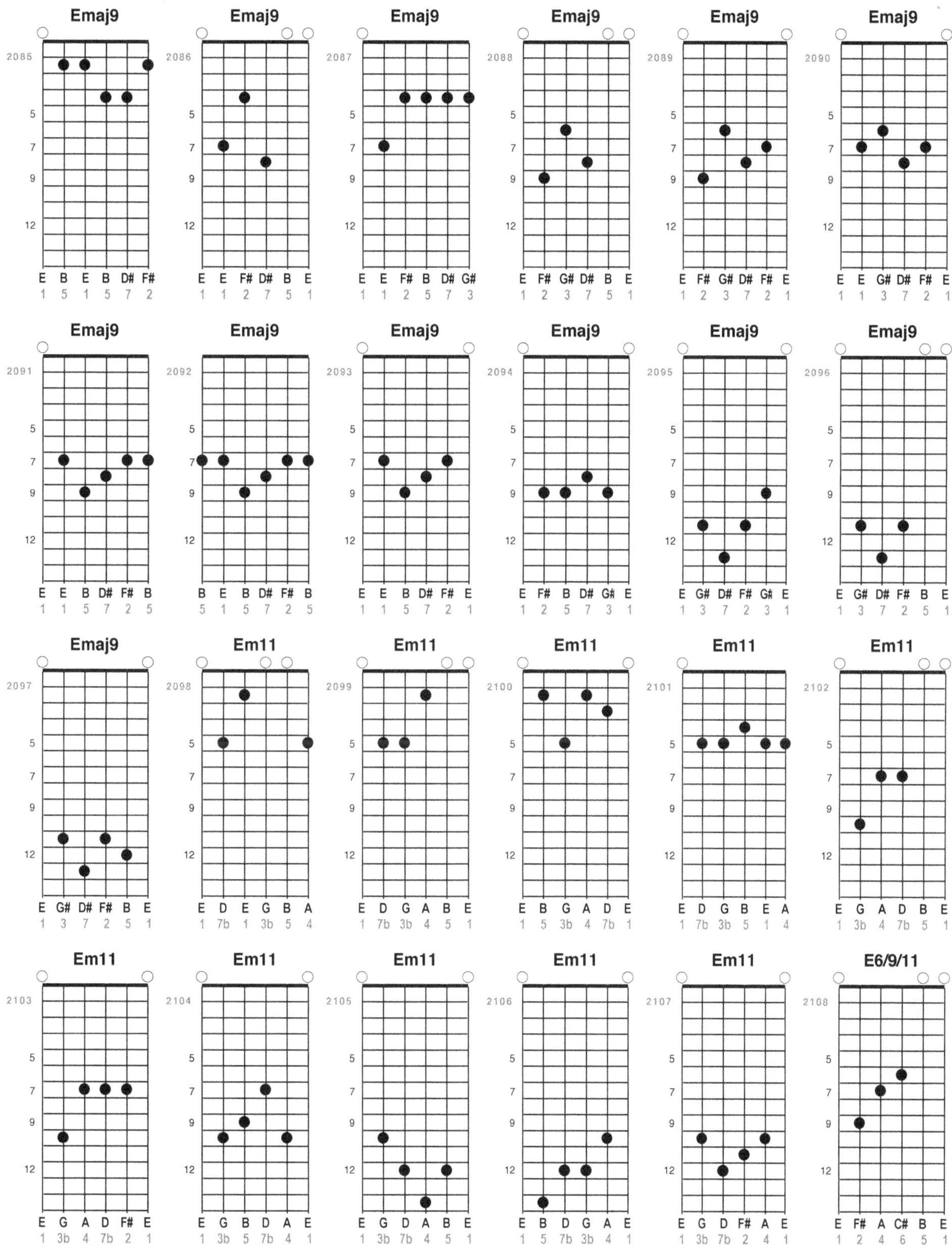
Emaj9
2085
E B E B D# F#
1 5 1 5 7 2
Emaj9
2086
E E F# D# B E
1 1 2 7 5 1
Emaj9
2087
E E F# B D# G#
1 1 2 5 7 3
Emaj9
2088
E F# G# D# B E
1 2 3 7 5 1
Emaj9
2089
E F# G# D# F# E
1 2 3 7 2 1
Emaj9
2090
E E G# D# F# E
1 1 3 7 2 1
Emaj9
2091
E E B D# F# B
1 1 5 7 2 5
Emaj9
2092
B E B D# F# B
5 1 5 7 2 5
Emaj9
2093
E E B D# F# E
1 1 5 7 2 1
Emaj9
2094
E F# B D# G# E
1 2 5 7 3 1
Emaj9
2095
E G# D# F# G# E
1 3 7 2 3 1
Emaj9
2096
E G# D# F# B E
1 3 7 2 5 1
Emaj9
2097
E G# D# F# B E
1 3 7 2 5 1
Em11
2098
E D E G B A
1 7b 1 3b 5 4
Em11
2099
E D G A B E
1 7b 3b 4 5 1
Em11
2100
E B G A D E
1 5 3b 4 7b 1
Em11
2101
E D G B E A
1 7b 3b 5 1 4
Em11
2102
E G A D B E
1 3b 4 7b 5 1
Em11
2103
E G A D F# E
1 3b 4 7b 2 1
Em11
2104
E G B D A E
1 3b 5 7b 4 1
Em11
2105
E G D A B E
1 3b 7b 4 5 1
Em11
2106
E B D G A E
1 5 7b 3b 4 1
Em11
2107
E G D F# A E
1 3b 7b 2 4 1
E6/9/11
2108
E F# A C# B E
1 2 4 6 5 1

TUNING: E A D G B E (Standard)

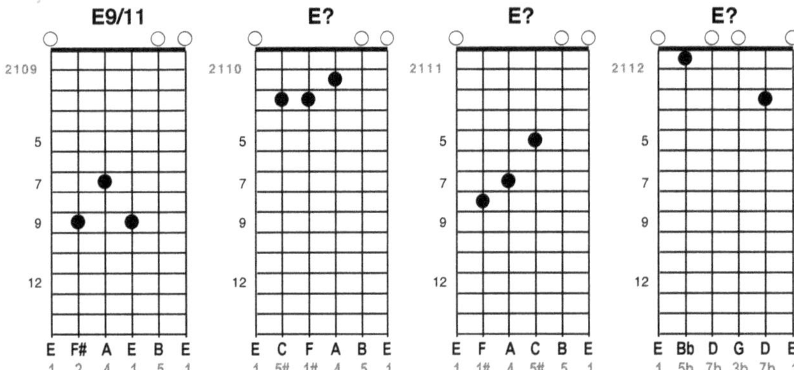
E9/11
2109
5
7
9
12
E F# A E B E
1 2 4 1 5 1
E?
2110
5
7
9
12
E C F A B E
1 5# 1# 4 5 1
E?
2111
5
7
9
12
E F A C B E
1 1# 4 5# 5 1
E?
2112
5
7
9
12
E Bb D G D E
1 5b 7b 3b 7b 1

The only name I can find for this common chord is the "Phrygian Suspended"

TUNING: E A D G B E (Standard)

F

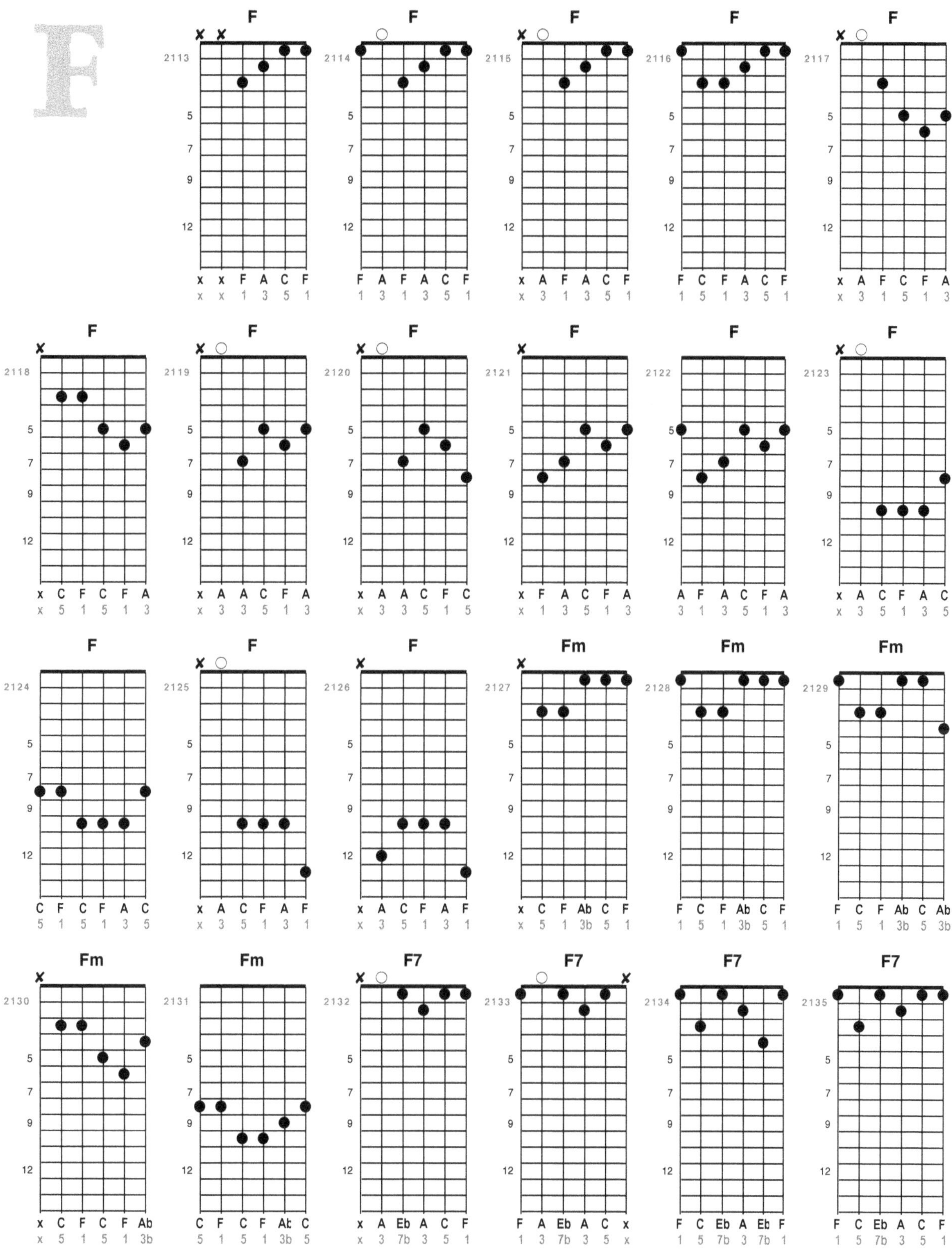

TUNING: E A D G B E (Standard)

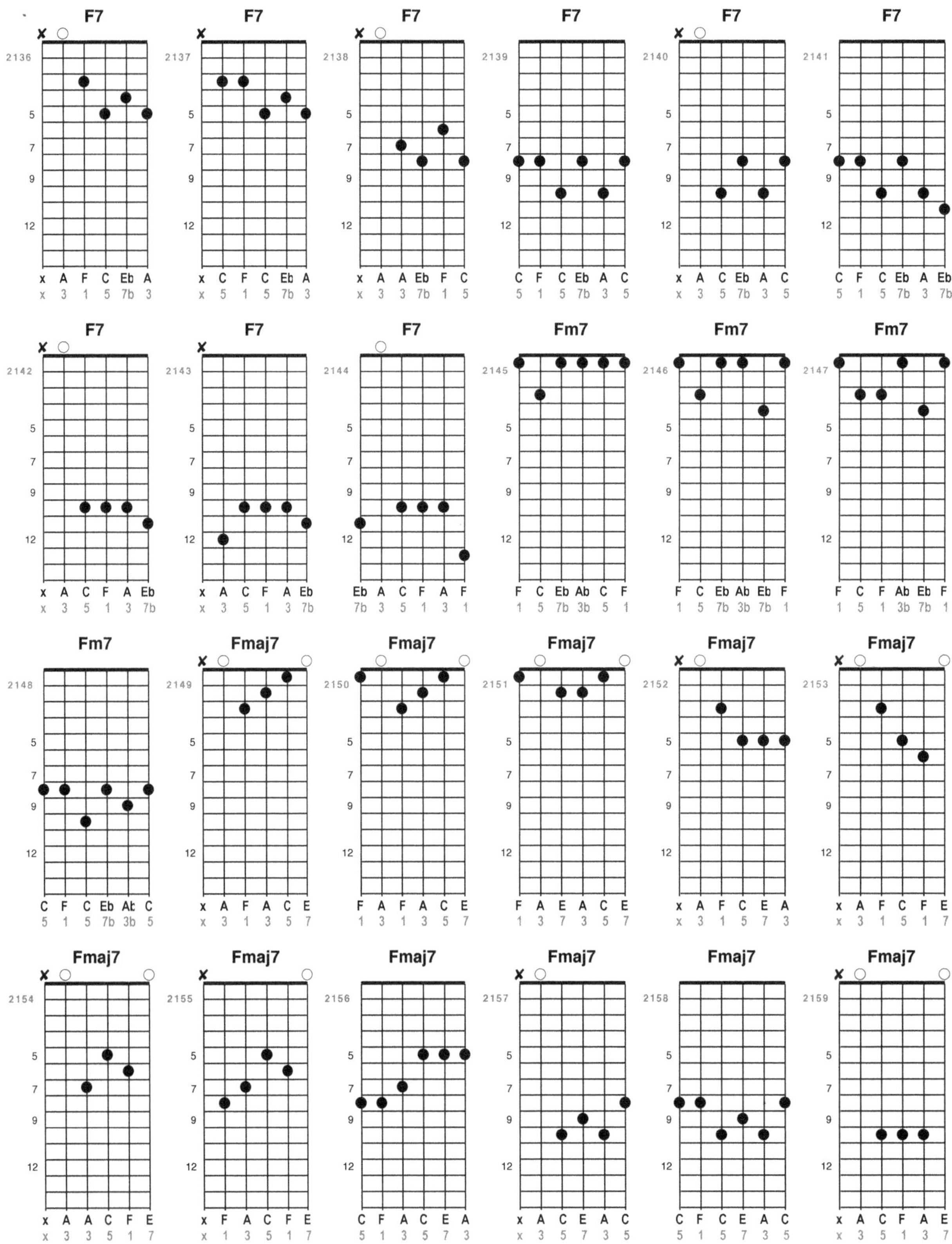
F7
2136
x A F C Eb A
x 3 1 5 7b 3
F7
2137
x C F C Eb A
x 5 1 5 7b 3
F7
2138
x A A Eb F C
x 3 3 7b 1 5
F7
2139
C F C Eb A C
5 1 5 7b 3 5
F7
2140
x A C Eb A C
x 3 5 7b 3 5
F7
2141
C F C Eb A Eb
5 1 5 7b 3 7b
F7
2142
x A C F A Eb
x 3 5 1 3 7b
F7
2143
x A C F A Eb
x 3 5 1 3 7b
F7
2144
Eb A C F A F
7b 3 5 1 3 1
Fm7
2145
F C Eb Ab C F
1 5 7b 3b 5 1
Fm7
2146
F C Eb Ab Eb F
1 5 7b 3b 7b 1
Fm7
2147
F C F Ab Eb F
1 5 1 3b 7b 1
Fm7
2148
C F C Eb Ab C
5 1 5 7b 3b 5
Fmaj7
2149
x A F A C E
x 3 1 3 5 7
Fmaj7
2150
F A F A C E
1 3 1 3 5 7
Fmaj7
2151
F A E A C E
1 3 7 3 5 7
Fmaj7
2152
x A F C E A
x 3 1 5 7 3
Fmaj7
2153
x A F C F E
x 3 1 5 1 7
Fmaj7
2154
x A A C F E
x 3 3 5 1 7
Fmaj7
2155
x F A C F E
x 1 3 5 1 7
Fmaj7
2156
C F A C E A
5 1 3 5 7 3
Fmaj7
2157
x A C E A C
x 3 5 7 3 5
Fmaj7
2158
C F C E A C
5 1 5 7 3 5
Fmaj7
2159
x A C F A E
x 3 5 1 3 7

TUNING: E A D G B E (Standard)

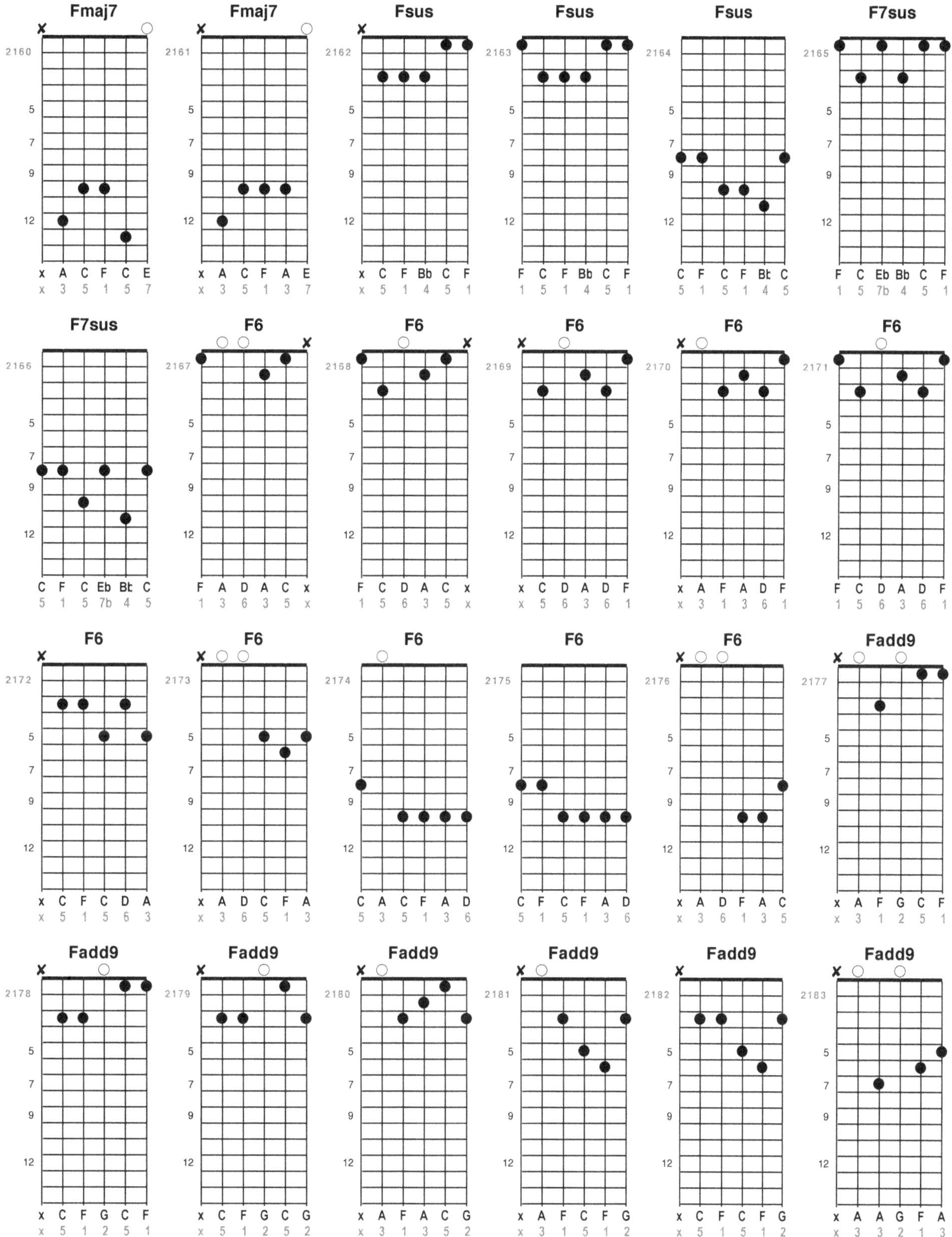

TUNING: E A D G B E (Standard)

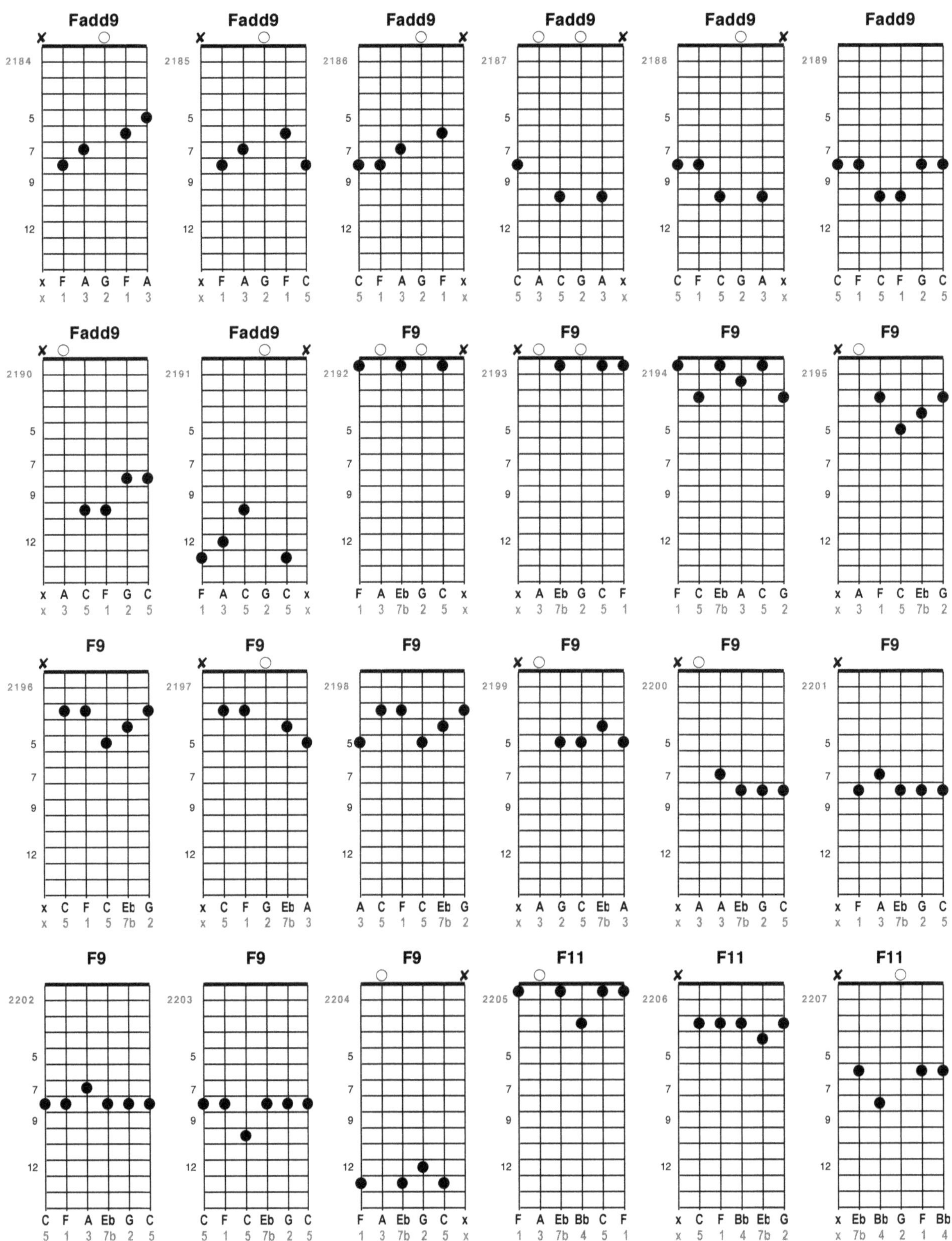
Fadd9
2184
x F A G F A
x 1 3 2 1 3
Fadd9
2185
x F A G F C
x 1 3 2 1 5
Fadd9
2186
C F A G F x
5 1 3 2 1 x
Fadd9
2187
C A C G A x
5 3 5 2 3 x
Fadd9
2188
C F C G A x
5 1 5 2 3 x
Fadd9
2189
C F C F G C
5 1 5 1 2 5
Fadd9
2190
x A C F G C
x 3 5 1 2 5
Fadd9
2191
F A C G C x
1 3 5 2 5 x
F9
2192
F A Eb G C x
1 3 7b 2 5 x
F9
2193
x A Eb G C F
x 3 7b 2 5 1
F9
2194
F C Eb A C G
1 5 7b 3 5 2
F9
2195
x A F C Eb G
x 3 1 5 7b 2
F9
2196
x C F C Eb G
x 5 1 5 7b 2
F9
2197
x C F G Eb A
x 5 1 2 7b 3
F9
2198
A C F C Eb G
3 5 1 5 7b 2
F9
2199
x A G C Eb A
x 3 2 5 7b 3
F9
2200
x A A Eb G C
x 3 3 7b 2 5
F9
2201
x F A Eb G C
x 1 3 7b 2 5
F9
2202
C F A Eb G C
5 1 3 7b 2 5
F9
2203
C F C Eb G C
5 1 5 7b 2 5
F9
2204
F A Eb G C x
1 3 7b 2 5 x
F11
2205
F A Eb Bb C F
1 3 7b 4 5 1
F11
2206
x C F Bb Eb G
x 5 1 4 7b 2
F11
2207
x Eb Bb G F Bb
x 7b 4 2 1 4

TUNING: E A D G B E (Standard)

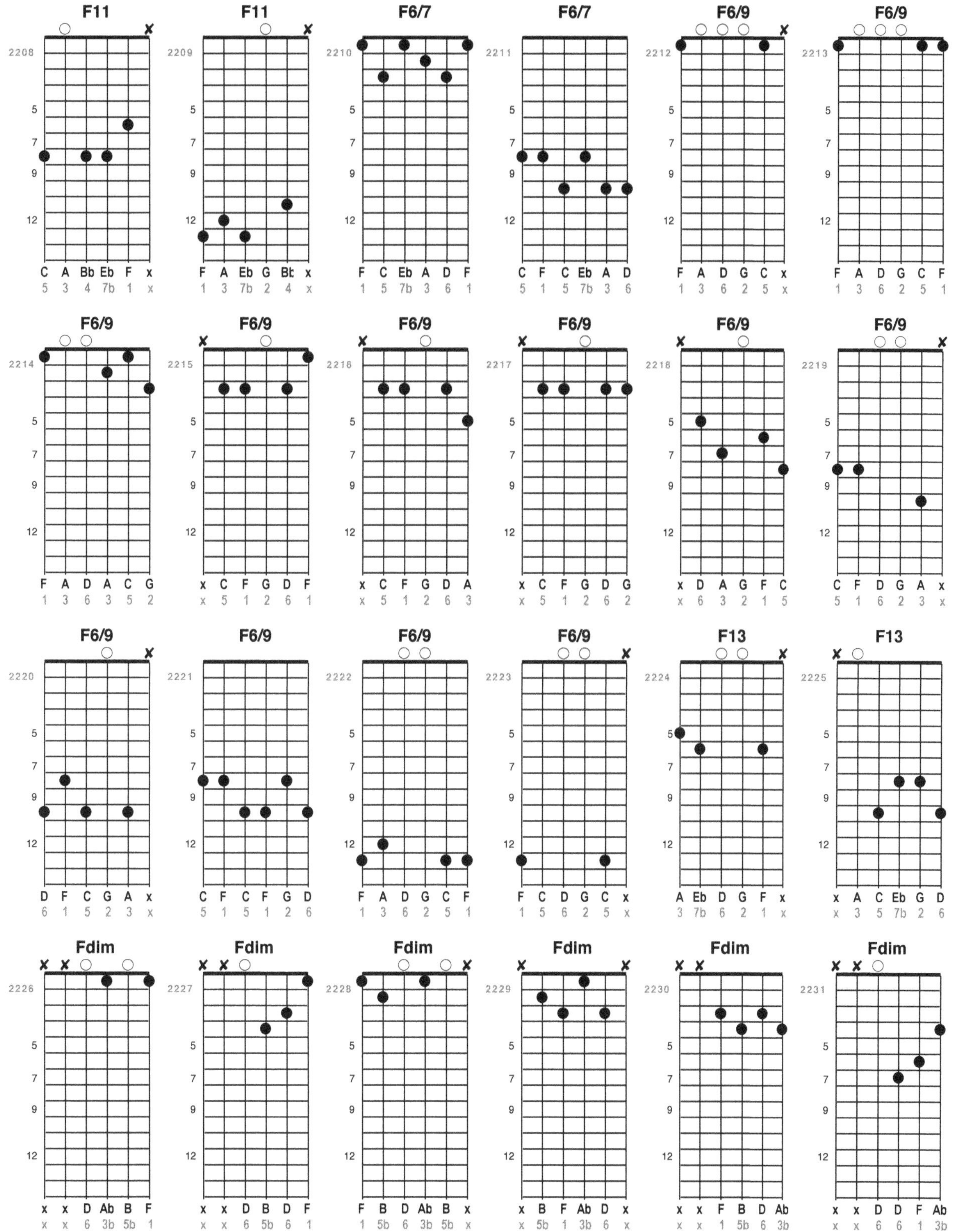
F11
2208
C A Bb Eb F x
5 3 4 7b 1 x
F11
2209
F A Eb G Bb x
1 3 7b 2 4 x
F6/7
2210
F C Eb A D F
1 5 7b 3 6 1
F6/7
2211
C F C Eb A D
5 1 5 7b 3 6
F6/9
2212
F A D G C x
1 3 6 2 5 x
F6/9
2213
F A D G C F
1 3 6 2 5 1
F6/9
2214
F A D A C G
1 3 6 3 5 2
F6/9
2215
x C F G D F
x 5 1 2 6 1
F6/9
2216
x C F G D A
x 5 1 2 6 3
F6/9
2217
x C F G D G
x 5 1 2 6 2
F6/9
2218
x D A G F C
x 6 3 2 1 5
F6/9
2219
C F D G A x
5 1 6 2 3 x
F6/9
2220
D F C G A x
6 1 5 2 3 x
F6/9
2221
C F C F G D
5 1 5 1 2 6
F6/9
2222
F A D G C F
1 3 6 2 5 1
F6/9
2223
F C D G C x
1 5 6 2 5 x
F13
2224
A Eb D G F x
3 7b 6 2 1 x
F13
2225
x A C Eb G D
x 3 5 7b 2 6
Fdim
2226
x x D Ab B F
x x 6 3b 5b 1
Fdim
2227
x x D B D F
x x 6 5b 6 1
Fdim
2228
F B D Ab B x
1 5b 6 3b 5b x
Fdim
2229
x B F Ab D x
x 5b 1 3b 6 x
Fdim
2230
x x F B D Ab
x x 1 5b 6 3b
Fdim
2231
x x D D F Ab
x x 6 6 1 3b

TUNING: E A D G B E (Standard)

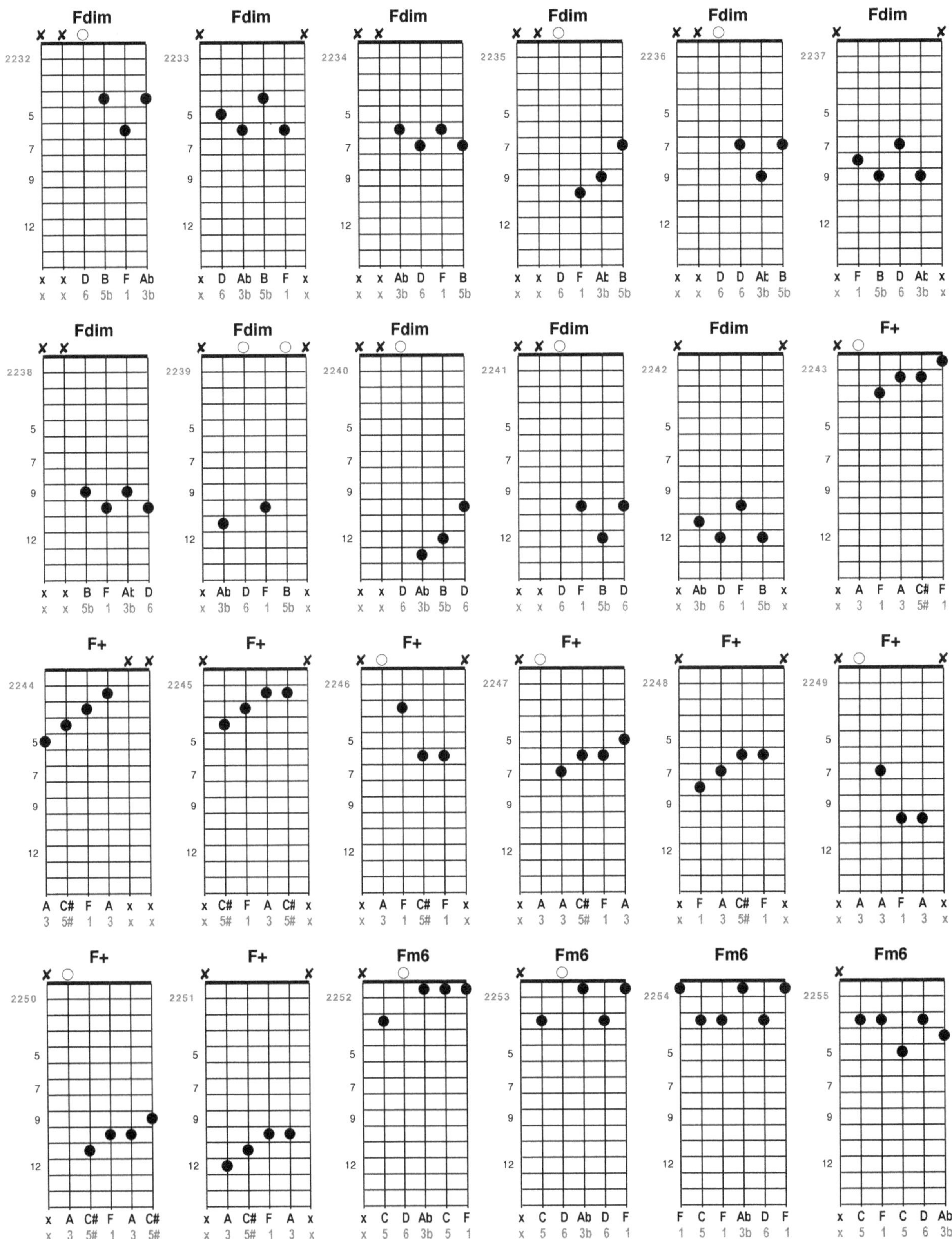

TUNING: E A D G B E (Standard)

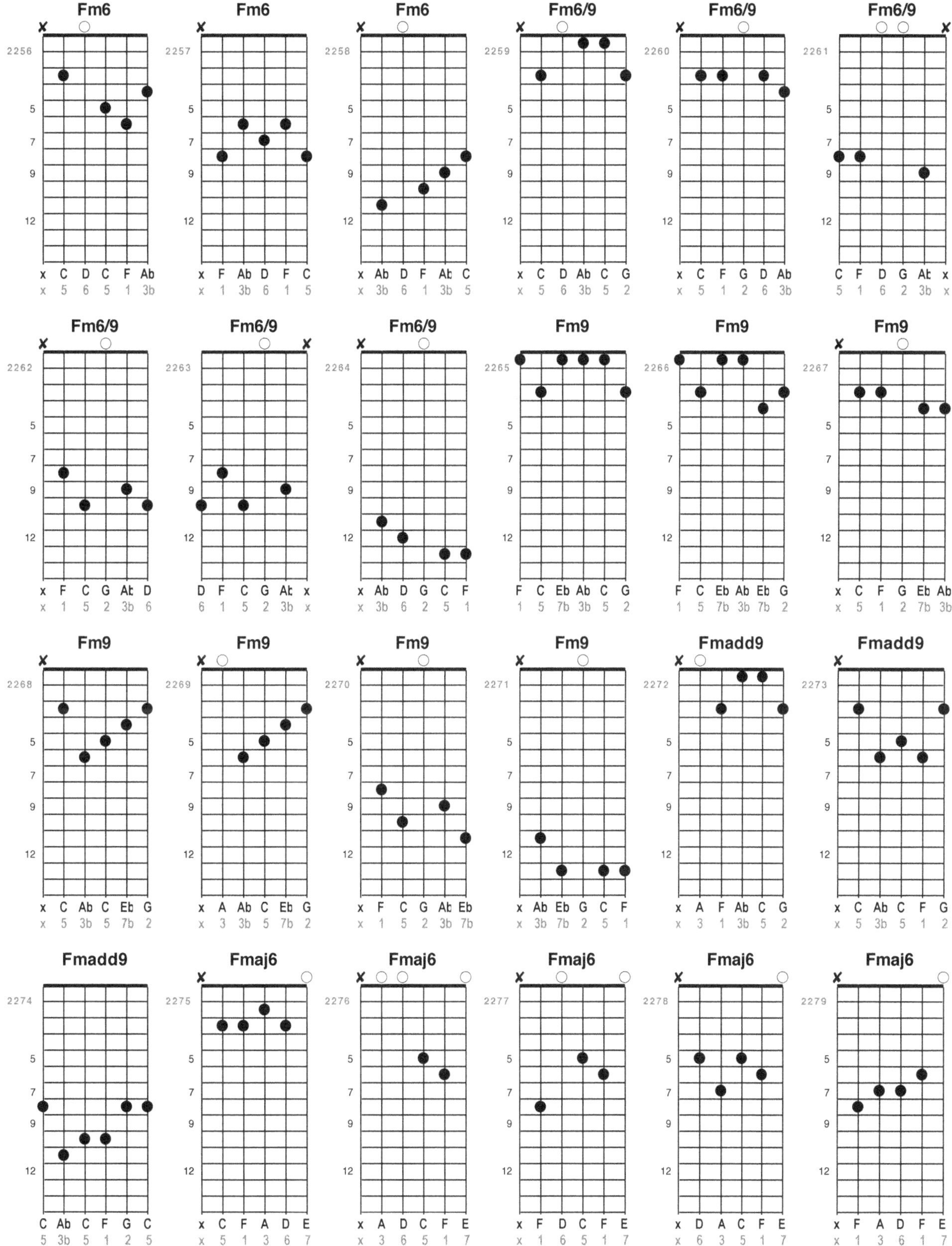
Fm6
2256
x C D C F Ab
x 5 6 5 1 3b
Fm6
2257
x F Ab D F C
x 1 3b 6 1 5
Fm6
2258
x Ab D F Ab C
x 3b 6 1 3b 5
Fm6/9
2259
x C D Ab C G
x 5 6 3b 5 2
Fm6/9
2260
x C F G D Ab
x 5 1 2 6 3b
Fm6/9
2261
C F D G Ab x
5 1 6 2 3b x
Fm6/9
2262
x F C G Ab D
x 1 5 2 3b 6
Fm6/9
2263
D F C G Ab x
6 1 5 2 3b x
Fm6/9
2264
x Ab D G C F
x 3b 6 2 5 1
Fm9
2265
F C Eb Ab C G
1 5 7b 3b 5 2
Fm9
2266
F C Eb Ab Eb G
1 5 7b 3b 7b 2
Fm9
2267
x C F G Eb Ab
x 5 1 2 7b 3b
Fm9
2268
x C Ab C Eb G
x 5 3b 5 7b 2
Fm9
2269
x A Ab C Eb G
x 3 3b 5 7b 2
Fm9
2270
x F C G Ab Eb
x 1 5 2 3b 7b
Fm9
2271
x Ab Eb G C F
x 3b 7b 2 5 1
Fmadd9
2272
x A F Ab C G
x 3 1 3b 5 2
Fmadd9
2273
x C Ab C F G
x 5 3b 5 1 2
Fmadd9
2274
C Ab C F G C
5 3b 5 1 2 5
Fmaj6
2275
x C F A D E
x 5 1 3 6 7
Fmaj6
2276
x A D C F E
x 3 6 5 1 7
Fmaj6
2277
x F D C F E
x 1 6 5 1 7
Fmaj6
2278
x D A C F E
x 6 3 5 1 7
Fmaj6
2279
x F A D F E
x 1 3 6 1 7
5
7
9
12

TUNING: E A D G B E (Standard)

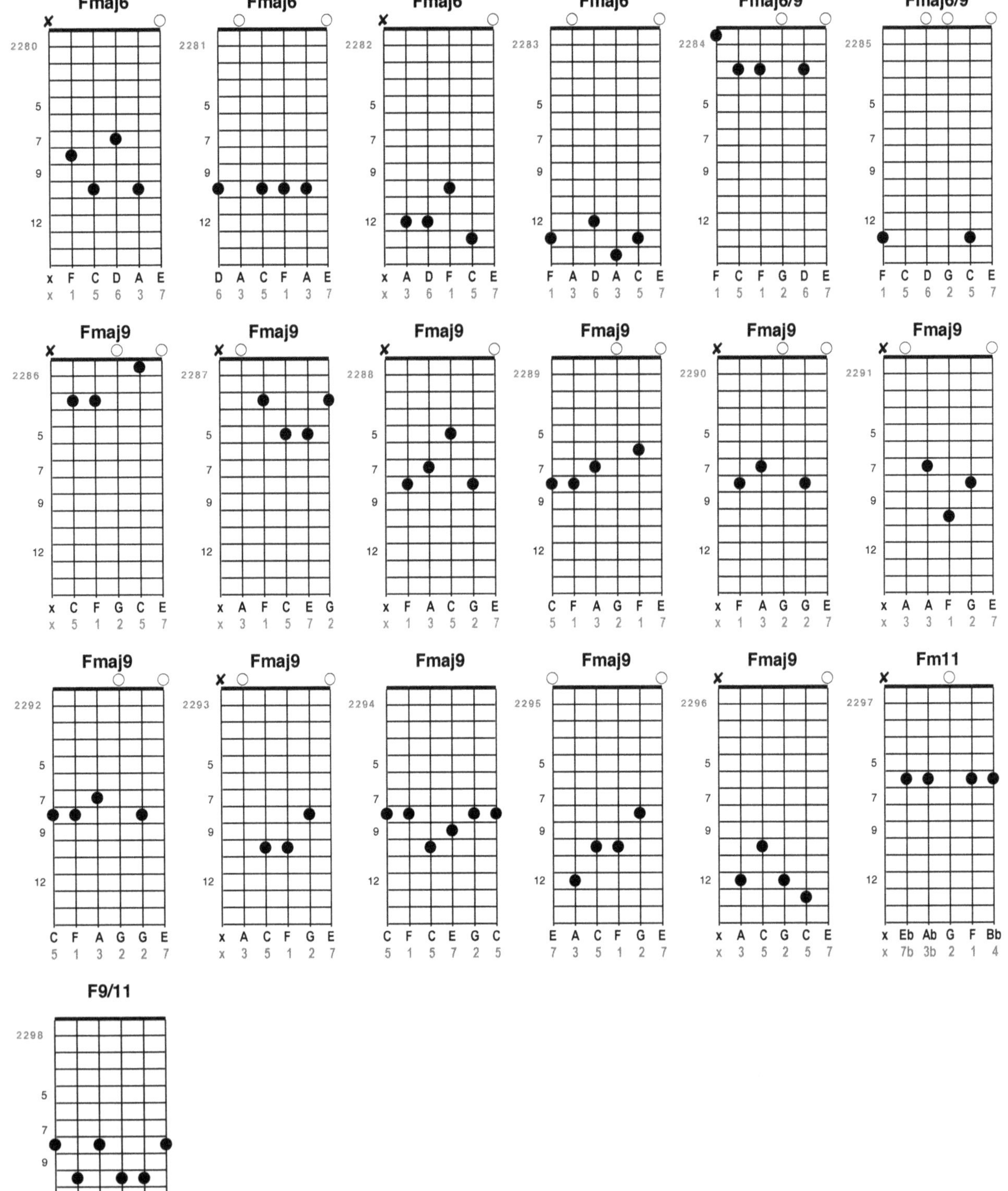
Fmaj6
2280
x F C D A E
x 1 5 6 3 7
Fmaj6
2281
D A C F A E
6 3 5 1 3 7
Fmaj6
2282
x A D F C E
x 3 6 1 5 7
Fmaj6
2283
F A D A C E
1 3 6 3 5 7
Fmaj6/9
2284
F C F G D E
1 5 1 2 6 7
Fmaj6/9
2285
F C D G C E
1 5 6 2 5 7
Fmaj9
2286
x C F G C E
x 5 1 2 5 7
Fmaj9
2287
x A F C E G
x 3 1 5 7 2
Fmaj9
2288
x F A C G E
x 1 3 5 2 7
Fmaj9
2289
C F A G F E
5 1 3 2 1 7
Fmaj9
2290
x F A G G E
x 1 3 2 2 7
Fmaj9
2291
x A A F G E
x 3 3 1 2 7
Fmaj9
2292
C F A G G E
5 1 3 2 2 7
Fmaj9
2293
x A C F G E
x 3 5 1 2 7
Fmaj9
2294
C F C E G C
5 1 5 7 2 5
Fmaj9
2295
E A C F G E
7 3 5 1 2 7
Fmaj9
2296
x A C G C E
x 3 5 2 5 7
Fm11
2297
x Eb Ab G F Bb
x 7b 3b 2 1 4
F9/11
2298
C G Bb F A C
5 2 4 1 3 5

TUNING: E A D G B E (Standard)

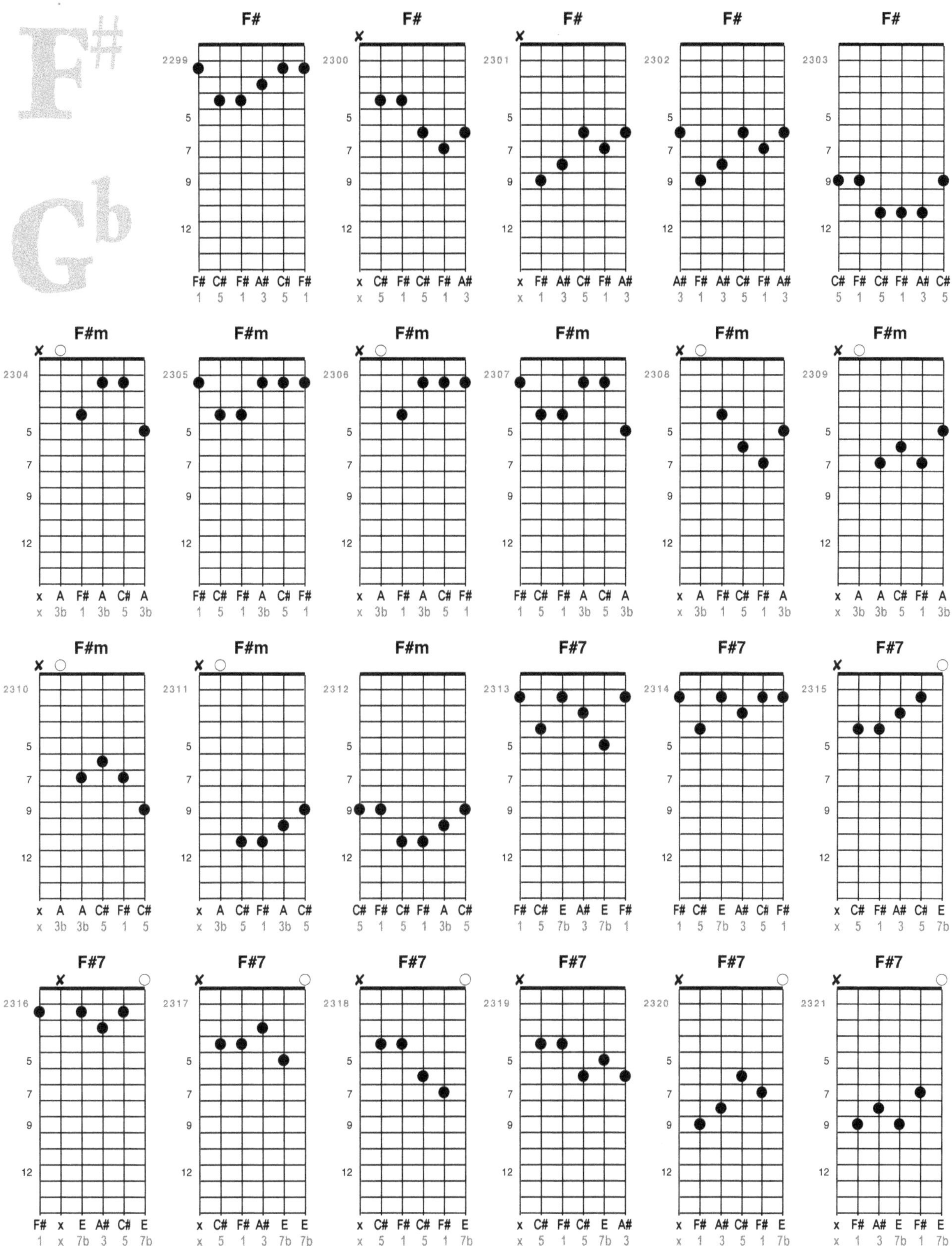
F#
Gb
F#
2299
F# C# F# A# C# F#
1 5 1 3 5 1
F#
2300
x C# F# C# F# A#
x 5 1 5 1 3
F#
2301
x F# A# C# F# A#
x 1 3 5 1 3
F#
2302
A# F# A# C# F# A#
3 1 3 5 1 3
F#
2303
C# F# C# F# A# C#
5 1 5 1 3 5
F#m
2304
x A F# A C# A
x 3b 1 3b 5 3b
F#m
2305
F# C# F# A C# F#
1 5 1 3b 5 1
F#m
2306
x A F# A C# F#
x 3b 1 3b 5 1
F#m
2307
F# C# F# A C# A
1 5 1 3b 5 3b
F#m
2308
x A F# C# F# A
x 3b 1 5 1 3b
F#m
2309
x A A C# F# A
x 3b 3b 5 1 3b
F#m
2310
x A A C# F# C#
x 3b 3b 5 1 5
F#m
2311
x A C# F# A C#
x 3b 5 1 3b 5
F#m
2312
C# F# C# F# A C#
5 1 5 1 3b 5
F#7
2313
F# C# E A# E F#
1 5 7b 3 7b 1
F#7
2314
F# C# E A# C# F#
1 5 7b 3 5 1
F#7
2315
x C# F# A# C# E
x 5 1 3 5 7b
F#7
2316
F# x E A# C# E
1 x 7b 3 5 7b
F#7
2317
x C# F# A# E E
x 5 1 3 7b 7b
F#7
2318
x C# F# C# F# E
x 5 1 5 1 7b
F#7
2319
x C# F# C# E A#
x 5 1 5 7b 3
F#7
2320
x F# A# C# F# E
x 1 3 5 1 7b
F#7
2321
x F# A# E F# E
x 1 3 7b 1 7b

TUNING: E A D G B E (Standard)

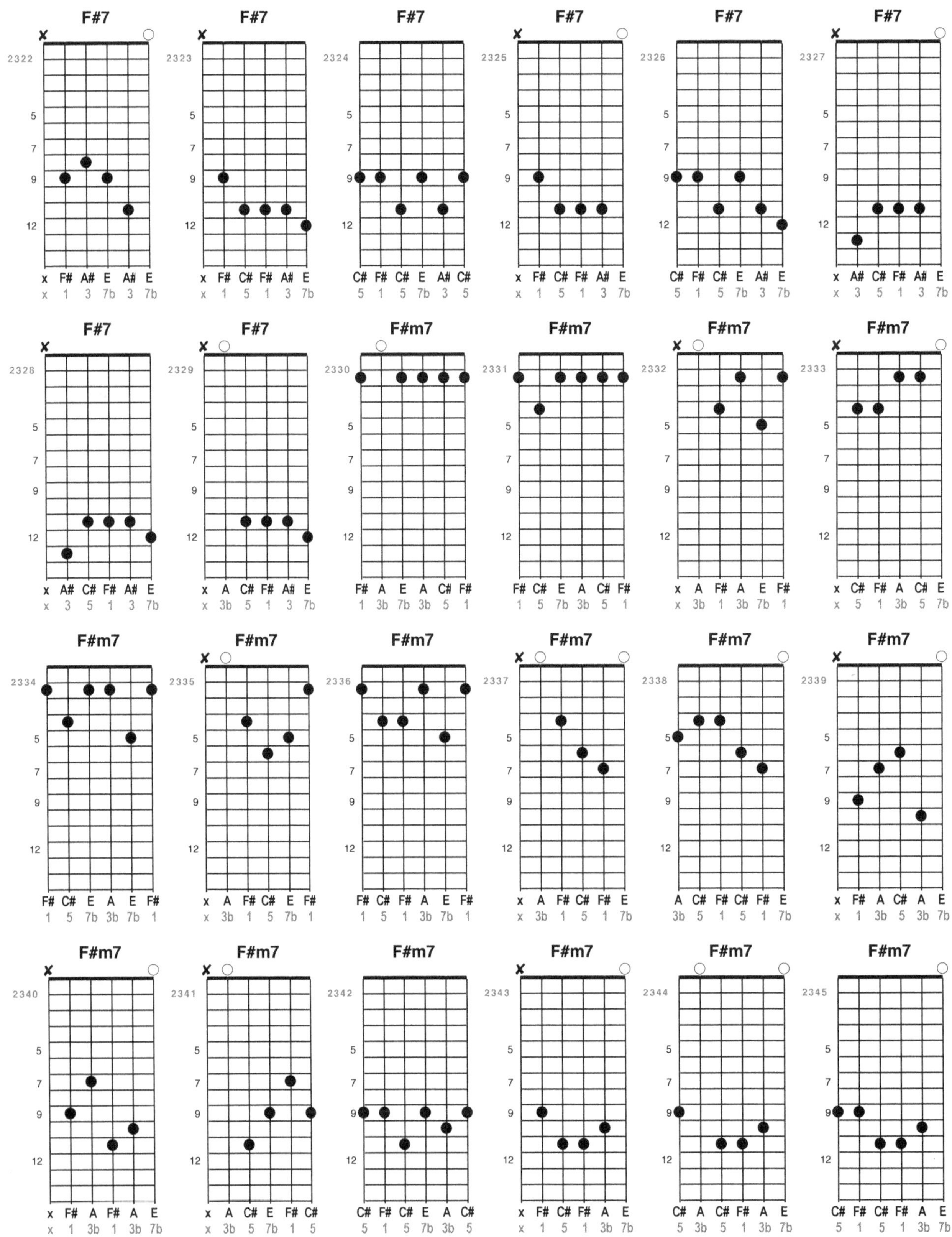
F#7
2322
x F# A# E A# E
x 1 3 7b 3 7b
F#7
2323
x F# C# F# A# E
x 1 5 1 3 7b
F#7
2324
C# F# C# E A# C#
5 1 5 7b 3 5
F#7
2325
x F# C# F# A# E
x 1 5 1 3 7b
F#7
2326
C# F# C# E A# E
5 1 5 7b 3 7b
F#7
2327
x A# C# F# A# E
x 3 5 1 3 7b
F#7
2328
x A# C# F# A# E
x 3 5 1 3 7b
F#7
2329
x A C# F# A# E
x 3b 5 1 3 7b
F#m7
2330
F# A E A C# F#
1 3b 7b 3b 5 1
F#m7
2331
F# C# E A C# F#
1 5 7b 3b 5 1
F#m7
2332
x A F# A E F#
x 3b 1 3b 7b 1
F#m7
2333
x C# F# A C# E
x 5 1 3b 5 7b
F#m7
2334
F# C# E A E F#
1 5 7b 3b 7b 1
F#m7
2335
x A F# C# E F#
x 3b 1 5 7b 1
F#m7
2336
F# C# F# A E F#
1 5 1 3b 7b 1
F#m7
2337
x A F# C# F# E
x 3b 1 5 1 7b
F#m7
2338
A C# F# C# F# E
3b 5 1 5 1 7b
F#m7
2339
x F# A C# A E
x 1 3b 5 3b 7b
F#m7
2340
x F# A F# A E
x 1 3b 1 3b 7b
F#m7
2341
x A C# E F# C#
x 3b 5 7b 1 5
F#m7
2342
C# F# C# E A C#
5 1 5 7b 3b 5
F#m7
2343
x F# C# F# A E
x 1 5 1 3b 7b
F#m7
2344
C# A C# F# A E
5 3b 5 1 3b 7b
F#m7
2345
C# F# C# F# A E
5 1 5 1 3b 7b

Troubadour Guitar Chords

TUNING: E A D G B E (Standard)

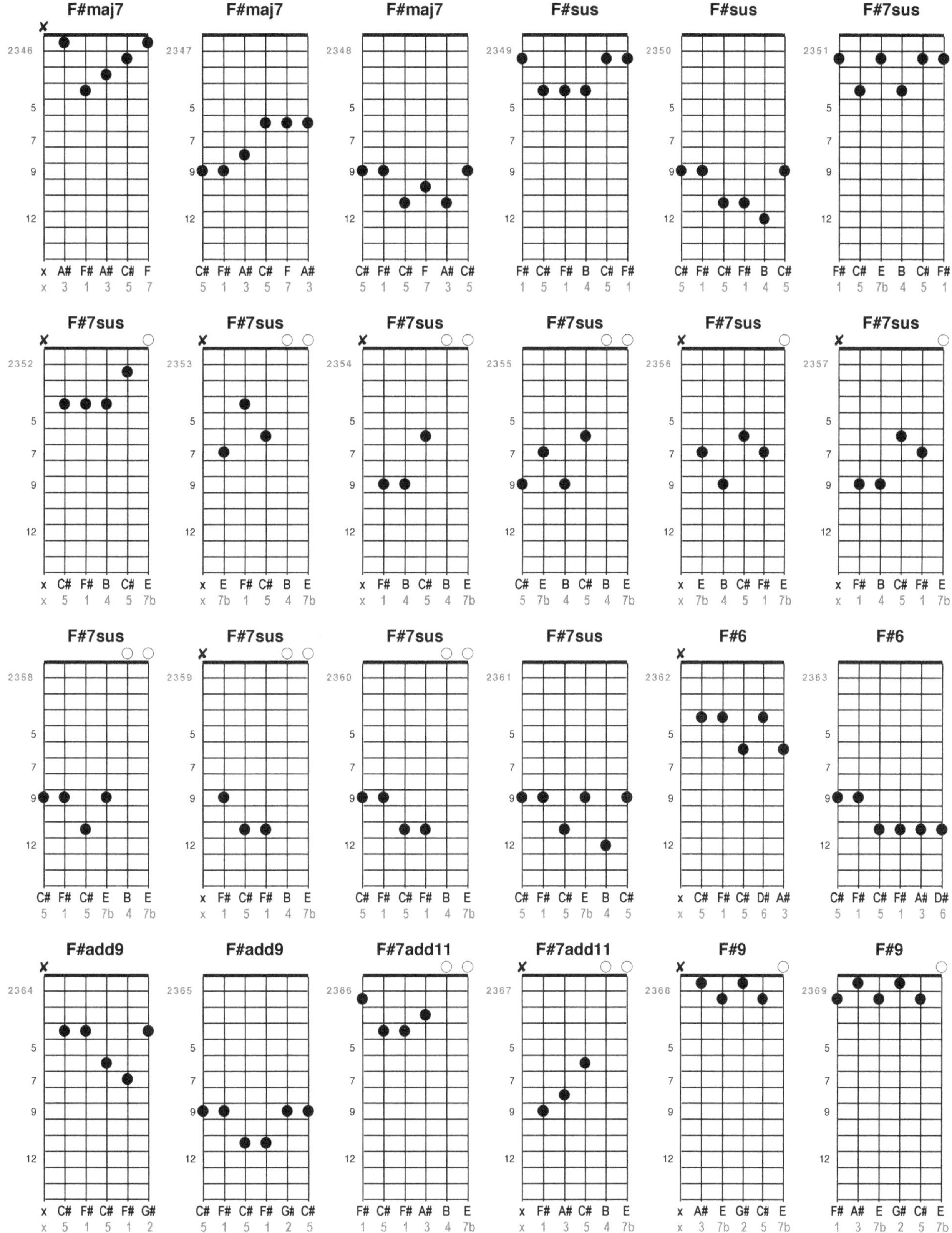

Troubadour Guitar Chords

TUNING: E A D G B E (Standard)

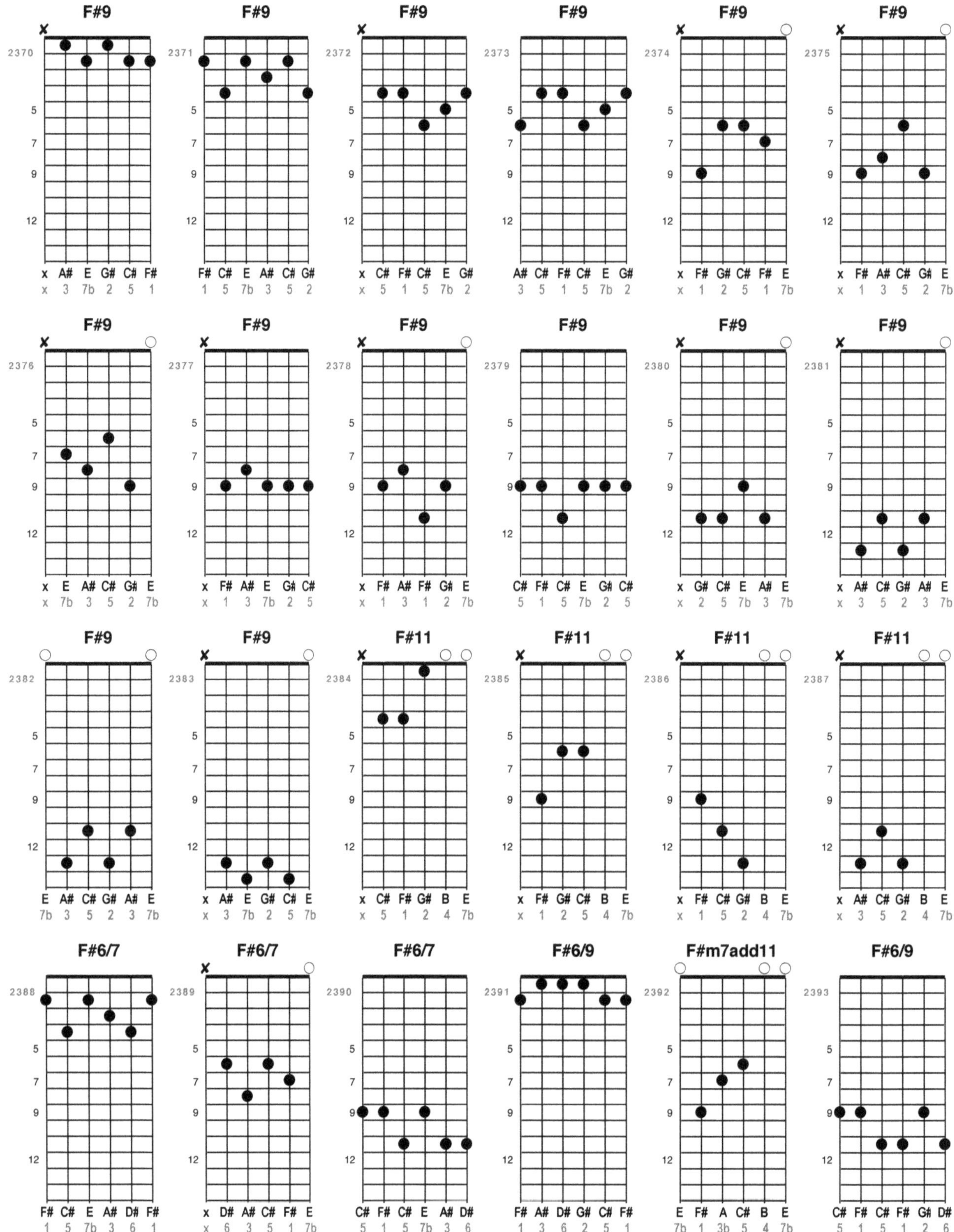
F#9
2370
x A# E G# C# F#
x 3 7b 2 5 1
F#9
2371
F# C# E A# C# G#
1 5 7b 3 5 2
F#9
2372
x C# F# C# E G#
x 5 1 5 7b 2
F#9
2373
A# C# F# C# E G#
3 5 1 5 7b 2
F#9
2374
x F# G# C# F# E
x 1 2 5 1 7b
F#9
2375
x F# A# C# G# E
x 1 3 5 2 7b
F#9
2376
x E A# C# G# E
x 7b 3 5 2 7b
F#9
2377
x F# A# E G# C#
x 1 3 7b 2 5
F#9
2378
x F# A# F# G# E
x 1 3 1 2 7b
F#9
2379
C# F# C# E G# C#
5 1 5 7b 2 5
F#9
2380
x G# C# E A# E
x 2 5 7b 3 7b
F#9
2381
x A# C# G# A# E
x 3 5 2 3 7b
F#9
2382
E A# C# G# A# E
7b 3 5 2 3 7b
F#9
2383
x A# E G# C# E
x 3 7b 2 5 7b
F#11
2384
x C# F# G# B E
x 5 1 2 4 7b
F#11
2385
x F# G# C# B E
x 1 2 5 4 7b
F#11
2386
x F# C# G# B E
x 1 5 2 4 7b
F#11
2387
x A# C# G# B E
x 3 5 2 4 7b
F#6/7
2388
F# C# E A# D# F#
1 5 7b 3 6 1
F#6/7
2389
x D# A# C# F# E
x 6 3 5 1 7b
F#6/7
2390
C# F# C# E A# D#
5 1 5 7b 3 6
F#6/9
2391
F# A# D# G# C# F#
1 3 6 2 5 1
F#m7add11
2392
E F# A C# B E
7b 1 3b 5 4 7b
F#6/9
2393
C# F# C# F# G# D#
5 1 5 1 2 6

TUNING: E A D G B E (Standard)

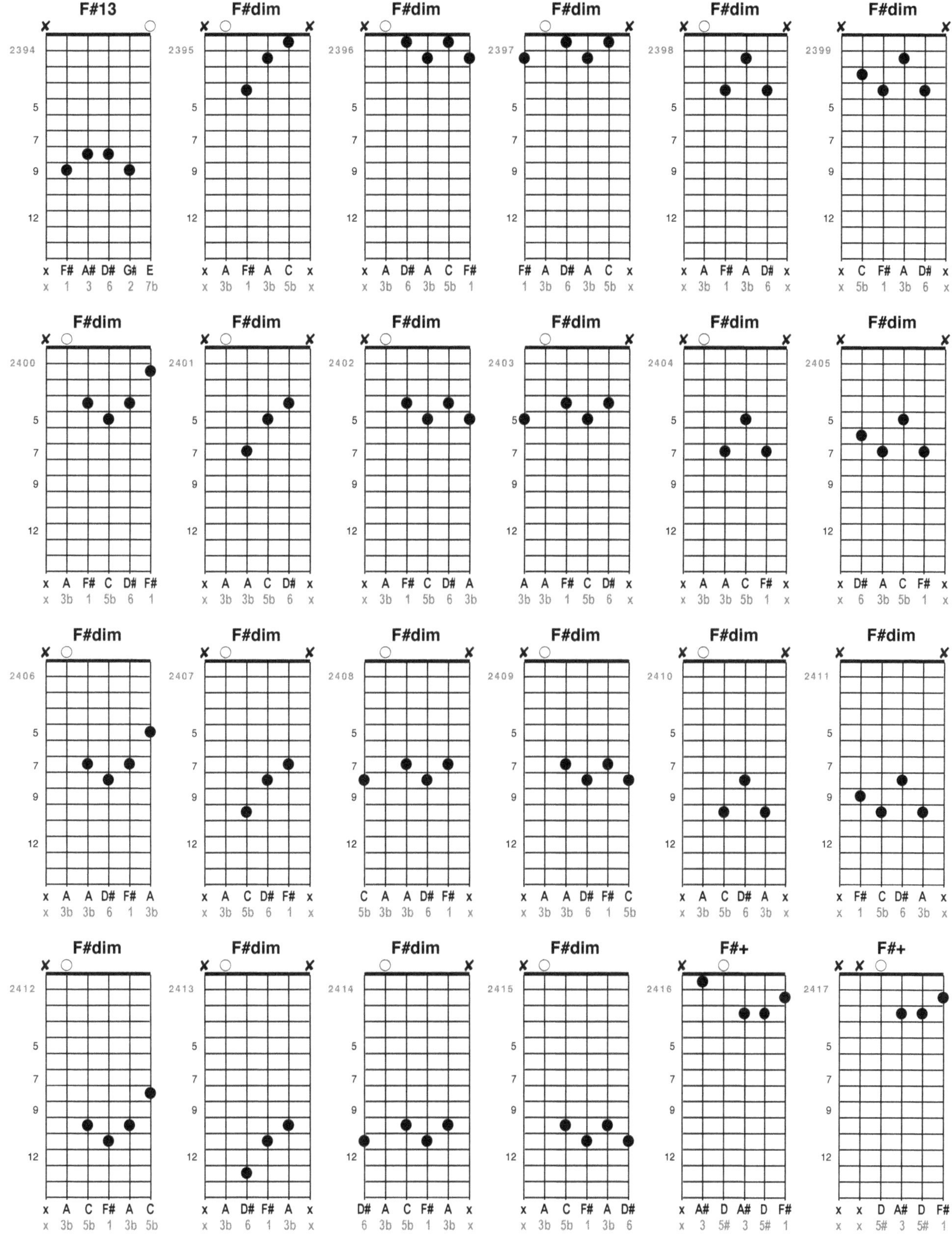
F#13
2394
x F# A# D# G# E
x 1 3 6 2 7b
F#dim
2395
x A F# A C x
x 3b 1 3b 5b x
F#dim
2396
x A D# A C F#
x 3b 6 3b 5b 1
F#dim
2397
F# A D# A C x
1 3b 6 3b 5b x
F#dim
2398
x A F# A D# x
x 3b 1 3b 6 x
F#dim
2399
x C F# A D# x
x 5b 1 3b 6 x
F#dim
2400
x A F# C D# F#
x 3b 1 5b 6 1
F#dim
2401
x A A C D# x
x 3b 3b 5b 6 x
F#dim
2402
x A F# C D# A
x 3b 1 5b 6 3b
F#dim
2403
A A F# C D# x
3b 3b 1 5b 6 x
F#dim
2404
x A A C F# x
x 3b 3b 5b 1 x
F#dim
2405
x D# A C F# x
x 6 3b 5b 1 x
F#dim
2406
x A A D# F# A
x 3b 3b 6 1 3b
F#dim
2407
x A C D# F# x
x 3b 5b 6 1 x
F#dim
2408
C A A D# F# x
5b 3b 3b 6 1 x
F#dim
2409
x A A D# F# C
x 3b 3b 6 1 5b
F#dim
2410
x A C D# A x
x 3b 5b 6 3b x
F#dim
2411
x F# C D# A x
x 1 5b 6 3b x
F#dim
2412
x A C F# A C
x 3b 5b 1 3b 5b
F#dim
2413
x A D# F# A x
x 3b 6 1 3b x
F#dim
2414
D# A C F# A x
6 3b 5b 1 3b x
F#dim
2415
x A C F# A D#
x 3b 5b 1 3b 6
F#+
2416
x A# D A# D F#
x 3 5# 3 5# 1
F#+
2417
x x D A# D F#
x x 5# 3 5# 1

TUNING: E A D G B E (Standard)

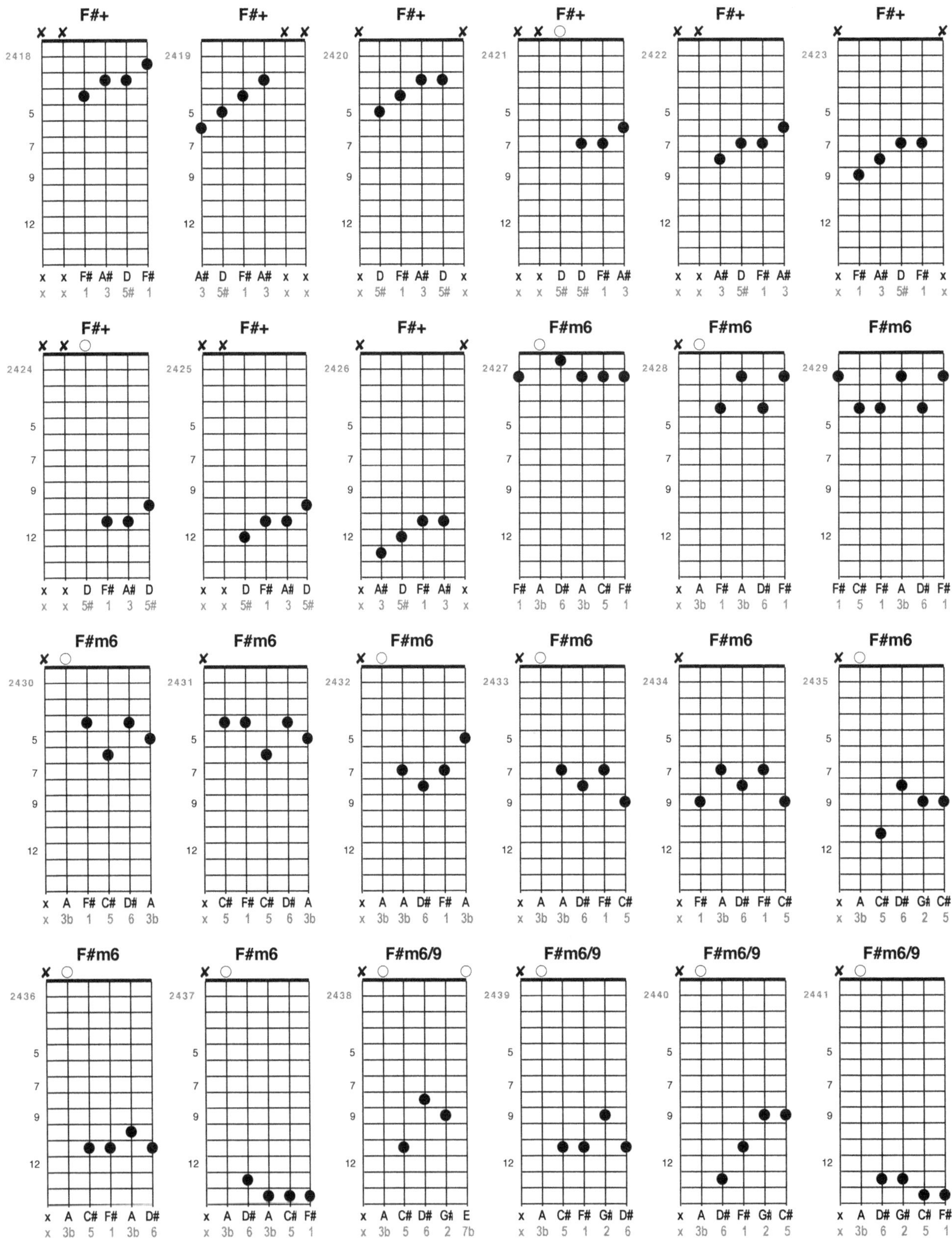
F#+
2418
x x F# A# D F#
x x 1 3 5# 1
F#+
2419
A# D F# A# x x
3 5# 1 3 x x
F#+
2420
x D F# A# D x
x 5# 1 3 5# x
F#+
2421
x x D D F# A#
x x 5# 5# 1 3
F#+
2422
x x A# D F# A#
x x 3 5# 1 3
F#+
2423
x F# A# D F# x
x 1 3 5# 1 x
F#+
2424
x x D F# A# D
x x 5# 1 3 5#
F#+
2425
x x D F# A# D
x x 5# 1 3 5#
F#+
2426
x A# D F# A# x
x 3 5# 1 3 x
F#m6
2427
F# A D# A C# F#
1 3b 6 3b 5 1
F#m6
2428
x A F# A D# F#
x 3b 1 3b 6 1
F#m6
2429
F# C# F# A D# F#
1 5 1 3b 6 1
F#m6
2430
x A F# C# D# A
x 3b 1 5 6 3b
F#m6
2431
x C# F# C# D# A
x 5 1 5 6 3b
F#m6
2432
x A A D# F# A
x 3b 3b 6 1 3b
F#m6
2433
x A A D# F# C#
x 3b 3b 6 1 5
F#m6
2434
x F# A D# F# C#
x 1 3b 6 1 5
F#m6
2435
x A C# D# G# C#
x 3b 5 6 2 5
F#m6
2436
x A C# F# A D#
x 3b 5 1 3b 6
F#m6
2437
x A D# A C# F#
x 3b 6 3b 5 1
F#m6/9
2438
x A C# D# G# E
x 3b 5 6 2 7b
F#m6/9
2439
x A C# F# G# D#
x 3b 5 1 2 6
F#m6/9
2440
x A D# F# G# C#
x 3b 6 1 2 5
F#m6/9
2441
x A D# G# C# F#
x 3b 6 2 5 1

TUNING: E A D G B E (Standard)

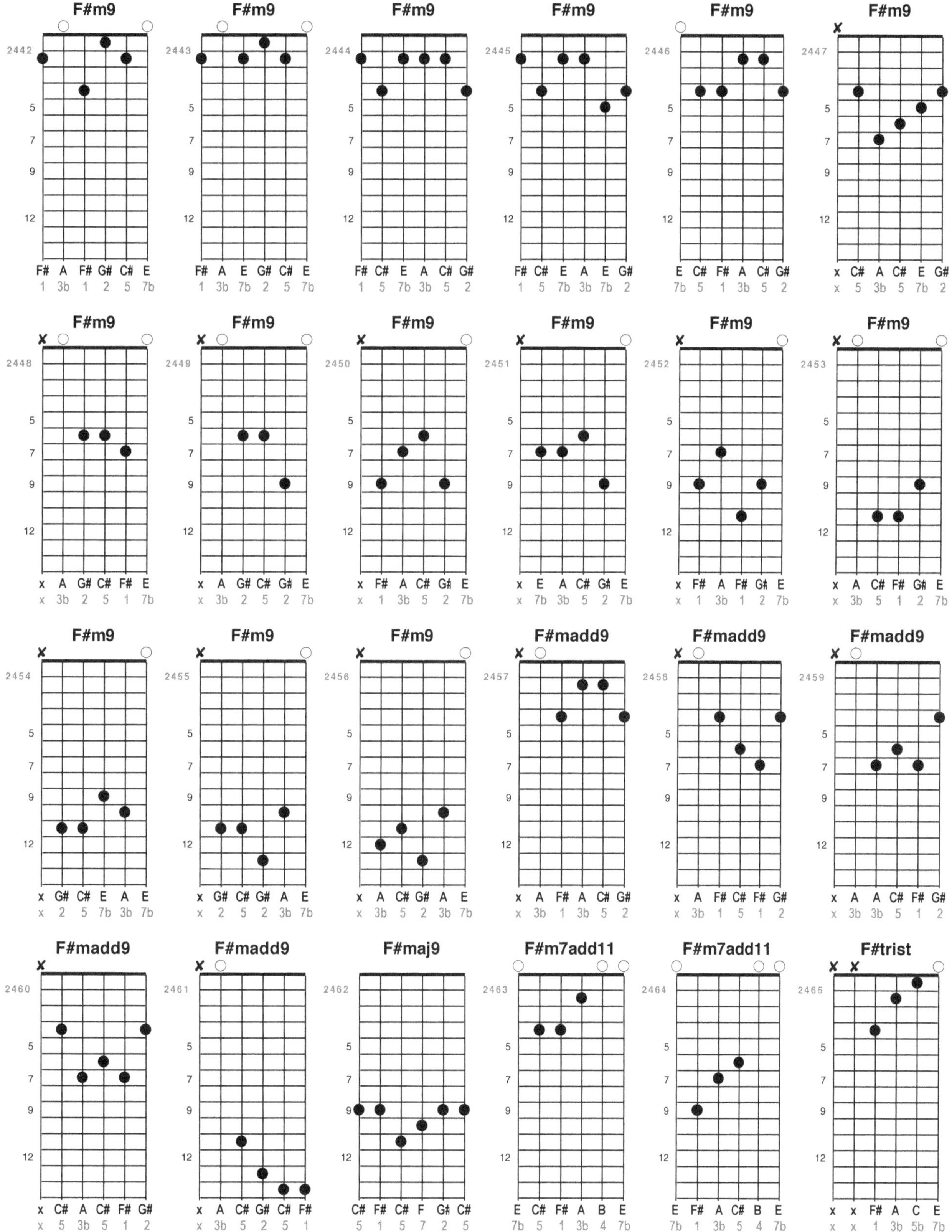

F#m9
2442
F# A F# G# C# E
1 3b 1 2 5 7b
F#m9
2443
F# A E G# C# E
1 3b 7b 2 5 7b
F#m9
2444
F# C# E A C# G#
1 5 7b 3b 5 2
F#m9
2445
F# C# E A E G#
1 5 7b 3b 7b 2
F#m9
2446
E C# F# A C# G#
7b 5 1 3b 5 2
F#m9
2447
x C# A C# E G#
x 5 3b 5 7b 2
F#m9
2448
x A G# C# F# E
x 3b 2 5 1 7b
F#m9
2449
x A G# C# G# E
x 3b 2 5 2 7b
F#m9
2450
x F# A C# G# E
x 1 3b 5 2 7b
F#m9
2451
x E A C# G# E
x 7b 3b 5 2 7b
F#m9
2452
x F# A F# G# E
x 1 3b 1 2 7b
F#m9
2453
x A C# F# G# E
x 3b 5 1 2 7b
F#m9
2454
x G# C# E A E
x 2 5 7b 3b 7b
F#m9
2455
x G# C# G# A E
x 2 5 2 3b 7b
F#m9
2456
x A C# G# A E
x 3b 5 2 3b 7b
F#madd9
2457
x A F# A C# G#
x 3b 1 3b 5 2
F#madd9
2458
x A F# C# F# G#
x 3b 1 5 1 2
F#madd9
2459
x A A C# F# G#
x 3b 3b 5 1 2
F#madd9
2460
x C# A C# F# G#
x 5 3b 5 1 2
F#madd9
2461
x A C# G# C# F#
x 3b 5 2 5 1
F#maj9
2462
C# F# C# F G# C#
5 1 5 7 2 5
F#m7add11
2463
E C# F# A B E
7b 5 1 3b 4 7b
F#m7add11
2464
E F# A C# B E
7b 1 3b 5 4 7b
F#trist
2465
x x F# A C E
x x 1 3b 5b 7b

Troubadour Guitar Chords

TUNING: E A D G B E (Standard)

G

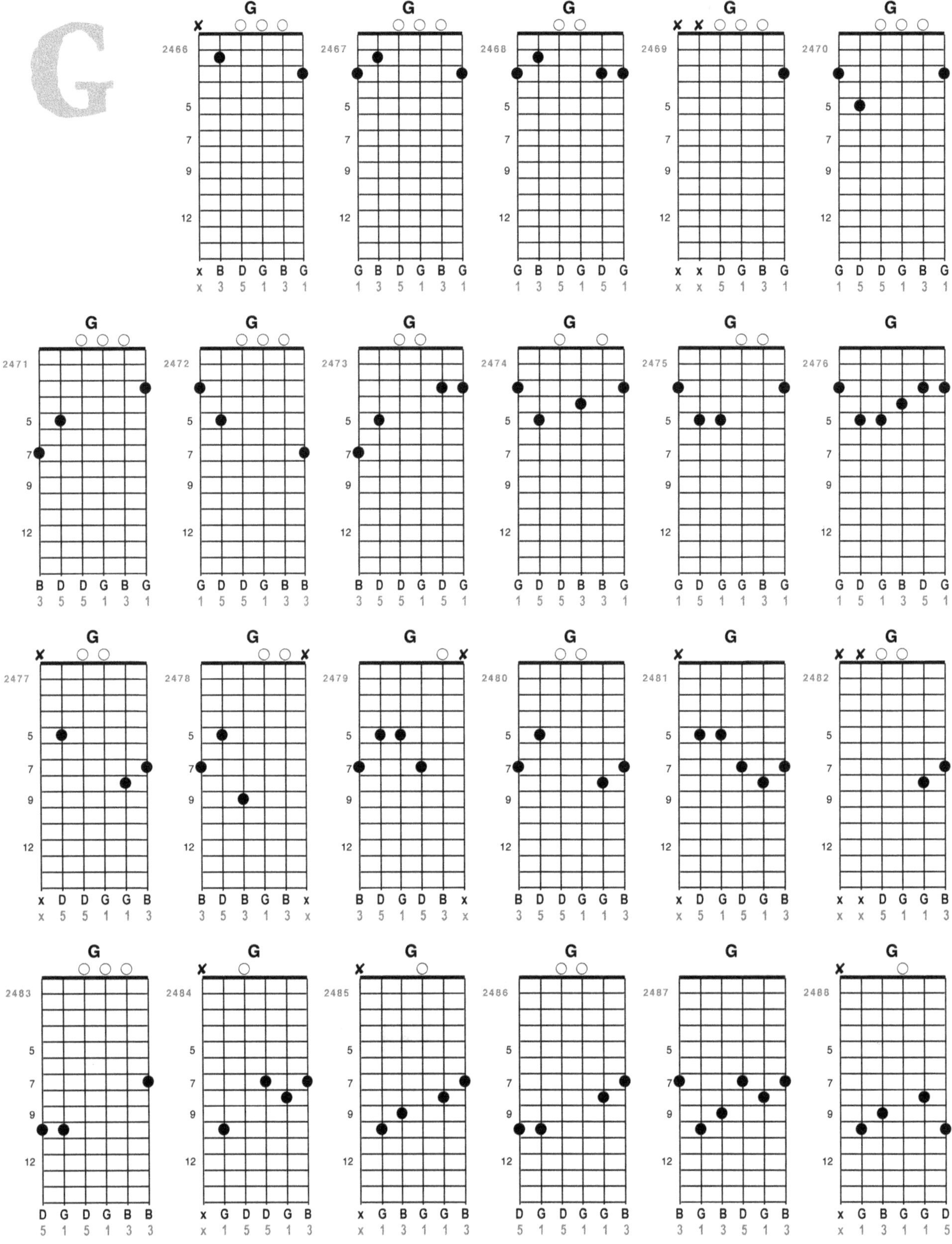

G
2466
x B D G B G
x 3 5 1 3 1
G
2467
G B D G B G
1 3 5 1 3 1
G
2468
G B D G D G
1 3 5 1 5 1
G
2469
x x D G B G
x x 5 1 3 1
G
2470
G D D G B G
1 5 5 1 3 1
G
2471
B D D G B G
3 5 5 1 3 1
G
2472
G D D G B B
1 5 5 1 3 3
G
2473
B D D G D G
3 5 5 1 5 1
G
2474
G D D B B G
1 5 5 3 3 1
G
2475
G D G G B G
1 5 1 1 3 1
G
2476
G D G B D G
1 5 1 3 5 1
G
2477
x D D G G B
x 5 5 1 1 3
G
2478
B D B G B x
3 5 3 1 3 x
G
2479
B D G D B x
3 5 1 5 3 x
G
2480
B D D G G B
3 5 5 1 1 3
G
2481
x D G D G B
x 5 1 5 1 3
G
2482
x x D G G B
x x 5 1 1 3
G
2483
D G D G B B
5 1 5 1 3 3
G
2484
x G D D G B
x 1 5 5 1 3
G
2485
x G B G G B
x 1 3 1 1 3
G
2486
D G D G G B
5 1 5 1 1 3
G
2487
B G B D G B
3 1 3 5 1 3
G
2488
x G B G G D
x 1 3 1 1 5

Troubadour Guitar Chords

TUNING: E A D G B E (Standard)

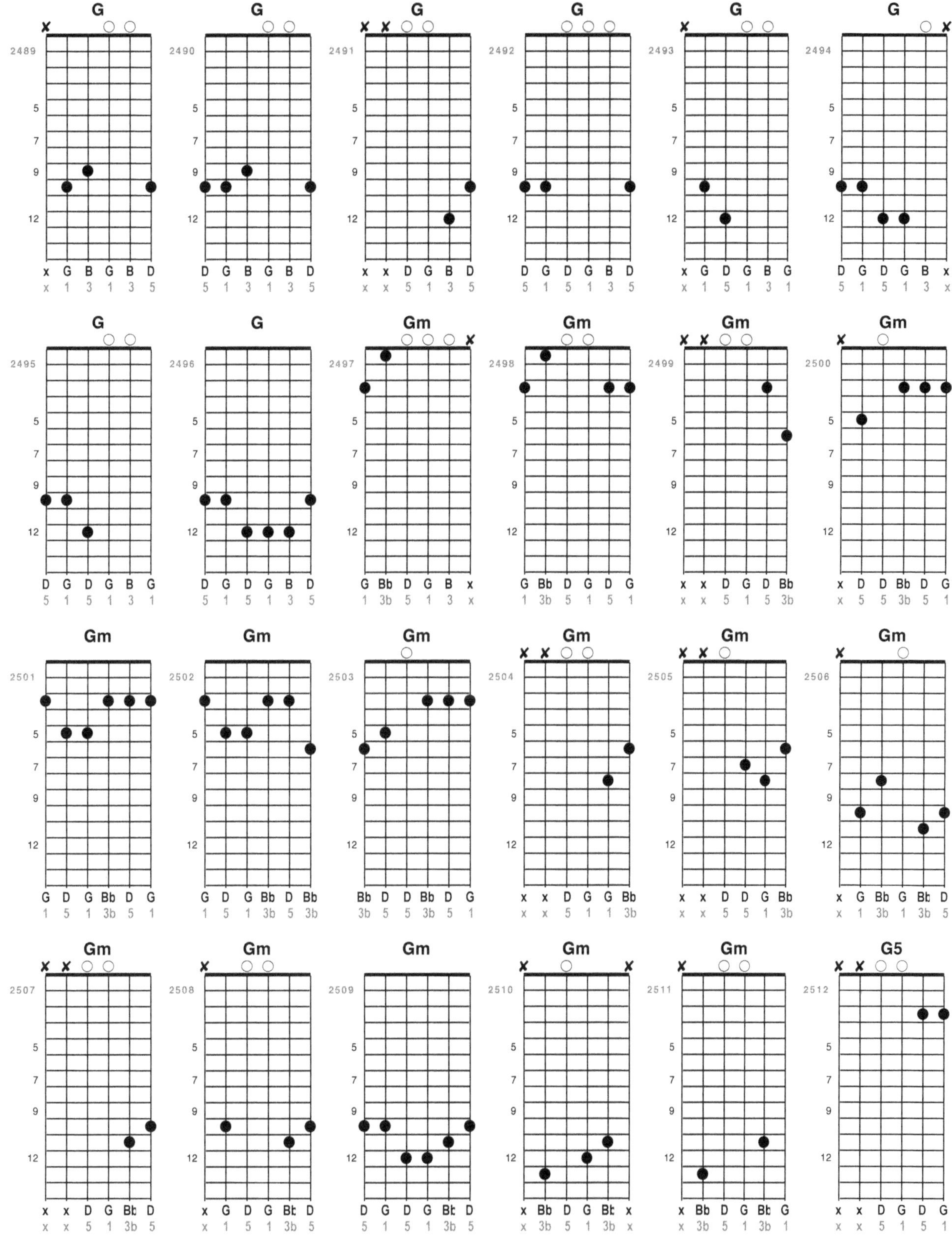

TUNING: E A D G B E (Standard)

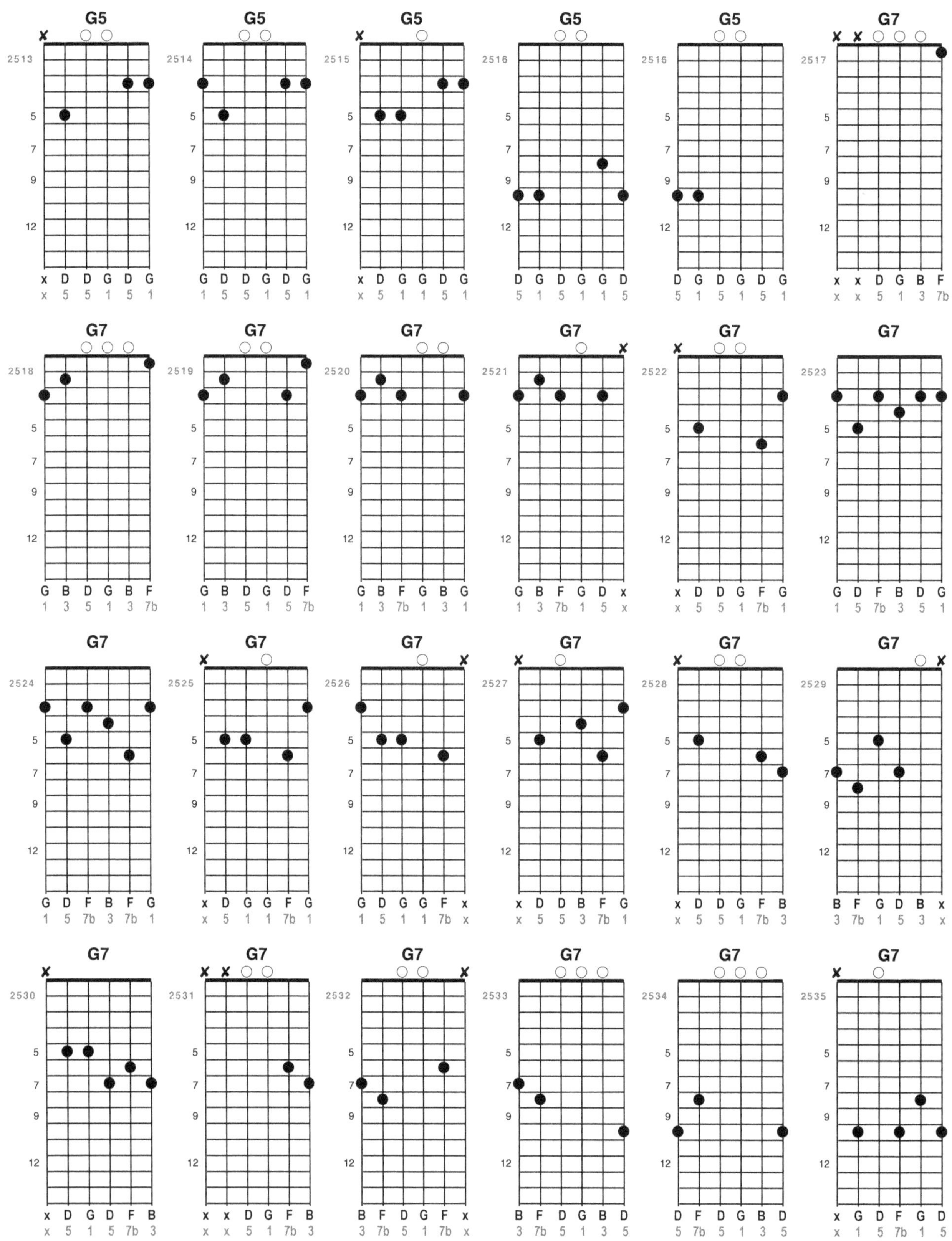

TUNING: E A D G B E (Standard)

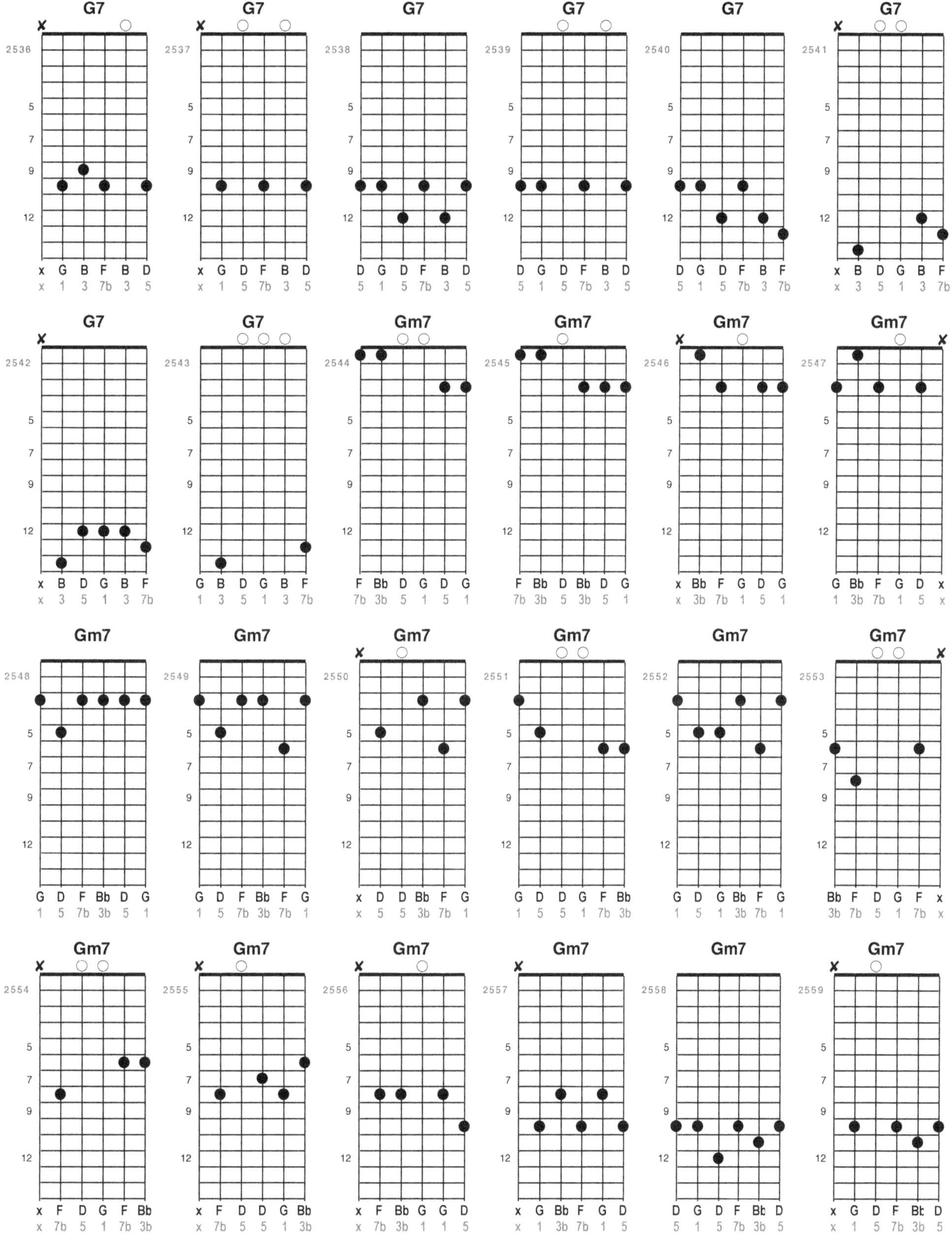
G7
2536
x G B F B D
x 1 3 7b 3 5
G7
2537
x G D F B D
x 1 5 7b 3 5
G7
2538
D G D F B D
5 1 5 7b 3 5
G7
2539
D G D F B D
5 1 5 7b 3 5
G7
2540
D G D F B F
5 1 5 7b 3 7b
G7
2541
x B D G B F
x 3 5 1 3 7b
G7
2542
x B D G B F
x 3 5 1 3 7b
G7
2543
G B D G B F
1 3 5 1 3 7b
Gm7
2544
F Bb D G D G
7b 3b 5 1 5 1
Gm7
2545
F Bb D Bb D G
7b 3b 5 3b 5 1
Gm7
2546
x Bb F G D G
x 3b 7b 1 5 1
Gm7
2547
G Bb F G D x
1 3b 7b 1 5 x
Gm7
2548
G D F Bb D G
1 5 7b 3b 5 1
Gm7
2549
G D F Bb F G
1 5 7b 3b 7b 1
Gm7
2550
x D D Bb F G
x 5 5 3b 7b 1
Gm7
2551
G D D G F Bb
1 5 5 1 7b 3b
Gm7
2552
G D G Bb F G
1 5 1 3b 7b 1
Gm7
2553
Bb F D G F x
3b 7b 5 1 7b x
Gm7
2554
x F D G F Bb
x 7b 5 1 7b 3b
Gm7
2555
x F D D G Bb
x 7b 5 5 1 3b
Gm7
2556
x F Bb G G D
x 7b 3b 1 1 5
Gm7
2557
x G Bb F G D
x 1 3b 7b 1 5
Gm7
2558
D G D F Bb D
5 1 5 7b 3b 5
Gm7
2559
x G D F Bb D
x 1 5 7b 3b 5

Troubadour Guitar Chords

TUNING: E A D G B E (Standard)

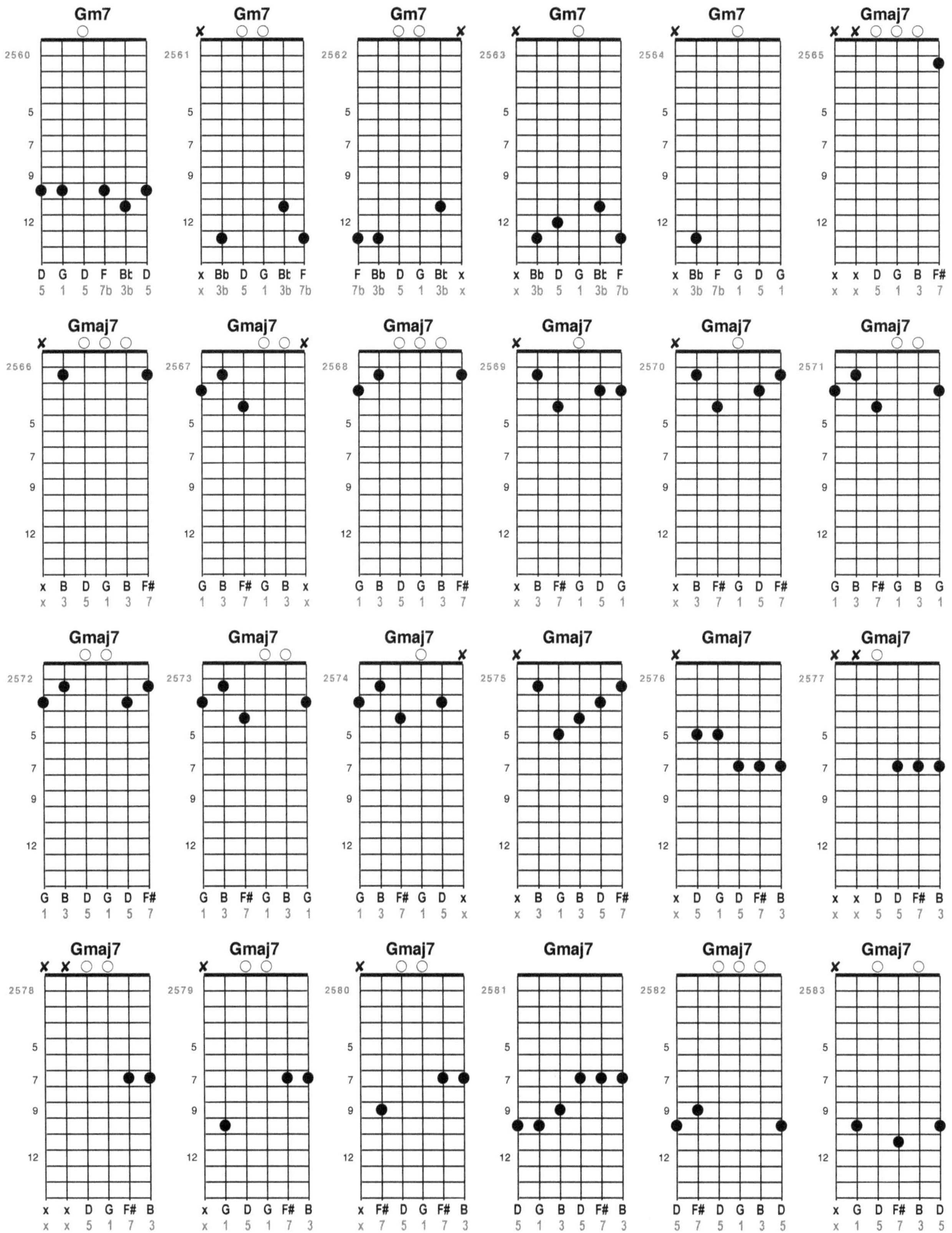

Gm7
2560
D G D F Bb D
5 1 5 7b 3b 5
Gm7
2561
x Bb D G Bb F
x 3b 5 1 3b 7b
Gm7
2562
F Bb D G Bb x
7b 3b 5 1 3b x
Gm7
2563
x Bb D G Bb F
x 3b 5 1 3b 7b
Gm7
2564
x Bb F G D G
x 3b 7b 1 5 1
Gmaj7
2565
x x D G B F#
x x 5 1 3 7
Gmaj7
2566
x B D G B F#
x 3 5 1 3 7
Gmaj7
2567
G B F# G B x
1 3 7 1 3 x
Gmaj7
2568
G B D G B F#
1 3 5 1 3 7
Gmaj7
2569
x B F# G D G
x 3 7 1 5 1
Gmaj7
2570
x B F# G D F#
x 3 7 1 5 7
Gmaj7
2571
G B F# G B G
1 3 7 1 3 1
Gmaj7
2572
G B D G D F#
1 3 5 1 5 7
Gmaj7
2573
G B F# G B G
1 3 7 1 3 1
Gmaj7
2574
G B F# G D x
1 3 7 1 5 x
Gmaj7
2575
x B G B D F#
x 3 1 3 5 7
Gmaj7
2576
x D G D F# B
x 5 1 5 7 3
Gmaj7
2577
x x D D F# B
x x 5 5 7 3
Gmaj7
2578
x x D G F# B
x x 5 1 7 3
Gmaj7
2579
x G D G F# B
x 1 5 1 7 3
Gmaj7
2580
x F# D G F# B
x 7 5 1 7 3
Gmaj7
2581
D G B D F# B
5 1 3 5 7 3
Gmaj7
2582
D F# D G B D
5 7 5 1 3 5
Gmaj7
2583
x G D F# B D
x 1 5 7 3 5

Troubadour Guitar Chords

TUNING: E A D G B E (Standard)

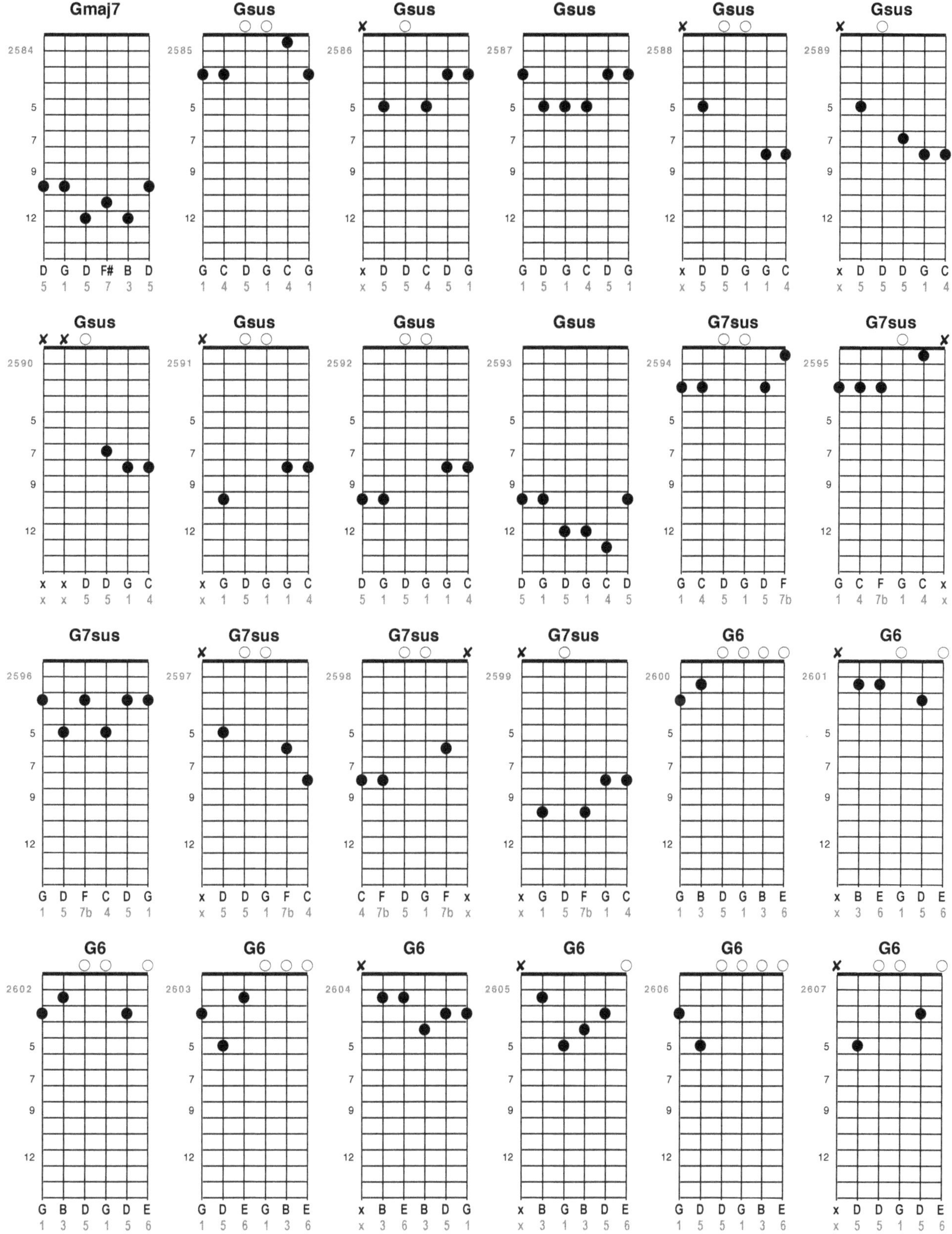

Gmaj7
2584
D G D F# B D
5 1 5 7 3 5
Gsus
2585
G C D G C G
1 4 5 1 4 1
Gsus
2586
x D D C D G
x 5 5 4 5 1
Gsus
2587
G D G C D G
1 5 1 4 5 1
Gsus
2588
x D D G G C
x 5 5 1 1 4
Gsus
2589
x D D D G C
x 5 5 5 1 4
Gsus
2590
x x D D G C
x x 5 5 1 4
Gsus
2591
x G D G G C
x 1 5 1 1 4
Gsus
2592
D G D G G C
5 1 5 1 1 4
Gsus
2593
D G D G C D
5 1 5 1 4 5
G7sus
2594
G C D G D F
1 4 5 1 5 7b
G7sus
2595
G C F G C x
1 4 7b 1 4 x
G7sus
2596
G D F C D G
1 5 7b 4 5 1
G7sus
2597
x D D G F C
x 5 5 1 7b 4
G7sus
2598
C F D G F x
4 7b 5 1 7b x
G7sus
2599
x G D F G C
x 1 5 7b 1 4
G6
2600
G B D G B E
1 3 5 1 3 6
G6
2601
x B E G D E
x 3 6 1 5 6
G6
2602
G B D G D E
1 3 5 1 5 6
G6
2603
G D E G B E
1 5 6 1 3 6
G6
2604
x B E B D G
x 3 6 3 5 1
G6
2605
x B G B D E
x 3 1 3 5 6
G6
2606
G D D G B E
1 5 5 1 3 6
G6
2607
x D D G D E
x 5 5 1 5 6

TUNING: E A D G B E (Standard)

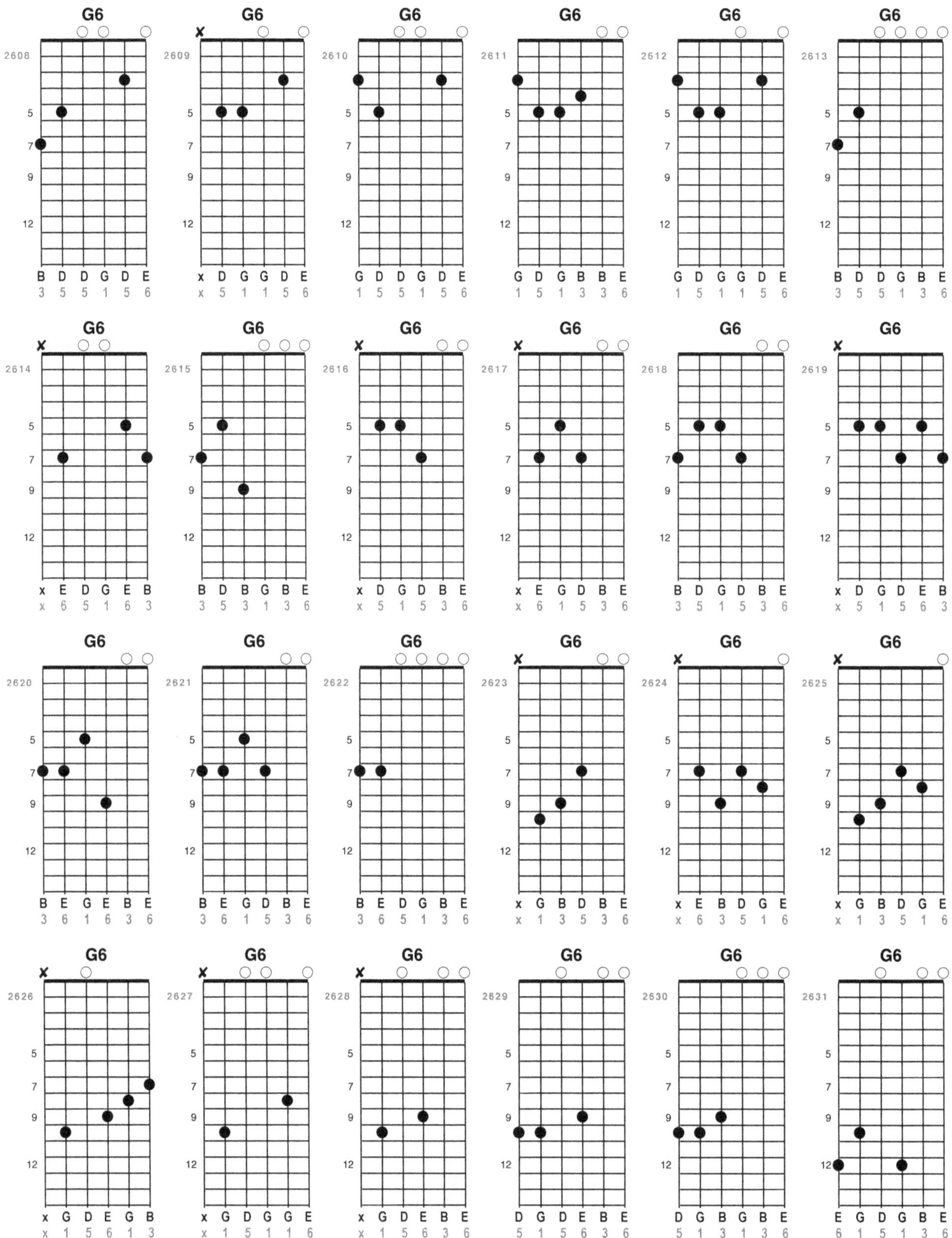

TUNING: E A D G B E (Standard)

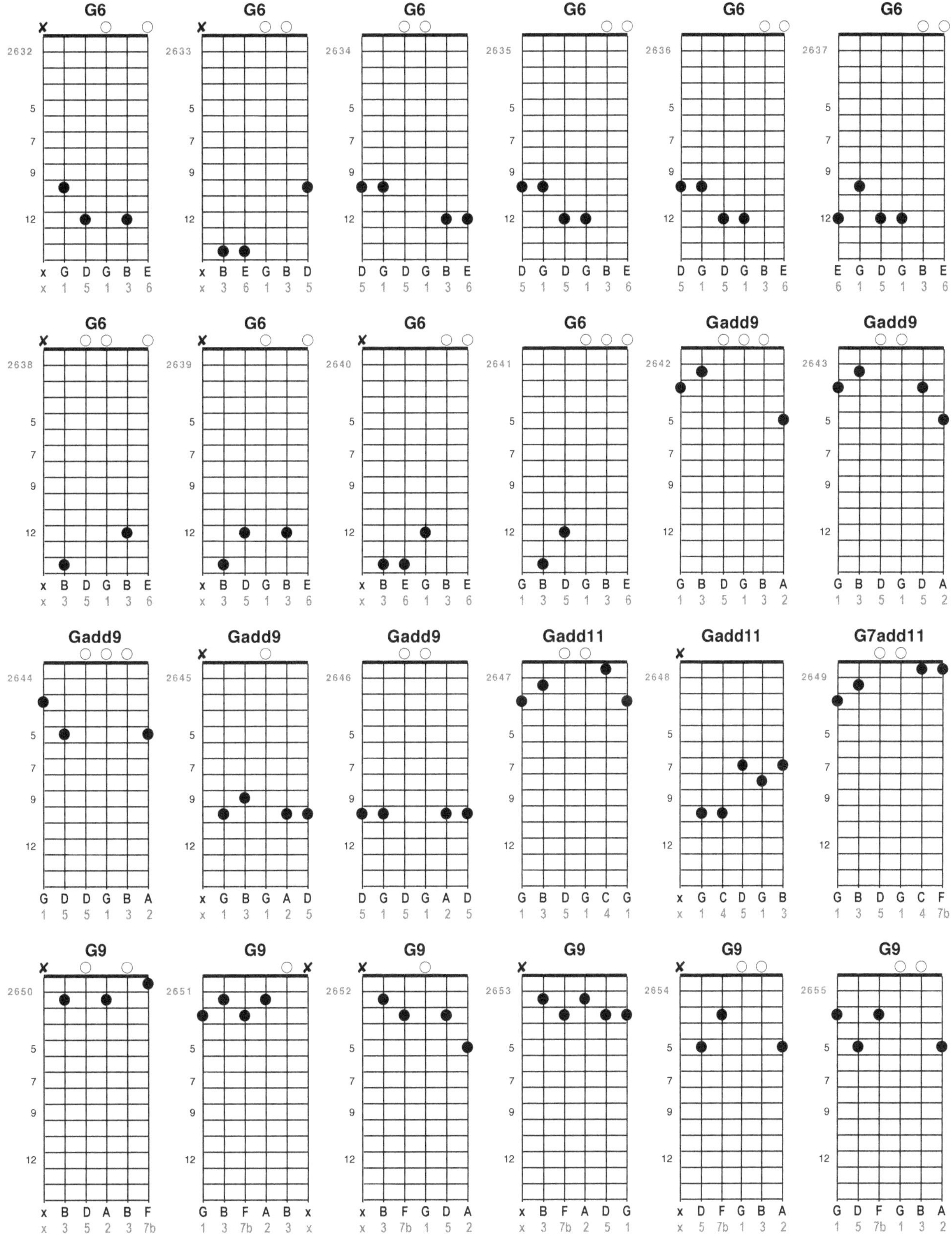
G6
2632
x G D G B E
x 1 5 1 3 6
G6
2633
x B E G B D
x 3 6 1 3 5
G6
2634
D G D G B E
5 1 5 1 3 6
G6
2635
D G D G B E
5 1 5 1 3 6
G6
2636
D G D G B E
5 1 5 1 3 6
G6
2637
E G D G B E
6 1 5 1 3 6
G6
2638
x B D G B E
x 3 5 1 3 6
G6
2639
x B D G B E
x 3 5 1 3 6
G6
2640
x B E G B E
x 3 6 1 3 6
G6
2641
G B D G B E
1 3 5 1 3 6
Gadd9
2642
G B D G B A
1 3 5 1 3 2
Gadd9
2643
G B D G D A
1 3 5 1 5 2
Gadd9
2644
G D D G B A
1 5 5 1 3 2
Gadd9
2645
x G B G A D
x 1 3 1 2 5
Gadd9
2646
D G D G A D
5 1 5 1 2 5
Gadd11
2647
G B D G C G
1 3 5 1 4 1
Gadd11
2648
x G C D G B
x 1 4 5 1 3
G7add11
2649
G B D G C F
1 3 5 1 4 7b
G9
2650
x B D A B F
x 3 5 2 3 7b
G9
2651
G B F A B x
1 3 7b 2 3 x
G9
2652
x B F G D A
x 3 7b 1 5 2
G9
2653
x B F A D G
x 3 7b 2 5 1
G9
2654
x D F G B A
x 5 7b 1 3 2
G9
2655
G D F G B A
1 5 7b 1 3 2

Troubadour Guitar Chords

TUNING: E A D G B E (Standard)

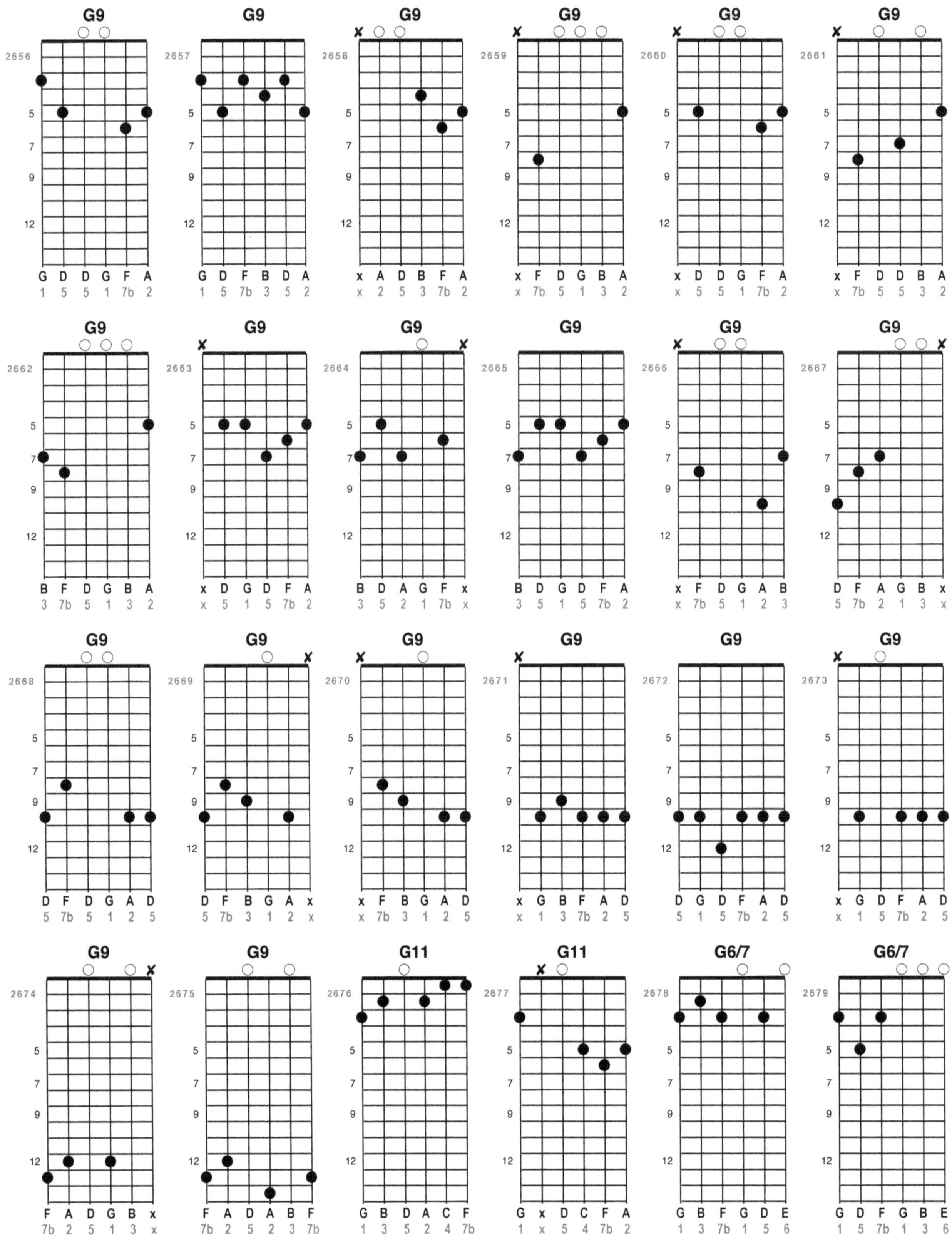
G9
2656
G D D G F A
1 5 5 1 7b 2
G9
2657
G D F B D A
1 5 7b 3 5 2
G9
2658
x A D B F A
x 2 5 3 7b 2
G9
2659
x F D G B A
x 7b 5 1 3 2
G9
2660
x D D G F A
x 5 5 1 7b 2
G9
2661
x F D D B A
x 7b 5 5 3 2
G9
2662
B F D G B A
3 7b 5 1 3 2
G9
2663
x D G D F A
x 5 1 5 7b 2
G9
2664
B D A G F x
3 5 2 1 7b x
G9
2665
B D G D F A
3 5 1 5 7b 2
G9
2666
x F D G A B
x 7b 5 1 2 3
G9
2667
D F A G B x
5 7b 2 1 3 x
G9
2668
D F D G A D
5 7b 5 1 2 5
G9
2669
D F B G A x
5 7b 3 1 2 x
G9
2670
x F B G A D
x 7b 3 1 2 5
G9
2671
x G B F A D
x 1 3 7b 2 5
G9
2672
D G D F A D
5 1 5 7b 2 5
G9
2673
x G D F A D
x 1 5 7b 2 5
G9
2674
F A D G B x
7b 2 5 1 3 x
G9
2675
F A D A B F
7b 2 5 2 3 7b
G11
2676
G B D A C F
1 3 5 2 4 7b
G11
2677
G x D C F A
1 x 5 4 7b 2
G6/7
2678
G B F G D E
1 3 7b 1 5 6
G6/7
2679
G D F G B E
1 5 7b 1 3 6

Troubadour Guitar Chords

TUNING: E A D G B E (Standard)

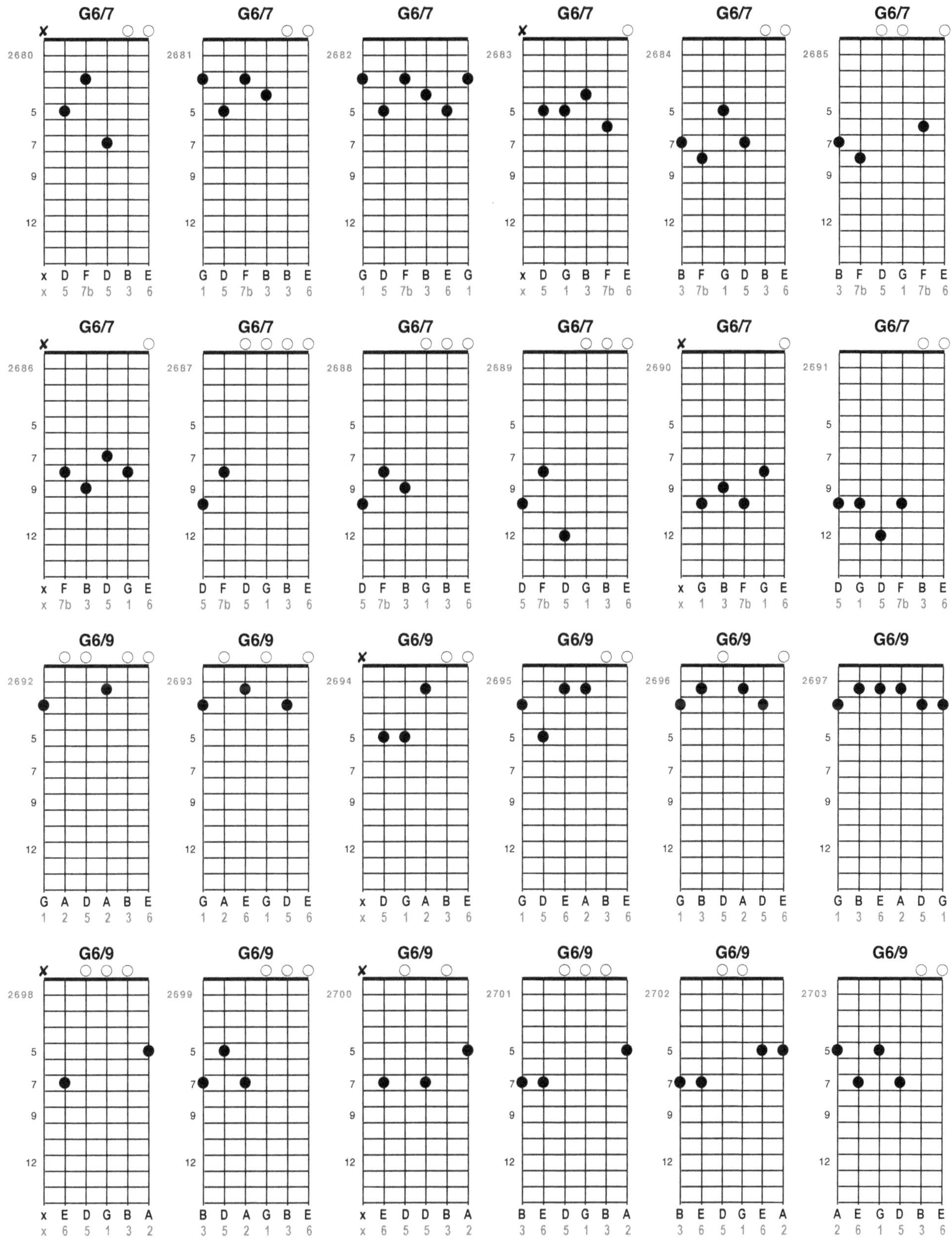

G6/7
2680
x D F D B E
x 5 7b 5 3 6
G6/7
2681
G D F B B E
1 5 7b 3 3 6
G6/7
2682
G D F B E G
1 5 7b 3 6 1
G6/7
2683
x D G B F E
x 5 1 3 7b 6
G6/7
2684
B F G D B E
3 7b 1 5 3 6
G6/7
2685
B F D G F E
3 7b 5 1 7b 6
G6/7
2686
x F B D G E
x 7b 3 5 1 6
G6/7
2687
D F D G B E
5 7b 5 1 3 6
G6/7
2688
D F B G B E
5 7b 3 1 3 6
G6/7
2689
D F D G B E
5 7b 5 1 3 6
G6/7
2690
x G B F G E
x 1 3 7b 1 6
G6/7
2691
D G D F B E
5 1 5 7b 3 6
G6/9
2692
G A D A B E
1 2 5 2 3 6
G6/9
2693
G A E G D E
1 2 6 1 5 6
G6/9
2694
x D G A B E
x 5 1 2 3 6
G6/9
2695
G D E A B E
1 5 6 2 3 6
G6/9
2696
G B D A D E
1 3 5 2 5 6
G6/9
2697
G B E A D G
1 3 6 2 5 1
G6/9
2698
x E D G B A
x 6 5 1 3 2
G6/9
2699
B D A G B E
3 5 2 1 3 6
G6/9
2700
x E D D B A
x 6 5 5 3 2
G6/9
2701
B E D G B A
3 6 5 1 3 2
G6/9
2702
B E D G E A
3 6 5 1 6 2
G6/9
2703
A E G D B E
2 6 1 5 3 6

Troubadour Guitar Chords

TUNING: E A D G B E (Standard)

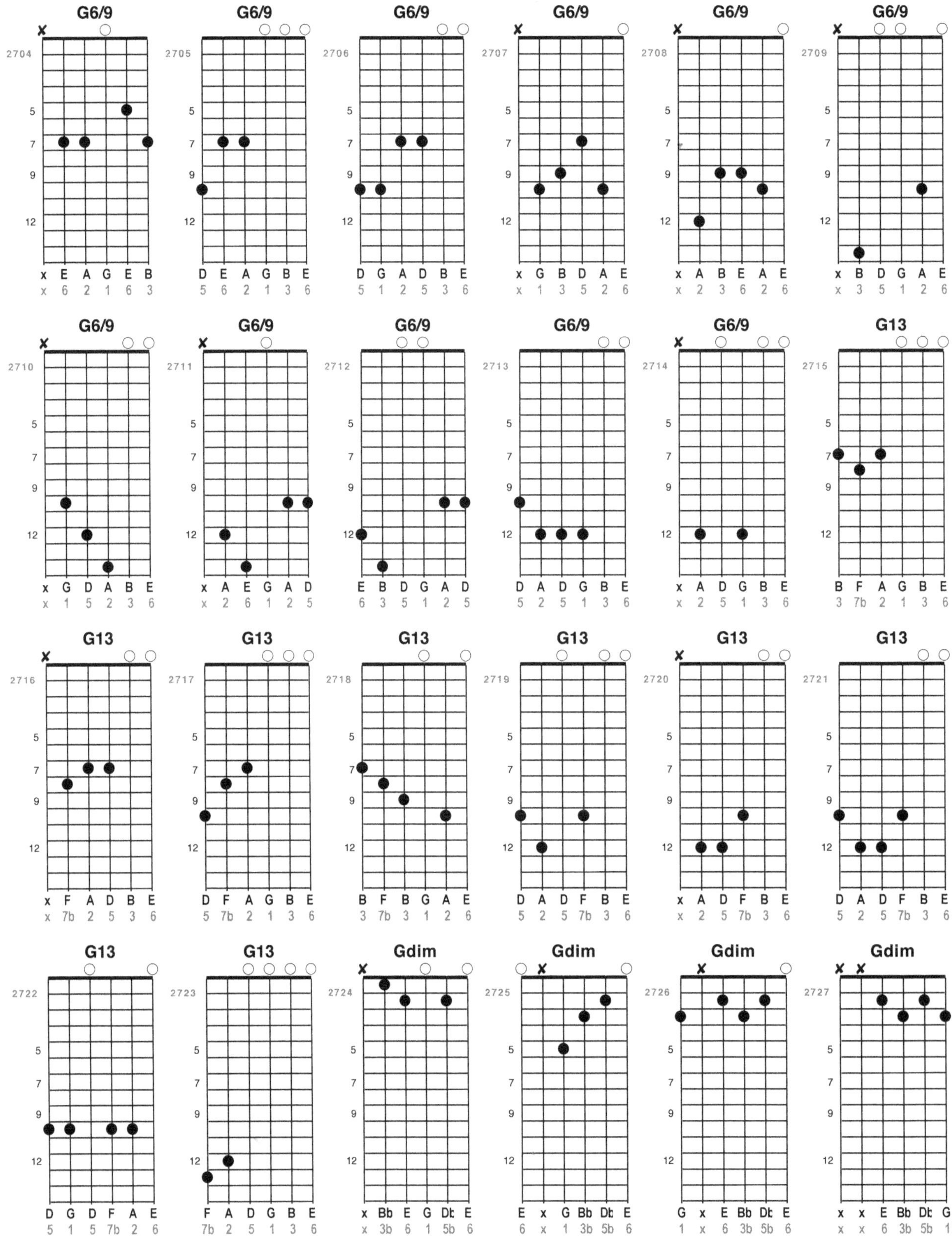

G6/9
2704
x E A G E B
x 6 2 1 6 3
G6/9
2705
D E A G B E
5 6 2 1 3 6
G6/9
2706
D G A D B E
5 1 2 5 3 6
G6/9
2707
x G B D A E
x 1 3 5 2 6
G6/9
2708
x A B E A E
x 2 3 6 2 6
G6/9
2709
x B D G A E
x 3 5 1 2 6
G6/9
2710
x G D A B E
x 1 5 2 3 6
G6/9
2711
x A E G A D
x 2 6 1 2 5
G6/9
2712
E B D G A D
6 3 5 1 2 5
G6/9
2713
D A D G B E
5 2 5 1 3 6
G6/9
2714
x A D G B E
x 2 5 1 3 6
G13
2715
B F A G B E
3 7b 2 1 3 6
G13
2716
x F A D B E
x 7b 2 5 3 6
G13
2717
D F A G B E
5 7b 2 1 3 6
G13
2718
B F B G A E
3 7b 3 1 2 6
G13
2719
D A D F B E
5 2 5 7b 3 6
G13
2720
x A D F B E
x 2 5 7b 3 6
G13
2721
D A D F B E
5 2 5 7b 3 6
G13
2722
D G D F A E
5 1 5 7b 2 6
G13
2723
F A D G B E
7b 2 5 1 3 6
Gdim
2724
x Bb E G Db E
x 3b 6 1 5b 6
Gdim
2725
E x G Bb Db E
6 x 1 3b 5b 6
Gdim
2726
G x E Bb Db E
1 x 6 3b 5b 6
Gdim
2727
x x E Bb Db G
x x 6 3b 5b 1

TUNING: E A D G B E (Standard)

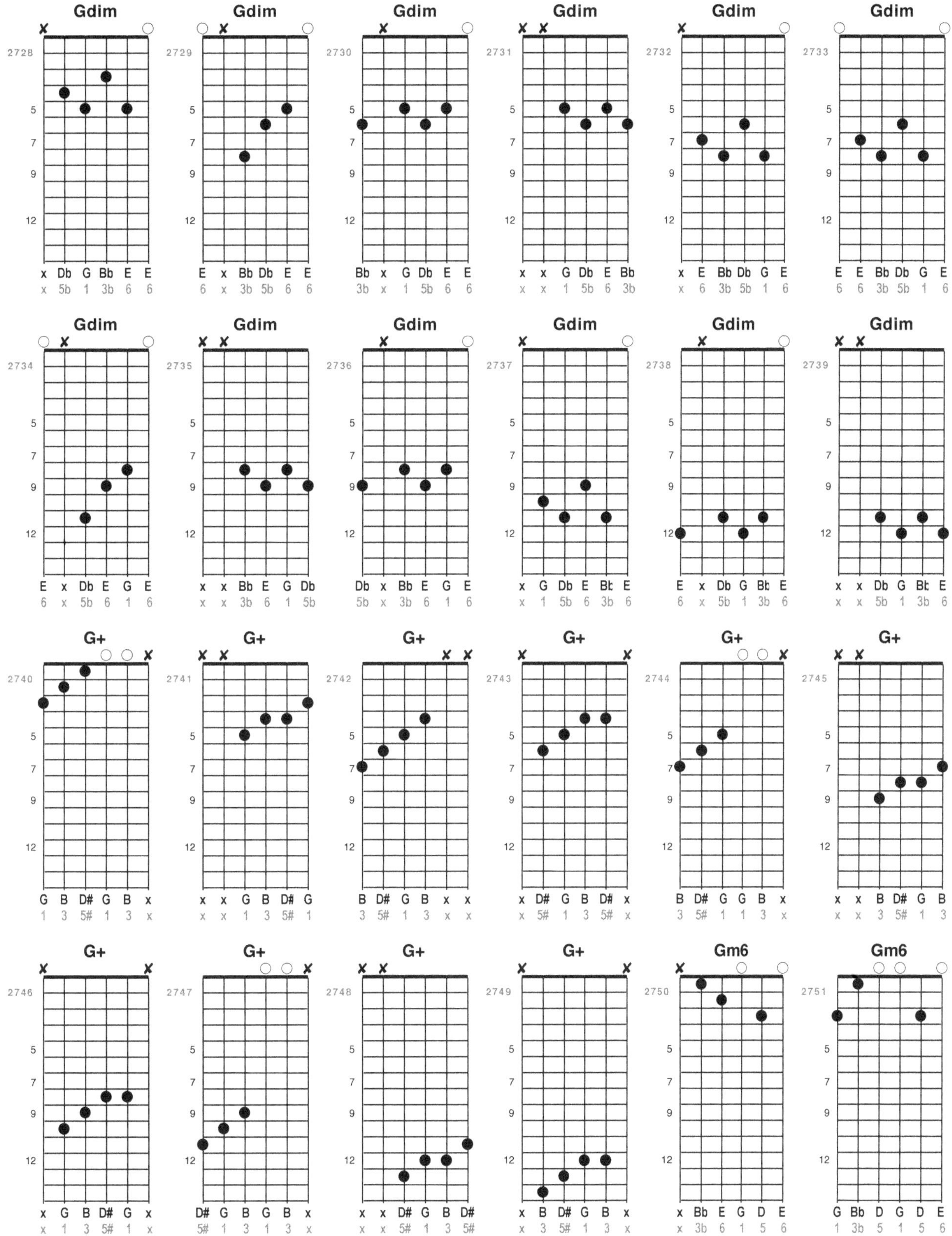
Gdim
2728
x Db G Bb E E
x 5b 1 3b 6 6
Gdim
2729
E x Bb Db E E
6 x 3b 5b 6 6
Gdim
2730
Bb x G Db E E
3b x 1 5b 6 6
Gdim
2731
x x G Db E Bb
x x 1 5b 6 3b
Gdim
2732
x E Bb Db G E
x 6 3b 5b 1 6
Gdim
2733
E E Bb Db G E
6 6 3b 5b 1 6
Gdim
2734
E x Db E G E
6 x 5b 6 1 6
Gdim
2735
x x Bb E G Db
x x 3b 6 1 5b
Gdim
2736
Db x Bb E G E
5b x 3b 6 1 6
Gdim
2737
x G Db E Bb E
x 1 5b 6 3b 6
Gdim
2738
E x Db G Bb E
6 x 5b 1 3b 6
Gdim
2739
x x Db G Bb E
x x 5b 1 3b 6
G+
2740
G B D# G B x
1 3 5# 1 3 x
G+
2741
x x G B D# G
x x 1 3 5# 1
G+
2742
B D# G B x x
3 5# 1 3 x x
G+
2743
x D# G B D# x
x 5# 1 3 5# x
G+
2744
B D# G G B x
3 5# 1 1 3 x
G+
2745
x x B D# G B
x x 3 5# 1 3
G+
2746
x G B D# G x
x 1 3 5# 1 x
G+
2747
D# G B G B x
5# 1 3 1 3 x
G+
2748
x x D# G B D#
x x 5# 1 3 5#
G+
2749
x B D# G B x
x 3 5# 1 3 x
Gm6
2750
x Bb E G D E
x 3b 6 1 5 6
Gm6
2751
G Bb D G D E
1 3b 5 1 5 6

TUNING: E A D G B E (Standard)

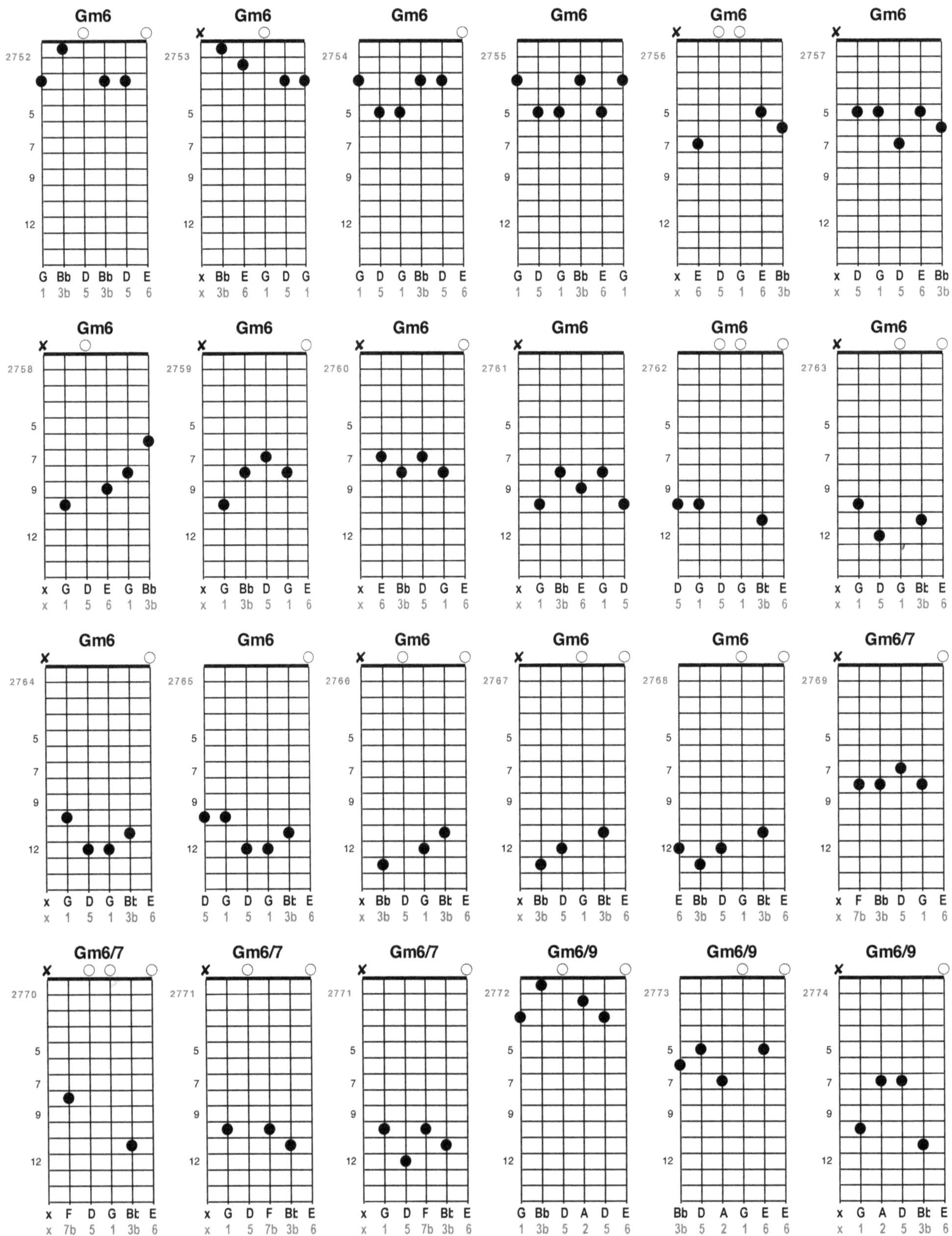
Gm6
2752
G Bb D Bb D E
1 3b 5 3b 5 6
Gm6
2753
x Bb E G D G
x 3b 6 1 5 1
Gm6
2754
G D G Bb D E
1 5 1 3b 5 6
Gm6
2755
G D G Bb E G
1 5 1 3b 6 1
Gm6
2756
x E D G E Bb
x 6 5 1 6 3b
Gm6
2757
x D G D E Bb
x 5 1 5 6 3b
Gm6
2758
x G D E G Bb
x 1 5 6 1 3b
Gm6
2759
x G Bb D G E
x 1 3b 5 1 6
Gm6
2760
x E Bb D G E
x 6 3b 5 1 6
Gm6
2761
x G Bb E G D
x 1 3b 6 1 5
Gm6
2762
D G D G Bb E
5 1 5 1 3b 6
Gm6
2763
x G D G Bb E
x 1 5 1 3b 6
Gm6
2764
x G D G Bb E
x 1 5 1 3b 6
Gm6
2765
D G D G Bb E
5 1 5 1 3b 6
Gm6
2766
x Bb D G Bb E
x 3b 5 1 3b 6
Gm6
2767
x Bb D G Bb E
x 3b 5 1 3b 6
Gm6
2768
E Bb D G Bb E
6 3b 5 1 3b 6
Gm6/7
2769
x F Bb D G E
x 7b 3b 5 1 6
Gm6/7
2770
x F D G Bb E
x 7b 5 1 3b 6
Gm6/7
2771
x G D F Bb E
x 1 5 7b 3b 6
Gm6/7
2771
x G D F Bb E
x 1 5 7b 3b 6
Gm6/9
2772
G Bb D A D E
1 3b 5 2 5 6
Gm6/9
2773
Bb D A G E E
3b 5 2 1 6 6
Gm6/9
2774
x G A D Bb E
x 1 2 5 3b 6

TUNING: E A D G B E (Standard)

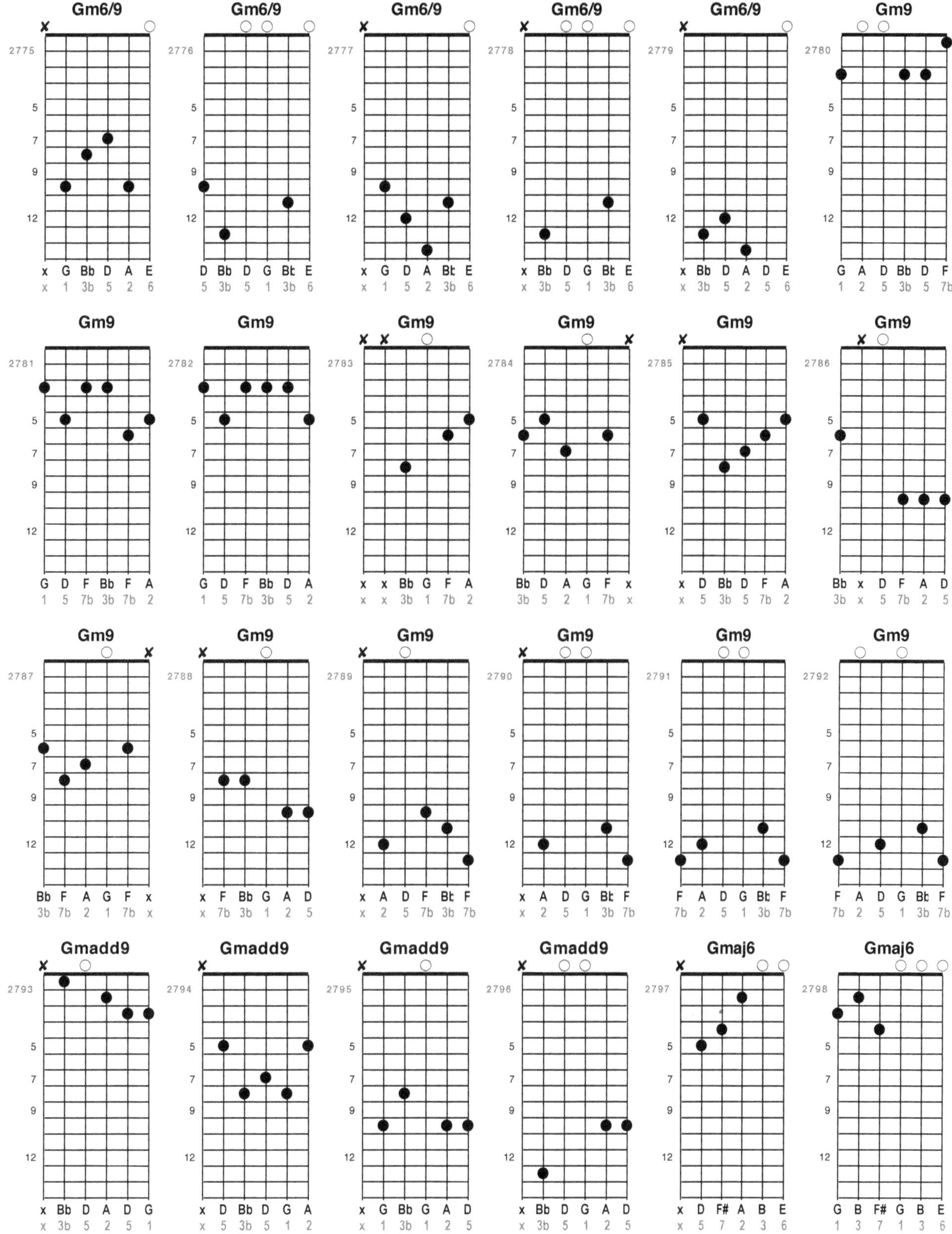

Gm6/9
2775
x G Bb D A E
x 1 3b 5 2 6
Gm6/9
2776
D Bb D G Bb E
5 3b 5 1 3b 6
Gm6/9
2777
x G D A Bb E
x 1 5 2 3b 6
Gm6/9
2778
x Bb D G Bb E
x 3b 5 1 3b 6
Gm6/9
2779
x Bb D A D E
x 3b 5 2 5 6
Gm9
2780
G A D Bb D F
1 2 5 3b 5 7b
Gm9
2781
G D F Bb F A
1 5 7b 3b 7b 2
Gm9
2782
G D F Bb D A
1 5 7b 3b 5 2
Gm9
2783
x x Bb G F A
x x 3b 1 7b 2
Gm9
2784
Bb D A G F x
3b 5 2 1 7b x
Gm9
2785
x D Bb D F A
x 5 3b 5 7b 2
Gm9
2786
Bb x D F A D
3b x 5 7b 2 5
Gm9
2787
Bb F A G F x
3b 7b 2 1 7b x
Gm9
2788
x F Bb G A D
x 7b 3b 1 2 5
Gm9
2789
x A D F Bb F
x 2 5 7b 3b 7b
Gm9
2790
x A D G Bb F
x 2 5 1 3b 7b
Gm9
2791
F A D G Bb F
7b 2 5 1 3b 7b
Gm9
2792
F A D G Bb F
7b 2 5 1 3b 7b
Gmadd9
2793
x Bb D A D G
x 3b 5 2 5 1
Gmadd9
2794
x D Bb D G A
x 5 3b 5 1 2
Gmadd9
2795
x G Bb G A D
x 1 3b 1 2 5
Gmadd9
2796
x Bb D G A D
x 3b 5 1 2 5
Gmaj6
2797
x D F# A B E
x 5 7 2 3 6
Gmaj6
2798
G B F# G B E
1 3 7 1 3 6

TUNING: E A D G B E (Standard)

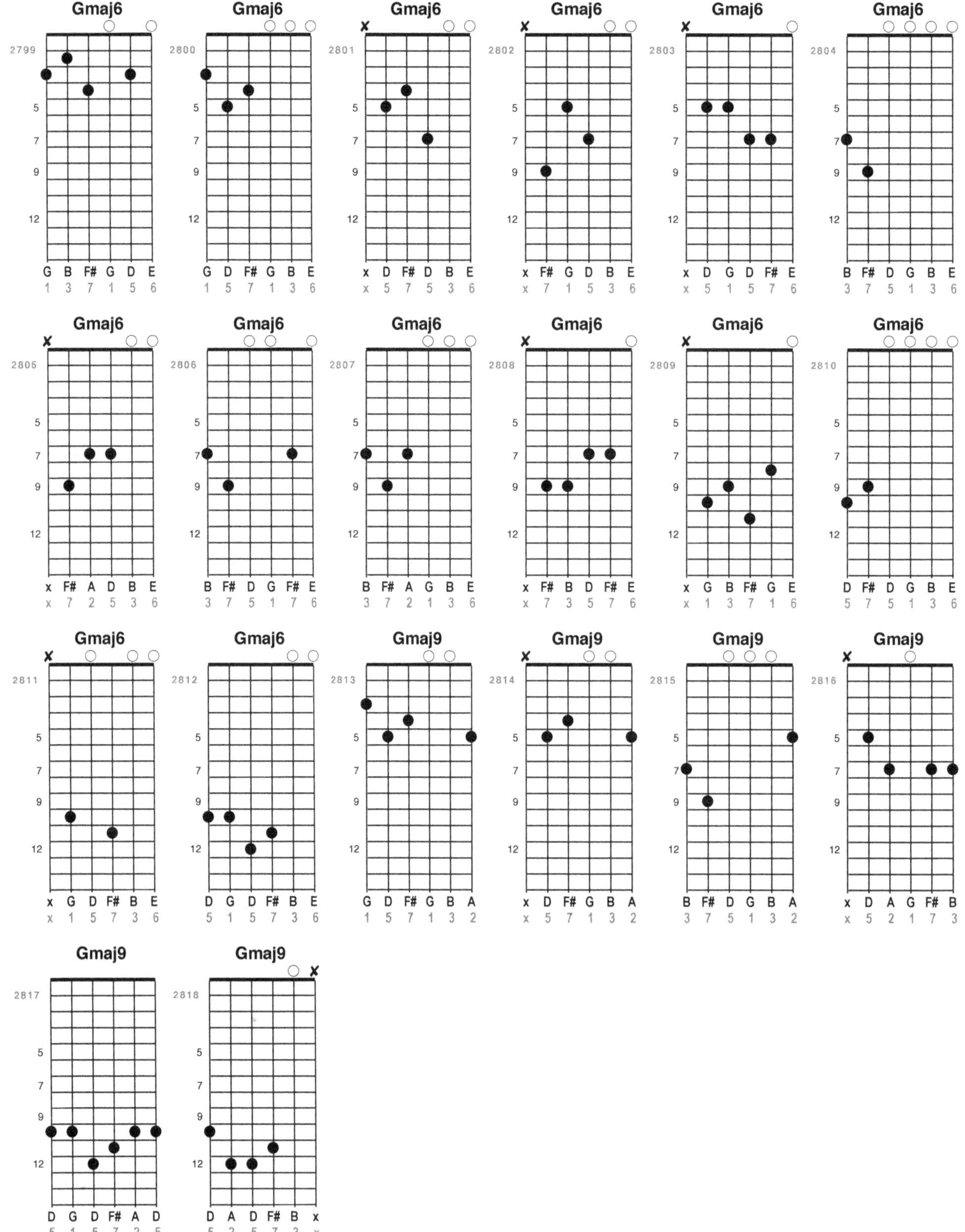
Gmaj6
2799
G B F# G D E
1 3 7 1 5 6
Gmaj6
2800
G D F# G B E
1 5 7 1 3 6
Gmaj6
2801
x D F# D B E
x 5 7 5 3 6
Gmaj6
2802
x F# G D B E
x 7 1 5 3 6
Gmaj6
2803
x D G D F# E
x 5 1 5 7 6
Gmaj6
2804
B F# D G B E
3 7 5 1 3 6
Gmaj6
2805
x F# A D B E
x 7 2 5 3 6
Gmaj6
2806
B F# D G F# E
3 7 5 1 7 6
Gmaj6
2807
B F# A G B E
3 7 2 1 3 6
Gmaj6
2808
x F# B D F# E
x 7 3 5 7 6
Gmaj6
2809
x G B F# G E
x 1 3 7 1 6
Gmaj6
2810
D F# D G B E
5 7 5 1 3 6
Gmaj6
2811
x G D F# B E
x 1 5 7 3 6
Gmaj6
2812
D G D F# B E
5 1 5 7 3 6
Gmaj9
2813
G D F# G B A
1 5 7 1 3 2
Gmaj9
2814
x D F# G B A
x 5 7 1 3 2
Gmaj9
2815
B F# D G B A
3 7 5 1 3 2
Gmaj9
2816
x D A G F# B
x 5 2 1 7 3
Gmaj9
2817
D G D F# A D
5 1 5 7 2 5
Gmaj9
2818
D A D F# B x
5 2 5 7 3 x

Troubadour Guitar Chords

TUNING: E A D G B E (Standard)

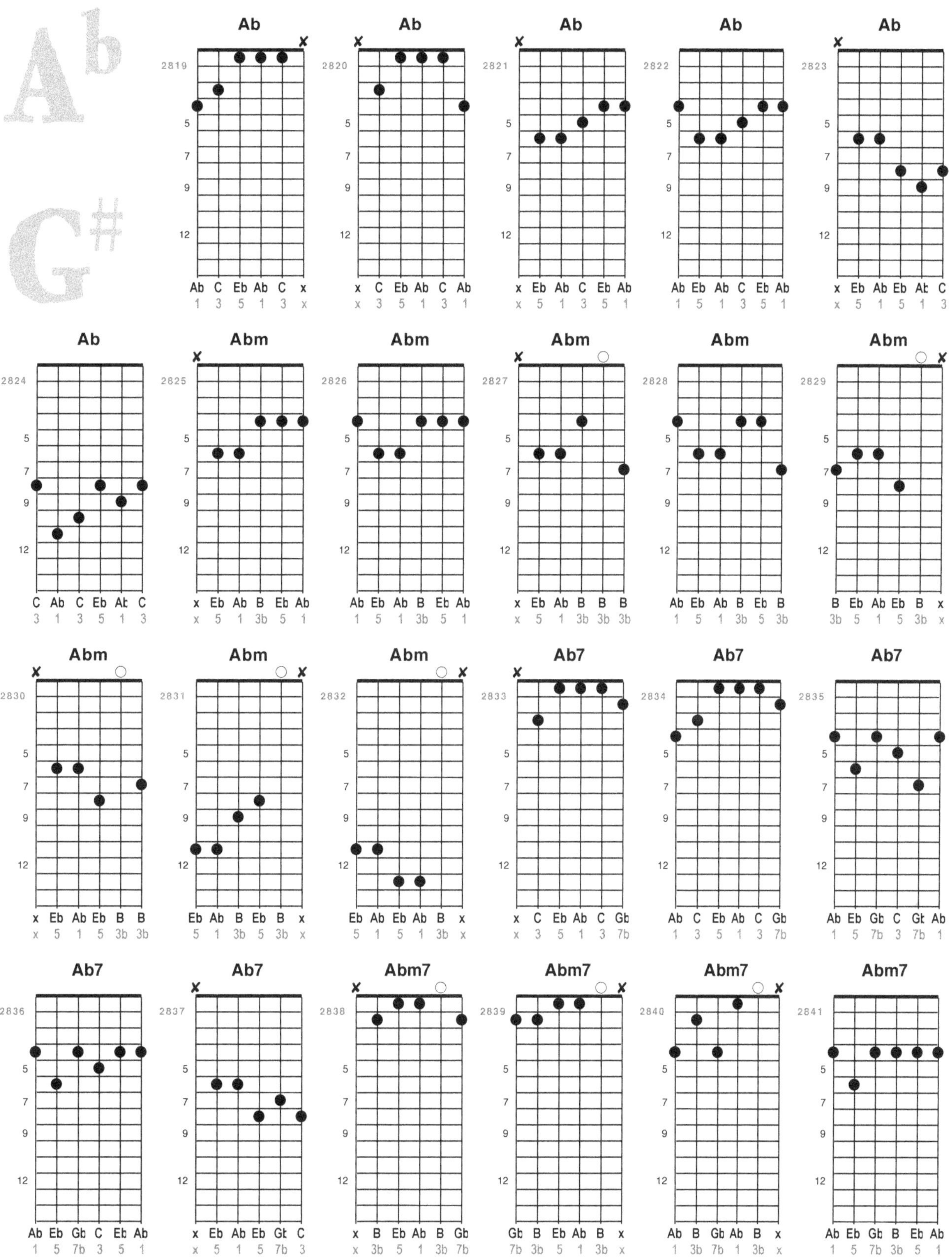

Ab
G#
Ab
2819
Ab C Eb Ab C x
1 3 5 1 3 x
Ab
2820
x C Eb Ab C Ab
x 3 5 1 3 1
Ab
2821
x Eb Ab C Eb Ab
x 5 1 3 5 1
Ab
2822
Ab Eb Ab C Eb Ab
1 5 1 3 5 1
Ab
2823
x Eb Ab Eb Ab C
x 5 1 5 1 3
Ab
2824
C Ab C Eb Ab C
3 1 3 5 1 3
Abm
2825
x Eb Ab B Eb Ab
x 5 1 3b 5 1
Abm
2826
Ab Eb Ab B Eb Ab
1 5 1 3b 5 1
Abm
2827
x Eb Ab B B B
x 5 1 3b 3b 3b
Abm
2828
Ab Eb Ab B Eb B
1 5 1 3b 5 3b
Abm
2829
B Eb Ab Eb B x
3b 5 1 5 3b x
Abm
2830
x Eb Ab Eb B B
x 5 1 5 3b 3b
Abm
2831
Eb Ab B Eb B x
5 1 3b 5 3b x
Abm
2832
Eb Ab Eb Ab B x
5 1 5 1 3b x
Ab7
2833
x C Eb Ab C Gb
x 3 5 1 3 7b
Ab7
2834
Ab C Eb Ab C Gb
1 3 5 1 3 7b
Ab7
2835
Ab Eb Gb C Gb Ab
1 5 7b 3 7b 1
Ab7
2836
Ab Eb Gb C Eb Ab
1 5 7b 3 5 1
Ab7
2837
x Eb Ab Eb Gb C
x 5 1 5 7b 3
Abm7
2838
x B Eb Ab B Gb
x 3b 5 1 3b 7b
Abm7
2839
Gb B Eb Ab B x
7b 3b 5 1 3b x
Abm7
2840
Ab B Gb Ab B x
1 3b 7b 1 3b x
Abm7
2841
Ab Eb Gb B Eb Ab
1 5 7b 3b 5 1

TUNING: E A D G B E (Standard)

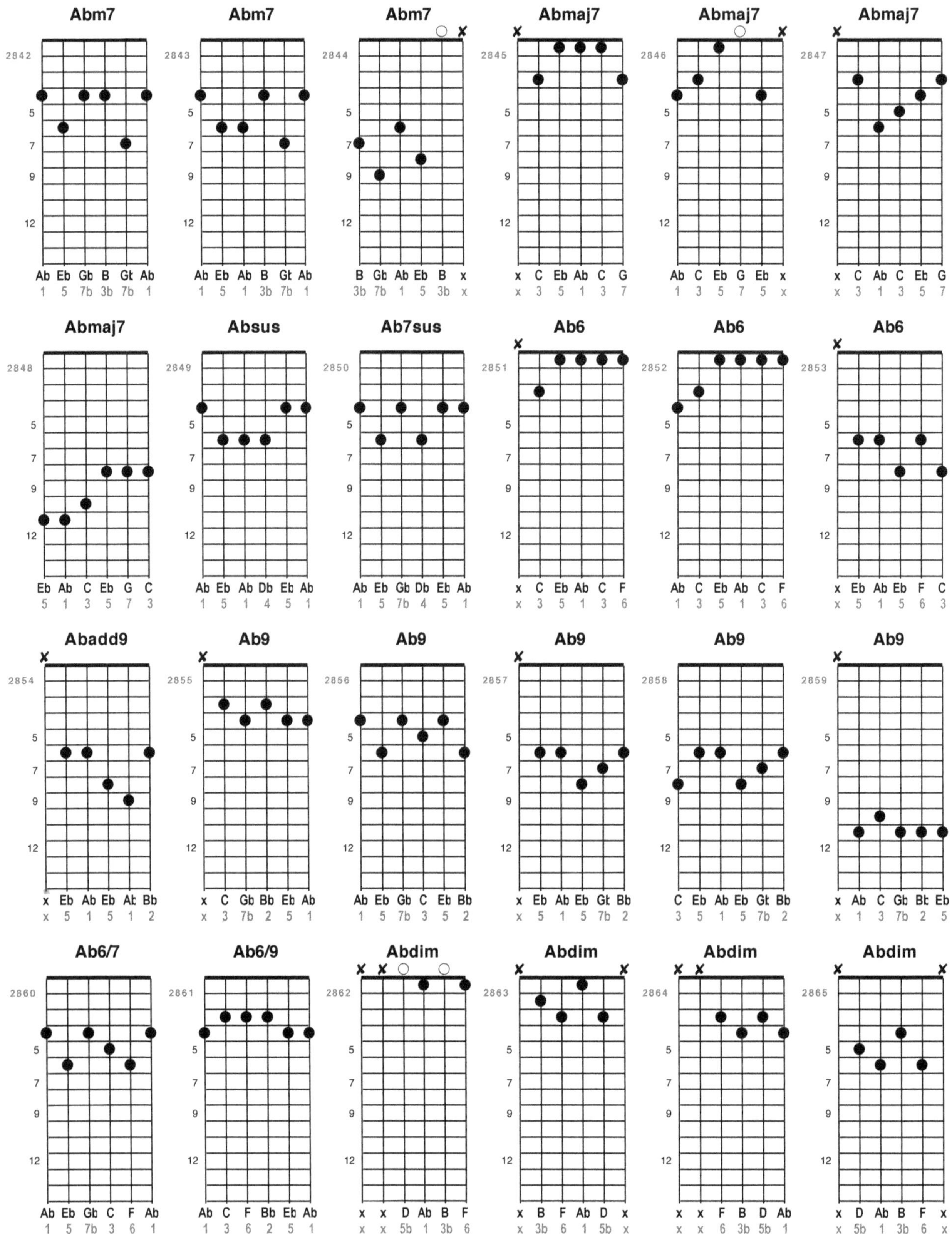

TUNING: E A D G B E (Standard)

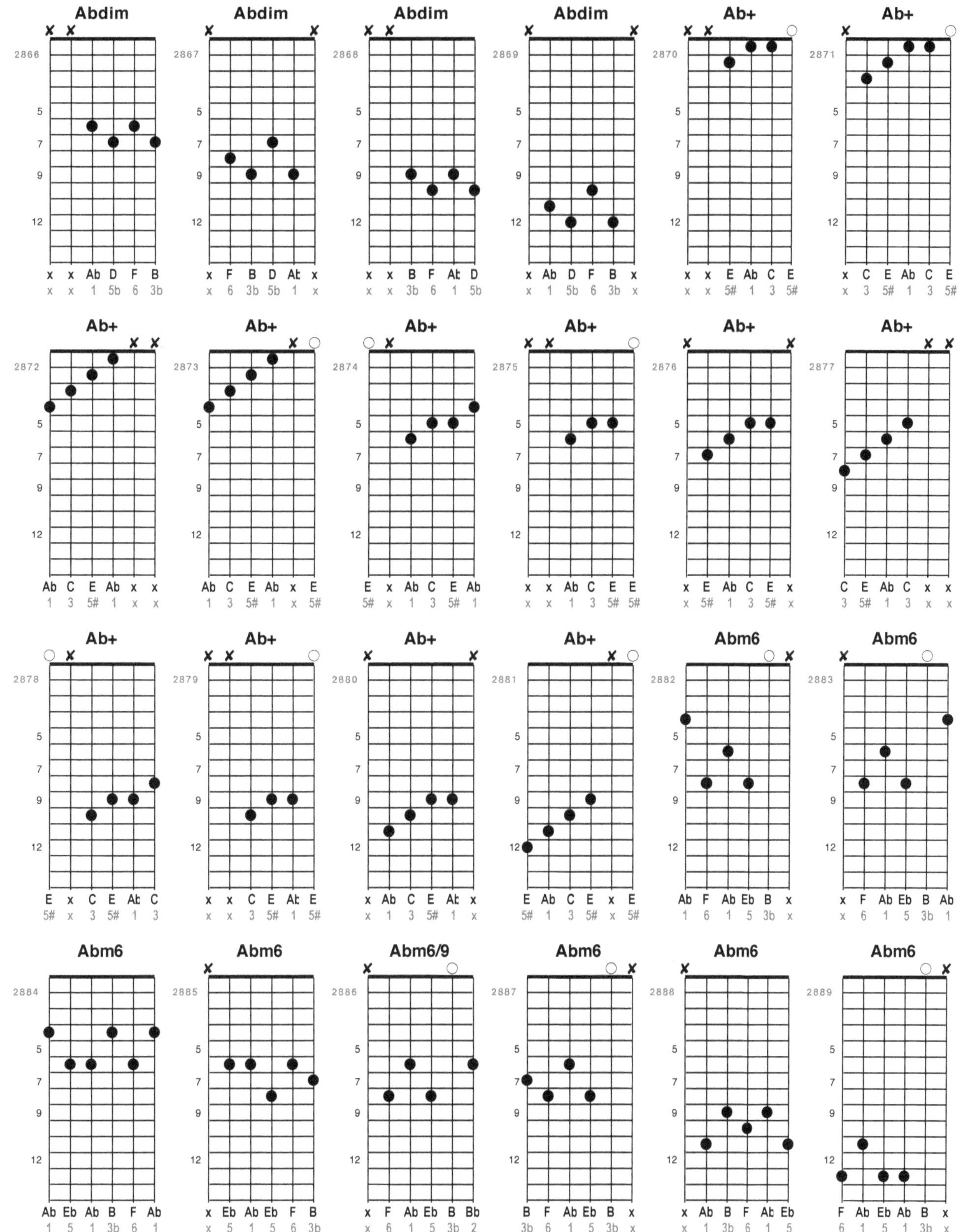
Abdim
2866
x x Ab D F B
x x 1 5b 6 3b
Abdim
2867
x F B D Ab x
x 6 3b 5b 1 x
Abdim
2868
x x B F Ab D
x x 3b 6 1 5b
Abdim
2869
x Ab D F B x
x 1 5b 6 3b x
Ab+
2870
x x E Ab C E
x x 5# 1 3 5#
Ab+
2871
x C E Ab C E
x 3 5# 1 3 5#
Ab+
2872
Ab C E Ab x x
1 3 5# 1 x x
Ab+
2873
Ab C E Ab x E
1 3 5# 1 x 5#
Ab+
2874
E x Ab C E Ab
5# x 1 3 5# 1
Ab+
2875
x x Ab C E E
x x 1 3 5# 5#
Ab+
2876
x E Ab C E x
x 5# 1 3 5# x
Ab+
2877
C E Ab C x x
3 5# 1 3 x x
Ab+
2878
E x C E Ab C
5# x 3 5# 1 3
Ab+
2879
x x C E Ab E
x x 3 5# 1 5#
Ab+
2880
x Ab C E Ab x
x 1 3 5# 1 x
Ab+
2881
E Ab C E x E
5# 1 3 5# x 5#
Abm6
2882
Ab F Ab Eb B x
1 6 1 5 3b x
Abm6
2883
x F Ab Eb B Ab
x 6 1 5 3b 1
Abm6
2884
Ab Eb Ab B F Ab
1 5 1 3b 6 1
Abm6
2885
x Eb Ab Eb F B
x 5 1 5 6 3b
Abm6/9
2886
x F Ab Eb B Bb
x 6 1 5 3b 2
Abm6
2887
B F Ab Eb B x
3b 6 1 5 3b x
Abm6
2888
x Ab B F Ab Eb
x 1 3b 6 1 5
Abm6
2889
F Ab Eb Ab B x
6 1 5 1 3b x

TUNING: E A D G B E (Standard)

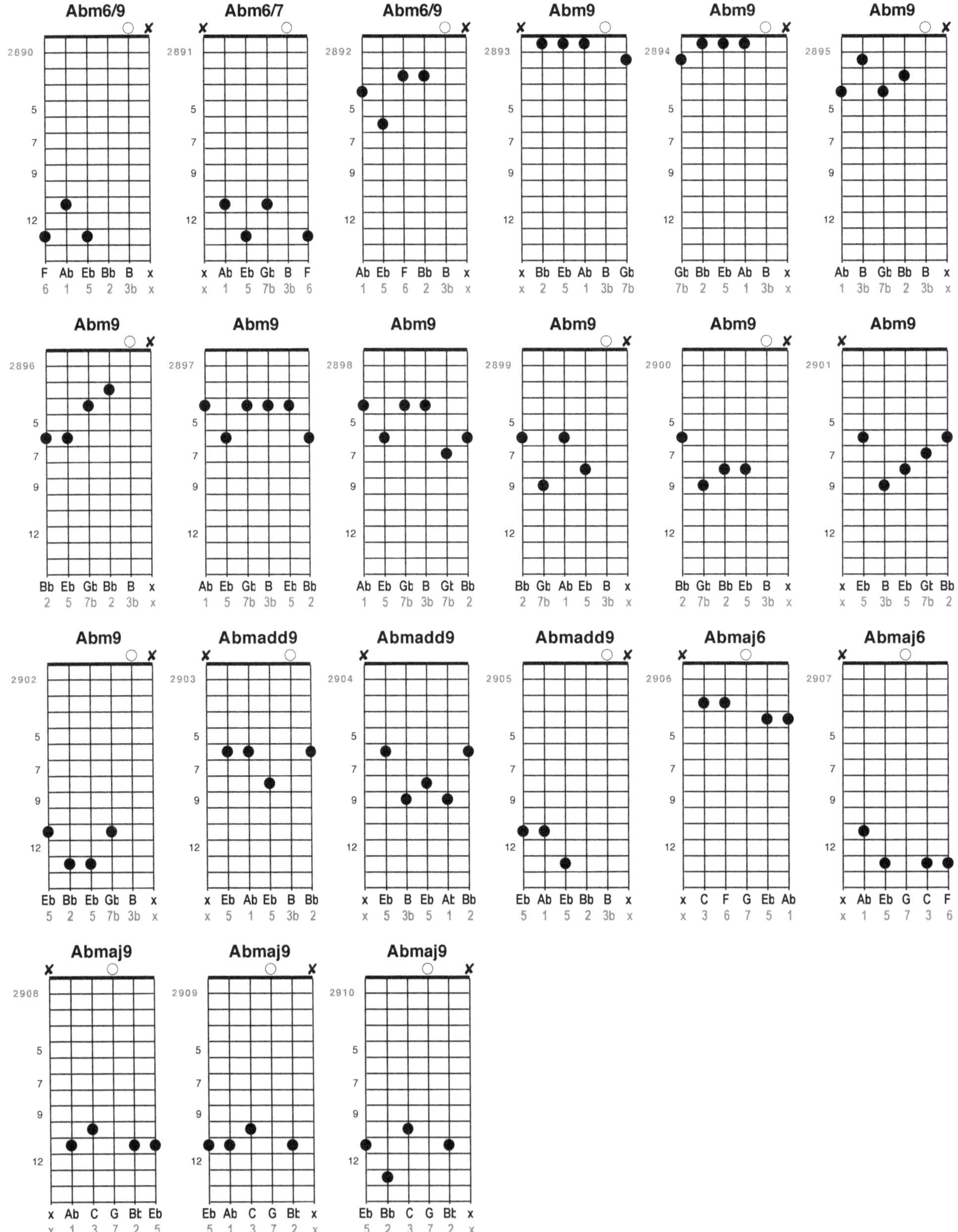
Abm6/9
2890
F Ab Eb Bb B x
6 1 5 2 3b x
Abm6/7
2891
x Ab Eb Gb B F
x 1 5 7b 3b 6
Abm6/9
2892
Ab Eb F Bb B x
1 5 6 2 3b x
Abm9
2893
x Bb Eb Ab B Gb
x 2 5 1 3b 7b
Abm9
2894
Gb Bb Eb Ab B x
7b 2 5 1 3b x
Abm9
2895
Ab B Gb Bb B x
1 3b 7b 2 3b x
Abm9
2896
Bb Eb Gb Bb B x
2 5 7b 2 3b x
Abm9
2897
Ab Eb Gb B Eb Bb
1 5 7b 3b 5 2
Abm9
2898
Ab Eb Gb B Gb Bb
1 5 7b 3b 7b 2
Abm9
2899
Bb Gb Ab Eb B x
2 7b 1 5 3b x
Abm9
2900
Bb Gb Bb Eb B x
2 7b 2 5 3b x
Abm9
2901
x Eb B Eb Gb Bb
x 5 3b 5 7b 2
Abm9
2902
Eb Bb Eb Gb B x
5 2 5 7b 3b x
Abmadd9
2903
x Eb Ab Eb B Bb
x 5 1 5 3b 2
Abmadd9
2904
x Eb B Eb Ab Bb
x 5 3b 5 1 2
Abmadd9
2905
Eb Ab Eb Bb B x
5 1 5 2 3b x
Abmaj6
2906
x C F G Eb Ab
x 3 6 7 5 1
Abmaj6
2907
x Ab Eb G C F
x 1 5 7 3 6
Abmaj9
2908
x Ab C G Bb Eb
x 1 3 7 2 5
Abmaj9
2909
Eb Ab C G Bb x
5 1 3 7 2 x
Abmaj9
2910
Eb Bb C G Bb x
5 2 3 7 2 x

Appendix: About Chord Structure

About Sharps and Flats

Most of us know that $D^{\#}$ (D-*sharp*) and $E^{\flat}$ (E-*flat*) are two different names for the same musical note that lies between D and E. There is even a fancy word for it: they are called "*enharmonic equivalents.*" On the piano, sharps and flats are black keys, while white keys have simple letter names. The naming system makes sense to a pianist who reads music, but is quite confusing to a troubadour guitarist, whose frets are the same color and who likely plays by ear.

Unfortunately, the musical notation system is most confusing to beginning troubadours, who happen to be the largest group of people playing musical instruments, so it is worth taking a little time to explain things.

When the word *sharp* or *flat* is used as a verb, it means to move up or down in pitch, and usually refers to an upward move of a single increment, which would be the next key on the piano or the next fret up the guitar neck. "*Sharp that note, please*" would tell you to move to the next higher note. A singer or violin player might also produce a note that is *flat*, which means it's too low in pitch by any amount. A guitar that is tuned *sharp* would mean that all the strings are tighter than normal. In a guitar chord situation we might mention the sharp fifth (#5) note of a C scale, which means that the normal 5th (G) is sharped up to G#. If we sharp a Bb it becomes a B.

It takes some study of music to understand why this dual-naming is done. The choice of whether to call a note A# or Bb is really determined in the musical context of a particular piece of music. In a guitar chord book, there is no context, so it is a little arbitrary what to name things. I called the section after C in this book C#, while others, especially those who are used to playing jazz with horns (who always play in flat keys like F, Bb, Eb etc.) who would have called it Db.

There are situations in music where a note is written as a double-sharp or double-flat, and there is such as thing as a G##, or even a B# and a Cb, though it would seem that a B# would just be a C natural. (The 7th scale position in the key of G# is an F##.) There isn't a good reason to use double accidentals in this book. There is even a third symbol (these three symbols are collectively called accidentals) known as the "natural." A natural symbol (♮) indicates that the musician is to ignore the flat or sharp symbol on that staff line temporarily. So a piece of music in G, that usually had all F's sharped to F#, might have an F natural note in it, which is the flat 7th note of the G scale, because the F# is the usual 7th note. Understanding that "flatting an F sharp note yields an F natural" is precisely the kind of thing that happens all the time in music, but this language is confusing to a campfire musician. Naturals are used commonly in sheet music because of the parameters imposed by the key signature at the beginning of each line of music, but they are not used in chord diagrams, and don't appear here.

It is painfully clumsy to call a note "D-sharp or E-flat" every time you mention it, and what is usually done is determined by a hierarchy of the so-called order of sharps and order of flats. F is the key that uses only one flatted note (black key) in its major scale, so to ensure that the F scale includes each of the 7 letters once and only once, its scale is written F-G-A-Bb-C-D-E-F. So "A-sharp" is much less commonly used for the note between A and B, and it is usually called "B flat." The key of Bb is the next most complex "flat key" and it has both a Bb and an Eb in its scale. For the same reason, we hear people talk about Eb much more than D#.

Likewise, among guitarists, F# and C# are used much more often than their enharmonic equivalents Gb or Db, and most musicians in conversation, instruction books or chord books, will use the more common of the 2 names. The order of flats is B-E-A-D-G-C and the order of sharps is F-C-G-D-A-E-B. This works reasonably well, until you go to the "farther" keys like C# and you will always reach some confusion about what to call some things. Choosing between the key name C# or Db can be fuzzy. In this book I used C#, because most guitarists think in sharps and not flats. This means that the musical 3rd of that scale is an E#. My system does not handle the augmented chord, where the #5 note should be a G## and my charts call it an A. If I called the key Db then the flat 7 note in a lot of chords would be a Cb, and the 5b in a diminished chord would be an Abb. There are similar

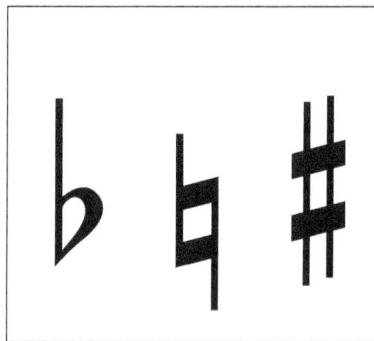

problems in the keys of F# and G#.

Rather than calling every accidental by 2 names, or doing something radical like calling every accidental a sharp, which makes logical but not musical sense, I chose to use the more common names for each chord and for the notes in the chord. The point of this book is to show you where your fingers go on the fretboard, and to help you understand the musical value of each note in the chord. If you are a novice troubadour, and are using this book, be aware that there is such a thing a D# chord, though you are generally better off calling it an Eb. A final thought: there are special typographic symbols for sharp ♯ and flat ♭, but I have chosen for the sake of simplicity in typesetting this book to just use a lower case B (b) for the flat symbol, even though I know there is a slightly different symbol. The flat and sharp symbols don't occur in normal typefaces, and it is very awkward to typeset them, especially in sentences like this, and the fonts used in e-books sometimes don't even allow them and they disturb the line spacing in the paragraphs that use them.

Bear in mind that not all chord have names, there are different names, symbols, abbreviations and nicknames for chords, and not all chords will actually contain every one of the notes in their "spelling." There are hundreds of ways to rearrange the notes in every type of chord. Knowing which notes can be doubled or omitted, and how to use the chords in musical situations is something that takes a lifetime to learn, and that few ever master.

About Naming Guitar Chords

Professors of music probably cringe when we guitarists start talking guitar chord theory, since a lot of what we do is a little contrary to the way Western music has been taught for centuries. It is only because of the proliferation and dominance of guitars in recent decades in American music that there has been a push to use and name guitar chords. Composers and pianists got by for centuries without doing what we all do now, which is to analyze the structure of all our chords, and to catalog and categorize them.

Bear in mind that not all chord have names, there are different names, symbols, abbreviations and nicknames for chords, and not all chords will actually contain every one of the notes in their "spelling." There are hundreds of ways to rearrange the notes in every type of chord. Knowing what notes can be doubled or omitted, and how to use the chords in musical situations is something that takes a lifetime to learn.

Only some chords have names, and people don't agree on the names or the notation systems used for chords that have been named. **Chords may have more than one name**, which is also confusing when you are compiling a book of guitar chords, and everyone who makes guitar chord books makes up names and uses all sorts of different symbols and terminology. It seems to be all organized, but it is in many ways a lawless jungle.

First We Name The Notes

The naming system for musical notes makes more sense once you have used it for a while, but it is confusing to a beginner, especially if you never studied piano and are a recreational guitarist. The piano and the notation system evolved together, and the whole notation system really doesn't make sense on just a guitar. The idea that some of the notes have 2 names is both useful and hard to swallow at first. The note between F and G is sometimes called F# and sometimes Gb. *Hmmm.*

In Western music, the octave is divided into 12 equal pieces called half-steps or semi-tones, or on guitar frets. The 12th fret of a stringed instrument has the same name as the open string, and it is 1/2 the string length exactly. (The ratio of the length of each fret of a guitar to the adjacent fret is the 12th root of 2, a thoroughly irrational number.) There is a certain amount of numerological mystery to all this, and most people who have studied either math or music know about the mysterious relationship of integers to music. The harmonic series: 1/2, 1/3, 1/4, 1/5, 1/6 etc has a lot to do with music, and represents the overtones of vibrating objects. The numbers 5, 7 and 12 appear a lot in musical ideas.

There are only 7 notes in most scales, and they are given the 7 letter names from A to G, with the accidentals (sharps & flats) sprinkled in. The only thing you really have to memorize is that there are no sharps or flats between B and C, and between E and F. Remember the piano keyboard layout, where some white keys are adjacent but most aren't. The rest of chord theory you can figure out from some simple rules.

Next We Look At The Intervals

The system for describing how each chord is built used to be based on what are called intervals, which is the musical distance between 2 notes. On a one-dimensional instrument like the piano it makes total sense to think this way. Traditional music theory talks of combining 2 intervals to make a 3-note chord, and stacking up larger groups of intervals, triads and even *tetrachords* (4-note chords) to build the more complex and extended chords. **We don't really need to know about intervals to use this book, and guitarists really don't think in terms of them, so I'll be brief here.**

Intervals are given names according to how many consecutive letters they span, which can be confusing. Any interval that spans the letter names C to D is a second, though it might be C-D (also a major 2nd) Cb-Db (major 2nd), C-Db (minor 2nd), C#-D (minor 2nd), C#-D# (major 2nd). Intervals get names: unison, 2nd, 3rd, 4th etc, and there are modifiers: *perfect*, *augmented*, and *diminished* for unisons, octaves, 4ths and 5ths, and *major* or *minor* for 2nd, 3rd, 6th or 7ths. All intervals can be augmented. All intervals but the unison can be diminished. Only seconds, thirds, sixths, and sevenths can be major or minor. Got it? Maybe there is a reason this system for describing chords isn't universal.

INTERVAL	Steps	Example
perfect unison	0	C-C
augmented unison	1	C-C#
minor 2nd	1	C-Db
major 2nd	2	C-D
augmented 2nd	3	C-D#
minor 3rd	3	C-Eb
major 3rd	4	C-E
augmented 3rd	5	C-E#
diminished 4th	4	C-Fb
perfect 4th	5	C-F
augmented 4th	6	C-F#
diminished 5th	6	C-Gb
perfect 5th	7	C-G
augmented 5th	8	C-G#
minor 6th	8	C-Ab
major 6th	9	C-A
augmented 6th	10	C-A#
minor 7th	10	C-Bb
major seventh	11	C-Bb
octave	12	C-C

Every chord can be described as a series of intervals. A *major triad* (3 notes) is made by stacking up 2 intervals of 4 and then 3 half steps (frets), known as a major 3rd plus a minor 3rd. Reversing the order of these two intervals builds a *minor triad.* Two minor 3rds stacked up makes a *diminished triad*, and two major 3rds create an *augmented triad.* Intervals make sense and are quite visual on the piano keyboard, where letter names are white keys and accidentals are black keys and on paper, since a staff is also a linear representation of pitch.

Trouble is, when we play a ninth chord on guitar, we are not playing the notes in numerical order– we play them the way we can. Our 9th chord might not have a 5th and it might have 2 of them, and it might have the 5th on the bottom and it might not.

Describing 6-string guitar chords with intervals is extremely messy, and not that helpful to a guitarist in explaining what is going on musically, because the guitar is not linear like a piano keyboard. Look at the 74 different A9 chords in this book. They all have a different sequence of intervals that make them up. But they all are made up of the same 5 notes: A-C#-E-G-B.

The interval-based system of describing chords is too clumsy to describe thousands of guitar chords, so a simpler but also slightly illogical numerical system is employed that uses the major scale numbers 1 through 7 combined with sharps and flats to mark the position of each note. I use this in this book, and so do most guitar chord publications.

The 12 Major Scales

Even if you play music that never uses a major scale, you'll still use the major scale numbers to describe the notes in the chords. That's how it is usually done, and it is what all the numbers in chord names and underneath each chord in this book are about. You need to at least understand what a *major scale* is.

A scale is nothing more than a group of notes arranged in order of pitch. There are dozens, possibly hundreds of kinds of scales that are associated with the various kinds of music in the world, and an exhaustive discussion of them is beyond the scope of this book.

In a so-called major scale, which is just one type of scale, the 7 notes are separated by half-steps (frets) in the pattern 2-2-1-2-2-2-1. Start on any guitar string, and climb up frets in this order and you'll finish at fret 12, and you'll hear a *do-re-mi* major scale. Remember this pattern.

There is a major scale built on each of the 12 note names, and since 5 of the 12 note names have dual names, we could map out 17 major scales instead of just 12. Because Eb is less clumsy than D#, and Bb is much more manageable than A#, we rarely hear about the key or the scale of A# or D#. The notes D# and A# appear in some of chords we play but we don't play in those keys. This is confusing. The B major 7th chord has an A# note in it, and the F#m chord has a D# note in it.

Guitars normally play in the keys of C, G, D, A and E, which are all "sharp keys." Jazz evolved with a lot of horns, which play in "flat keys" like Bb and Eb. Jazz theory uses a lot more flats, and in guitar chord theory that is not part of a jazz curriculum, we have a tendency to just use sharps and kind of ignore flats. This is why I use C# instead of Db. You could almost get by in guitar by just calling every accidental a sharp. So I put the Db scale next to the C# scale.

Let's have a look at the major scales, since these generate all the chord spellings in the book. **Each letter name appears once and only once in each scale.** This is a big part of the reason why the sharps and flats are used.

Now We Can Map the Chord Structures

The major chord (which we previously described as an interval of a major 3rd plus a minor 3rd stacked on a note...) can also be defined as the 1st, 3rd and 5th notes of a major scale. The C major chord is the 1-3-5 notes of the first row in the scales chart (previous page), which is the notes C-E-G. Likewise, a D chord has the 1-3-5 notes of the D scale (see chart) which means D-F#-A. Each other type of chord also has a numeric spelling, as shown in the next chart.

The Basic Major Scales (both C# and Db are shown)

Root 1	2	3	4	5	6	7	sharps/ flats
C	D	E	F	G	A	B	none
C#	D#	E#	F#	G#	A#	B#	7#
Db	Eb	F	Gb	Ab	Bb	C	5b
D	E	F#	G	A	B	C#	2#
Eb	F	G	Ab	Bb	C	D	3b
E	F#	G#	A	B	C#	D#	4#
F	G	A	Bb	C	D	E	1b
F#	G#	A#	B	C#	D#	E#	6#
G	A	B	C	D	E	F#	1#
Ab	Bb	C	Db	Eb	F	G	4b
A	B	C#	D	E	F#	G#	3#
Bb	C	D	Eb	F	G	A	2b
B	C#	D#	E	F#	G#	A#	5#

What comes next is a little confusing... When we play in the key of G, our three most common chords are G-C-D, referred to as the *tonic* (1or I) the *sub-dominant* (4 or IV) and the *dominant* (5 or V.) The names of those chords come from the G scale, since we are playing in the key of G. The 1-4-5 positions of the G scale are G-C-D. That's not confusing.

But each of those 3 chords is made up of 3 notes. The G chord itself is made up of the 1-3-5 notes (not the 1-4-5-- that was for chords, not notes) of the G scale, which are G-B-D. Look at all the G chords in this book-- they are all made up of various combinations of those 3 notes only. The C chord is the 1-3-5 notes (C-E-G) of the C scale and the D chord is likewise made up of the 1-3-5 (D-F#-A) notes of the D scale. This is confusing at first, to name the notes in every chord according to the major scale built on its root note name, regardless of what key the song is in.

There are of course lots of other types of chords in the world that are not in this book, and there are fuzzy and gray areas within certain types of chords.

An 11th chord, for example may have the 1-3-5-7-9-11 scale notes in it, and it may just have some of them. It's hard to know when to call it an 11th and when it is an "add11."

There will always be some chords where it is unclear what to call them, and ambiguous chords are often musically interesting and useful. When you get a chord with 5 or 6 notes in it, and you start scrambling the order and omitting notes, those same notes can often be understood as another kind of chord entirely. What the chord is named has everything to do with how it is used in a piece of music, and in a book like this they are not being used in specific songs, and are just "laboratory specimens."

The Order of Notes in a Chord

The real workings of chord theory are determined by how a chord is used in a piece of music, and studying them too closely out of context can be pointless. There are also a lot of examples of unusual voicings of chords that sound great in certain songs or as part of a progression of chords, but that might sound odd when played by themselves.

On guitar, we take what we can get, and we don't have the same choices of notes that pianists have for the order of notes. We may use a chord whose voicing is not ideal because it is all we can reach, and we may also push ourselves to play a hard fingering because it has a better or different sound.

The note names and scale degrees are shown for all the chords in this book. It offers an unprecedented look at the inner workings of all these chords.

Chord Name	Scale Degrees	*Example : C Scale*	Symbol or Abbrev.
major	1 - 3 - 5	C-E-G	C, Cmaj CΔ
minor	1 - 3^{b} - 5	C-E^{b}-G	Cm C-
modal	1 - 5	C-G	C5
diminished (dim7)	1 - 3^{b} - 5^{b} or 1-3^{b}-5^{b}-7bb (6)	C-E^{b}-G^{b} B^{bb} (A)	Cdim or C°
augmented	1 - 3# - 5#	C-F-G#	C+, Caug
suspended fourth	1 - 4 - 5	C-F-G	Csus, Csus4
sixth (added sixth)	1 - 3 - 5 - 6	C-E-G-A	C6
(dominant) seventh	1 - 3 - 5 - 7b	C-E-G-Bb	C7 Cdom7
major seventh	1 - 3 - 5 - 7	C-E-G-B	Cmaj7 Cma7 CM7 CMa7 C j7 CΔ7 CΔ
minor seventh	1 - 3^{b} - 5 -7b	C-E^{b}-G-Bb	Cm7 C-7
seventh suspended	1 - 4 - 5 - 7b	C-F-G-Bb	C7sus, C7sus4
add nine	1 - 3 - 5 - 2	C-E-G-D	Cadd9 , Csus2
minor add nine	1 - 3b - 5 - 2	C-Eb-G-D	Cmadd9
add eleven	1 - 3 - 5 - 4	C-E-G-F	Cadd11, Cadd4
minor add eleven	1 - 3b - 5 - 4	C-Eb-G-F	Cmadd11
(dominant) ninth	1 - 3 - 5 - 7b - 2	C-E-G-Bb-D	C9
major ninth	1 - 3 - 5 - 7 - 2	C-E-G-B-D	Cmaj9, Cma9, CM9 C j9 CΔ9
minor ninth	1 - 3b - 5 - 7b - 2	C-Eb-G-Bb-D	Cm9
major sixth	1 - 3 - 5 - 6 - 7	C-E-G-B-A	Cmaj6, Cma6, CM6 C j6 CΔ6
minor sixth	1 - 3b - 5 - 6	C-E^{b}-G-A	Cm6
6/7 (dominant sixth)	1 - 3 - 5 - 6 - 7b	C-E-G-Bb-A	C6/7
6/9	1 - 3 - 5 - 6 - 2	C-E-G-A-D	C6/9
eleventh	1 - 3 - 5 - 7b- 2- 4	C-E-G-Bb-D-F	C11
major eleventh	1 - 3 - 5 - 7- 2- 4	C-E-G-B-D-F	Cmaj11, Cma11, CM11 C j11 CΔ11
9/11	1 - 3 - 5 - 2- 4	C-E-G-D-F	C9/11
minor eleventh	1 - 3b - 5 - 7b- 2- 4	C-Eb-G-Bb-D-F	Cm11
thirteenth	1 - 3 - 5 - 6 - 7b- 2	C-E-G-Bb-D-A	C13
minor thirteenth	1 - 3b - 5 - 6 -7b- 2	C-Eb-G-Bb-D-A	Cm13
major thirteenth	1 - 3 - 5 - 6 - 7- 2	C-E-G-B-D-A	Cmaj13, Cma13, CM13 C j13 CΔ13
6/11	1 - 3 - 5 - 6 - 4	C-E-G-A-F	C6/11

The Root / Bass Note

When we compare two or more notes, our ear usually uses the lower pitched note as a reference and compares the higher notes to it. (This is why if just our lowest string is out of tune, it makes us want to tune the others to it.) **The lowest note of a chord is by far the most important in shaping the flavor and sound of a chord.** Pay attention and keep track of your bass notes. You will notice that most of the chords in this book have 1's or 5's in the bass, though there are a few with unusual bass notes that I liked. Even the musical 3rd can sound odd if it is in the bass. Compare the C chords, with 1, 3 or 5 in the bass.

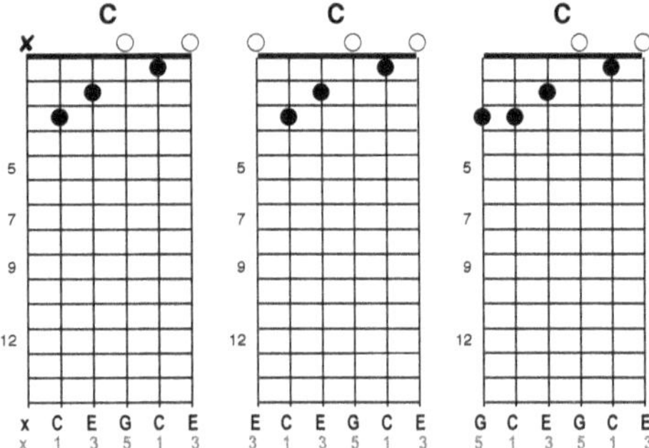

C
C
C
x C E G C E
x 1 3 5 1 3
E C E G C E
3 1 3 5 1 3
G C E G C E
5 1 3 5 1 3

Now listen to the Em chord with the root bass and with the 3rd in the bass. It's almost unusable as a standalone chord:

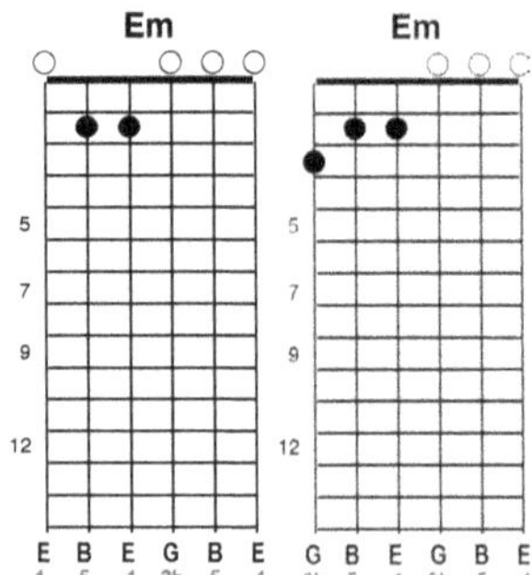

Em
Em
E B E G B E
1 5 1 3b 5 1
G B E G B E
3b 5 1 3b 5 1

If a 6th, 7th or 9th is in the bass, it may render the chord barely usable. The D major chord with the E bass should be some kind of *Dadd9* chord, but it is really just a "non-chord." We can't compare it to the sound of adding the D note an octave higher on the 4th string, since we can't play that E without removing our D low note on the 4th string. But we can compare the sound of adding a D note to a C chord in 2 octaves. Notice how much better it sounds when added in the treble. Even adding the D in the middle is pretty "muddy."

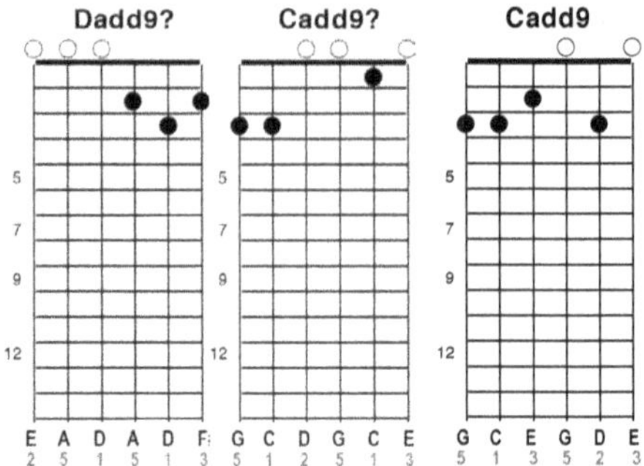

Dadd9?
Cadd9?
Cadd9
E A D A D F♯
2 5 1 5 1 3
G C D G C E
5 1 2 5 1 3
G C E G D E
5 1 3 5 2 3

As a general rule, you will get stronger chords if there are roots or 5ths in the bass, with the more "exotic" notes in the treble.

About Dissonance and Pitch

Play an E and an F simultaneously, or any musical interval of a "minor 2nd," which means 2 adjacent keys on the piano. They are quite dissonant. On a guitar play the 6th fret of the B string [F] and the open high E string at the same time. Now separate the notes E-F by an octave and play them again. (This time play fret 2 of the 4th string [E] and the 1st fret of the high E string [F]. The result is much less dissonant. If you play the open bass E [E] and fret 1 of the high E string [F] simultaneously and separate the E from the F by another octave, the interval E-F is not really dissonant anymore.

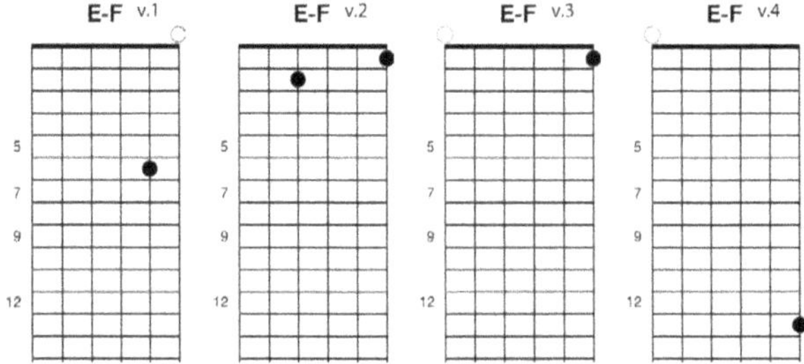

E-F v.1
E-F v.2
E-F v.3
E-F v.4

Finally, if you play the bass E string and the 13th fret F on the high E string, this is also the same interval of E-F, except now the two are separated by 3 octaves. It is not dissonant at all.

Sometimes chords and inversions of chords sound fine if they are spread across several octaves, even though the same letter-named notes would not sound as good if they were closer together in overall pitch.

The location of the notes in the chord has a big effect on the sound. If you find a chord you like or don't like in this book, study the structure more carefully.

About Numbers like 9^{ths} and 11^{ths}

You've probably noticed that the numerals 1-7 mark the musical function of the chords in this book, yet the chords have names like 9th, 11th and 13th. This is one of those "gray areas" where things are not totally logical, but it is standard practice. To be rigorous, when you add a D note to a C chord, you should call it a 2nd if it is in a lower octave and a 9th if it is higher, and you might wonder why we don't call adding a D note another octave higher a 16th. The answer is that we don't. The language used, like a lot of linguistic things, evolves and changes as it is passed through the people that use it. Musicians tend to use the term "9th chord" when there is a 1-3-5 chord with both a 7th and a 2nd added, but if there is no 7th, and it is just 1-3-5-2 it is called an *"add9," "add2"* or *"sus2."* I use the term *add9* in this book, though just as many people call it an add2, and some people use both. Likewise, musicians have adopted the terms 11th and 13th, but you just don't hear talk of 18th or 20th chords, and the distinctions and definitions are often blurred.

There is no legislation or regulation, and not much in the way of organized attempts to standardize things. After decades of independent teachers and publishers inventing notation and terminology, there is quite a lot of diversity in the way music theory is written and discussed. The *Berklee College of Music* in Boston is doing a lot to make the study of contemporary music theory more uniform.

Inversions, Voicings and Doubling

What is also not clear, and something for which there is no terminology, is what happens when there are notes "missing." This happens all the time in guitar, since we have such limitations in fingerings, especially when trying to play extended chords that may have 5 or 6 notes in their "official" form when we only have 4 fingers and 6 strings. What if it is 1-5-7b-2 or 1-3-7b-2? Are they still 9th chords? In this book I say *yes.*

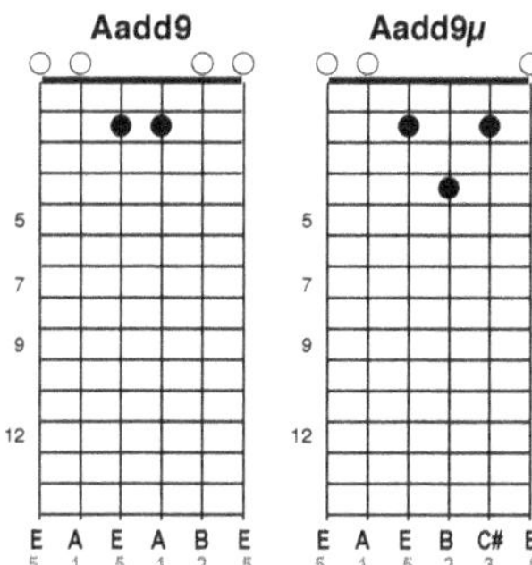
Aadd9
Aadd9μ
5
7
9
12
E A E A B E
5 1 5 1 2 5
E A E B C# E
5 1 5 2 3 5

These two *Aadd9* chords are quite different in sound, because one has just 1-2-5 notes and the other has 1-2-3-5. The popular rock band *Steely Dan* made extensive use of these kinds of chords, and called them "*mu*" chords, since there was no common name for this kind of structure.

Music theory books teach that an "uninverted" or root position C triad has the notes C-E-G, while a 1st inversion C chord has the spelling E-G-C and a 2nd inversion is G-C-E. The term "inversion" is sometimes used to mean the order of notes or voicing, though technically it refers to which is the lowest note in the group.

Look at any groups of chords in this book, and you will see quite a diversity of repeated, scrambled and missing numbers. This is the beauty and mystery of guitar chords, and in this book they are all laid out in front of you.

Those Pesky 4's and 11's

If we add a 4th scale note to a major chord, 1-3-5-4 or 1-3-4-5 we get what most often is called an add11. Adding the 4 in the lower pitches muddies up the sound a lot, unless we remove the 3rd, and just have 1-4-5, which is usually called a suspended 4th or sus4.

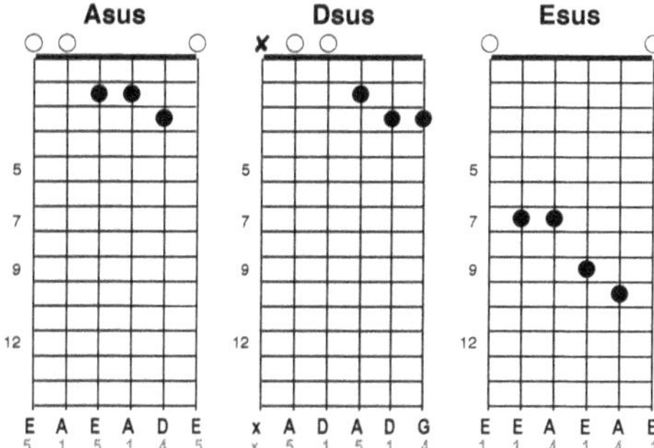
Asus
Dsus
Esus
5
7
9
12
E A E A D E
5 1 5 1 4 5
x A D A D G
x 5 1 5 1 4
E E A E A E
1 1 4 1 4 1

There are all kinds of chords with 4's sprinkled around, and they tend to have missing notes and irregular structure. The Esus here has no 5th. Is it still an Esus?

The *sus4* is an unstable chord that wants to resolve back to the major. *The Who's* song *Pinball Wizard* is full of them.

It's quite common to have the 3rd replaced with the 4th, and also have a flat 7th. This chord is called the 7th suspended, or 7sus, and there are a lot of them in troubadour's lives.

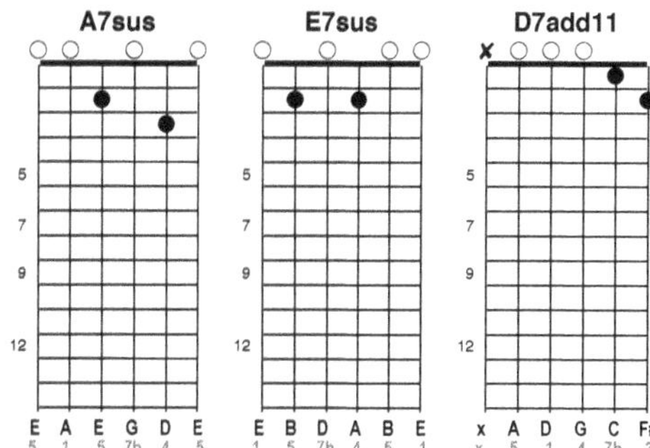
A7sus
E7sus
D7add11
5
7
9
12
E A E G D E
5 1 5 7b 4 5
E B D A B E
1 5 7b 4 5 1
x A D G C F#
x 5 1 4 7b 3

Adding the 4th and the flat 7 without removing the 3rd is often called *7add11* since it is not the same as a *7sus*. I use this category in this book.

But what if we add the 4 in a high octave and don't remove

the 3rd? We get a different-sounding kind of *add11* harp-like chord. They are hard to play but sound great. Because of how standard tuning works, these are rare, and there are a lot more of these kinds of "overlapping" voicings that show up when you use open tunings or partial capos:

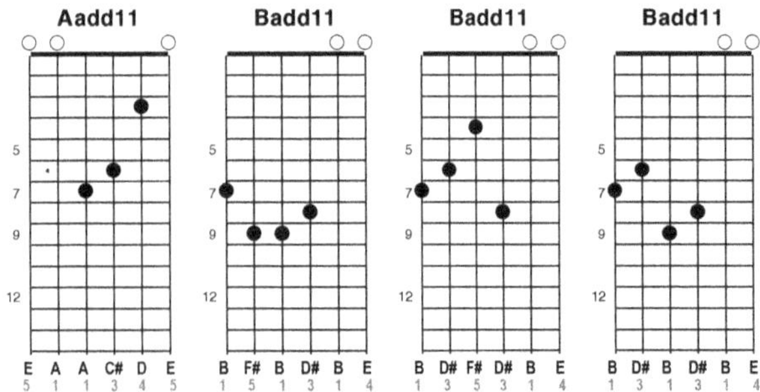
Aadd11
Badd11
Badd11
Badd11
E A A C# D E
5 1 1 3 4 5
B F# B D# B E
1 5 1 3 1 4
B D# F# D# B E
1 3 5 3 1 4
B D# B D# B E
1 3 1 3 1 4

What is normally called an 11th chord in music theory is a chord that has a 1-3-5 foundation, and then it has a 7th, 9th and also an 11th added on. This is a 6-note chord that is much easier on piano than guitar. It's a very different sounding chord than an add11. There are actually a lot of A11 chords. Here are a couple, plus a C11. Notice that they are all missing some notes:

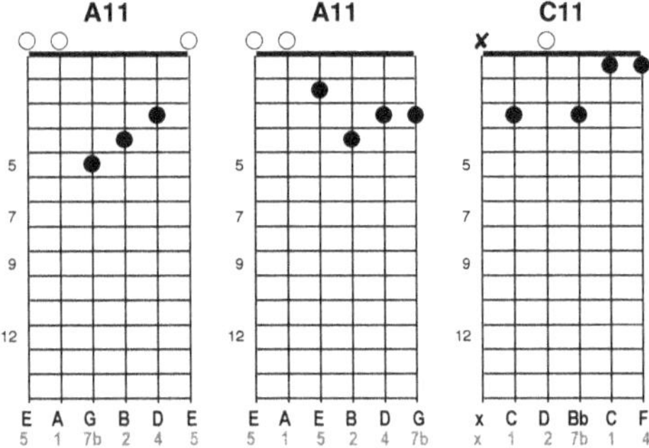
A11
A11
C11
E A G B D E
5 1 7b 2 4 5
E A E B D G
5 1 5 2 4 7b
x C D Bb C F
x 1 2 7b 1 4

Identifying a Chord

It's one thing to look for ways to play a particular chord on the fingerboard, but it's another task entirely to find a chord, and then wonder what it might be called or how it might be used. Our ears are a big part of this, and we should learn to hear the telltale sound of each type of chords. Many chords are "cut and dried" and everyone agrees what they are called. Others can be ambiguous. No doubt some of you will object to the names I have given to some chords, especially if you are used to using an enharmonic equivalent. The point at which a Em7 chord becomes a G6 is sometimes unclear. If it has a big E bass note on the bottom that will tilt the balance toward calling it an Em7, and if there is a G on the bottom, it will be more of a G6. But what about these D6 and Bm7 chords?

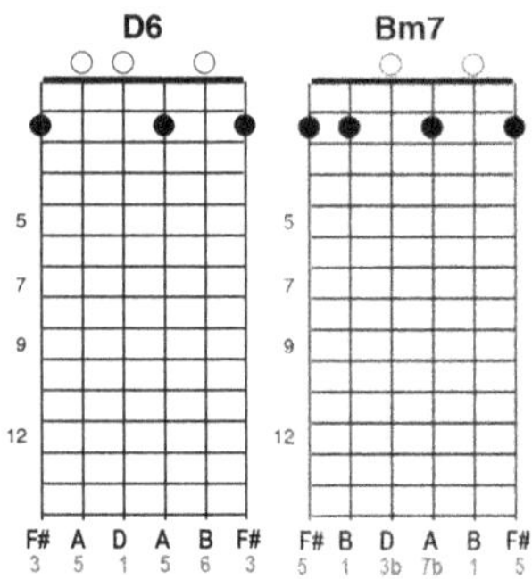
D6
Bm7
F# A D A B F#
3 5 1 5 6 3
F# B D A B F#
5 1 3b 7b 1 5

They are much closer in sound, since both have the F# on the bottom. If you lifted that B note on the A string up and down it would not sound that different, but would technically switch the chord from D6 to Bm7. Change a note, add an E on top, and it really becomes a Bm11 with no 9th in it, then add the 9th C# on the B string if you like, or remove the low F# bass note and it's an E7sus.

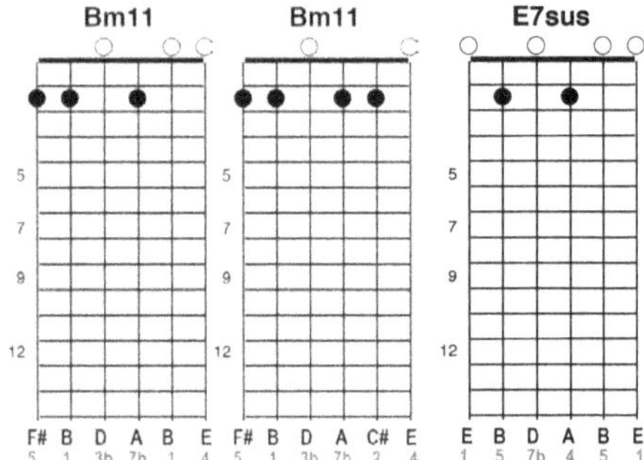
Bm11
Bm11
E7sus
F# B D A B E
5 1 3b 7b 1 4
F# B D A C# E
5 1 3b 7b 2 4
E B D A B E
1 5 7b 4 5 1

Here is another good example. It's a chord I use to follow 2 frets above an E minor in my instrumental version of Gershwin's *Summertime*:

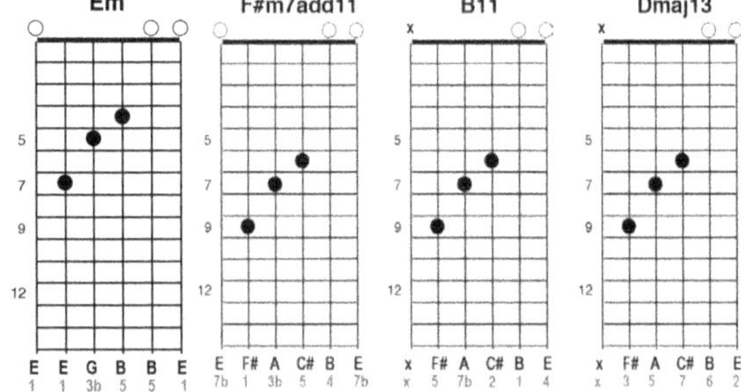
Em
F#m7add11
B11
Dmaj13
E E G B B E
1 1 3b 5 5 1
E F# A C# B E
7b 1 3b 5 4 7b
x F# A C# B E
x 5 7b 2 1 4
x F# A C# B E
x 3 5 7 6 2

Depending on which note you choose to be the root, you get three totally different names. You tell me what to call it.

Chords Without Good Names

A great example of a chord without a good name is a chord that has been around as long as standard tuning itself. It is the chord you get when you move an E major chord up a half step and still leave the 1-2 and 6 strings open. Or when you slide an A chord up a half step:

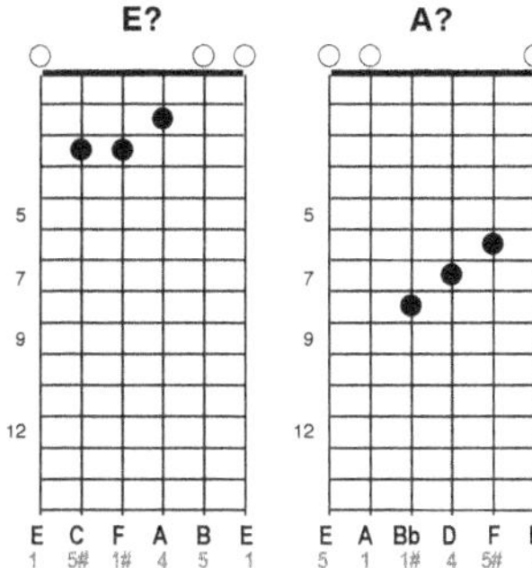
E?
A?
5
7
9
12
E C F A B E
1 5# 1# 4 5 1
E A Bb D F E
5 1 1# 4 5# 5

It is a very common chord in Spanish and Flamenco music, and there is probably one in the soundtrack of every spaghetti Western movie. It just doesn't fit regular music theory explanations. Instead of E-B-E-G#-B-E (E major chord) you now have E-C-F-A-B-E, which means you sort of still have an E chord, since that is the root, but it has a 4th (A), a "sharp 5" or "flat 6" (C) and what might be called a "sharp 1" or a "flat 2." This chord sounds great when you play first an E chord, then this chord, and then go back to the E chord. It is sometimes called a "*Phrygian suspended*" chord, but the technical explanation of that chord usually just calls it a "sus4 flat9" (b9) which does not mention the other note C. If you play guitar in *Phrygian* mode, you know all about this kind of chord, but other troubadours you run into probably won't know what to call it any more than you do.

Another great example of a chord that has no name and isn't really a useful and functioning chord is the 6 open strings of a standard-tuned guitar: E-A-D-G-B-E. No one uses it in songs or instrumental music, but we all have heard it a lot. Because it has a bass string note of E and a D (7b) and a G (3b) it could be called some kind of extended E minor 7th, with numerical spelling from the E scale as 1-4-7b-3b-5-1. That A note in the bottom end doesn't belong, and the bass end is a poor place to put a 4th. So if you instead thought of it as an A-rooted chord, then the low E string would be a 5th, and the chord would have the spelling: 5-1-4-7b-2-5 which would make it a lousy voicing of an A11th chord, since it has the flat 7th and 2 (9th). But it has no 3rd in this latter situation, which makes it less convincing. Without the E bass note it could be a D-root chord, with added 6/9/11 notes.

There are plenty of other chords you will find that just don't have good names and that don't fit common patterns. The "C-A-G-E-D" chord is one I have been bumping into a lot lately. With those note names in various orders and depending on which bass root note is prominent you can call it a C6/9, Am9, D11, Em11#5, or even something like G6/9/11.

Try to just enjoy the sounds of chords, and use them in your music, and keep an open mind about what to call them. Other people may use different terminology.

More Musical Resources By Harvey Reid

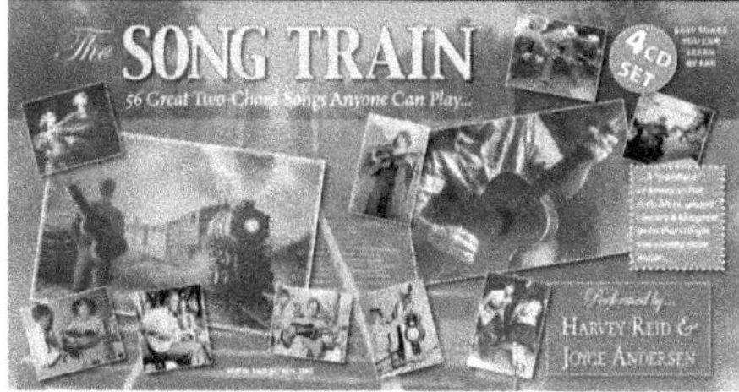
The SONG TRAIN
56 Great Two-Chord Songs Anyone Can Play...

THE SONG TRAIN (2007) is a landmark resource for beginning guitarists by Harvey Reid & Joyce Andersen. 4-CD boxed set with 80-page color hardback book, contains 56 one & two chord songs. Half the songs are copyrighted, by the likes of Bob Dylan, Hank Williams, Chuck Berry etc, so it offers beginners easy but great songs they can play. Folk, blues, gospel, rock, celtic, country and gospel songs, and an amazing cross-section of American music. **www.songtrain.net**

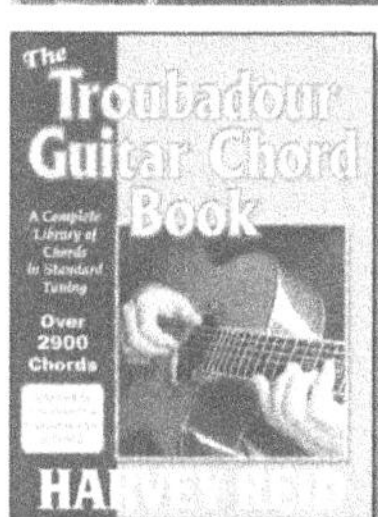
The Troubadour Guitar Chord Book
Over 2900 Chords

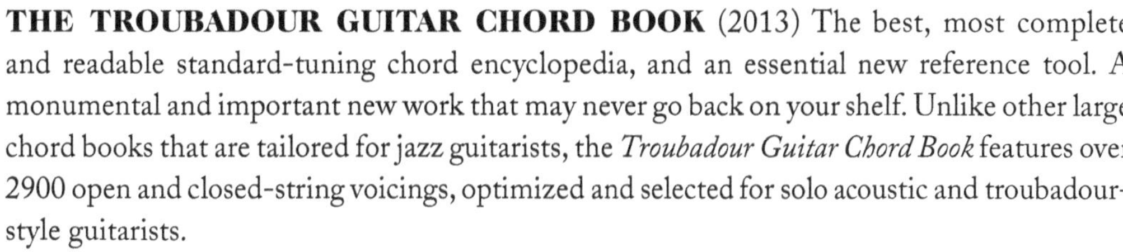

THE TROUBADOUR GUITAR CHORD BOOK (2013) The best, most complete and readable standard-tuning chord encyclopedia, and an essential new reference tool. A monumental and important new work that may never go back on your shelf. Unlike other large chord books that are tailored for jazz guitarists, the *Troubadour Guitar Chord Book* features over 2900 open and closed-string voicings, optimized and selected for solo acoustic and troubadour-style guitarists.

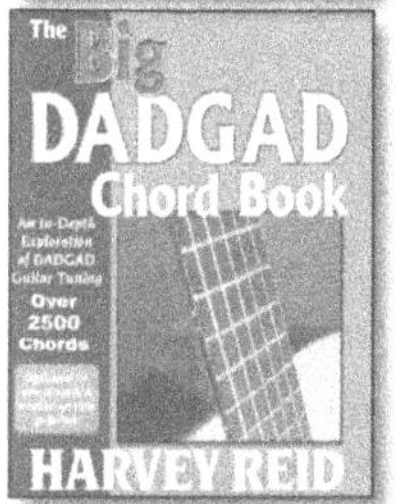
The Big DADGAD Chord Book
Over 2500 Chords
HARVEY REID

THE BIG DADGAD CHORD BOOK (2014) The best, most complete and readable chord encyclopedia in DADGAD tuning, with 2500 chords mapped out. Another indispensable reference book for anyone who plays in this popular tuning. Also features full-fingerboard diagrams, with every note and scale degree shown for every chord.

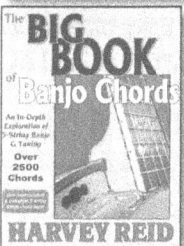

The BIG BOOK of Banjo Chords
Over 2500 Chords
HARVEY REID
BIG BOOK Mandocello Chords
HARVEY REID

THE BIG BOOK OF BANJO CHORDS (2015) The most complete, detailed and versatile book of chords for standard banjo G tuning. The fingerboard shown like never before, with 5th string notes shown.

THE BIG BOOK OF MANDOCELLO CHORDS (2015) The most complete, detailed and versatile book of chords for standard C-G-A-D tuning. Also includes 11 of the first ideas ever published for partial capos on mandocello.

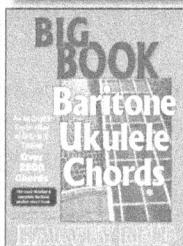

Baritone Ukulele Simplified
HARVEY REID

BIG BOOK Baritone Ukulele Chords

THE BIG BOOK OF BARITONE UKULELE CHORDS (2015) The most complete, detailed and versatile book of chords for standard D-G-B-E tuning.

BARITONE UKULELE SIMPLIFIED (2015) Explores 9 different new tunings and partial capo ideas that reveal for the first time how to play instant music with great-sounding but simpler chord shapes. This is the first book to introduce partial capos on a ukulele.

SLEIGHT OF HAND (1983) The first book of partial capo guitar arrangements, still in print. 16 solo guitar arrangements using a universal partial capo. Intermediate to advanced level, mostly for fingerstyle guitar, but has 2 flatpicked fiddle tune arrangements (*Sally Goodin'* and *Devil's Dream*) In TAB and standard notation. *Suite: For the Duchess, Für Elise, Scarborough Fair, Minuet in Dm, Flowers of Edinburgh, Simple Gifts, Sally Goodin', Irish Washerwoman, Pavanne, Minuet in Dm, Red-Haired Boy, June Apple, Jesu Joy of Man's Desiring, Devil's Dream, Sally Goodin', Scherzo, Shenandoah, Greensleeves, Sailor's Hornpipe, Fisher's Hornpipe*

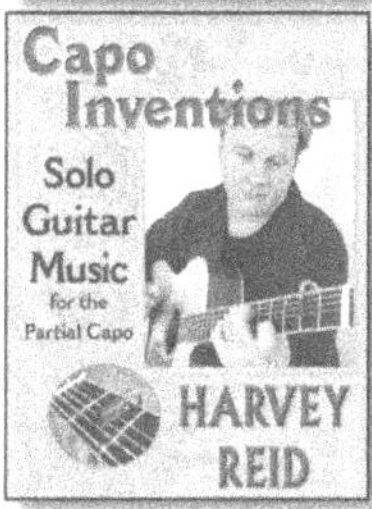
Capo Inventions
Solo Guitar Music
for the Partial Capo
HARVEY REID

CAPO INVENTIONS (2006) 14 intermediate to advanced arrangements from Reid's catalog of guitar recordings. Precisely transcribed for solo guitar, these pieces all use a 3-string *Esus* type partial capo. In TAB and standard notation. *Skye Boat Song, Highwire Hornpipe, Windy Grave, Hard Times, The Unknown Soldier, Suite: For the Duchess, The Arkansas Traveler, The Minstrel Boy, Red in the Sky, Prelude to the Minstrel's Dream, Norway Suite: Parts 1 &2, Star Island Jig, Macallan's Jig.*

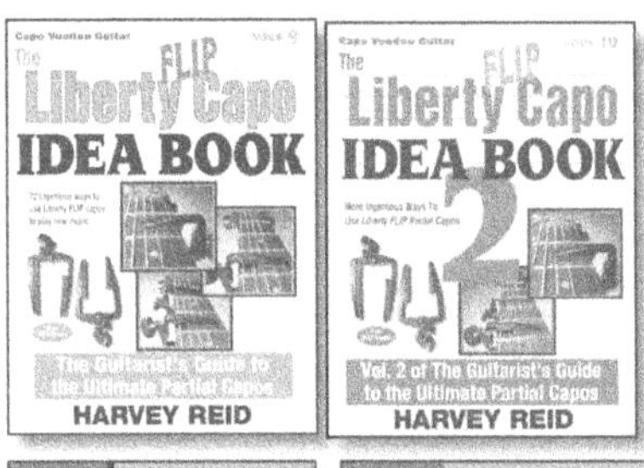
The FLIP Liberty Capo IDEA BOOK
The Guitarist's Guide to the Ultimate Partial Capos
HARVEY REID
The FLIP Liberty Capo IDEA BOOK 2
Vol. 2 of The Guitarist's Guide to the Ultimate Partial Capos
HARVEY REID

THE LIBERTY "FLIP" CAPO IDEA BOOKS (2014-15) Two volumes, totaling almost 400 pages, with over 113 ideas of partial capo configurations that can be done with a pair of *Model 43* and *Model 65 Liberty* partial capos. These were developed by Harvey Reid, and are the new generation of sleek and versatile partial capos that clamp 6, 5, 4 or 3 strings on most guitars, banjos, ukes and mandolins. Volume I shows 72 ideas, mostly in standard tuning, and with a taste of combining capos with altered tunings. Volume 2 combines capos with altered tunings.

Secrets of the 3-String Partial Capo
HARVEY REID

Capo Voodoo BOOK 6
More Secrets of the 3-String Partial Capo
HARVEY REID

SECRETS OF THE 3-STRING PARTIAL CAPO (2010) 24 mind-bending ways to use the popular 3-string *Esus* (*E-suspended*) type partial capo. ***This book may no longer be available after the arrival of the Liberty Capos.*** **18 of these ideas are now in the *Liberty Capo IDEA BOOK*, and the other 6 appear in the *Liberty "FLIP" Capo IDEA BOOK Vol.2.***

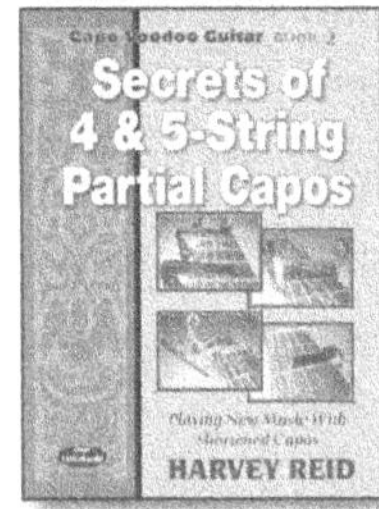
Secrets of 4 & 5-String Partial Capos
HARVEY REID

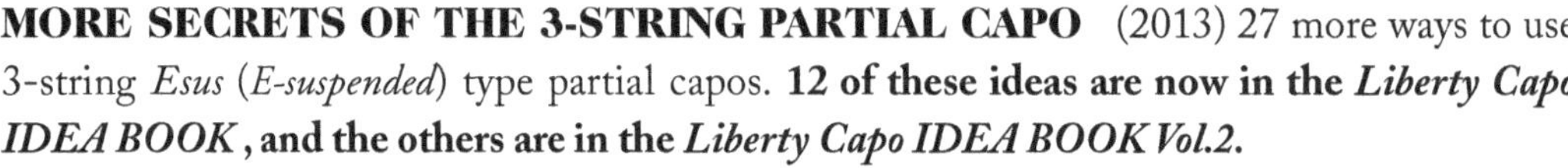

MORE SECRETS OF THE 3-STRING PARTIAL CAPO (2013) 27 more ways to use 3-string *Esus* (*E-suspended*) type partial capos. **12 of these ideas are now in the *Liberty Capo IDEA BOOK*, and the others are in the *Liberty Capo IDEA BOOK Vol.2.***

SECRETS OF THE 4 & 5-STRING PARTIAL CAPOS (2011) Another treasure trove of ideas, for the *Planet Waves*, *Shubb*, or *Kyser* shortened 4 or 5-string capos. (Also valuable for *Third Hand, Liberty "Flip"* or *Spider* universal capos.) Most people who have one of these capos know a few ways to use them. Here are an amazing 47 ideas that use a 4 or 5-string capo to generate new music. Over 1600 chords. ***This book may no longer be available after the arrival of the Liberty Capos.*** **30 of these 47 ideas are now in the *Liberty Capo IDEA BOOK*, and the other 17 appear in the *Liberty Capo IDEA BOOK Vol.2.***

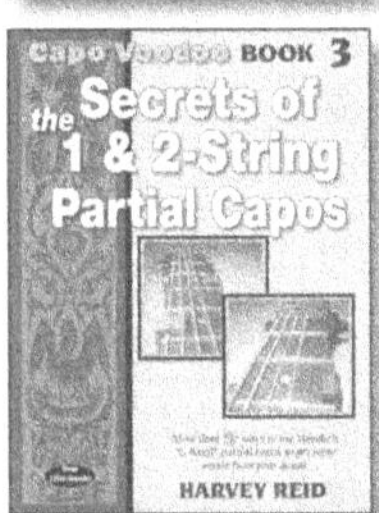
Capo Voodoo BOOK 3
the Secrets of 1 & 2-String Partial Capos
HARVEY REID

SECRETS OF THE 1 & 2-STRING PARTIAL CAPOS (2012) How to use the unique *Woodie's G-Band* 1 and 2-string partial capos. 33 clever ways to use these capos in a number of tunings and in combination with other partial capos, with over 1100 chords. 98 pages are packed with photos, ideas and capo knowledge that is only available here. Even the makers of the capos don't know about these ideas.

Capo Voodoo BOOK 4
Secrets of Partial Capos in DADGAD Tuning
HARVEY REID

SECRETS OF PARTIAL CAPOS IN DADGAD TUNING (2012) Most people think of partial capos as a substitute for open tunings, and don't realize that they can be combined. Harvey Reid shows you over 25 ingenious ways to use partial capos to expand the musical possibilities of DADGAD tuning (4 of them use the similar CGDGAD tuning.) Get new chords, fingerings, voicings, resonances and unlock a new, mysterious world of new music hiding in your fingerboard. **17 of these ideas are now in the *Liberty Capo IDEA BOOK Vol.2.***

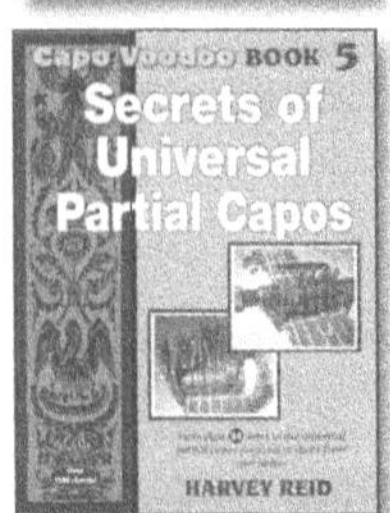
Capo Voodoo BOOK 5
Secrets of Universal Partial Capos
HARVEY REID

SECRETS OF UNIVERSAL PARTIAL CAPOS (2012) 45 ways to get new music from your guitar that can only be done with universal partial capos. This hidden world of music in your fingerboard includes a number of tunings and combinations with other partial capos. Over 1500 chords. Packed with photos, clear explanations and capo strategy will save you years of searching. **Because the *Model 43 Liberty* capo clamps 4 middle strings, 13 of these ideas are now duplicated in the *Liberty Capo IDEA BOOKS, Vol. 1-2.***

Secrets of Partial Capos in Drop D Tuning
HARVEY REID

SECRETS OF PARTIAL CAPOS IN DROP D TUNING (2014) The most common tuning is *Drop D*: D A D G B E, and like any tuning, it can be combined with partial capos to add another dimension to the guitar. This book presents 24 ways to use one or more partial capos of all types to generate more new music. **9 of these ideas are now in the *Liberty Capo IDEA BOOK*, and 7 more appear in *Vol.2.*** The others use a universal or *G-Band* capo.

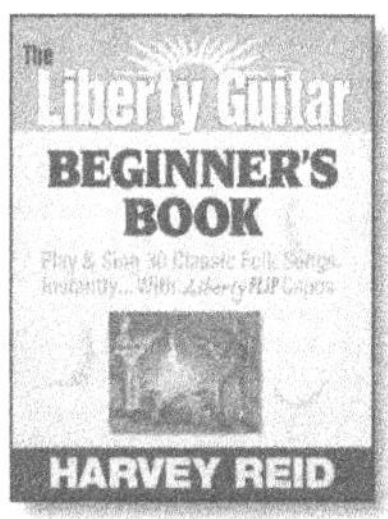
The
Liberty Guitar
BEGINNER'S
BOOK
HARVEY REID

THE LIBERTY GUITAR BEGINNER'S BOOK (2015) Play 30 classic folk songs instantly with super-simple, great-sounding chords. For children or adults, this book carefully explains how to use *Liberty Tuning* to play chords and sing songs in 6 different major and minor keys. You need a guitar, a full capo, and a *Liberty FLIP Model 43* capo.

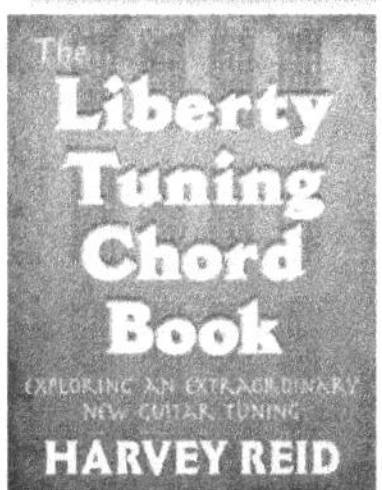
The
Liberty
Tuning
Chord
Book
HARVEY REID

THE LIBERTY TUNING CHORD BOOK (2013) In his partial capo research, Harvey Reid discovered a simple new guitar tuning that introduces a remarkable geometrical symmetry and simplicity to the guitar fingerboard that no one ever dreamed existed. Here is a thorough examination of what this amazing tuning can do, with over 1200 chords, sorted, mapped out and organized to help you find your way in *Liberty Tuning*. Lots of tips, advice & clear explanations. For guitar teachers, beginners and anyone who already plays guitar and wants to learn about this important discovery.

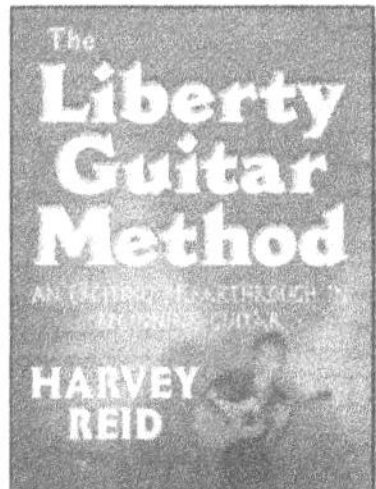
The
Liberty
Guitar
Method
HARVEY
REID

THE LIBERTY GUITAR METHOD (2013) Total beginners can play music like never before. It's easy to do and sounds great. Learn to use *Liberty Tuning* to play great-sounding, simple 2-finger chords to songs by Bob Dylan, Hank Williams, John Prine, Johnny Cash, Chuck Berry, The Beatles, Adele, and more. You won't believe it 'til you try it. *Hush Little Baby, This Land is Your Land, Your Cheating Heart, A Hard Rain's A Gonna Fall, Amazing Grace, The Cuckoo, Folsom Prison Blues, Angel From Montgomery, Maybellene, Let It Be, Imagine, Someone Like You, The Wedding Song, House of the Rising Sun*

The
"Liberty"
SONG TRAIN
HARVEY REID

THE LIBERTY SONG TRAIN (2013) Learn how to use *Liberty Tuning* to play all 56 two-chord songs in the epic *Song Train* collection with just 2-finger chords, in the same keys as they were done on the *Song Train* recordings. Beginning guitar has never been easier. Careful explanations, with lots of helpful tips, strategy and advice. If you have the *Song Train* 4-CD collection, you need this companion book.

Liberty Guitar
HARVEY REID &
JOYCE ANDERSEN

LIBERTY GUITAR FOR KIDS (2013) It's a huge breakthrough in children's guitar. Children as young as 4 can learn to strum simple 2-finger *Liberty Tuning* chords and play guitar like never before. Classic traditional plus modern children's songs arranged in keys young voices can sing in. No need to wait until the children grow bigger or waste your money on crummy small children's guitars. Learn how even small children can instantly start strumming songs on adult guitars. It's really amazing. *London Bridge, Row Row Row Your Boat, Farmer in the Dell, Hush Little Baby, This Land is Your Land, Oh Susannah, Standing in the Need of Prayer, Hey Lolly Lolly, Comin' Round the Mountain* and more.

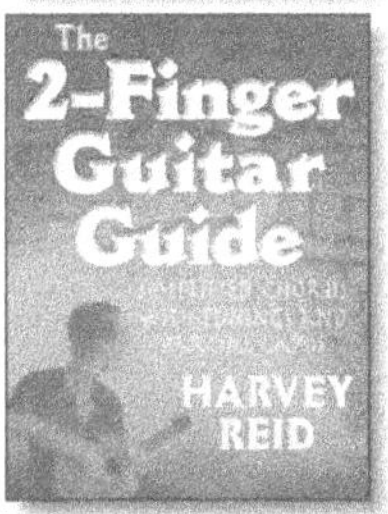
The
2-Finger
Guitar
Guide
HARVEY
REID

THE 2-FINGER GUITAR GUIDE (2013) A careful study of simplified guitar chords, this book takes you through each of the common tunings and partial capo configurations that can be used to play simplified guitar chords. Learn the advantages and disadvantages of each of 28 different guitar environments, including the amazing *Liberty Tuning* and related hybrid tunings. If you have a shortage of fingers on the fretting hand, or if you work with hand injuries, special music education or music therapy, this is the definitive guide to showing what can be done musically with just 2-finger chords.

Support Harvey Reid's ground-breaking work in guitar. Buy his books, music, videos, and capos.

www.PartialCapo.com www.LibertyGuitar.com

Available from Amazon.com and other retail outlets

www.woodpecker.com

About the Author

Harvey Reid has been a full-time acoustic guitar player since 1974, and has performed over 6000 concerts throughout the US and in Europe. He won the 1981 *National Fingerpicking Guitar Competition* and the 1982 *International Autoharp* contest, and has released 32 highly-acclaimed recordings of original, traditional and contemporary acoustic music.

He is best known for his solo fingerstyle guitar work, but he is also a solid flatpicker (he won Bill Monroe's *Beanblossom* bluegrass guitar contest in 1976), a versatile singer, lyricist, prolific composer, arranger and songwriter. He also plays mandolin, mandocello and bouzouki. Reid recorded the first album ever of 6 & 12-string banjo music, and his CD ***Solo Guitar Sketchbook*** made Guitar Player Magazine's Top 20 essential acoustic guitar CD's list. His CD ***Steel Drivin' Man*** was chosen by Acoustic Guitar Magazine as one of **Top 10 Folk CD's** of all time, along with Woody Guthrie, Ry Cooder and other hallowed names. His music was included in the blockbuster BBC TV show *A Musical Tour of Scotland*, and Reid was featured in the Rhino Records **Acoustic Music of the 90's** collection, along with a "who's who" line-up of other artists including Richard Thompson, Jerry Garcia & Leo Kottke.

In 1980 Reid published ***A New Frontier in Guitar***, the first book about the partial capo, and in 1984 he wrote ***Modern Folk Guitar***, the first college textbook for folk guitar. Quite possibly the first modern person to publish and record with the partial capo, he is almost certainly the most prolific arranger and composer of partial capo guitar music, and is responsible for most of what is known about the device. He lives in southern Maine with his family.

www.ingramcontent.com/pod-product-compliance
Lightning Source LLC
Chambersburg PA
CBHW080512110426
42742CB00017B/3088

9781630290115